D1431976

MITTELEUROPA: BETWEEN EUROPE AND GERMANY

MITTELEUROPA
Between Europe and Germany

Edited by

Peter J. Katzenstein

Berghahn Books
Providence • Oxford

First published in 1997 by

Berghahn Books
Editorial offices:
165 Taber Avenue, Providence, RI 02906, USA
3, Newtec Place, Magdalen Road, Oxford, OX4 1RE, UK

Library of Congress Cataloging-in-Publication Data
Mitteleuropa : between Europe and Germany / Peter J. Katzenstein, ed.
    p.   cm.
   Includes bibliographical references and index.
   ISBN 1-57181-124-9 (alk. paper)
   1. Geopolitics--Europe, Central. 2. Europe, Eastern--Relations-
-Germany. 3. Germany--Relations--Europe, Eastern. 4. Post-
communism--Europe, Central. 5. Post-communism--Europe, Eastern.
6. Europe, Central--Civilization--20th century. 7. Europe, Eastern--
Politics and government--1989-   I. Katzenstein, Peter J.
DAW1051.M57   1997
943--dc21   97-29740
                                         CIP

British Library Cataloguing in Publication Data
A CIP catalogue record for this book is available from
the British Library.

Printed in the United States on acid-free paper

CONTENTS

LIST OF TABLES

PREFACE

This book is closely intertwined with my intellectual autobiography. Raised in the Federal Republic after World War II, I received all of my university training abroad, in the United Kingdom and the United States. When I accepted my first full-time teaching position at Cornell University, I was hired as the Government Department's central European specialist. The category "central Europe" left me groping. Although my dissertation had dealt with Austrian history, I had been no more than a casual student of the Federal Republic, and I knew nothing about Switzerland. I thus was relieved when my perplexed question led to the reassuring answer that central Europe was constituted by all the political entities between Narvik and Sicily, an imprecise American rendering, I suppose, of the nationalist German stanza "*von der Etsch bis an den Belt*" (from Jutland in the north to the River Adige in the south).

During my first year at Cornell I developed a course on central European politics organized around the two key categories then informing German area studies: the national and the social questions. When Chancellor Brandt resigned in 1974 I drafted a paper which distilled what I had learned. In the end I decided not to publish this paper—indeed, not to write further on West German politics until I had found a framework less culture- and area-bound than the one which I had culled from the best scholarship for my very first course and my first academic paper.

In hindsight I can see that this turned out to be a shrewd move. It certainly did not look like it at the time, at least not in the eyes of some of my academic elders who were justifiably worried about my intellectual trajectory. Still, without knowing it, I had chosen an approach maximizing my comparative advantage, happily stuck as I was in bucolic upstate New York, three thousand miles from my subject of study. For viewing an object from afar while removed from constant immersion in the political developments of the day encourages the recognition of new political contours and fault lines. Mountains begin to look like molehills and molehills like mountains. Thus I tried to rethink West German politics in categories also designed, however imperfectly, to engage the political structures and strategies of other states. This effort was facilitated by the re-emergence of political economy as a legitimate academic discipline in the 1970s and of political institutions as a viable analytical perspective in the 1980s.

The peaceful revolution of 1989, German unification, and the breakup of the Soviet Union once again created a central Europe that excited my political imagination in a way that state socialism in East Germany and Eastern Europe before 1989 never had. My other research projects did not make it possible for me to acquire in-depth knowledge of central Europe (Poland, Hungary, and the later to be divided Czechoslovakia). But I was determined to make contacts and to include that part of Europe in a research project that inquired into the relation between German unification and European integration. *Mitteleuropa: Between Europe and Germany* is thus intimately linked to *Tamed Power: Germany in Europe* (Ithaca: Cornell Universtiy Press, 1997), which contains a chapter on central Europe that the authors of all the country chapters in this volume wrote together.

Draft papers for most of the chapters in this book were written and revised for subsequent workshops held at Cornell (February 1994), Budapest (June 1995), and Bratislava (March 1996). I would like to thank all of the participants who attended these workshops and whose comments and criticisms have helped to improve the individual chapters and the overall focus of this project.

Without the necessary financial support it would have been impossible to convene these workshops. I would like to thank, specifically, the generosity of the Council for European Studies which supported this project with two different grants; the German Marshall Fund (Grant A-0063); the American Council of Learned Societies; the Friedrich-Ebert Foundation; the Institute for European Studies at Cornell's Einaudi Center for International Studies; and Cornell's Walter S. Carpenter, Jr. Chair of International Studies.

This project ended where it had begun in November 1989, in Berlin. I was extremely fortunate to have spent the academic year of 1995–96 at the Wissenschaftskolleg Berlin. An oasis for scholars the world over, the Kolleg offered an ideal environment for thinking through all aspects of the project, for editing and re-editing most of the chapters, for planning the Bratislava workshop, and for outlining the books' introductory chapter. I would like to thank Wolf Lepenies, the director, and the entire staff of the Kolleg for having treated me much better than I could ever have dreamed of and than I deserved.

A major purpose of this project was to bring younger scholars from central Europe into contact with their colleagues from Europe and the United States. The hope that these contacts would lead to future collaboration has already been met even before this book is going to press.

My specific thanks go to all of the authors who have contributed to this book. Throughout the last three years they have remained interested and committed to this project under occasionally trying personal circumstances. They were enthusiastic in experimenting with the American notion of field research, of going beyond the use of printed source material; they were good-natured to a fault in meeting my numerous requests for revisions; and they were extremely understanding of the necessity for the tedious process of stylistic editing. Most importantly, they exemplified how joint scholarship can evolve into mutually rewarding professional relationships, a deeper sense of intellectual companionship, and, in some instances, into enduring personal friendships.

Finally, I would like to thank Marion Berghahn who took quickly to this project and made sure that unusual circumstances would not delay its publication. The staff at Berghahn Books made me appreciate once again that small is not only beautiful but also efficient.

Peter J. Katzenstein
Ithaca, New York

1. GERMANY AND MITTELEUROPA

An Introduction

Peter J. Katzenstein

The return of central Europe is a sign of profound political change. Like the name Adolf, the concept of *Mitteleuropa* had all but vanished from the political vocabulary in Bonn, Berlin and Vienna after Hitler's "thousand-year" empire went up in smoke and flames. In Prague and Budapest, on the other hand, the idea of central Europe, as Timothy Garton Ash writes, "continued to be cherished between consenting adults in private."[1] As in the West, however, central Europe was eviscerated from public discourse. Stirrings of political reform, vigorous debate by Polish, Czech, and Hungarian intellectuals, and the end of the Cold War have given the concept current coinage once again. "Mitteleuropa is coming back."[2]

But will it be more than a short-term engagement? Germany, for example, remains politically unsettled. While the new capital of united Germany will be Berlin, about a third of Germany's federal ministries, including defense, will continue to have their main seats in Bonn. The Bonn republic was not Weimar. And united Germany will not be a Berlin republic.

The new Germany will be multicephalic with numerous political, financial, communication, and cultural centers. United Germany is unlikely to be haunted by the traditional German question

For their helpful comments, criticisms, and suggestions on an earlier draft of this chapter I would like to thank Valerie Bunce, Timothy Byrnes, Marc Ellingstad, Péter Gedeon, Elena Iankova, and Andrei Markovits.

1. Timothy Garton Ash, "Does Central Europe Exist?" in George Schöpflin and Nancy Woods, eds., *In Search of Central Europe* (London: Polity Press, 1989), p. 191.

2. Walter Russell Mead, "The Once and Future Reich," *World Policy Journal* 7 (1990): 603. See also James Kurth, "Germany and the Reemergence of Mitteleuropa," *Current History* 94, 595 (November 1995): 381–86, and "United Germany in Eastern Europe: The New Eastern Question," *Problems of Post-Communism* 42, 1 (January-February 1995): 51–55.

of how to accommodate under one political roof ethnic Germans living in different central and eastern European states. The international dimensions of Germany's national question appear to have been settled for the foreseeable future. But other German questions, as Elizabeth Pond and David Schoenbaum note in their recent book, are far from settled.[3] The uncertainties of the political and economic transformations affecting central European politics are even greater. Will post-Communism push ahead with the task of institutionalizing a democratic capitalism? And how will this process be aided or disrupted by international developments in the East? Less than a decade after the end of the Cold War there are no unambiguous answers to these questions.

Yet there is a range of possible responses. Contemporary geostrategic and geoeconomic perspectives are not necessarily limited to drawing tired historical analogies with the 1930s. Acknowledging the dramatic changes that have transformed Germany in the second half of the twentieth century, these perspectives envision not militant domestic pressures for eastward expansion (*"Drang nach Osten"*), but irresistible international pressures for eastern stabilization (*"Zwang nach Osten"*). From this vantage point, German purchases of Polish farmland and the muted political demands of some German political organizations seeking to alter the status of the Russian enclave of Kaliningrad are not harbingers of a new phase of irredentist German politics.[4] Rather, Germany's growing Eastern orientation will be dictated by powerful international developments that no German government will be able to resist. Unavoidable political instabilities and possibly violent conflicts will make German foreign policy seek to build political buffers on its Eastern border. Furthermore, the growing competitive pressures that German producers are experiencing in world markets will make them flock to central and eastern Europe as a natural economic *hinterland*. Hence an international vacuum will recreate German hegemony in central Europe.

This book offers a different response. The preliminary evidence offered here indicates that the end of the Cold War and German unification are not returning Germany and central Europe to historically troubled, asymmetric, bilateral relationships. Rather, changes in the character of German and European politics as well

3. Elizabeth Pond and David Schoenbaum, *The German Question and Other German Questions* (New York: St. Martin's, 1996).
4. Michael Kumpfmüller, "Königsberg und andere Kleinigkeiten," *Die Zeit* (8 April 1994): 13.

as the transformations now affecting Poland, Hungary, the Czech Republic, and Slovakia point to the emergence of multilateral relationships linking Germany and central Europe to an internationalizing Europe.[5] Furthermore, the collapse of markets and political instabilities in Russia and the Commonwealth of Independent States (CIS) help make this shift self-evident to most leaders and mass publics in central Europe.

With the end of the Cold War the central European states are seeking to engage Europe and Germany on many levels. Berlin-Bonn lie on the road leading to Brussels; without Germany's active support, membership in the European Union (EU) will be slow in coming. And Brussels is a kind of reassurance against excessive reliance on Berlin-Bonn; the central European states seek to shelter their bilateral dependence on Germany in multilateral European arrangements. In brief, the central European states are emulating in the 1990s a strategy that other smaller European states had deployed with great success in earlier times.[6] Central European politics is thus defined by its German and European relationships rather than by its traditional position between East and West.

Central Europe: A Geopolitical Terrain and an Ideological Construct

Our map of Europe and the world was devised by Gerardus Mercator in Germany in 1569. It dates back to a historical era when Europe discovered, dominated, and exploited the world. And at the center of that Eurocentric map was central Europe and Germany.[7]

Within this cartographic perspective the hyperbolic assertion *am deutschen Wesen soll die Welt genesen* (German qualities will cure the world) appeared to make sense. Germany and Europe looked like the center of the world based, as we now know, on inaccurate representations of size as well as unequal axes and positions. In

5. Peter J. Katzenstein, ed., *Tamed Power: Germany in Europe* (Ithaca: Cornell University Press, 1997).

6. Ibid.

7. According to Timothy Garton Ash, French geographers determined a place north of Vilnius to be the center of Europe. It is marked by a black granite slab engraved with the longitude (25° 19′) and latitude (54° 54′) and the words *Europos centras*. As Ash reports, "I stand on it with what eighteenth-century travelers used to call sublime emotion, and nearly fall off. It's slippery out there, on the center of Europe." Timothy Garton Ash, "Journey to the Post-Communist East," *The New York Review of Books* (23 June 1994): 18.

contrast to Mercator, the maps of the German historian Arno Peters show all areas—countries, continents, and oceans—according to their actual size. The map's north-south lines run vertical, permitting us to see geographic points in their precise directional relationship. And its east-west lines run parallel, permitting us to determine easily the relationship of any point on the map to its distance from the equator. Peters's new and more accurate map corrects the striking visual over-representation of the northern hemisphere over the south, which makes Europe's 3.8 million square miles loom large over South America's 6.9 million, and the Soviet Union's 8.7 million square miles dwarf Africa's 11.6 million. More important for the purpose of this chapter and book, Peters's map removes central Europe and Germany from the center of the world. Instead, these geographic areas are now located at the world's northern rim. This induces an altogether salutary shift in political perspective. The premise of this book is to avoid what one could call Nelson's perspective, reversing the telescope and putting it on the blind eye. The northern rim of the world has been of great importance in recent times. It is not marginal. But it is not central either.

Acknowledging that central Europe exists, there is no agreement about where it starts precisely, and where it ends. Is its center in Berlin, Prague, Vienna or further east? Are the Baltic states part of central Europe? What about Serbia, Croatia, Slovenia, Romania, and Bulgaria? There are no precise or uncontestable answers to these questions. But this much is certain: while the coordinates of world politics are shifting away from Europe, central Europe remains politically important because it evokes powerful memories of some of the major disasters of the twentieth century: fascism, two world wars, and the holocaust. Furthermore, central Europe was the staging area of the Cold War and the most likely flashpoint where that war might have turned hot.[8]

Europe is a geopolitical terrain of considerable importance. Both before and after the Cold War, the north German plains and the eastern states of united Germany are central to past, and possibly future, conflagrations. The positioning and plans of NATO and Warsaw pact troops until the end of the 1980s, and the political controversies about NATO enlargement in the 1990s, illustrate the importance of geographical space in central Europe. Intent on creating a zone of stability to its east, Germany is particularly concerned with the enlargement of NATO. Facing severe problems to

8. Andrei S. Markovits and Simon Reich, *The German Predicament: Memory and Power in the New Europe* (Ithaca: Cornell University Press, 1997).

their south, France and Spain have no particular interest in the rapid expansion of the EU. Germany does. And Germany has been helped by the United States. Driven by electoral concerns and the liberal impetus of the foreign policy of the Clinton administration, U.S. policy in 1996 has accelerated movement toward NATO enlargement, thus reinforcing German preferences.

The border that is separating Germany and central Europe has been transformed since 1989. A journalistic account of various stops along Germany's 800 mile-long eastern border underlines the importance of economic inequality, political indifference, ethnic stereotypes, and historical amnesia. This is a border patrolled by police, not military forces. Smuggling, illegal immigration, prostitution, and automobile theft constitute the new security threats.[9]

Territorial spaces and their borders are material as well as social facts. In the 1980s intellectuals in particular sought to recreate the political space that a central Europe, shorn of all German, liberal imperialist connotations, might create for a regional cultural identity that could further the process of political reform.[10] Like Europe's other subregions, central Europe is a specific ideological construct that is open to varied and contested political interpretations.[11] For many decades Scandinavia and southern Europe retained specific collective identities that overlapped in part with European and national ones. Only with the acceleration of the European integration process and the end of the Cold War have these subregional identities weakened significantly.

A corresponding process is apparently underway in central Europe. As Valerie Bunce illustrates in chapter 6, since 1993 Europe, not central Europe, has become the major focus of the security and economic policies of Poland, Hungary, the Czech Republic, and, possibly, Slovakia. Europe symbolizes democratic welfare states that are at peace with themselves and their neighbors. Meeting the requirements that the EU has set forth for membership is not merely an instrumental goal for the central European states, it is also a way of enacting an identity that, with the collapse of socialism, has no international rival. "Isolationists" who oppose the "cosmopolitans"

9. "Grenze ohne Schatten," *Der Spiegel* 41/1996: 134–63, and 42/1996: 142–63.

10. Important contributions to that debate are translated and interpreted in Schöpflin and Wood, *In Search of Central Europe.*

11. For an application of a similar analytical perspective to Europe and Asia, see Peter J. Katzenstein, "Introduction: Asian Regionalism in Comparative Perspective," in Peter J. Katzenstein and Takashi Shiraishi, eds., *Network Power: Japan and Asia* (Ithaca: Cornell University Press, 1997), pp. 7–12.

in domestic politics—to adopt the terminology of Włodek Anioł, Timothy Byrnes, and Elena Iankova in chapter 2—invoke different issues, such as religion and nationalism. To date, however, these isolationists have not succeeded in articulating politically a collective identity for central Europe that rivals that of Europe.

If Europe is a positive pole of attraction that affirms the central European "self," Russia, Iver Neumann argues, is its constituting "other."[12] Regional identities are based not only on inclusive affirmations but on exclusive demarcations. Specifically what is at stake for central European identity politics are the underlining principles of political and social pluralism, political democracy and capitalist efficiency that contradict the political homogenization, as well as authoritarianism and state socialism of past Soviet and potential future Russian policies. Differentiated from the Soviet Union and Russia, central Europe is thus a way station in a Europeanization process that marks the transformation of these four states in different, though broadly comparable, ways.

This wish to differentiate is also noticeable in Germany. It typically refers directly or obliquely, to a civilizational divide between Roman Catholicism and Eastern Orthodoxy. What divided the Habsburg Monarchy historically remains important in Germany's contemporary public discourse, even though that division does not fit very neatly the geographic facts either of the Baltic states or of the western Ukraine.[13] In the 1980s central Europe re-emerged as a political category in West Germany's public debate, primarily on the Left. Social Democrats like Peter Glotz sought to undermine the divisive effects of the Iron Curtain by looking to central Europe as one bridge among several that might help to reintegrate Europe and Germany.[14]

Because Russia is the state from which central European states, with the possible exception of Slovakia, wish to differentiate themselves, does this open central Europe to the increasing cultural influence of Germany? Hynek Jeřábek and František Zich, document in chapter 4 the extent to which German ownership of the

12. Iver B. Neumann, "Russia as Central Europe's Constituting Other," *East European Politics and Societies* 7, 2 (Spring 1993): 349–69, and Neumann, *Russia and the Idea of Europe* (London: Routledge, 1996). See also Matthias Zimmer, "Return of the *Mittellage*? The Discourse of the Centre in German Foreign Policy," *German Politics* 6, 1 (April 1997): 23–38.

13. Samuel P. Huntington, "The Clash of Civilizations?" *Foreign Affairs* 72, 3 (Summer 1993): 22–49.

14. Peter Glotz, "Deutsch-böhmische Kleinigkeiten oder: Abgerissene Gedanken über Mitteleuropa," *Die Neue Gesellschaft/Frankfurter Hefte* 33 (1986): 584–85.

regional press in the Czech Republic has created a potential opening for what might turn out to be an illegitimate foreign influence.[15] But because the influence of regional print media is countered by an international electronic media that is mostly dominated by American interests, the Czech government has not regarded the German takeover of the regional press as threatening.

The relation between the German and English languages among secondary and university students in central Europe amplifies the same point. Although there are significant variations by country, English is everywhere the preferred first foreign language. And American mass culture enjoys in central Europe, as in Germany, an unquestioned hegemonic position. Demand for German language for business is at record levels; Germany's official and private cultural presence in central Europe is on a marked upswing; and German cultural diplomacy is toying with a more assertively political approach to presenting Germany abroad. Yet embedded in the global hegemony of the many products of American mass culture, German cultural influence, though strong and rising in central Europe, will not be able to emerge from a position of junior partner even as Germany's economic influence increases.[16]

Furthermore, the multilateral bent in Germany's cultural diplomacy runs deep. Working on major projects with other West European states, and with several local organizations, is standard operating procedure for parapublic German institutions such as the Goethe Institute and the Center for Advanced Study, Berlin.[17]

15. The Polish data are comparable. A parliamentary debate in February 1995 revealed that 56 percent of all national publications and 50 percent of all regional ones, with about 70 percent of the total print run in both instances, were foreign-owned. The *Passauer Neue Presse* has acquired almost a monopoly position in the regional press of the Czech Republic and is also very prominent in Poland. Włodek Anioł, personal communication, 13 June 1995.

16. Andrei S. Markovits and Carolyn Höfig, "Germany as a Bridge: German Foreign Cultural Policy in a Changing Europe," paper presented as part of the seminar series of the American Institute for Contemporary German Studies on "Germany's Role in Shaping the New Europe: Architect, Model, Bridge," Washington D.C., 9 January 1996, pp. 35–46. See also Markovits and Reich, *The German Predicament*, pp. 183–202, which are jointly authored with Höfig.

17. I gathered the information on the Goethe Institute's approach in interviews conducted in Warsaw, Budapest, and Prague between 1992 and 1994. The experience of the Center for Advanced Study is reported in Wolf Lepenies, "Wie stärkt man lokale Wissenskulturen? Drei Fallbeispiele aus Budapest, Warschau und Bukarest," paper prepared for a meeting of the working group "Wissenschaften und Wiedervereinigung," Berlin-Brandenburgische Akademie der Wissenschaften, Berlin, 5–6 October 1995.

Central Europe's cultural orientation will be to the West, including Germany, rather than on Germany exclusively. In brief, central Europe is experiencing simultaneous processes of internationalization and Europeanization that contain a strong German component.

Germany and Central Europe in History

This is a surprising development. For there exists an alternative historical vision of a middle way, of an in-between Europe or *Zwischeneuropa*, of small, sovereign, and democratic states that constitute the core of European culture and thus help to anchor Western Europe against undue Americanization and an overbearing Russia.[18] Tomás Masaryk's definition of central Europe, for example, articulated during World War I, included many different national groups from northern, eastern, and southern Europe; but it excluded Germans and Austrians. For Friedrich Naumann, by contrast, central Europe was, in the words of Timothy Garton Ash, "all about the Germans and Austrians, with the others included only insofar as they were subjects of the German and Austro-Hungarian empires."[19]

In a broader historical perspective central and eastern Europe are marked by belated processes of industrialization, nation-building, and modernization processes that left these societies with both deep social and economic inequalities and a concentration of economic and political resources that provided a fertile basis for state socialism.[20] This legacy reinforced a mosaic pattern of various nationality groups that lived in close proximity to one another in what Karl Deutsch called a "polka-dot" pattern that is arguably different from the "patchwork-quilt" pattern characteristic of Western Europe.[21] The polka-dot pattern was the result of a flow of west-to-east migration in the thirteenth and fourteenth centuries. Although the migrants did not think of themselves as German, the similarity, for example, in the legal codes that they brought with them earned them the name "German" in the eyes of

18. Schöpflin and Woods, *In Search of Central Europe*. Peter Stirk, ed., *Mitteleuropa: History and Prospects* (Edinburgh: Edinburgh University Press, 1994). Henry Cord Meyer, *Mitteleuropa in German Thought and Action 1815–1945* (The Hague: M. Nijhoff, 1955).

19. Ash, "Post-Communist East," p. 16.

20. Werner Conze, *Ostmitteleuropa* (Munich: C.H. Beck, 1992).

21. Karl W. Deutsch, *Nationalism and Its Alternatives* (New York: Knopf, 1969), pp. 37–66.

local populations. The territories in east-central Europe thus settled were united under the Order of Teutonic Knights and existed under the protectorate of the Emperor and the Pope, in contrast to those in the eastern part of Germany which were part of the Holy Roman Empire.

Europe's religious wars and the modernization policies of Peter the Great and Catherine II led to a second wave of migration that dispersed ethnic Germans into the inner reaches of Russia. A network of commercial, financial, and political privileges stretched unevenly across countryside and city throughout eastern-central Europe, subject to local variations that were magnified by the absence of an imperial center.

In the nineteenth and twentieth centuries this complex pattern of central-eastern European and German relations was simplified into the bifurcation between the *Kleindeutsche* (small German) and the *Grossdeutsche* (large German) solutions to Germany's national question. Prussia stood for the former, the Habsburg monarchy for the latter solution. The political defeat of Austrian plans for a central European federation at the hands of Prussia, and German unification under Prussian leadership in 1871 in the wake of three wars, provided a temporary answer to Germany's national question. Germany and Prussia adopted a policy of forced assimilation that engendered deep hostilities, especially among members of the Polish population residing in the eastern parts of Imperial Germany.

Published during World War I Friedrich Naumann's book *Mitteleuropa* popularized plans that had circulated especially in Austria-Hungary in the late nineteenth century. Naumann drew up a plan for a federal union of central Europe that aimed at incorporating the western parts of Russia, Poland, and the Baltic states. Other plans were geographically more expansive and sought to consolidate southeast Europe under German leadership. These plans were spurred by the conviction that rivalry with the United States, Britain, and Russia required Germany to enlarge the territorial and demographic base of this potential fourth "world state" through the establishment of close links with central and eastern Europe.[22] In the view of its German and Austrian proponents such plans would create a flexible international political order, marked by a spirit of political compromise, in which various nationalities and states would be able to coexist peacefully; in the view of its foreign critics this was crass imperialism designed to cement German

22. Rainer Eisfeld, "Mitteleuropa in Historical and Contemporary Perspective," *German Politics and Society* 28 (Spring 1993): 39.

power on the continent. From either perspective such plans were embedded in the process of capitalist development that increasingly came to penetrate central and eastern Europe.

Germany's defeat in World War I and the breakup of Austria-Hungary created a *cordon sanitaire* of states in central and eastern Europe increasingly referred to as east-central Europe or *Zwischeneuropa*. It restored Poland's sovereignty and gave independence to a rump Austria, Hungary, and Czechoslavakia as well as to the Balkan states. The Wilsonian principle of national self-determination was violated in numerous instances—for example, in the case of Austria, in western Poland, Hungary, and in Bohemia and Moravia. Ethnic Germans thus found themselves living under non-German governments. The revision of the Versailles treaty regarding Germany's eastern border became an important policy objective for both the governments of Weimar Germany and Nazi Germany.

Central Europe thus became part of a revisionist political agenda that, without relinquishing its economic-imperialist character, acquired radical nationalist overtones. Based on its outright rejection of the Versailles and St. Germain treaties, German and Austrian political revisionism accorded Germany the role as central Europe's undisputed political and economic leader and, eventually, sanctioned military aggression and political annexation.[23] Liberals advocated an imperialism of free trade that put Germany at the center of an informally organized zone of economic influence intimately linked to an open international economy. Proponents of autarchic economic development put Germany at the center of an economic bloc that was protectionist in its external orientation and hierarchical in its internal organization.[24]

After 1933 Nazi Germany opted unequivocally for the second option. It instituted bilateral trade and monetary clearing arrangements designed to cement a system of asymmetric vulnerabilities between Germany and its smaller neighbors to the east.[25] German

23. Konrad H. Jarausch. "From Second to Third Reich: The Problem of Continuity in German Foreign Policy," *Central European History* 12, 1 (March 1979): 68–82. Peter J. Katzenstein and Takashi Shiraishi, "Conclusion: Regions in World Politics. Japan and Asia-Germany in Europe," in Katzenstein and Shiraishi, *Network Power*, pp. 375–78.

24. Volker Berghahn, "German Big Business and the Quest for a European Economic Empire in the Twentieth Century," in Volker Berghahn, Reinhard Neebe, and Jeffrey J. Anderson, *German Big Business and Europe in the Twentieth Century* (Providence, R.I.: Brown University, 1993), pp. 1–38.

25. Peter M.R. Stirk, "Ideas of Economic Integration in Interwar Mitteleuropa," in Stirk, *Mitteleuropa*, pp. 86–111. Anthony McElligott, "Reforging Mitteleuropa in the

domination over central Europe and further east was an act of destructive colonization that brought about wars of ethnic cleansing, resettlements of vast tracts of land, outright annexation of western Poland, and the creation of a vicious apartheid regime in central Poland. And the German SS, military, police, and courts closely cooperated in conducting a genocidal war and the running of the death camps in which Germans murdered millions of Jews and members of other minority groups.

The total failure of this policy and the unconditional surrender of Nazi Germany in May 1945 signified an end to German expansionism in central Europe. More than ten million ethnic Germans became refugees who resettled in a rump Germany in 1945. Subsequent decades have witnessed a slow draining of the reservoir of ethnic Germans from central and eastern Europe that has continued up to the present day. In a broader perspective, 1945 heralded the loss of an informal German "empire" comparable to the very different kinds of losses that Britain and France experienced after World War II.

Varieties of Corporatism in Central Europe

The Cold War redefined all aspects of European politics. It divided Germany. It eviscerated the very notion of central Europe for several decades; and it recreated a new kind of central Europe in the form of Austria and Switzerland, states that were capitalist, democratic, and neutral and thus not part of either NATO or the EC. Since World War II, Austria and Switzerland have exhibited a specific style of politics marked by negotiated compromises premised on a far-reaching depoliticization of political conflicts in the interest of stability.[26]

For this reason it is noteworthy that scholars who are beginning to analyze the emerging political characteristics in the post-Communist polities in central Europe point to some surprising

---

Crucible of War: The Economic Impact of Integration under German Hegemony," ibid., pp. 129–58. Robert Mark Spaulding, Jr., "German Trade Policy in Eastern Europe, 1890–1990: Preconditions for Applying International Trade Leverage," *International Organization* 45, 3 (Summer 1991): 343–68. *Idem, Osthandel and Ostpolitik: German Foreign Trade Policies in Eastern Europe from Bismarck to Adenauer* (Providence, RI: Berghahn Books, 1997).

26. Peter J. Katzenstein, *Corporatism and Change: Austria, Switzerland and the Politics of Industry* (Ithaca: Cornell University Press, 1984). Andreas Busch, "The Politics of

similarities with the politics of democratic corporatism in Austria and Switzerland. In their analysis of post-socialist pathways, David Stark and László Bruszt, for example, compare privatization politics in Hungary, the Czech Republic, and the former GDR.[27] They focus on how politicians deal with the interdependencies of assets and the chains of liabilities. For Stark and Bruszt "deliberative association" is a process of creating binding agreements over large stakes and long periods of time. They identify a style of politics that recognizes, to different degrees in different contexts, the network characteristics of assets and liabilities and sees these as central to the politics of privatization.

For example, Germany's agency for privatization, the *Treuhandanstalt*, found itself in charge of privatizing virtually all of the state-owned assets of the GDR. Although it began with an explicit rejection of all network ties, prompted by social protests and electoral competition, Stark and Bruszt argue that the agency eventually shifted course and created social ties in negotiating fora that are responsible for restructuring networks of firms. In Hungary a rich legacy of inter-enterprise links has generated dense, extensive, and complex networks of ownership between various enterprises, thus mitigating some of the enormous uncertainties in the post-socialist era. As Stark and Bruszt argue, the government neglected these networks and proceeded to privatize on a firm-by-firm basis, thus spawning a wave of bankruptcies and a severe financial crisis that in turn forced a dramatic change in policy and an extensive government bail out. Finally, despite the free-market rhetoric of Prime Minister Klaus, the Czech government recognized the network properties of assets and liabilities from the outset. It favored both active anti-bankruptcy policies on the one hand and new forms of inter-organizational ownership on the other.

Price Stability: Why the German-Speaking Nations are Different," in Francis G. Castles, ed., *Families of Nations: Patterns of Public Policy in Western Democracies* (Aldershot: Dartmouth, 1993), pp. 35–91. Andrei S. Markovits, "Austrian-German Relations in the New Europe: Predicaments of Political and National Identity Formation," *German Studies Review* 19, 1 (February 1996): 91–111. Markovits and Reich, *German Predicament*, pp. 101–08.

27. *Postsocialist Pathways: Transforming Politics and Property in East Central Europe* (New York: Cambridge University Press, forthcoming). For a useful schematic description of central European privatization schemes, see also Catherine Mann, Stefanie Lenway, and Derek Utter, "Political and Economic Consequences of Alternative Privatization Schemes," University of California, Center for German and European Studies, Working Paper 5.14 (June 1993).

In short, the empirical form of network ties varies from case to case. As Stark and Bruszt describe, in Hungary a tight coupling of direct ties between enterprises has occurred; in the Czech Republic close links exist between banks and investment funds at the meso level; and in East Germany the powerful effect of a politics of deliberative association has reversed the legal approach that the *Treuhand* took initially. As chapter 5 argues below, a politically hotly contested privatization program in Slovakia appears to follow a traditional, German, bank-led model that is also distinguished by network characteristics. In these cases the organizational, institutional, and political responses to the network properties of assets and liabilities yield political economies that, at this early stage, resemble the liberal Anglo-Saxon model much less than Austria's and Switzerland's democratic corporatism.

Elena Iankova's analysis of the social partnership evident in what she calls a "transformative corporatism" in Bulgaria and Poland points in the same direction.[28] Her survey of post-socialist, central and eastern European politics points to pervasive indications of a tripartite corporatist politics that has varying political effects. Hungary's version, for example, was relatively weak. The tripartite National Council for Reconciliation of Interests, established in 1988, focuses on consensual wage bargaining and the negotiation of a host of social issues. Revived in 1990 in the interest of buffering the shock of market competition, it is comprised of representatives of six unions and employer organizations. Czechoslovakia's federal tripartite Council of Social and Economic Accord was constituted in 1990 and, after the country's split-up, was succeeded in 1993 by Czech and Slovak successor organizations. In Poland tripartite negotiations accelerated after the signing of the Enterprise pact of February 1993 and the formation of the National Commission on Social-Economic Issues in February 1994. It brings around one table representatives of the government, the confederation of Polish employers, NSZZ-Solidarity, the All-Polish Trade Union Alliance, and seven other national unions. In Bulgaria, Romania, and the successor states to the Soviet Union similar corporatist arrangements have also sprung up.

28. Elena Atanassova Iankova, "The Transformative Corporatism of Eastern Europe," paper presented at the conference "The Politics of Regional Restructuring," Cornell University, Center for International Studies, 18–19 October 1996, and "Social Partnership after the Cold War: The Transformative Corporatism of Eastern Europe," Ph.D. dissertation, School for Industrial and Labor Relations, Cornell University, 1997.

Iankova, furthermore, shows in her detailed research in Bulgaria and Poland that these councils are not merely empty institutional shells at the national level. They are replicated at regional levels, in different industrial branches and within particular enterprises. The network structure of the political economies of central Europe that Stark and Bruszt uncovered and interpreted in their study of privatization, Iankova finds to be very prominent on issues of macroeconomic policy and wage bargaining. In her view, beyond all national, regional, local, and sectoral variations (marked, for example, by a more adversarial form of social dialogue in Poland than in Hungary, the Czech Republic, and Slovakia) tripartite corporatism in central and eastern Europe has developed a similar transformative design.

The rapid and almost simultaneous emergence of transformative corporatism, Iankova argues, is due to the convergence of three factors that, in a different historical context, had brought forth a different kind of corporatism in Austria and Switzerland.[29] First, one legacy of socialism was a collectivist culture that is reflected in the emergence of new, centralized unions and, more slowly, of new employer associations. Second, in all central European states the opening to Western markets and high levels of international indebtedness created strong pressures for domestic concertation policies. Finally, in an era of great uncertainty corporatism facilitates the signing of social pacts and agreements that are vitally important in the absence of consolidated norms of conduct. In brief, under great political and economic pressure and in an environment of high uncertainty both unions and employers agreed with the post-Communist governments that, in radically new circumstances, centralized decision making is a virtue.

It is too early to judge confidently whether the central European experience will generate in due course political mechanisms sufficiently strong to sustain corporatist structures and practices. But with Bulgaria and Poland as exemplars, Iankova's research on transformative corporatism generates a novel perspective that points to some important similarities with Austria and Switzerland.

Their democratic corporatism has three defining traits.[30] First, business and labor subscribe to an ideology of social partnership that subordinates the natural antagonism of different producer groups to an overarching consensus on a peaceful and stable

29. Iankova, "Transformative Corporatism," pp. 6–14.

30. Peter J. Katzenstein, *Small States in World Markets: Industrial Policy in Europe* (Ithaca: Cornell University Press, 1985). Katzenstein, *Corporatism and Change.*

politics. Political conflict, while not eliminated, occurs within a framework that, however vaguely, is designed around a shared notion of the public good. Second, the major interest groups are very centralized. Indeed, the very concept of "peak association"—in which associations, not individuals are organized—is a central European institutional innovation that dates back to the nineteenth century. Interest group leaders typically enjoy very strong powers and control over a membership that rarely challenges its political prerogatives. And these groups typically organize broad segments of the relevant social sectors. Yet the image of order that this institutional order conveys is misleading. Political struggle is intense, but many of these conflicts occur within organizations in private rather than between them in public, thus preventing a cluttering of the public agenda with fights, for example, between various segments of labor or business. This type of corporatist structure remains democratic. Periodic electoral competition interrupts a potentially dangerous consensus among the elites running these organizations. Finally, democratic corporatism features a particular style of political bargaining that is informal, voluntary, and uninterrupted. This bargaining process facilitates consensus by permitting trade-offs across different policy sectors.

In their many differences Switzerland and Austria exemplify a liberal and social variant of democratic corporatism. In Switzerland international business and finance dominate national business, the unions, and the political Left. In Austria, conversely, a large union and a very large public sector prevail over internationally oriented business interests by diminishing margins. Thus Switzerland chooses liberal foreign trade, large direct investments abroad, and the reliance on a large number of foreign workers while Austria prefers a cautious pursuit of free trade, subsidization of domestic investment, and an active labor market policy. And Switzerland favors a relatively privatized social policy system and limited public expenditures, whereas Austria chooses large public expenditures, publicly funded social policies, and an incomes policy supported by both employers and unions. But these differences between international and national adaptation to change, and between private and public compensation for change, reflect only one-half of a picture that differentiates between liberal and a social variants of corporatism.

The other half is conveyed by the fact that in both countries business and labor accommodate their divergent interests, on different terms, in centralized institutions. In both countries producer groups, state bureaucracies and, at times, political parties are linked through multiple institutional channels that often make it virtually impossible to distinguish the public from the private sector. In both countries producer groups are well-organized in typically centralized and all-encompassing peak associations. Reaching a consensus between the divergent viewpoints expressed within these organizations is a key to the institutional stability of the national policy network and the predictability of the policy process. Yet some differences in institutional form remain apparent. The state bureaucracy, for example, is larger and more centralized in Austria than in Switzerland. And the degree of centralization tends to be somewhat larger in the dominant social sector—business in Switzerland and the unions in Austria—than in the subordinate sectors. But both Switzerland and Austria seek to link their institutions, including political parties, to policy networks that reliably shield the policy process from exogenous shocks and unpredictabilities.

The consensual and democratic political arrangements that emerged in Austria after World War II and that were reinforced by a series of far-reaching constitutional amendments adopted by Switzerland soon after 1945 resulted from the traumatic convulsions of the 1930s and 1940s. The Great Depression, fascism, war, and occupation convinced Austrian and Swiss voters and leaders that moderation in the exercise of power was a marriage of virtue with necessity.

In Austria a strong political consensus emerged after the war which viewed that country as occupied between 1938 and 1955, first by the Nazis and later by the Allied Powers. It matters little that the empirical evidence does not support this historical myth about the years 1938–45.[31] Only in the 1980s did the Waldheim affair put seriously into question this instance of collective historical re-interpretation. The Austrians learned an important lesson specifically from the brief civil war of 1934 and more generally from the events of the 1930s and 1940s. Left and Right agreed that it was dangerous and undesirable to push political conflicts too far. Domestic tranquillity and prosperity as well as international neutrality became the object of Austrian policies and politics. Democratic corporatism became the anchor.

Although it was spared Austria's difficult experiences, Switzerland's experience of the perilous 1930s and 1940s, the depression,

---

31. Peter J. Katzenstein, *Disjoined Partners: Austria and Germany since 1815* (Berkeley: University of California Press, 1976), pp. 163–176.

and the threat of war nonetheless left a deep imprint. Lacking a broad political consensus, rule by emergency decree became almost normal in the abnormal 1930s. But the victory of reformism over radicalism on the political Left and the trade union movement encouraged the political incorporation and pacification of all major social sectors by the mid-1940s. This broadened the political base of Swiss liberalism and eventually transformed it into a liberal version of democratic corporatism.

In the evolution of democratic corporatism it is difficult to overestimate the role which the liberal international economy has played since 1945.[32] As is true of other small industrial states, the economies of Switzerland and Austria are remarkably open to the international economy. Increasing international liberalization provided ample opportunities in growing export markets, but it also greatly increased the competitive pressures that were placed on all of the major producer groups and political actors. In their daily lives everyone in Switzerland and Austria was constantly reminded of how open and vulnerable their economies really are. Corporatist practices thus became valued as tools that are essential for the consensual fashioning of national strategies in an international economy that is typically perceived as a rigorous taskmaster that leaves little room for self-indulgence or self-pity. Economic competitiveness and social welfare were viewed as being inextricably linked. Political adjustment to the changes imposed by developments in the international economy have been made easier by the fact that corporatist institutions were the conduits by which the welfare policies of compensation were expanded during the postwar period—some in response to the pressures of the international economy, others as the result of the internal dynamics of democratic corporatism.

In the 1980s and 1990s this pattern has undergone important changes, especially in Austria. The Austrian decision to join the EU in 1995 has increased international competition. And a partial destabilization of the Austrian party system is apparent in the growth of a number of small parties.[33] More specifically, in the case of Austria democratic corporatism in the 1990s is now seriously challenged by a populist right-wing party that packages its xenophobia and furtive support of the Nazi past in a heavy dose

32. Katzenstein, *Small States in World Markets.*
33. Hans-Georg Betz, "Continuity and Change in Austria, Switzerland and Germany," unpublished paper, Paul H. Nitze School of Advanced International Studies, Johns Hopkins University, n.d.

of anti-European rhetoric. In Switzerland, by way of contrast, it is uncertainty about the course the country should navigate in an integrating Europe that is increasing numerous political cleavages. These challenges to its hegemony notwithstanding, democratic corporatism continues to define Austrian and Swiss politics more accurately than does any other label.

Institutional Affinities of Germany with Corporatism

German politics arguably has a greater similarity with democratic corporatism than do the politics of any other larger capitalist states. Germany's semi-sovereign state helps bring about this convergence in politics and policy.[34] Government and state bureaucracy are closely connected to the political process of consultation, by way of an ideological framework of social partnership that links parapublic institutions with broadly based, centralized producer groups and with political parties that are decidedly centrist in outlook. The extreme Right has been delegitimated by the horrors of the Nazi past. The extreme Left never overcame the liability of espousing a socialist ideal that to most West Germans was hidden behind a cement wall and barbed wire. The sharply narrowed spectrum of partisan preferences that has dominated German politics since 1949 has reinforced an ideology of social partnership that eventually superseded the language of class conflict.

The organization of German politics is quite decentralized. This can be traced to several factors: historical legacies of a decentralized German polity, American political precepts, such as federalism and judicial review, and emerging political characteristics, such as the growing significance of the *Bundesrat* and the increasing role of the judiciary in policy making during the last forty years. German politics, to be sure, features some countervailing centralizing tendencies, most important among which are legal norms that help to shape a complex system of intergovernmental relations and general political practices.

Many other German institutions are, by contrast, quite centralized in their structure and highly encompassing in their membership. This is especially true of the major producer organizations.

---

34. Peter J. Katzenstein, *Policy and Politics in West Germany: The Growth of a Semisovereign State* (Philadelphia: Temple University Press, 1987).

German business had begun organizing in the form of peak associations as early as the 1870s. And after 1945 West German unions
also decided on a more centralized organizational structure along
industry lines. And although Germany's banking system is no
longer viewed adequately as a contemporary version of Hilferd-
ing's finance capitalism, its organization and the legal rules under
which it is permitted to operate still give it a position of great
importance in the Germany polity.

Germany's similarity to democratic and other forms of corporatism is underlined by parapublic institutions that are open to
centralized interest groups as well as party leaders and senior civil
servants. Examples include Chambers of Industry, Commerce,
and Agriculture, professional associations, public radio and television stations, and a variety of research institutes and universities. Parapublic institutions are both political actors and policy
arenas. Some of these institutions, such as the social welfare funds,
date back to the nineteenth century. Others, such as the Bundesbank, were created by the Allies after 1945. Especially on economic
and social questions these institutions have acted like political
shock absorbers. They tend to limit the scope for innovation in the
formulation of policies, and they limit political controversies in
the process of policy implementation.

German politics shares characteristic traits with both social and
liberal variants of corporatism. As is true of Switzerland, German
business is powerful and has an international cast. And a strong
federalism introduces an element of decentralization into electoral
politics and intergovernmental relations. Moreover, as in Austria
political parties play a prominent role, and the position of the
labor movement is very significant. Finally, German politics shares
with both Switzerland and Austria a penchant for organizing politics along stable institutional lines that encourage incremental
changes in policy.

At the same time there exist significant differences. For example, institutional networks linking political actors in the Federal
Republic are less centralized and less tight than those in Switzerland and Austria. Political bargaining across issue areas is less
frequent and more difficult. This is due to the normative and
political importance of the state in German politics and is not
characteristic of Switzerland and Austria. The German state provides a normative reference point that in Switzerland is confined
to the institution of direct democracy. In Switzerland only in
times of crisis is the federal government granted emergency

powers that help it to define and implement policy. Austria's political parties, on the other hand, have penetrated the state bureaucracy so totally as to have robbed the state of almost all vestiges of autonomy. If any one Austrian institution is singled out which could claim to provide a normative order for politics, it would be the social and economic partnership between the major producer groups as opposed to the state. Thus neither the Swiss emasculation of the state in normal times, and its enhancement in times of crisis, nor the Austrian neutralization of the state resemble the role the state plays in Germany. If one considers Switzerland and Austria as exemplars of liberal and social variants, Germany could be called a third, attenuated example of democratic corporatism.

After 1945 Germany had little choice but to acknowledge its profound vulnerability. Defeated and divided, it was the staging area for the Cold War that threatened to annihilate Germany should that war ever turn hot. Germany was a medium-sized power with resources inadequate to bring about national unification. A quiet agreement kept the Allied powers united throughout the Cold War. It was summarized by the flippant, though accurate, *aperçu* "if you keep down your Germans, we will keep down ours." Furthermore, as in Austria and Switzerland, international economic pressures have had a comparable though weaker effect. The concept of vulnerability describes very well the situation of West Germany after 1945. Totally defeated in war, the country was made much smaller by its division. The traditional breadbasket in the eastern territories ceded to Poland and in the GDR were no longer available. West Germany was thus condemned to export in order to pay for the foodstuff it now had to import as well as the raw materials necessary to fuel its manufacturing sector. Eventually its four major manufacturing sectors—automobiles, chemicals, electrical equipment, and machinery—all exported more than half of their total production to foreign markets. Germany became the world's leading exporter in the late 1980s. But its export-led growth strategy induced a structural dependence on the international economy over which it had, with few exceptions, precious little control.

The direct effects of German unification have made remarkably little difference to the country's institutional networks, thus keeping the similarity with other types of central European corporatism in place. This was largely due to the constitutional provision under which Germany united. In choosing Article 23 rather than Article 146 the German government made sure that Western institutions would remain unaltered rather than open to renegotiation by the governments of the FRG and GDR. Consequently, West German institutions in all spheres of state and society have spread to the five new *Länder*—including the judiciary, the local and state bureaucracy, the armed forces and police, the federal system of government, political parties, interest groups, social welfare funds, vocational training, labor market boards, universities, and research and development systems. From this perspective German unification is a story of transferring institutions from west to east.[35]

But institutions that are transferred to new settings remain open to eventual transformation. The extent of change that is now concealed can be measured indirectly by the explosive growth of Germany's national debt. Germany bought political tranquillity at an economic price that is sustainable in the longer term only if important aspects of the German political economy are greatly modified. As West Germany's capacity and willingness to subsidize the economic and social changes in the east diminishes, institutional and political discontinuities may become apparent in political practices matching the division of the country in their collective consciousness.

This does not mean, as a small group of neo-conservatives writing on German foreign affairs argues, that the Berlin Republic will have no commonalities with the Bonn Republic. With a number of ministries, most importantly defense, staying put in Bonn and with many federal offices moving from Berlin to Bonn, the capital of the new Germany will be hyphenated. But it is quite plausible to expect that some policy domains will be opened to market processes as the fiscal capacities of the German social market economy are strained under the triple impact of unification, European integration, and increasing global competition; that the traditional sectoralization of policy making typifying Germany will go hand in hand with more centralization; and that a harsher public climate will coexist with or pervade informal networks of cooperation that

35. Scott Gissendanner, "*Die dritte Republik* or the Same Old Federal Republic? What the German Social Science Literature has to Say about German Unification and Its Systemic Effects," Max-Planck Society, Arbeitsgruppe Transformationsprozesse in den neuen Bundesländern, Humboldt University, Berlin, September 1996. Klaus von Beyme, "The Failure of a Success Story: German Reunification in Light of Policy Evaluation," Center for German and European Studies, Georgetown University, October 1994.

have been a hallmark of German politics since the 1960s. This would herald the coming of a Third German Republic under auspices quite different from those foreseen in the late 1980s.[36] It is unlikely, though possible, that such changes would fundamentally undercut the institutional similarities between German, Swiss, and Austrian versions of corporatism.

Central Europe between Germany, the European Union, and NATO Enlargement

The central European states are strongly oriented westwards through overlapping relationships that link them to Germany, the EU and NATO. After 1989 most experts expected that Germany would come to prevail economically in its own backyard by recreating through politics and markets a contemporary analog to the economic hegemony that it had enjoyed in central and eastern Europe before World War II. The picture which is beginning to emerge a few years after the end of the Cold War is more complicated. Growing bilateral ties with Germany, especially in the economic sphere, are mitigated by different national strategies that seek to anchor central Europe in a Europe encompassing Germany and, on security issues, a Western alliance that ties Europe to the United States.

Central Europe and Germany

Before unification the GDR was, after the Soviet Union, the largest partner in the Council for Mutual Economic Assistance (CMEA). And while foreign trade was relatively unimportant in state socialist economies following policies of import substitution, the FRG was central Europe's most important Western trade partner. As Markovits and Reich write, "it is extremely difficult to identify *any* category of commerce and trade in which the Federal Republic has not consistently been the most important Western presence in Eastern Europe."[37] Ranking behind only the Soviet Union, the FRG and the GDR in 1989 accounted for a total of 14.9 percent of

36. Peter J. Katzenstein, ed., *Industry and Politics in West Germany: Toward the Third Republic* (Ithaca: Cornell University Press, 1989).
37. Markovits and Reich, *German Predicament*, p. 172.

Czechoslovak trade, 17.4 percent of Hungarian trade, and 19 percent of Polish trade.[38] The collapse of trade relations in the Soviet bloc and central Europe in 1990 and 1991 set the stage for a breathtakingly quick economic reorientation of the central European economies towards German and European markets. Between 1989 and 1992, for example, West German imports increased by 166 percent (Czechoslovakia), 108 percent (Poland), and 66 percent (Hungary) while exports increased by 173 percent (Czechoslovakia), 72 percent (Poland) and 23 percent (Hungary). By contrast, in 1992 central European trade with the former GDR, now part of united Germany, reached only 20 percent of its 1989 level.[39] Between 1993 and 1995 Germany's foreign trade with central and Eastern Europe increased by a further 30 percent, a figure that was larger than for any other region of the world. By 1995 German exports to central and eastern Europe exceeded exports to the United States by a slight margin and imports by a substantial one.[40] By contrast, the importance of the Russian market in the foreign trade of central Europe had shrunk to about 5 percent of total trade; only in Hungary was the proportion slightly larger (8 percent).[41]

Germany is also the most important source of foreign direct investment and technology imports. In Poland and Czechoslovakia, for example, German firms moved with great speed and accounted for 30 to 40 percent of all joint ventures in the early months of 1990.[42] It is not surprising that, in light of historical memories, the Polish and Czech governments have tried to counterbalance German

---

38. András Inotai, "The Economic Impact of German Reunification on Central and Eastern Europe," *AICGS Seminar Paper* 1 (June 1992), pp. 2–3 and table 1. For a variety of data covering the years 1989/90–1992/93, see also *Relations between Germany and East Central Europe until 2000: Prospects and Policy Options: Proceedings of an International Conference* (Budapest: Institute for World Economics of the Hungarian Academy of Sciences, 1994), pp. 65–67, 80–84, 90–93, 98–99. Se also Patricia Davis and Peter Dombroswki, "Appetite of the Wolf: German Foreign Assistance for Central and Eastern Europe," *German Politics* 6, 1 (April 1997): 1–22.

39. Klaus-Dieter Schmidt and Petra Naujoks, "Western Enterprises on Eastern Markets: The German Perspective," *Kiel Working Paper* No. 607 (Kiel: Kiel Institute of World Economics, December 1993), pp. 10–11.

40. *Die Zeit* 31 (26 July 1996): 18. Markovits and Reich, *German Predicament*, p. 174. Marc Ellingstad, "German Domination in Central Europe: Room for Potential Concern," JATE Sociology Department, Szeged, Hungary, p. 5.

41. Trade among the central European economies has declined in all four countries after 1989 and remains very limited, despite the political efforts of organizing a free trade area. Only the trade between the Czech Republic and Slovakia is an exception; it is almost twice as large as the total trade in the rest of the region.

42. Markovits and Reich, *German Predicament*, p. 176. Ellingstad, "German Domination," p. 5.

investments with those from other states. In Hungary such compensating policies do not exist even though German and Austrian firms account for more than one-third of the total number of joint ventures.[43] Trailing only the United States, Germany is the region's second largest investor with more than $7 billion in cumulative investments in central and eastern Europe. This figure reflects not only big projects like VW's investment in Skoda, discussed in chapter 4 below, of German Telekom's and Audi's investments in Hungary. It is, rather, medium-sized firms that are driving Germany's investment push in central Europe. In the Czech Republic German companies had, by 1994, invested in more than 5,000 joint ventures, compared to only 600 for the United States.[44] With much larger wage than productivity differentials, investment opportunities are very enticing for smaller German firms. And these firms do not carry the heavy historical baggage that accompanies large German investment projects like VW's joint venture with Skoda. These economic statistics should be interpreted in the context of the size of Germany's total investment of about DM700 billion in 1993. The total foreign investment of all OECD states in central Europe, to which Germany contributes about one-third, accounted for only about 1 percent of Germany's total domestic investment.[45]

Germany seeks to stabilize the social and political conditions to its east by assisting the process of economic transformation and liberalization through various aid programs. In this respect Germany's position in central Europe and further east is unrivaled. By January 1995 Germany had provided DM45.4 billion to the central and eastern European states, in addition to the DM100 billion allocated to assist the successor states of the Soviet Union; most of these funds were provided in the form of tied loans, granted at concessionary interest rates.[46]

German influence is spread not only directly through aid but also indirectly through institutions. German foreign policy operates in a dual mode. The government's traditional foreign policy

43. Markovits and Reich, *German Predicament*, p. 177.

44. Anjana Shrivastava, "Smaller Firms Lead German Push to East," *The Wall Street Journal* (14 June 1995): A15.

45. "Nur wenige fliehen," *Der Spiegel* 6/1995: 94–95. Schmidt and Naujoks, "Western Enterprises on Eastern Markets," p. 13.

46. Reinhard Wolf, "The Doubtful Mover: Germany and NATO Expansion," in David Haglund, ed., *Will NATO Go East? The Debate over Enlarging the Atlantic Alliance* (forthcoming; currently, unpublished paper, University of Halle, February 1996), p. 4, footnote 3. Markovits and Reich, *German Predicament*, pp. 177, 180.

is complemented by Germany's societal foreign policy (*gesell-schaftliche Aussenpolitik*). Most of the major German institutions conduct their own foreign relations. Typically, they engage partner institutions in other countries thus creating or reinforcing a pattern of transnational relations. This gives German political actors ample opportunities to intervene obliquely in the domestic affairs of the central European states, without throwing their weight around unduly. This is a distinctive style of foreign policy that, writes Jeremiah Riemer, "has been institutionalized and internalized."[47] The creation of electoral systems in central Europe, for example, was assisted by many European parties, "especially the German CDU and SPD, but also British conservatives and American Democratic and Republican strategists."[48] And like their U.S. colleagues, German lawyers were being busily consulted as central and eastern European states drafted new constitutional provisions.

Going beyond electoral and constitutional affairs where Germany's party foundations have been very active in central Europe, institutional effects are also readily apparent in the field of business. The corporate and banking systems in central Europe, for example, are developing along the lines of Germany's universal banks which not only take deposits and make loans but also trade and sell securities and other financial products. According to Mark Nelson, Germany spent heavily between 1990 and 1994 on programs seeking to draft the laws and regulations by which capitalism evolves in central and eastern Europe.[49] In the monetary realm, specifically, German influence is relatively uncontested. And the Bundesbank served as an institutional model for several national banks in central Europe, including Hungary as Péter Gedeon discusses in chapter 3. Following in the footsteps of other German institutions, it has offered extensive training to about 500 central bankers from central and eastern Europe. Each of the central European states floats against a trade-weighted

47. Jeremiah Riemer, "West Germany and the Transition in Eastern Europe," paper prepared for the Annual Meeting of the American Political Science Association, San Francisco, September 1990, p. 20. See also, Peter J. Katzenstein, "The Smaller European States, Germany, and Europe," in Katzenstein, ed., *Tamed Power,* chapter 8, pp. 20–22 (manuscript).

48. Ronald H. Linden, "The New International Political Economy of East Europe," *Studies in Comparative Communism* 25, 1 (March 1992): 7.

49. Mark M. Nelson, "Two Styles of Business Vie in East Europe: Americans, Germans have a Motive in Trying to Mold Laws," *The Wall Street Journal* (3 April 1995): A10. Nelson reports an implausibly high figure of $5.68 billion.

average of foreign currencies in which the DM or ECU account for about two-thirds.[50]

Strong as the German position has rapidly become in central Europe during the 1990s, it is not uncontested. An alternative institutional model is offered by the more free-wheeling Anglo-American banking model which the United States promoted at considerable cost.[51] And despite its phenomenal growth since 1990, German trade accounts for only about one-third of the total external trade and investment figures of the central European economies.[52] This figure is, broadly speaking, in line with Germany's economic weight in the EU.[53] It remains to be seen whether central Europe's economic dependence on Germany will further increase in the coming years or whether it will taper off at levels that are roughly comparable to those of other Western European economies. Early EU enlargement and the lowering of EU tariff barriers would facilitate such a development.

Central Europe and the EU

With the political and economic revolutions of 1989, the collapse of the CMEA, and the disintegration of the Soviet Union, central European trade has shifted with remarkable speed to the EU. While domestic GDP in central Europe declined by about one-fifth between 1989 and 1992, from a very low base Czechoslovakia's imports from the EU rose by 96 percent, Poland's by 62 percent, and

50. The Polish zloty has since May 1995 fluctuated within a band of ±7 percent against a basket of five currencies (45 percent dollar; 35 percent DM; 20 percent other). The Hungarian forint has been on a crawling peg since 1995 with a band of ±2.25 percent around a weighted currency basket (70 percent ECU and 30 percent dollar). For the Czech koruna the band is ±7.5 percent and the trade weights are 65 percent ECU and 35 percent dollar. With identical trade weights, for the Slovak koruna the band is only ±3 percent.

51. Nelson, "Two Styles of Business Vie in East Europe." Nelson mentions an unrealistically high figure of four billion dollars which the United States supposedly spent between 1993 and 1995.

52. Raimo Värynen, "Post-Hegemonic and Post-Socialist Regionalism: A Comparison of Central Europe and East Asia," paper prepared for the ISA-JAIR Joint Convention in Makuhari, Japan, 20–22 September 1996, p. 21.

53. Joseph M. Grieco, "Variation in Regional Economic Institutions in Western Europe, East Asia and the Americas: Magnitude and Sources" (Duke University, Political Science Department, 1994), pp. 20–24, 30–36, and tables 2, 3, 7–9. Alan Siaroff, "Interdependence versus Asymmetry? A Comparison of the European and Asia-Pacific Economic Regions," paper presented at the ISA-West Meetings, Seattle, 14–15 October 1994.

Hungary's by 40 percent. Despite these strong increases the central European economies accounted for less than 1.5 percent of the EU's total external trade in 1992 and this figure has increased only slightly since then.[54] Since the start of the 1990s Western corporations have invested about $25 billion in the four Visegrad countries.[55]

Of similar importance are the institutional links that the central European states have forged with the EU.[56] Movement away from the Communist system was complemented by movement towards the European model. "The most powerful force exerted both on the political systems and the peoples of East Europe," writes Ron Linden, "was the pull of the idea of Europe itself. As the revolutions of 1989 spread, the sentiment was increasingly voiced by those making the changes that they wanted their country to be 'European,' to join or rejoin a political continent from which they had been forcibly cut off."[57] The EC foreign ministers, in turn, issued in December 1991 a declaration which specified the conditions for diplomatic recognition of the central and eastern European states and the successor states to the Soviet Union: respect for the rule of law; for democracy and human rights as laid down in the provisions of the UN Charter, the Final Act of Helsinki setting up the CSCE, and that organization's Charter of Paris adopted in November 1990; and for guarantees for the rights of ethnic and national groups and minorities as specified in the general framework of the CSCE.

In July 1989 the EC took over the coordination of the aid programs of the G-24 for central and eastern Europe. It signed bilateral trade agreements with the central European states in 1990–91. In 1990 the EU initiated a special assistance program for Poland and Hungary; in January 1991 it granted the central European states

54. Alexis Galinos, "Central Europe and the EU: Prospects for Closer Integration," *RFE/RL Research Report* 3, 29 (22 July 1994): 21. See also András Inotai, "Central and Eastern Europe," in C. Randall Henning, Eduard Hochreiter, and Gary Clyde Hufbauer, eds., *Reviving the European Union* (Washington D.C.: Institute for International Economics, April 1994), pp. 139–64, and Barry P. Bosworth and Gur Ofer, *Reforming Planned Economies in an Integrating World Economy* (Washington D.C.: The Brookings Institution, 1995), pp. 119–46. John Pinder, *The European Community and Eastern Europe* (New York: Council of Foreign Relations Press, 1991).

55. Ellingstad, "German Domination in Central Europe," p. 4.

56. Thomas A. Baylis, *The West and Eastern Europe: Economic Statecraft and Political Change* (Westport, Conn.: Praeger, 1994). Wolfgang H. Reinicke, *Building a New Europe: The Challenge of System Transformation and Systemic Reform* (Washington D.C.: Brookings Institution, 1992). "After Communism: What?" *Dædalus* 123, 3 (Summer 1994).

57. Linden, "New International Political Economy," p. 7.

Generalized System of Preferences (GSP) status normally reserved for developing economies; subsequently, in 1991, it eliminated some quantitative restrictions on steel and iron and increased the quotas for the import of textiles and garments; and after eighteen months of negotiations the EU signed Association Agreements (the so-called "Europe Agreements") in December 1991 which also sought to institutionalize a regular policy dialogue while specifying conditions on questions of economic and political reforms and guarantees of human rights. By the end of 1991 central European firms enjoyed EU tariff preferences over non-European firms. But because the EU exempted sensitive sectors such as agriculture, textiles, and steel from trade liberalization, sectors in which they enjoy the largest comparative advantage, the central European states have had a more restricted access to the EU market than do some of the associate Mediterranean members of the EU.

In the summer of 1993, at its Copenhagen summit, the EU made additional policy concessions while specifying a catalogue of conditions that the central European states had to meet prior to becoming full EU members. Subsequently, in May 1994, the EU offered its central and eastern European associate members an "associate partnership" in the West European Union (WEU), the EU's security and defense organizations.

The applications that Poland, Hungary, and the Czech Republic subsequently filed for full membership have met stiff resistance from several members of the EU. Imports in sensitive sectors, such as agriculture, steel, chemicals, and garments, are meeting stiff protectionist resistance in the EU. After sharp increases in central European exports in these sectors between 1989 and 1992, the European Association Agreements of 1991 brought export growth to a halt. Thus imports from central Europe in sensitive sectors barely topped 2 percent of the EU's total imports in 1992.[58] Finally, for strategic and economic reasons France and the southern European states do not see the EU's eastern enlargement as a high-priority issue. Strategically, they worry about a possible destabilization of North African politics through Islam. And on economic grounds France fears that Polish membership could wreck the system of the Common Agricultural Policy (CAP), while Spain, Portugal, and Greece are fearful of diminishing subsidies from the EU's structural and cohesion funds.[59] On a per capita basis Hungary's income

58. Galinos, "Central Europe and the EU," pp. 20–21.

59. András Inotai estimates that the total transfer of EU funds to the central European economies would amount to about sixty to 90 percent (or ten to sixteen billion

was $2,720 in 1991 as compared to $2,470 for Czechoslovakia and $1,790 for Poland; these figures amounted, respectively, to 45, 41, and 30 percent of Portugal's per capita income, which itself is only half of Spain's. Having greatly benefited from EU membership, the southern European states, together with France, are not eager to help create the unavoidable political pressures for redistribution favoring central Europe in an enlarged EU.[60] German policy will thus be crucial in determining the pace of the EU's incorporation of central Europe.

Central Europe and NATO

With the end of the Cold War, for a brief moment in 1990 the debate about the future security structure of Europe was genuinely open.[61] NATO, the Conference for Security and Cooperation in Europe (CSCE), and the WEU (as the foreign policy arm of the EC) all offered different institutional possibilities. Among these the United States preferred redefining and broadening NATO's mission, beyond the collective defense provisions of Article V, to act as guarantor of European security; Germany favored upgrading the importance of the CSCE, an institution that it had helped found in 1975, into the center of a new pan-European security structure embedding East and West; and France hoped to enhance the importance of the EC and WEU in providing for European security. Political reactions to the initial crises of the post-Cold War era in 1991 (the Gulf War, the beginning of the war in Yugoslavia, and the failed coup in the Soviet Union) all helped bring about a NATO-centered security structure.

ECU) of the current subsidies paid to the southern European states. The longer the delay before the central European states become full-fledged members, the smaller the needed transfer payments. See his paper, "From the Association Agreements to Full Membership? The Dynamics of Relations between the Central and Eastern European Countries and the European Union," paper presented at the Fourth Biennial International Conference of European Community Studies Association, 11–14 May 1995, Charleston, South Carolina, p. 13.

60. Christian Deubner, Heinz Kramer, Elke Thiel, "Die Erweiterung der Europäischen Union nach Mittel- und Osteuropa," SWP-AP 2818 (Stiftung Wissenschaft und Politik, Ebenhausen, November 1993), p. 24.

61. Allen Sens, *The Security of Small States in Post-Cold War Europe: A New Research Agenda?*, Working Paper No. 1, University of British Columbia, Institute of International Relations, January 1994. See also the debate between Charles A. Kupchan and Clifford A. Kupchan, "Concerts, Collective Security, and the Future of Europe," *International Security* 16, 1 (Summer 1991): 114–61, and Richard K. Betts, "Systems for Peace or Causes of War?" *International Security* 17, 1 (Summer 1992): 5–43.

Yet in the fall of 1989 this outcome was not preordained. Adopted in November 1990, the CSCE Charter of Paris was based on the assumption that states would be willing to comply with the procedures, rules, and norms laid down by CSCE mechanisms and institutions. Small organizational headquarters dealing with security, dispute and conflict resolution, and elections and democracy were set up, respectively, in Prague, Vienna, and Warsaw, soon to be marginalized by the crises in the post-Cold War era. The CSCE Helsinki Summit Declaration emphasized human and democratic rights and, seeking a global affiliation, in effect made the CSCE a regional organization of the UN.[62]

In an initial move designed to facilitate contacts with central Europe, NATO's London Summit set up liaison officers between central Europe and NATO in June 1990. NATO created the North Atlantic Cooperation Council (NACC) in late 1991 as the main forum for dialogue and cooperation on security issues affecting NATO and the former member states of the WTO. By fall 1992, at its Oslo summit, NATO agreed that it should act on behalf of the CSCE. This was a precursor for NATO's Partnership for Peace (PFP). The Partnership offered a vehicle for concrete military cooperation between NATO and the former members of the WTO, including operational cooperation in defense budgeting, joint planning and exercises, peacekeeping operations, disaster relief and crisis management. This is also a possible, though not an automatic, pathway toward eventual NATO membership for states that have successfully consolidated their transitions to market-oriented, democratically organized political systems and that have refurbished their militaries and acquired the capabilities necessary to operate under joint NATO command. The chief tasks for the central European states are establishing a clear civilian control over the military; fundamental changes in strategic doctrine and operational planning; and significant changes in procurement and logistics.[63]

62. Lecture delivered by Martin Palous, former foreign minister of Czechoslovakia, "Security Issues in Eastern and Central Europe," Cornell University, Institute for European Studies, 18 April 1994.

63. Thomas S. Szayna and F. Stephen Larrabee, *East European Military Reform after the Cold War: Implications for the United States* (Santa Monica: RAND, National Defense Research Institute, 1995). *Conversion of the Military Production: Comparative Approach* (Bratislava: Friedrich-Ebert Foundation, 1993). Szemlér, *Relations between Germany and East Central Europe*, pp. 7–53. Zoltan Barany, "The Military and Political Transitions in Eastern Europe," unpublished manuscript, Department of Government, University of Texas at Austin, n.d.

During his trip to Europe in July 1994, President Clinton stated that it is "no longer a question of whether, but when and how." The U.S. Presidential election in 1996 fixed the date with Senator Dole and the President both agreeing that enlargement should happen before the year 2000. Poland, Hungary, and the Czech Republic have expressed a strong interest in being admitted to NATO at an early date. Security concerns, especially about the stability of Russian democracy and the peacefulness of Russian foreign policy, have mattered greatly. So does a strong sense that to be part of the West means to be part not only of the EU but also of NATO. For reasons that chapter 5 discusses in some detail, alone among the central European states Slovakia may not be included in the initial group to be admitted to full NATO membership.

For the same reasons that the central European states wish to join NATO at an early date, government and opposition in Russia are strongly opposed.[64] NATO's Eastern enlargement would tilt the balance of power further against a much weakened Russian military; and, barring a fixed timetable for Russian NATO membership, it would symbolize that even a capitalist and democratic Russia was not part of the West. For this reason the German government has not taken a uniform position on this issue. While Defense Minister Rühe has been a strong advocate of early NATO enlargement, Chancellor Kohl and Foreign Minister Kinkel have adopted a more cautious line which leaves open the interpretation that they favor enlargement as a long-term process that eventually would also include Russia and thus might transform NATO from a collective defense to a collective security institution.[65] To date, Germany's Eastern policy is thus predicated on an unwillingness to choose between NATO enlargement with or without Russia. Whether earlier or later, with the United States and Germany both committed to their joining NATO, the central European states, with the possible exception of Slovakia, are well on their way to becoming NATO members.

Preview

Chapters 2–5 cover a total of fourteen cases dealing with many of the economic, social, and ethnic problems that the central European states are facing in the 1990s. The concluding chapter 6 argues

64. Though less vocal, the Ukrainian government also fears being left out of an emerging European security architecture and thus having to cope with Russia on its own.

65. Wolf, "The Doubtful Mover."

that, for a number of reasons, the dynamics of central European integration existed only before 1993; since then the central European states have been powerfully affected by European and international rather than subregional factors.

Włodek Aniol, Timothy Byrnes, and Elena Iankova argue in chapter 2 that Poland's return to Europe is marked by the strong cross-currents between Polish nationalists, organized around the trade union and the Catholic Church, which helped bring the Communist system down and cosmopolitans, many of whom are voters of post-Communist parties, who are deeply attracted by the model of a secular welfare state and a capitalist democracy. Poland's Western orientation is reflected in the affinity between its transformative corporatism that helps govern its political economy, its embracing of European norms and conventions dealing, for example, with issues of identity (the German ethnic minority)[66] and security (migration). Returning to Europe can mean importing liberal norms, as in the case of ethnic minorities, or adopting restrictive policies, as in the case of migration. But in all instances it means choosing a multilateral over a bilateral approach. Poland's Catholic Church meanwhile has in mind not merely adjusting to European norms but civilizing of Western Europe, multilaterally if possible and unilaterally if necessary, through the revitalization of a religious faith and morality long lost in a secular and commercial world.

Péter Gedeon argues in chapter 3 that, compared to Poland, the role of the Church in Hungary is much weaker as is the legacy of fearing Germany. In the case of privatization and the inflow of foreign investment, for example, German influence is no source of political debate or concern. In the area of social policy the German model shows a certain amount of influence but this effect is undermined by the contradictory constraints of democratic politics and economic efficiency. Both constraints limit Hungary's emulation of the German welfare state. The crucial international actors affecting Hungary's social policy are the IMF and the World Bank. They are very active in helping develop the formation of a new social policy regime in Hungary. The situation differs in the case of Hungary's National Bank (NBH). Here the German institutional model is powerful, although democratic politics has mediated this influence. As a result of legal regulations the autonomy of the NBH does not match that of the Bundesbank, and the government

66. See also Grzegorz Ekiert, "The Return of the German Minority to Poland," *German Politics and Society* 26 (Summer 1992): 90–108.

made efforts to circumvent the legal restrictions under which it operates. But under circumstances of economic crisis a hardening of external constraints in international markets may counterbalance the effect of democratic politics and pressure the government to observe more strictly the institutionalized autonomy of the National Bank.

In chapter 4 Hynek Jeřábek and František Zich argue that VW's acquisition of Skoda illuminates the growing international links that tie the Czech economy to German, European, and world markets. Both Skoda and the Czech government badly wanted an infusion of Western capital and know-how in order to secure the future of a corporation occupying a strategic position inside the Czech economy. However, VW's takeover has exposed Skoda to economic dependence. This opens the Czech economy to international influences few envisaged when the initial deal was signed. Hard times in Wolfsburg sharply reduced the growth and technological potential of this crucial Czech company. Czech media have internationalized even more rapidly than the automobile industry. German influence was virtually unchecked in the regional press, with one Bavarian publishing company quickly acquiring monopoly control over the regional press in Bohemia. In electronic media, on the other hand, the issuance of a license to the first private national television station in 1993 opened the Czech market not to German but to American investors who provided two-thirds of the capital of CET 21.

Finally, the historically laden issue of Czech-German relations in the Czech borderlands and the position of the Sudeten Germans illustrates how progress toward Czech membership in the EU is complicated by a political issue that has bedeviled central European politics for many decades. Euroregions as a concrete counter have none of the political salience that the Sudeten Germans evoke with their political demands for official recognition as a dialogue partner for the Czech government. The difficulties in official German-Czech relations explain why by March 1996 half of the Czech public viewed Germany as a danger for the Czech economy, a slight increase as compared to 1992. The proportion of those viewing Germany as a source of political danger jumped by ten points to 39 percent.[67] A joint declaration agreed to in December 1996 and signed in January 1997 by Prime Minister Klaus and Chancellor Kohl trades German apologies for its invasion and

---

67. *Frankfurter Allgemeine Zeitung* (10 April 1996): 1.

annexation of Czechoslovakia in 1938–39 for Czech apologies for the expulsion of three million Sudeten Germans at the end of World War II.[68] Now ratified, this declaration may help to gradually improve bilateral relations as both governments have now agreed not to burden their future relationship with the burdens of the past.

Daneš Brzica, Zuzana Poláčková, and Ivo Samson argue in chapter 5 that, beyond the double transformation of moving to democracy and capitalism, Slovakia is experimenting, for the first time in a thousand years, with sovereign statehood. Thus the fight for power in Slovakia's domestic politics is intense and the reluctance of the government to embrace an integration strategy is palatable. For reasons of national identity Slovakia is interested in charting its own way, separate from the Czech Republic. It sees itself as a bridge between East and West. In some policy areas, such as the conversion of its armaments industry, the Slovak government has moved with dramatic speed to shut down most of its production facilities in record time, thus creating enormous unemployment problems in several regions of the country. Rather than following through with the voucher privatization that Czechoslovakia had started, the decision of the government to maintain national control over privatized firms has been the source of intense domestic conflict and some nervousness in international capital markets. Because it fits current political needs Slovakia, more than the other central European states, is intent on institutionalizing a bank-led German rather than a market-led Anglo-American system. Slovak policy regarding the Hungarian ethnic minority is not firmly committed to European norms and practices. Slovakia has permitted the issue of minority rights to be at the center of the political agenda since the country gained its independence in 1993. Finally, in its security policy the Slovak government, more than the Polish government, stresses traditional military concerns and has chosen to maintain cordial relations with Russia while viewing NATO with some suspicion. On most counts then Slovakia is less strongly oriented toward western Europe than are Poland, Hungary, and the Czech Republic.

The international relations of central Europe, Valerie Bunce argues in chapter 6, have seen a substantial change in a very short time. Seeking to revive historical memories and consolidate the gains of the revolution of 1989, the central European states undertook

---

68. Craig R. Whitney, "Germans and Czechs Try to Heal Hatreds of the Nazi Era," *The New York Times* (22 January 1997): A3.

numerous attempts at institution building in the region between 1990 and 1992. In November 1989 Austria, Czechoslovakia, Hungary, Italy, and the former Yugoslavia signed the Pentagonale Agreement which Poland joined in 1991 and the Ukraine in 1992; Belarus, Bulgaria, Romania, and Germany's Bavaria have asked to participate in specific projects. Poland, Hungary and Czechoslovakia signed in February 1990 the so-called Trilateral Cooperation Agreement. Evoking the historical memory of the 1335 meeting between their three kings, the Visegrad summit of February 1991 codified the trilateral cooperation between these three central European states, specifically a strengthening of economic and defense ties as well as the development of a common approach to NATO and the EU. In 1992 this organization was renamed the Central European Initiative (CEI), even though the four central European states and the Ukraine signed in February 1993 an agreement covering broader cooperation. Various cooperative ventures are covering a wide array of policy sectors dealing with, among other things, energy, migration, the environment, research and development, culture, tourism, transport, telecommunications, information, and small enterprises. Finally, the establishment of the Central European Free Trade Area (CEFTA) in 1992 prepared the ground for a decision to abolish tariffs in the region by 1998.

But as chapter 6 argues, since 1993 these attempts have flagged as central Europe became in the eyes of the Czech government in particular a hindrance for rapid integration with Western Europe. Because the Czechs, in their own self-perceptions, are Europeans, not central Europeans, European, not central European multilateralism is for the Czech government the preferred way of linking up quickly to Germany and Europe. This contrasts sharply with the policy the Ukrainian government has adopted in its relations with Russia and the CIS. Despite its apparent weakness it has opted for bilateralism. Even though it receives the lion's share of U.S. aid in central-eastern Europe, the Ukrainian government rejects the notion that multilateralism will somehow constrain Russia as the stronger power. It fears that multilateralism will become a vehicle through which Russian power in the CIS will be magnified. Central European governments have no similar fears in their relations with the EU and Germany. Central European integration was also hindered by the constant irritation that the minority issue has generated in the relations between Hungary and Slovakia since 1993. In short, as has been true of Scandinavia in recent years, central European cooperation was stymied by the dynamic of European integration which has eaten away at integration processes in all of Europe's subregions.

The case studies in this book illustrate two broad sets of factors that are affecting the political choices of the central European states. International factors are shaping the definition of interests of Poland and the Czech Republic. In the case studies presented in chapters 2 and 4 Polish interests are shaped by the primacy of international norms, Czech interests by the primacy of economic internationalization. Because the seven case studies are only illustrative, we cannot be sure that this reflects a more general difference between the two countries. The analytical difference between international norms and economic internationalization is, however, significant since, to varying degrees, these two factors are affecting all four central European states.

In contrast, chapter 3 argues for the relatively greater importance of domestic factors in Hungary's policies of economic and social experimentation. Similarly, chapter 5 illustrates the importance of domestic politics in the Slovak Republic which, on issues such as privatization and minority rights, appears to be motivated substantially by a domestic politics of regime consolidation. Although the Hungarian and Slovak case studies are only illustrative, they point to the range of conditions under which domestic politics greatly matter in all four central European states.

Finally, these chapters illustrate the different weight of the memories of past German policies, less powerful in Poland than in the Czech Republic, and virtually absent in Hungary and the Slovak Republic.[69] The effects that the policies and developments of recent years are having on the reconstruction of the relationships between Germany and the central European states remain unclear today. But because they are occurring in a Europe, and with a Germany, that is much more internationalized than was true before 1945, the evidence of this book suggests that the developments and policies of the 1990s are cutting against a deep historical grain.

Friedrich Naumann's vision of central Europe "sought a comprehensive political solution for the national and social problems of his era ... a postwar German society interrelated with other nations

---

69. Markovits and Reich, *The German Predicament*, pp. 109–19. Petr Príhoda, "Wenn die Erinnerung die Zukunft blockiert," *Die Zeit* (10 May 1996): 8.

of Middle Europe and living with them in a new context of social and cultural relationships."[70] I have argued here that central Europe is no longer a political program. It may well be in the process of becoming a set of distinctive domestic structures that we can analyze as types of corporatist politics that differ but are related to the types that have evolved in Austria, Switzerland, and Germany. The effect of international politics on this western-central European corporatism has been profound as a liberal international economy has contributed to the consolidation and perpetuation of democratic corporatism in the cases of Germany, Austria, and Switzerland. The EU and international markets more generally are probably having an analogous effect on Poland, Hungary, the Czech Republic, and Slovakia in the 1990s and beyond.

In the postwar era central Europe shrank to Germany, with Austria and Switzerland as little noticed appendages. A transatlantic historical consensus measured the German problem in terms of its deviation from the Western path to modernity. The peaceful citizen revolutions which helped bring about the end of the Cold War, the liberation of central Europe, and German unification open up the possibility, indeed the necessity, of rethinking afresh "the German question," and other German questions in central Europe and in Europe at large.[71]

Naumann's conception of central Europe entailed the view of politics as a zero-sum game. "We know that when we win, others must lose. Yet this fact should not keep us from wanting to win."[72] German nationalism and imperialism, its dynamic society and its Nietzschean lust for power, no longer preoccupy and threaten the world as they once did.[73] And central European affairs have moved to the margins of world politics. This development is remarkable in light of the profound upheavals and horrors which Germany has caused in the past and which central and eastern Europe have suffered. Multilateral regimes are inhibiting unilateral German

70. Henry Cord Meyer, "Naumann and Rathenau: Their Paths to the Weimar Republic," in Leonard Krieger and Fritz Stern, eds., *The Responsibility of Power: Historical Essays in Honor of Hajo Holborn* (Garden City: Doubleday, 1967), pp. 302, 306.

71. Michael Geyer and Konrad H. Jarausch, "The Future of the German Past: Transatlantic Reflections for the 1990s," *Central European History* 22, 3/4 (September/December 1989): 229–59. For an early attempt that seeks to place German questions in a new light after 1989, see Pond and Schoenbaum, *The 'German Question' and other German Questions*.

72. Meyer, "Naumann and Rathenau," pp. 304–5.

73. David Calleo, *The German Problem Reconsidered: Germany and the World Order, 1870 to the Present* (Cambridge: Cambridge University Press, 1978).

initiatives along the lines of traditional power politics. This is also occurring in the way power is organized in German domestic politics. Power and wealth in central Europe are beginning to be thought of not only in relative but also in absolute terms. Yet if this way of thinking is to become firmly institutionalized, the convergence of central Europe with Western Europe as well as their integration will have to be taken to a new and higher level.

2. POLAND
Returning to Europe

Włodek Aniol, Timothy A. Byrnes, Elena A. Iankova

Poland began its return to Europe with the rise of mass discontent and relatively spontaneous revolts against the policies of the Communist regime in 1956, 1968, 1970, and 1976. Soviet pressure and domestic repression, of course, denied success to these recurrent rebellions and protest movements. And because the United States and the Soviet Union respected each others' sphere of influence,[1] only domestic opposition movements could liberate central and eastern Europe from its dictatorial regimes. In the early 1980s only one Soviet bloc country contained any internal force which constituted a serious threat to the state socialist regimes and to the preeminence of the Soviet Union in the region. For in Poland after 1976 a politically potent labor movement,[2] infused with a strong Polish nationalism which had turned against Russia and the Soviet Union, was supported by dissident intellectuals and a powerful Catholic Church. The ascent of the first independent mass organization, the Solidarity trade union with a membership of about ten million, was the turning point in the courageous struggle of the Polish people for liberalization within the Soviet empire. Moreover, Poland's mass oppositional movement proved crucial in helping to bring about fundamental change

1. David S. Mason, *Revolution and Transition in East-Central Europe* (Boulder: Westview Press, 1996), p. 9. Chris Harman, *Class Struggles in Eastern Europe 1945–83* (London: Bookmarks, 1988), p. 17.

2. The Workers Defense Committee (KOR) formed in 1976 and the precursor of Solidarity, the Committee of Free Trade Unions, was established in 1978. When the Independent Self-Governing Trade Union "Solidarity" was founded on 17 September 1980 it already had three million members.

throughout the region. For Poland's political opposition weakened the whole Soviet bloc in the 1980s, and this helps explain the sudden, volcanic eruptions that shook the Soviet empire in 1989, which quickly led to the collapse of political regimes throughout the region. Poland's mass-based political opposition made it probable that its Communist government would be replaced not through violent revolution but through a negotiated process of reform.[3] Political compromise to some extent blurred the distinction between old and new political arrangements, thus concealing the true import of the portentous changes that 1989 brought to Poland and to the rest of central and Eastern Europe. Poland's transformative corporatism is a case in point. It is also an institutional example of how Poland has charted its own distinctive return to Europe.

The democratic revolution of 1989 has given Poland new opportunities "to return to Europe," to re-establish traditional links with the West. Having overcome half a century of dependence on the Soviet Union, Poland now wants to be incorporated fully in the network of Western European and North Atlantic interdependence. At present, Poland is no longer facing the threat of becoming once again a satellite state. But if it were to remain on the economic periphery of the West, relegated to a gray security zone, this would amount to condemning Poland to a continued existence in a new, though qualitatively different, structure of dependence.[4]

Poland's policy of Western integration has great importance for both national security and economic prosperity.[5] Although it involves many economic and social issues, Poland's relationship with the European Union (EU) is, above all, a political one. Growing links with the Union support both national security and democratic transformation. Furthermore, Poland's economic recovery and social stability are heavily dependent on not only economic aid and technical support from the West, but also on the fashioning of an adequate security arrangement with the North

3. Eric Hobsbawm, *The Age of Extremes: A History of the World, 1914–1991* (New York: Pantheon Books, 1994), p. 487.

4. Roman Kuźniar, "The Geostrategic Factors Conditioning Poland's Security," *The Polish Quarterly of International Affairs*, 2, 1 (Winter 1993): 19.

5. See, for example, "Statement by Mr. Krzysztof Skubiszewski, Minister for Foreign Affairs of the Republic of Poland, on Poland's foreign policy in 1993 to the Diet of the Republic of Poland, Warsaw, 29 April 1993," *Materials and Documents* 2, 5 (1993): 131.

Atlantic Treaty Organization (NATO) or the West European Union (WEU).[6] Poland's return to Europe thus touches on a full range of political, economic, social, and security issues. Enhanced cooperation with Western European and trans-Atlantic partners and institutions serves three purposes: it increases the sense of security, particularly as central-eastern Europe faces new tensions and conflicts; it helps Poland overcome a development and technological gap that separates it from the West; and it keeps Poland on the road to institutionalizing fully democracy, the rule of law, and a market economy.

As has been true for more than a millennium, Germany occupies a special place in Poland's relations with the West. The history of Polish-German relations contains dark chapters: Germany's allegedly eternal *Drang nach Osten* (eastward drive), the invasions by the Teutonic Order in the fourteenth to fifteenth centuries, three partitions of Poland toward the end of the eighteenth century that were much to the profit of Prussia, and the horrible German occupation of Poland as the main site of the holocaust during World War II. But, at the same time, this relationship has also seen its brighter moments. Since the Middle Ages important intellectual trends, including Catholic theology and the ideas of the Reformation, the Enlightenment, and Humanism, advanced eastward carried by the German language. Then too, successive waves of German settlers brought to Poland legal patterns, merchant capital, and modern technologies.

Poland's most direct route to achieving membership in the EU and NATO in the 1990s leads through Germany. It is not only a matter of geographical proximity, but also of inescapable economic, political, and social links. Germany's economic strength is an important factor that draws Poland into the process of Western European integration abroad while simultaneously stimulating economic growth and modernization at home.

This path is not free of risk. Central Europe is a traditional zone of German influence, and in the aftermath of the disintegration of the Soviet Union, Russia has lost control over events in this region. Germany can be expected to fill some of the economic and political vacuum that now exists. Some argue that united Germany will

6. In accordance with "The principles of Polish security policy and the defense strategy of the Republic of Poland," issued by the National Defense Council on 2 November 1992, the main strategic external objectives of this policy are economic and political integration with the European Community and membership in NATO.

now reconstruct a new version of "Mitteleuropa."[7] Poland thus might be relegated once again to an economic hinterland and in the role of a political satellite.

Germany, however, is among the strongest supporters of Poland's return as a full-fledged member in various Western institutions which have anchored its transformation since World War II.[8] For reasons of its own national security and social stability, Germany is interested in moving the borders of the EU and NATO further eastward, while at the same time hoping to avoid an isolation of Russia in the process.

Germany's membership in the EU, NATO, and other European and Western institutions is thus extremely important. A better functioning EU, with stronger institutions to which member states have transferred important competencies, is in the best interest of Poland. A loose system of intergovernmental co-operation, on the other hand, harbors the danger of domination by the strongest states of Europe. It remains subject to power politics in which some are "more sovereign than others."[9] Although it may be more difficult for Poland to qualify for full membership, a more tightly integrated EU would anchor united Germany in a broader European unit that could only enhance Polish security.

Public opinion polls conducted in Poland in 1990 showed the predominance of negative German stereotypes; they also revealed, however, a remarkable willingness to develop relations with the Federal Republic of Germany.[10] But with the passing of time the Poles have begun to look westward more anxiously. In particular, opposition to the increasing scope of activities of Western corporations in Poland has increased.[11] Specifically, anxiety concerning

7. Jacques Rupnik, "Central Europe or Mitteleuropa?" *Daedalus*, 119, 1 (Winter 1990).

8. See Peter J. Katzenstein, ed., *Tamed Power: Germany in Europe* (Ithaca: Cornell University Press, 1997).

9. Ferdinand Kinsky, "Germany's European Policy and Impact on Central Europe," paper presented at the CEU Conference on "Germany in the Central-East European Crisis Zone," Stirin, 19–22 September 1993, pp. 6–7.

10. Aldona Kloskowska, "Neighbourhood Cultures: Some Aspects of Difficult Historical Neighbourhoods," *International Sociology*, 7, 1 (March 1992).

11. In February 1992, 37 percent of the respondents in a public opinion poll opposed foreign investment, compared to 30 percent in November 1991 and 24 percent in September 1991. Disapproval of foreign projects in Poland is expressed primarily by older, less-educated, and poor people. For more details on this poll, conducted by the Pentor Institute, a Polish-American survey research institute, see *The Warsaw Voice*, 1 (March 1992): 4.

German investments in Poland is reflected in the stereotyped view that "the Germans are buying up Poland."

This shift in public opinion illustrates a deeper aspect of Polish politics regarding Western Europe and Germany. This chapter illustrates that Polish politics is divided into two camps, one internationalist and the other nationalist. Internationalism is promoted by "Europeans" and "cosmopolitans" who constantly invoke the theme of "returning to Europe." Internationalists want to catch up and integrate with an economically efficient, democratic, and secular Europe. For them, Germany is a bridge between the West and Poland, a force pulling the country westward.

A second camp consists of "isolationists," "true Poles," and "nationalists" who view closer links with an integrating Europe as a threat. They fear limitations imposed on Poland's sovereignty. They are apprehensive about political, economic, and cultural dependence on the West, and on Germany in particular. And they resent the loss of the Catholic Church's influence in Polish society.

This cleavage is not yet constitutive of Polish politics, and the main political divisions that have been the basis for building coalitions since 1989 continue to follow other lines. To date, a Solidarity background on the one hand and a Communist past on the other have been more important in shaping possible political alliances. But as the weight of the past recedes, coalitional patterns organized around this new axis are certain to become more central.

The presidential election of November 1995 illustrated the political struggle over a relatively open and a relatively closed Poland. Although most candidates running for the presidency were firmly in favor of joining NATO and the EU, some expressed doubts about Poland's moves to join the West. During the campaign one could hear voices warning against a blind acceptance of Europe that might conflict with Poland's national interests. And the economic implications of integration with the EU raised alarm, especially regarding Polish agricultural policy.[12]

The results of the second round of the elections showed Polish society to be split down the middle. While traditional, Catholic, rural Poland, located mostly in the south and east, voted for the incumbent Lech Wałesa, the more outward-looking, modernizing, and entrepreneurial sector of the country, the north and west (interestingly, the most Germanized parts of Poland) backed Aleksander Kwaśniewski, who won the election by a small margin.

---

12. See Andrzej Szczypiorski, "Straszenie Europą" ["Europe as Bogeyman"], *Polityka*, (23 September, 1995): 3.

This divide has much to do with social divisions and different public attitudes regarding Poland's "return to Europe." Opinion polls reveal that, in the process of integration, a significant sector of the public supports the view that Poland should not merely be "absorbed" but should rather retain a specific national identity.[13]

Poland's powerful Catholic Church is the core institution and symbol for this sense of national identity. It stands strongly behind its specific civilizational mission. The Church was a mainstay of opposition against the Communist regime to which it never surrendered. It played an instrumental part in the growing opposition movement that eventually toppled Communism in Poland and beyond. And it has a clear vision of the Catholic as opposed to the secular Europe to which it would like to link Poland. Thus just as a Catholic Poland set limits to political authoritarianism in Poland in the past, it is likely to set limits to secular internationalism in the future. Poland's European orientation is indelibly bound up with the civilizational mission which is acutely felt by one of the most important institutions in the Polish polity.

This chapter traces Poland's return to Europe in three case studies that amplify these themes by examining in greater detail the policy and politics of Poland's Western orientation in four areas: 1) the emergence of a transformative corporatism to help govern the process of economic transformation; 2) the role of the Catholic Church in public life; 3) migration policy; and 4) the protection of ethnic minorities, with special reference to the situation of Poland's German minority.

13. In a public opinion poll conducted by Pentor in late 1991 the Poles were asked whether Poland would gain or lose economically if it were to join the EC. The answers were: gain—15 percent; gain more than lose—52 percent; lose more than gain—16 percent; lose—2 percent; hard to say—15 percent. See *The Warsaw Voice* (12 January 1992): 5. At the same time, 52 percent of the population believed Poland should move towards a Christian-national model, while 47 percent supported a West European model. This means that the majority of the society did not accept a march towards a Western model of public life. Ibid., p. 8.

In October 1995, 84 percent of the Poles declared their support for joining the European Union, and more than three-fourths of the population backed Poland's membership in NATO. At the same time, as many as 62 percent did not agree with the opinion that "Poland should join Europe and accept the way of life existing there, even at the expense of her own tradition." See *Rzeczpospolita* (25 October 1995): 5.

Transformative Corporatism and Poland's Return to Europe

The central role that Poland's Solidarity union played in the process of undermining the entire Soviet bloc was fully manifested for the first time in the historical compromise that Solidarity and the government negotiated in Szczecin, Gdansk, and Jastrzebie in August–September 1980. These agreements preserved the leading role of the party in the governance of the state, but they also acknowledged the right of independent political organizations to exist. By December 1981, however, fearing the threat of armed Soviet intervention,[14] the government declared martial law.

Martial law did not stop Solidarity's attempt to democratize Poland in a non-revolutionary, non-violent manner. This strategy led to slow but considerable and subsequently irreversible changes. One achievement of the 1980–81 mass movement was the creation of the Ministry for Liaison with Trade Unions which functioned throughout the 1980s. A Trade Union Act adopted in 1982 sanctioned the recognition of collective labor disputes and the right to strike. More important, the events of 1980–81 widened the cracks within the Soviet empire. Especially after Gorbachev initiated a process of liberalization in the form of *glasnost* and *perestroika* in 1985, the Soviet empire could no longer be propped up by military means.

A wave of strikes in the spring and summer of 1988 brought about a radical shift in the balance of power between regime and opposition. This became public knowledge in early 1989, during the round-table negotiations between the ruling elite and opposition leaders. An agreement signed on 5 April 1989 ratified several explosive political concessions the government felt compelled to make. The agreement provided for Solidarity's legal reinstatement, guaranteed trade union pluralism at the workplace, and promised genuine parliamentary pluralism. The price the opposition paid for these concessions was high. "Contractual" parliamentary elections guaranteed a Communist majority; and the creation of a new office of the president (with power over the armed forces and control over foreign policy), to be held by General Jaruzelski, was meant to ensure continued Communist domination over the government.

14. David S. Mason, *Revolution and Transition in East-Central Europe* (Boulder: Westview Press, 1996), p. 5.

However, the June 1989 elections brought a total victory for Solidarity. Although the Solidarity union had been legally recognized as late as 17 April 1989, its candidates won all of the Sejm seats they could contest and ninety-nine of the one hundred seats in the resurrected Senate. This election victory was the beginning of a chain reaction that toppled regimes throughout the region by the end of the year. An agreement subsequently negotiated between the democratic opposition and the reformists within the Communist party paved the way for Poland's peaceful, early exit from state socialism.[15] By the end of August 1989 the first non-Communist government, headed by Poland's Tadeusz Mazowiecki, had seized power in the Soviet bloc, dramatically accelerating the unfolding process of regime collapse throughout the Soviet empire. By the end of 1989, with the exception of Romania, the peaceful victory of the opposition over state socialism throughout central and Eastern Europe had been completed.

The period of transformation that followed Poland's "return to Europe" was expressed in domestic processes of democratization, liberalization and "marketization." Although the reinstatement of liberal politics and free markets constitutes a return to "the West" in its broader ideological definition, these adjustments do not lead inexorably to a single capitalist model. Instead, the collapse of state socialism reminds us of the many rival capitalisms that now exist or are in the process of emerging. Poland and the post-Communist countries in central and eastern Europe are contributing to this pluralization of capitalism with specific, national varieties of what is referred to here as "transformative corporatism."[16]

Transformative corporatism is a specific form of linking state and market in post-Communist countries which, in an era of unsettling change, takes into account both conflictual societal interests and the maintenance of a modicum of social peace through processes of bargained exchange between government and social groups. Transformative corporatism seeks to combine the economic efficiency of markets with the power of government intervention. Moreover, it attempts to neutralize the destructive tendencies of unregulated markets and the inflexibilities of a planned economy. In central and eastern Europe transformative

---

15. David Ost, *Solidarity and the Politics of Anti-Politics: Opposition and Reform in Poland since 1968* (Philadelphia: Temple University Press, 1990).

16. See also Elena A. Iankova, "Social Partnership after the Cold War: The Transformative Corporatism of Post-Communist Europe," Ph.D. dissertation, Cornell University, May 1997.

corporatism is the bridge that links capitalist markets and state power. At the crossroads of contradictory interests, transformative corporatism makes possible liberal markets, market efficiencies, and profits through the political pressures exerted by state officials and emerging business and employer organizations. It makes planned, adequate wages possible through the pressure trade unions exert on the process of corporatist interest coordination; then too, at the very least, it holds open the possibility for a socially responsible redistribution of publicly owned assets through the involvement of public and private sectors in processes of bargained exchange.

The transformative corporatism that characterizes the central and eastern European model of capitalism resembles Western European corporatism in three ways. First, as is true of transformative corporatism, the corporatist practices that emerged in western Europe after World War II were designed to facilitate economic recovery. Second, transformative corporatism resembles the political stabilization pacts that helped bring about democratic transitions in southern Europe in the 1970s. Finally, transformative corporatism resembles in some important ways the democratic corporatist practices which evolved in many Western European countries in the 1960s and 1970s.

However, important differences exist between these two models of corporatist governance. These differences, when compared to the political experiences of Western and southern Europe, are due to two factors: the more complicated processes of simultaneous political and economic transformation that central and eastern Europe are experiencing, and the greater political uncertainties attending this double transformation.[17] A high degree of uncertainty in the post-Communist transformation process is the major factor that facilitated the emergence of corporatist practices in central and eastern Europe and what shaped the partial convergence of the various post-Communist states into the common mold of transformative corporatism. Despite undeniable national and subnational variations in the process of transformation, the central and eastern European countries have adopted remarkably similar transformative corporatist institutions and practices. These include diverse and often contradictory elements of interest coordination.

17. On the role of political uncertainty in post-Communist societies, see Valerie Bunce and Maria Csanadi, "Uncertainty in the Transition: Post-Communism in Hungary," *East European Politics and Societies*, 7, 2 (Spring 1993): 240–75.

Three characteristics distinguish the central and eastern European variety of corporatism during this period of transformation from the Western European variant of democratic corporatism. The first is its dual, cooperative-conflictual character which contrasts with the predominantly cooperative nature of democratic corporatism operating in relatively stable political economies.[18] The dual character of central and eastern European corporatism reflects the contradictory strains contained in the process of economic and political transformation, strains encompassing ideology (liberalism, partnership ideology, and an emerging form of *etatiste* ideology), politics (liberal politics and social democracy), and economics (unregulated markets, Keynesian welfare policies, and state intervention). These differing ideologies reflect the debate over the relative importance of market processes and interventionist policies. They are publicly accepted and inform public policies throughout central and eastern Europe. Liberalism and the virtues of unregulated competition are believed by its advocates to be a necessity if the transformation process is eventually to create stable market economies. For its part, social partnership offers instead a negotiated guideline for all groups during the transformation process. Because these contrasting ideologies are embedded in a single set of institutions, it has given rise to the contradictory, cooperative-conflictual nature of transformative corporatism and to porous boundaries separating liberal pluralism from a corporatism stressing social partnership.

The second characteristic of transformative corporatism refers to negotiated relationships between organized interests and the state. Compared to the democratic corporatism of relatively stable market economies, bargained exchange between these parties is more frequent and the process of negotiation is both more intensive and extensive. A third feature of transformative corporatism is the monopoly of group representation and the centralization of groups. Corporatist negotiations in Western Europe are often conducted by centralized unions and business organizations which exercise full control over their members; at times such corporatist negotiations are in fact assumed to rest on the monopoly of representation. Transformative corporatism, by contrast, exhibits greater variation in the degree of centralization and gives less importance to the monopoly of representation by union and employers' organizations.

18. Peter J. Katzenstein, *Small States in World Markets: Industrial Policy in Europe* (Ithaca: Cornell University Press, 1985).

Transformative Corporatism at the National Level

The Polish variant of transformative corporatism emerged in the hostile political environment of a state socialist regime. Compared to other central and eastern European countries its emergence was gradual and painful. Both before and after 1989 Poland's emerging transformative corporatism had broader political objectives which went beyond economic goals typical of democratic corporatist states operating in Western Europe. Before 1989 transformative corporatism was part of an organized effort to overthrow the Communist regime; after 1989 it helped in consolidating democracy and in establishing a market economy.

Transformative corporatism in Poland has developed in various organizational forms. On the heels of the adoption of neo-liberal reform measures, unemployment emerged as the greatest social problem of Poland's transformation. During the transformation process successive governments attempted to combine the implementation of a free market economy with an active social and employment policy. In 1989, 1991, and 1994 the Sejm articulated the principle of full employment in legislation dealing with problems of employment.

The government set up an institutional structure to deal with employment issues that has a dual character: administrative and tripartite-corporatist. Labor offices at national, provincial (*voivodship*), and regional (*rejon*) levels were set up as part of the state bureaucracy. Tripartite employment councils at these levels were also established to complement the government's administrative structure and to counterbalance the instabilities of emerging labor markets. The Main Employment Council was set up in 1990. The Council has twenty-four members, with equal numbers allocated to representatives from unions and employers' organizations, the state bureaucracy, and local government. The Council is a consultative body which advises the Minister of Labor and Social Policy on issues of employment. The activities of the Council deal mainly with initiatives to achieve full employment. The Council also advises the government on projects of the Labor Fund[19] and on draft legislation regarding employment issues.

---

19. The Labor Fund is administered by the minister of labor and social policy. It pays, among other things, for unemployment benefits, the costs of training and retraining unemployed workers, social insurance contributions, loans for the creation of new jobs, and vocational training programs for apprentices.

Other tripartite fora were also established, including the Commission on Labor Law Reform, the Tripartite Commission for Cooperation with the International Labor Organization, and the National Council on Social Aid Issues. An institutionalized social dialogue addressing the issue of social peace at a time of declining living standards emerged in 1994, four years later than in other post-Communist countries such as Hungary, Bulgaria, and Czechoslovakia. The explanation for Poland's tardiness lies in the complicated relations among its social partners and in the persistence, after 1989, of a basically undifferentiated civil society which had fought the Communist regime in the 1980s. After 1989, Solidarity, as the single organizational expression of civil society, experienced a profound identity crisis. Solidarity generated in quick succession five different governments, all of which drew their main support from the parent movement. In fact, even the founding members of the Confederation of Polish Employers (KPP) had been Solidarity activists before 1989. The pluralization of political structures, however, occurred more quickly than the articulation of distinct interests that these groups had or represented. The eventual split in Poland's labor movement was an inevitable by-product of having seized control of the powers of government.

Activists at central and regional levels who combined their work in the union movement with politics, supported corporatist arrangements that sought to minimize the risks of costly strikes. The initial organic and paternalistic relationship between Solidarity and "its" governments rendered unnecessary the formal institutionalization of corporatism and fostered the emergence of "informal" and "parliamentary" forms of cooperation. In 1991, for example, the government passed three laws to regulate its relationship with interest groups: the Act on Trade Unions, the Act on Employers' Organizations, and the Act on the Resolution of Collective Labor Disputes. The 1991 labor legislation favored the establishment of a national-level, non-monopolistic (for all trade unions and employer organizations), and informal and consultative corporatism. It stipulated that all draft laws and acts of government, prior to being submitted to parliament for debate and adoption, had to be taken under advisement by trade unions and employer organizations. In the absence of any formal, tripartite institutions this led to regular, informal meetings of officials from the Ministry of Labor, trade unions and, occasionally, from employer organizations such as the Confederation of Polish Employers. By 1990 the Ministry for Liaison with Trade Unions had merged with the Ministry of Labor, where a special department for contacts with trade unions was established.

A big problem for the government was Solidarity's reluctance to engage in negotiations jointly with the All-Poland Trade Union Alliance (OPZZ). The union-government talks were mainly between Solidarity and the Solidarity government, excluding, at least as understood by the Solidarity elites, all political forces "hostile to reform." Strikes were widely viewed as a part of a political campaign that sought to derail reform efforts. For this reason the early stages of Poland's transformation saw the emergence of a politicized, de facto monopoly of union representation, in contrast to other post-Communist countries which, through agreements negotiated by the social partners immediately following the 1989 revolution, granted all unions equal rights to participate in round-table negotiations with the government. However, the negotiations leading up to Poland's Enterprise Pact of February 1993 for the first time involved a wide variety of union organizations. Poland's corporatist arrangements were also extended to parliament, where Solidarity enjoyed direct representation.[20]

Soon after 1989 the declining living standards of the majority of the population forced trade union activists at the enterprise level to insist on a more conflictual stance towards the government that included the use of strikes as a political weapon. Poland's economic shock treatment in January 1990 resulted in sharp increases in both unemployment and prices, a wage freeze and decreases in real wages, and reduced living standards for salaried employees and older people living on pensions. Between 1989 and 1990 alone, the cost of living for workers and employees increased by 50 percent faster than did wages and salaries.[21] However, at the beginning of the neo-liberal reform process the general consensus at the elite level was largely shared by Solidarity activists on the shop floor; industrial peace prevailed. According to the Central Bureau of Statistics, the total number of strikes declined from 900 in 1989 to only 250 in 1990; in 1991 this figure increased only marginally to 305. Thereafter, however, a wave of grass-roots social discontent began to sweep Poland, and the number of work stoppages exploded. In

20. This tendency was further strengthened after September 1993 with parliament's shift to the Left and the direct participation of OPZZ in parliament as part of the ruling Democratic Left Alliance (SLD) coalition.

21. Larry L. Wade, Alexander J. Groth, and Peter Lavelle, "Estimating Participation and Party Voting in Poland: The 1991 Parliamentary Elections," *East European Politics and Societies*, 8, 1 (Winter 1994): 94–121.

1992 the number of strikes had increased twenty-fold and exceeded the 6,000 mark. Poland reached the peak of its wave of strikes in 1993 when 7,443 strikes occurred. In 1994 the number of strikes declined dramatically to only 429.[22] Most strike demands concerned wages and the excess wage tax (*popiwek*) which established a wage norm for a given firm or sector and then taxed all wage increases above that up to 100 percent.[23]

Thus the cooperative-conflictual nature of transformative corporatism, manifest in other post-Communist societies mainly in the relations *between* governments and unions, in Poland found political expression *within* the organizational structure of Solidarity, thus generating acute tensions between various levels of the union's organization. Both government and union elites found themselves challenged by the rising social discontent and unrest. The wave of strikes in the summer of 1992 marked a culmination in the contradiction between an elite-based corporatism at the top of the Polish polity and a pluralist conflict at the bottom.

The solution to this contradiction was to put an end to the paternalistic relationship between Solidarity and the government. Torn between the criticism of government policies by its militant cadres and a dissatisfied mass membership on the one hand, and the support of government policies by its leadership on the other, Solidarity concluded an agreement with the government in June 1992 concerning the regulation of collective labor disputes between the state and the union. Solidarity's leadership further distanced itself from the government's policies by becoming more militant in its strategy and tactics, organizing, for example, a major strike among school and hospital workers and even threatening a general strike. At the same time the government also attempted to distance itself from Solidarity by proposing comprehensive negotiations with both employers' organizations and with Solidarity as well as other trade unions concerning the privatization of state enterprises. The lifting of the practical barriers to participation in government-union

22. *Rocznik Statystyczny 1995* (Warsaw: Glówny Urzad Statystyczny, 1995), p. 130. See also Anna Buchner-Jeziorska, "Konflikt pracy w Polsce okresu transformacji," *Przeglad Socjologiczny*, 43 (1994): 75–93; Jolanta Kulpinska and Wielislawa Warzywoda-Krusynska, "Social Costs of Transformation," *Economic and Social Transformation in Poland*, Proceedings of the Conference on Econometric and Social Transformation in Poland, Lodz, 22–23 May 1995.

23. Kazimierz Kloc, "Polish Labor in Transition (1990–1992)," *Telos* 92 (Summer 1992): 139–48. Witold Morawski and Jerzy Hausner, "Tripartism in Poland," paper presented at the ILO conference on Tripartism in Central and Eastern Europe, Budapest, 26–27 May 1994.

talks, the conclusion of the Enterprise Pact, the formal institution-alization of a social dialogue through the creation of the National Tripartite Commission on Socio-Economic Issues—all constituted important steps towards a successful normalization of the contra-dictory character of Poland's transformative corporatism.

Signed in February 1993, the Enterprise Pact made Poland's tri-partite relations both more formal and inclusive. The negotiations were greatly facilitated by the "Social Dialogue" project that the EU, with the participation of experts from the ILO, ran in Poland in 1991–93, funded by the PHARE project.[24] Workshops attended by representatives of all the organizations that later signed the Pact were an important preliminary step for the substantive nego-tiations concerning the conclusion of the Enterprise Pact. The reluctance of Solidarity to negotiate with the government together with other trade unions, especially the OPZZ, did not block a suc-cessful conclusion of the Enterprise Pact. For as it turned out, unique compromise emerged between Solidarity and the govern-ment. In order to stop industrial unrest, the government and the employers' organization KPP held separate negotiations with the different unions. Thus three versions of the Enterprise Pact were signed simultaneously: with NSZZ Solidarity; with OPZZ; and with seven branch unions.

In its content the Enterprise Pact was a compromise between neo-liberals striving for an acceleration of privatization and trade unions seeking to oppose them. The Enterprise Pact consists of three parts: issues dealing with privatization; the financing of state enterprises; and social problems. The Pact's main purpose was to gain trade union acceptance of the privatization program of state-owned enterprises. In exchange, workers were granted free distribution of 10 percent of the stocks in privatized enter-prises as well as a right to participate in privatization through a guaranteed one-third of the seats on the Boards of Directors of pri-vatized enterprises. Bi- and tripartite mechanisms of control over the implementation and functioning of the agreements were also set up, such as a corporatist Fund Board for supervision and con-trol over the Guaranteed Workers' Benefits Fund,[25] and a tripartite

24. Elzbieta Sobotka, "The Role of the Tripartite Commission for Social and Economic Affairs in the Development of Labour Relations in Poland," in Michal Sewerynski, ed., *Polish Labour Law and Collective Labour Relations In the Period of Transformation* (Warsaw: Ministry of Labour and Social Policy, 1995), pp. 89–105.

25. Established in December 1993, the Fund protects workers' claims in the event of bankruptcy and other unusual contingencies.

commission charged with the task of monitoring economic processes and macro-economic policies.[26] Based on the Pact, the government submitted twenty major bills to parliament; and the signatories to the Pact, primarily the government, took the responsibility to support these bills in parliamentary debates.

The dissolution of the Polish parliament in 1993 resulted from Solidarity's grass-roots pressure that almost immediately followed the successful negotiation of the Enterprise Pact. This was clear evidence of both the contradictory nature of Poland's corporatism and the beginning of its normalization. Solidarity's identity crisis was thus resolved at a high price, resulting in a split between government and union that replaced the division within Solidarity. The establishment of a Tripartite Commission on Socio-Economic Issues in February 1994, as envisaged in the Enterprise Pact, was the next step. The Commission became a forum for constant negotiations. Since February 1994 a newly elected "post-Communist," left-wing government, the Confederation of Polish Employers, and several unions (NSZZ Solidarity, OPZZ, and seven branch unions) have been sitting around the same table negotiating on most of the pressing social and economic issues. The Commission was established to deal with, among other things, wages and employment issues in the public sector, social benefits, the instruments of wage policy, and the relation between consumption and investment. The Commission set up six working groups dealing with wages and social security, employment and the prevention of unemployment, the reform of social insurance and insurance benefits, health care, housing, and culture and education. As of March 1996 the Commission had met twenty-nine times. An important achievement of the Commission was the Agreement of 3 January 1995 regulating wage levels in the public sector, thus ending prolonged strikes.

Transformative Corporatism at Lower Levels

While in Western Europe corporatism remained predominantly a national-level affair,[27] in central and eastern Europe transformative corporatism typically was replicated at regional and sectoral levels. Yet in contrast to other post-Communist countries, sectoral corporatism did not develop in Poland. Solidarity's predominantly

26. *Pact on State-Owned Enterprise in the Process of Transformation* (Warsaw: Ministry of Labour and Social Policy, 1993).

27. Sectoral corporatism in Germany and some tripartite, regional employment councils in some Western European countries are partial exceptions to this generalization.

regional structure and the 1991 labor legislation, with its de facto exclusion of the state from the bargaining process below the national level, blocked the emergence of sectoral corporatism in Poland for all intents and purposes. But because the state remained the dominant employer in Polish industry and acted under strong social and political pressure, it could not help but become directly involved in worker disputes. In most cases industrial protests spawned vertical corporatist arrangements. Contentious issues were pushed upwards from lower levels for resolution, engaging social partners operating at higher levels. Increasingly, various ministries in Poland began to orchestrate issue-specific social dialogues. Tripartite meetings, for example, were organized for miners from Silesia, and these meetings led to the conclusion of the Katowice Contract.[28] Such corporatist meetings were also organized in other regions facing difficult restructuring problems, in the Lodz region (*region*), for example, which is dominated by textile production. Such meetings, however, were not the regular and institutionalized arrangements they are, for example, in Bulgaria.

Poland's regional social dialogues cover three major areas. First, territorial corporatist employment councils assist the national Main Employment Council in dealing with problems of employment. Second, regional social dialogues lead to regional collective agreements on wages and on the employment relationship in the public sector. Finally, in regions with particularly difficult restructuring and unemployment problems, social dialogues have emerged spontaneously among the local actors seeking to find solutions to difficult problems in situations of rising social tensions. The experience in Lodz, one of Poland's main industrial centers, illustrates that all three forms of regional social dialogue can be consequential in alleviating the economic and social problems of particular regions.

The collapse of Lodz's only major industry, textiles, resulted in high regional unemployment rates, reaching 17 to 20 percent, among the highest in Poland. Today Lodz faces extraordinarily difficult restructuring problems. A 48-hour general strike, organized by the Solidarity Regional Board in March 1993 with the support of the OPZZ union, marked the culmination to several weeks of local protest. The strike was the first one in Poland in which workers demanded a speeding up of economic changes and local

28. Jan Wojtyła, "Social Dialogue in the Process of Regional Restructuring: The Example of Upper Silesia," *Polish Labour Law and Collective Labour Relations in the Period of Transformation* (Warsaw: Ministry of Labour and Social Policy, 1995), pp. 107–24.

restructuring. In the spring of 1993 it resulted in the appointment of a Government Plenipotentiary for the Restructuring of Lodz Region, as well as the creation of a corporatist Regional Council for the Restructuring of Lodz Region which advises and consults with the government plenipotentiary to facilitate the process of regional restructuring. Specifically, the Council develops concrete plans for the implementation of the plenipotentiary's program. The Council is a broad corporatist body comprising not only local governments, unions and employer organizations, but also legislators, bankers, representatives of research centers and scientific academies, and all of the local institutions that deal with restructuring issues. The Council was very active, especially in 1993 and 1994, before lapsing in 1995. Under pressure from Solidarity-Lodz in 1996, vertical negotiations were held at the Ministry of Labor, in which all unions from the region, the local employers organization (KPP), and representatives of local governments and the Ministry of Labor all participated. An agreement was reached to renew Council activities from September 1996 onwards. As part of this agreement the government agreed to provide additional subsidies to facilitate the process of restructuring.

The Lodz Provincial Employment Council is a second regional corporatist forum. The provincial employment councils in Poland were developed as advisory-consulting bodies to the *voivod* (provincial government). They follow closely employment trends in the *voivodship*, assess the efficacy of the Labor Fund's expenditures, and advise on financial plans drawn up by provincial labor offices. The provincial employment councils have sixteen members, staffed equally from the provincial organizations of unions and employers as well as from the organs of state administration and self-governing communes. The chair of the provincial employment council is the *voivod*.

As the Polish experience shows, transformative corporatism involves numerous functions at lower levels of government. It encompasses an effort to decentralize political mechanisms of problem solving, as well as an attempt to involve central decision makers in problems that local or regional actors are having difficulties coping with.

Conclusion

The development of post-Communist, transformative corporatism is shaped by three major factors that will not be further explored here:[29] the process of political and economic transformation with all its uncertainties and contradictions; the legacies of the state socialist past; and international influences, including the role of international lending institutions such as the International Monetary Fund (IMF) and the World Bank, the role of the International Labor Organization's (ILO) philosophy of tripartism and the practical assistance its experts offer throughout central and eastern Europe, and the European Union's (EU) PHARE "Social Dialogue" Project.

Poland's post-Communist transformation points to a negotiated adjustment process. Because transformative corporatism takes into account both conflictual societal interests and the need for a modicum of social peace, it represents fundamental processes of bargaining between states and interest groups and strives to integrate states with markets. It thus offers a viable perspective in Poland's future is taking the form of a capitalism that combines elements of both the safety and predictability of a state-guided social market economy with the efficiency and uncertainty of unfettered market adjustments. Furthermore, Poland's transformative corporatism enhances the prospects of social peace through the inclusion of the major interest groups in its policy making. In brief, the emerging properties of Poland's polity point to a distinctive form of political economy that resembles some of the main features of Western European polities without duplicating them. In its return to Europe, Poland's transformative corporatism has thus added novel elements to Europe's political architecture.

The Catholic Church and Poland's "Return to Europe"

The fall of communism has posed powerful challenges to the Catholic Church in Poland. During the Communist era, the Church served as an indispensable vehicle of opposition to the political system. At times, in fact, the Church's hierarchy acted as a kind of alternative authority structure, an authentically Polish counterpoint to the Soviet-imposed regime. In the democratic Poland that has emerged since 1989, however, the role of the Church is much less clearly defined. The pluralism that has exploded in Poland in recent years has raised the potential for a progressive secularization of

29. See Iankova, "Social Partnership after the Cold War."

society, and for an eventual rejection of the nation's deeply Catholic cultural heritage. In fact, leaders of the Polish Church, in both Rome and Warsaw, already detect signs of such developments in the headlong rush to rejoin Europe, in the uncritical acceptance of what Pope John Paul II has called Europe's "civilization of desire and consumption."[30]

Poland's isolation from Western Europe over the last fifty years has preserved a cultural distinctiveness that the Church is committed to preserving, as well as a pervasive religiosity that the Church would like to see reignited throughout the continent. For these reasons, Polish Catholic leaders prefer to speak not of Poland's "return to Europe" (indeed, the Pope has dismissed such a formulation as a "humiliation")[31] but rather of Poland's reassertion of its historic role as the bulwark of Roman Christianity in central Europe. Standing astride both the religious and political dividing lines of Europe, the Polish Church wants Poland to serve as an instrument of the re-evangelization of the Orthodox East, and as a spiritual and moral exemplar to the secular West.

This grand vision of Catholic Poland's role in the emerging new Europe has had a profound effect on the Church's approach to Polish politics in recent years. The Church has welcomed the emergence of a democratic Poland. But it has aggressively defended its institutional interests in the new political order, and it has just as aggressively asserted its views on central political issues—from abortion, to economic restructuring, to entrance into the European Union. The Church's leaders correctly view themselves as having been central agents in the political transformation that took place in 1989. They are now insisting on playing an equally central role in determining the direction that this transformation will take in the future.

There is nothing preordained, of course, about the Polish Church's public and insistent participation in Polish politics. The Spanish Church, for example, adopted a very different approach to the rebirth of democracy in its own country during the 1970s. The Church had, to say the least, a long and storied history of active political involvement in Spain. Moreover, the Church played an important role in the political transformation in Spain through its increasingly vocal opposition to Franco's regime. Nevertheless, the Spanish Catholic hierarchy played a remarkably

30. *New York Times* (8 June 1991): A3.
31. Ibid.

restrained role in Spanish politics immediately following the transition to democracy.[32]

The Spanish bishops did not quite retreat to a monastic asceticism in regard to politics. But they did limit themselves to what some of them termed an "active neutrality" in terms of both partisan electoral politics and a host of controversial public policy issues.[33] The leaders of Spanish Catholicism were very sensitive to the historically close relationship between the Church and right-wing political forces and committed themselves to preventing a return of the virulent anticlericalism of the Spanish Republic. As a result, the bishops not only eschewed personal intervention in Spanish politics, but they also largely "abandoned [their] traditional attempt to enter political society through the mobilization of the Catholic laity."[34] The bishops were active in encouraging a smooth transition to democracy and in calling for a retention in Spanish society of traditional Catholic values. But they were neutral in regard to the particular political direction the transition should take. The Church, in a sense, turned inward following the change in political regime, allowing religion and morality to be "privatized" in Spanish society.[35]

The leadership of the Polish Church envisions no such outcome in the rebirth of democracy on its soil. Coming out of a quite different national and ecclesiastical history, the Polish bishops are demanding much more than a spiritually forthright but politically neutral role in post-Communist Poland. To the contrary, the Church's close identification with Polish nationalism, its powerful role in the dawning of Polish democracy, and not incidentally, its special relationship with a Vatican headed by a Polish pope, have all combined to call forward a Polish episcopate deeply involved not only in Polish politics and public policy, but also in the fundamental debate over Poland's proper place in the society of European nations.

32. There is a substantial literature on the role of the Church in Spanish politics both before and after the transformation to democracy. See, for example, Juan J. Linz, "Religion and Politics in Spain: From Conflict to Consensus Above Cleavage," *Social Compass* 27 (1980): 255–77; Richard Gunther and Roger A. Blough, "Religious Conflict and Consensus in Spain: A Tale of Two Constitutions," *World Affairs* 143 (1981): 366–412; Stanley G. Payne, *Spanish Catholicism: An Historical Overview* (Madison: The University of Wisconsin Press, 1984); and Jose Casanova, *Public Religions in the Modern World* (Chicago: The University of Chicago Press, 1994), pp. 75–91.

33. Payne, *Spanish Catholicism*, p. 216.

34. Casanova, *Public Religions in the Modern World*, p. 89.

35. Ibid., p. 90.

Catholic Poland

Scott Paltrow has argued that the Catholic Church's prominent role in contemporary Polish society is a function of three historical developments:[36] the identification of church and nation represented by Mieszko I's baptism in 966; the association of the Church with Polish nationalism during the partitions, occupations, and foreign dominations of the last two hundred years; and the creation of a homogeneously Catholic nation by the Jewish holocaust of World War II, and by the large-scale expulsions and forced migrations mandated by Stalin's post-war movement of Poland's national borders to the west. As a result of these developments, Poland today is a nation whose population is 98 percent Catholic and whose national identity is closely identified with Roman Catholicism.

Like all sweeping historical generalizations, however, the identification of Polish nationalism with Roman Catholicism is in many ways as much a caricature as a characterization. The interests of the Church and the interests of the nation have not always coincided. The complexity of the Church's historic status in Poland was never more clearly revealed than during the era of partition between 1795 and 1918. In one sense, the Church played a central role in the survival of the Polish nation during this period as Catholicism served as a fundamental pillar of Polish resistance to Austrian, Prussian, and Russian rule. In another sense, however, the Church's support for Polish independence was attenuated during the partition by the Vatican's overriding institutional interests in placating the occupying powers and in dampening the more virulent and violent manifestations of Polish nationalism.

This tension in the relationship between Polish nationalism and the Polish Catholic hierarchy was eliminated, however, during World War II by the Church's prominent participation in the general suffering of the Polish nation. As bishops and priests were murdered in large numbers, survivors like Stefan Wyszyński, chaplain to the Polish underground and future primate of Poland, squarely identified their Church with armed resistance to Nazi rule and with the dramatic resurgence in Polish nationalism the occupation created. Indeed, for Cardinal Wyszyński, and for the Church he led until his death in 1982, Catholicism was an integral element of

36. Scott J. Paltrow, "Poland and the Pope: The Vatican's Relations with Poland, 1978 to the Present," *Millennium: Journal of International Studies* 15, 1 (Spring 1986): 3.

Polish nationalism, just as a "Catholic Poland" was an indispensable signal of the limits of twentieth-century totalitarianism.

Cardinal Wyszyński and other Catholic leaders of this period did more than simply endorse Polish nationalism, however. They also advanced their nationalism as a necessary prerequisite to the eventual emancipation of Eastern and central Europe from Soviet rule, as well as to the ultimate re-emergence of an authentically Christian Europe. They believed, as many Poles through the ages have believed, that their nation is destined to play a special role in human history. They made sense of their nation's history by characterizing it as a human, national recapitulation of the suffering and death of Jesus Christ. And they comforted themselves with the conviction that just as the despair of Good Friday was followed by the redemption of Easter, so Poland's trials and dismemberment would be followed by national rebirth and international renewal.

As we indicated above, the official Catholic Church has not always played a dominant role in this national passion play. But during the Communist era, Cardinal Wyszyński intimately identified his Church with the aspirations of the Polish nation and eloquently declaimed the historic role Polish Catholicism would play through its endurance and vitality. His job, as primate and patriot, was to defend the Polish Church not only for its own sake, but also for the sake of Poland's future—and, indeed, for European Christendom's survival of both tyranny and apathy.

In truth, Wyszyński played a rather complicated and delicate role in Polish politics as the decades of Communist rule wore on. He was, to be sure, a sharp and consistent critic of the regime. But he was also a patriot, ever mindful of Poland's limited sovereignty and its potentially explosive relationship with the Soviet Union. By the 1970s, Wyszyński was acting largely as a mediator between an increasingly vulnerable regime and its opponents in an ever more restive civil society. As he did so, Wyszyński became fearful that his calculated balancing act would be toppled by Vatican officials who understood neither the confounding complexities nor the pregnant possibilities of the Polish circumstance.[37]

What neither Wyszyński nor those Vatican officials realized as they sparred through the 1970s, however, was how soon they would all be superseded in importance by a single man. When

---

37. For a discussion of Wyszyński's troubled relationship with the Vatican's *ostpolitik*, see Hansjokob Stehle, *Eastern Politics of the Vatican 1917–1979* (Athens: Ohio University Press, 1981), especially pp. 341–56.

Karol Cardinal Wojtyła of Cracow was named Pope John Paul II on 16 October 1978, he not only followed Paul VI on the throne of St. Peter's, he also supplanted Stefan Cardinal Wyszyński as the most influential leader of Polish Catholicism.

Pope Wojtyła

John Paul II's primary role in the transformation of European politics was to reveal the utter failure of Soviet Communism to impose its will on the hearts of Poles and other central Europeans. If, as Stalin once said, Communism fits Poland like a saddle fits a cow, then John Paul II's papacy represented the enduring distinctiveness of the Polish cow. His very existence as a stubbornly independent and fiercely pious Polish Catholic, and the ecstasy with which his election was greeted in his homeland, symbolized the survival of a culturally and socially independent Poland despite more than three decades of Soviet-imposed Communist rule. Wyszyński had nurtured this independence from the relative isolation of Warsaw, often in the face of distrust and misunderstanding from the Vatican. But Wojtyła would embody, celebrate, and advance this independence with all the considerable and varied tools available to the modern papacy.

For Wojtyła, however, even more so than for Wyszyński, Polish cultural and religious autonomy were valued not so much for their own sake, but for the role they would play in recreating and reunifying European Christendom. Karol Wojtyła was deeply committed to the messianic mission of the Polish nation, and as Pope John Paul II he would be able to advance this mission in ways that he and his countrymen could barely have imagined before. Indeed, the pope apparently viewed his very ascension to the papacy as a powerful sign of God's endorsement of his Polish vision of the future:

> Is it not Christ's will [he asked during his first pilgrimage to Poland in 1979], is it not what the Holy Spirit dispenses, that this Polish Pope, this Slav Pope, should at this precise moment manifest the spiritual unity of Christian Europe.[38]

This Polish pope, in short, views his role in human history in markedly sweeping terms. He considers himself to have been chosen by God to be a central actor in both the healing of the great Christian schism and in the unification of the European continent

38. Quoted in Paltrow, "Poland and the Pope," p. 16.

around Catholic principles and practice. He has, in the words of Patrick Michel, a "grand design of unity, of the reconquest and re-Catholization of Europe, of which the Church in Poland is at once the starting point, the powerhouse and the ideal."[39] Wyszyński, as primate, preserved the Polish Church. Wojtyła, as pope, seeks to use the Polish Church as a model and building block of a much more ambitious project.

Is it any wonder, given this world view, that Pope John Paul II, and other leaders of Polish Catholicism following his lead, have responded so strongly and so distinctively to the prospect of Poland's "return to Europe?" They refuse to view Poland as a supplicant seeking admission to a community of nations. To the contrary, they see their nation as a central player in the creation of this community, properly understood, and an important element in this community's survival into the future. According to this reading of European history, Poland's responsibility to preserve its distinctiveness, its Catholicity if you will, in the face of the secular commercialism of Western Europe is as clear and compelling as was Poland's responsibility to resist communism and foreign domination before 1989. Put another way, the Church is not so much interested in Poland's rejoining Europe as it is in inviting Europe to rejoin Poland in a renewed commitment to its shared Christian heritage.

Poland in Europe

Since the fall of Communism in 1989, the pope has ever more vigorously advocated his vision of a new era of Christian union in Europe. And he has passionately defended Poland's right to join this union on its own terms.

> We [Poles] have a right to be in Europe [he said in 1991], and to develop among other nations, according to our own identity, standing on the grounds of what we ourselves worked out during this difficult stage of history. We have the right especially because others look at the Polish way, sometimes critically, but often with hope.[40]

John Paul has not only defended Poland's place in Europe, he has also challenged the Polish nation to rededicate itself to Catholicism, and to its historic, evangelical mission.

---

39. Patrick Michel, *Politics and Religion in Eastern Europe: Catholicism in Hungary, Poland, and Czechoslovakia* (Cambridge: Polity Press, 1991), p. 133.
40. *Tygodnik Powszechny* (9 September 1990).

Do not let yourself get caught up by the civilization of desire and consumption [he said during his first visit to post-Communist Poland]. Is it civilization or anti-civilization, a culture or an anti-culture.... My dear brothers and sisters, I wish as Bishop of Rome to protest at such a definition of Europe, of Western Europe.... This insults the great world of Christian culture from which we have drawn, from which we have co-created for the price of our sufferings. We do not have to enter Europe, because we helped to create it, and we did so with greater effort than those who claim a monopoly on Europeaness.[41]

The pope is not, of course, the only leader of the Catholic Church who speaks of the need to resist secular trends in contemporary Poland, or of the right of a distinctively Catholic Poland to live in Europe on its own terms. The Catholic weekly, *Niedziela*, for example, dismissed the call for Poland to return to the center of modern Europe as an invitation to return "to the center of modern barbarity."[42] And Józef Cardinal Glemp, Wyszyński's successor as primate, argued before one hundred thousand pilgrims at Jasna Góra Monastery in 1995 that Poland's entry into the European Union should be seen as a "moral issue," not merely an economic one. Poles, he warned, should be wary of the threat EU membership could pose to Polish national identity.

There are two ways for the poor to enter the group of the rich. The first is to make an impression with their character, diligence, and personality. The second is to get rid of their character, their clothes, and their way of life, changing into compulsory full dress or jeans and imitating everything that makes a man rich.[43]

Pope John Paul II, Cardinal Glemp, and the other Polish bishops are not advocating the continued isolation of Poland from Western European society. In fact, like most Poles, they believe their homeland to be culturally and historically part of the West, and they are anxious to reconnect the bonds broken by forty-five years of Soviet domination. What they are arguing, however, is that Poland should navigate its way back to the European community without relinquishing either its own Catholic identity or its self-styled evangelical mission. They do not want to drift toward Western secularism; they want to build a Catholic Poland

41. *New York Times*, (8 June 1991): A3.
42. *Niedziela* (20 February 1994).
43. This sermon was reported in *Zycie Warszawy* on 16 August 1995 under the headline "To Which Europe? At Jasna Gora, Primate Glemp Highly Criticized the Poles Striving to Join Europe," *FBIS-EEU* (17 August 1995): 32.

that can in the long term serve as a model for other nations, both east and west of the old Cold War divide.

The Church in Poland Today

Such a mission for the church, of course, does not allow for the kind of passive, defensive approach adopted by the Spanish episcopate during the late 1970s. To the contrary, it requires the church's sustained and active participation in the political life of contemporary Poland. The church's leaders, for example, have held lengthy and detailed talks with the government concerning the language of the new Polish Constitution. They have also lobbied long and hard for the signing of a new concordat with the Vatican, and then much less successfully, for the ratification of that instrument by the leftist, so called post-Communist government that took power in September, 1993.

The Catholic Church in Poland has also been deeply involved in partisan politics in democratic Poland, and in efforts to have Polish public policy reflect the Church's traditional moral teachings. The most recent partisan episode was the Church's unsuccessful effort to prevent the election last year of Aleksander Kwasniewski as president of the Polish Republic. Kwasniewski, a junior minister in the last Communist government, defeated incumbent Lech Wałesa in a run-off despite a pastoral letter asking Poles not to vote for officials of the former regime, and a declaration on the eve of the vote that the nation faced a choice in Wałesa and Kwasniewski between Christianity and neo-paganism.[44]

In terms of public policy, the Church has spent as much effort and energy on abortion as it has on any other issue. In fact, no issue captures either the style of the Polish Church's activities in post-Communist Poland, or the magnitude of the Polish Church's task at the moment, more clearly than abortion does.[45] For the Polish episcopate, opposition to abortion serves as a kind of short hand for support of the Catholic heritage of the Polish nation. Those who oppose legal abortion are deemed by the Church to be patriots committed to the creation of an authentically independent Poland.

---

44. See *Open Media Research Institute Daily Digest*, No. 168, Part II (29 August 1995), and *Foreign Broadcast Information Service -East Europe* (20 November 1995), pp. 58–61.

45. For background on the abortion debate, and on the Church's role in it, see Hanna Jankowska, "Abortion, Church and Politics in Poland," in *Feminist Review* 39 (1991): 174–81.

Those who endorse legal abortion, on the other hand, are dismissed as either secularists devoted to the assimilation of Poland into an amorphous European whole, or even worse, as Communists nostalgic for the degradations and indignities of the Stalinist era.

After the fall of Communism, the Polish Church was initially fairly successful in its efforts to restrict access to abortion. According to a law passed with the Church's vocal endorsement in 1993, abortions were allowed only in response to rape, incest, and fetal deformity, or in the rare cases where carrying the pregnancy to term would threaten the life or physical health of the pregnant woman.[46] Abortions for "difficult personal circumstances," or "societal hardship," though supported by a majority of the population, were made illegal.[47]

The Church's victory on this issue, however, was short-lived. The new, so-called "post-Communist" government that took power after the 1993 parliamentary elections very quickly moved to ease access to abortion in Poland once again. The new parliament passed a law in 1994 that allowed legal abortion during the first twelve weeks of pregnancy if the woman is in a "difficult" social or financial situation. This law, strenuously opposed by the Church, was first vetoed by President Lech Wałesa, but then signed in late 1995 by Wałesa's successor, Aleksander Kwasniewski.[48]

This latest law, however, is not likely to be the last word on the legality of abortion in Poland either. The Church, not surprisingly, continues to push for further restriction. And another change in government after the 1997 election might well bring another shift in Poland's abortion law. Regardless of the legal status of abortion at any given moment, however, the issue of abortion is sure to remain a divisive one in Polish politics in the foreseeable future.

As it is in so many different national and cultural contexts, the abortion debate in Poland is really about much more than abortion alone. It is also about the ability of the Catholic Church to influence public policy more generally, and it is most fundamentally about the future of Polish society itself. Legal and readily available abortion,

---

46. *New York Times* (8 January 1993): A7.

47. According to a public opinion poll conducted in June 1995 by the Center of Public Opinion Research, 83 percent of Poles support legal abortion in cases of rape or incest and 86 percent support it if the pregnancy endangers the woman's health. Fifty-three percent endorse legal abortion if the woman is in difficult circumstances, and 33 percent support abortion on demand. See *Open Media Research Institute Daily Digest*, No. 137, Part II (17 July 1995).

48. Jakub Karpinski, "Polish President Signs Abortion Law," *Open Media Research Institute Daily Digest Part II*, 21 November 1996.

in short, runs directly counter to the Church's vision of a new, and at long last authentically Polish, Poland. Legal and readily available abortion in Poland also runs directly counter to the pope's project of advancing the cause of European Christianity generally through the consolidation of Polish Catholicism specifically.

The criminalization of abortion and other policy changes such as the reintroduction of Catholic instruction into public schools are important to the leaders of Polish Catholicism not only because these leaders believe such policies are morally righteous, but also because they believe such policies are essential prerequisites to Poland's playing its proper role in the European community of nations. How can Poland serve as the "starting point, the powerhouse, and the ideal" of a re-evangelized European continent if the Church cannot even have its way in Poland itself?[49]

One of the central projects of European integration is the assimilation of individual nationalisms into some form of a larger supranational identity. While the prospects for such an assimilation in the aggregate are, to say the least, uncertain, it is likely that the Catholic Church will pose a potentially troublesome barrier to such an assimilation in the Polish case. Like cultural leaders in many other countries, the Polish Catholic bishops are anxious to retain and protect Polish national distinctiveness as they embark upon a new and deeper relationship with the European community of nations. However, unlike most other cultural leaders, the Catholic bishops also want that distinctiveness, in their case Poland's national Catholic identity, to serve as the cornerstone of a fundamental transformation of the wider community itself. Theirs is a vision that is as grand as the idea of European union. But it is also a vision that fundamentally challenges the principles and processes on which that union has been based for four decades.

The Europeanization of Polish Migration Policy

Polish migration policy is an important element of Poland's integration strategy towards Western Europe for two reasons. First, migration is an important instrument for fastening the manifold relations linking Poland with Western Europe. Broadened experiences, new contacts, and upgraded skills all facilitate Poland's move towards full membership in the EU. Second, Poland's aspiration to

49. See Michel, *Politics and Religion in Eastern Europe*, p. 133.

membership in the EU needs to be followed up by the creation of compatible legal and administrative regulations in many policy sectors, including migration. Even if, for economic or technical reasons, an immediate transplanting of all relevant international norms to Poland is not possible, it is very important that the general direction of the new regulations introduced in Poland be in agreement with evolving European standards regarding the movements of people, border control, and the legal status of aliens, including migrant workers and refugees.

This is especially true seeing as for more than a decade west European states have made efforts to coordinate and harmonize national regulations and policies on migration, particularly within the Schengen Group. Solutions introduced in Poland should therefore bear an increasing similarity to those agreed upon by the Western countries. Indeed, the process of the Europeanization of Poland's migration policy is already under way, and the direct repercussions which the latest, restrictive changes in European and German migration policies have had for Poland are a good example.

The Security Dimension of Migration

Contemporary migration is a typical transnational phenomenon. It is not only an internal concern, but one intertwined with transnational politics. Domestic immigration laws and policies have unavoidable external implications, and a true study of the contemporary movements of peoples in Europe requires a broad understanding of the nature of international relations that is not limited to viewing merely the diplomatic relations among states.[50]

European migration has taken on increasingly important security dimensions as the total annual immigration to Western Europe has grown rapidly since the late 1980s. It rose from about one million in 1985 to about 2.7 million in 1992. Moreover, the share of illegal migration as a proportion of the total flows has increased from 20 percent in 1985 to 40 percent in 1992.[51]

50. See, for example, Christopher Mitchell, "International Migration, International Relations and Foreign Policy," *International Migration Review*, 23, 3 (Fall 1989): 682.

51. Jonas Widgren, "The Need for a New Multilateral Order to Prevent Mass Movements from Becoming a Security Threat in Europe," paper prepared for the conference organized by the Center for Strategic and International Studies, Taormina, Italy (1–3 April 1993), p. 3.

Abuse of the right of asylum has increasingly become the main way for economic migrants to enter and legally reside in European countries. Legislative and administrative changes have cut the total number of asylum seekers in Western Europe by more than half, from 693,000 in 1992 to 315,000 in 1994. However, the number of refugees, displaced persons, and others that have fled from areas of armed conflict has increased considerably throughout Europe. To a large extent they have been coming from the successor states of Yugoslavia. In 1994, the number of such people remaining in the successor states was about 3.5 million; about 0.6 million citizens from these states have been granted temporary protection in other European countries.[52]

Disorganized and disorderly large-scale migration naturally causes numerous and diverse problems for both the receiving countries and the countries of origin. Such movements can generate many dangerous social, economic, and political tensions and instabilities and should, therefore, be viewed from the perspective of a broadly understood European security policy.

Poland's own security policy has increasingly taken the migration factor into account. The growing number of foreigners coming into the country has been accompanied by many-sided problems, including a growth in crimes committed by foreigners. Special fears have also arisen from the threat of importing organized forms of crime: trade in weapons and radioactive materials, drug trafficking, mafia-organized car thefts, and money laundering.

Yet so far, at least, the fear of crime associated with the influx of foreigners has been exaggerated and is unjustified. Between 1991 and 1994, the number of foreigners arrested or serving time in Polish prisons remained at around 1,100, which is less than 0.5 percent of the total prison population. In March 1994, of the 1,076 foreigners held in Polish jails, 950 were being temporarily detained and only 114 were sentenced to serve prison terms; most of them were from Ukraine (459), Russia (168), Belarus (157), and Germany (53).[53]

On the other hand, there has been a rapid growth in the number of foreigners working illegally in Poland. Considerable numbers of "tourists" from the former Soviet Union—primarily Ukrainians, Belarussians, and Russians—are working illegally for very low wages in construction, agriculture, and other manual occupations.

---

52. See United Nations/ECE, *International Migration Bulletin*, No. 6, (Geneva: United Nations/ECE, May 1995), pp. 2–5.

53. See *Rzeczpospolita* (21 April 1994).

Some estimates indicate that as many as two hundred thousand foreigners from the East work in Poland without a permit.[54]

The number of those caught attempting to cross Polish borders illegally, especially the western border with Germany, is relatively high. In 1992 the Polish Border Guard caught a total of 33,581 people, compared to 13,589 in 1991. Most of them were citizens of Romania (23,401) and Bulgaria (6,395). The vast majority wanted to cross the western border (30,387).[55] The 1993 numbers were lower—some 18,200. These included about seven thousand Romanians, 1,600 Bulgarians, 1,400 Ukrainians, and one thousand Russians.[56]

People from southeast Europe treat Poland mostly as a transit country to reach their ultimate destination, Germany or Scandinavia. However, if legal channels of emigration to the rich Western countries were blocked, or if the destabilization in Eastern Europe and in the Balkans were to accelerate, Poland could easily become a country of destination as it in fact has been in recent years for a growing number of migrants. This is primarily due to a gradual tightening of Western European legal and administrative regulations concerning the entry and length of stay of migrants, as well as an increasing social xenophobia.

A rising wave of illegal migrants could become a threat to Poland's public security and social stability, and Poles have understandably begun to look anxiously eastward. Poland seems to be especially attractive for the inhabitants of the former Soviet Union for a number of reasons: its central location in Europe and its long Eastern border (820 miles), which is only symbolically protected on the Polish side and which Poland shares with as many as four post-Soviet republics; the relatively frequent visits paid to Poland by the citizens of the former USSR and thus their relatively good working knowledge of local conditions; the cultural proximity and linguistic similarity of Poland and Polish which facilitates their adaptation; the presence in the CIS of more than two million Poles who, in times of acute crisis, might choose to emigrate in hopes of preferential treatment in Poland; and, finally, the liberal entry regulations for citizens of the CIS, who do

54. See Jan B. de Weydenthal, "Immigration into Poland," *RFE/RL Research Report*, 3, 24 (17 June 1994): 40.

55. *Recent Developments in Policies Relating to Migrations and Migrants*. Papers submitted by the members of the European Committee on Migration (CDMG) of the Council of Europe, Strasbourg (1 September 1993), p. 47.

56. These are the figures provided by the Ministry of Internal Affairs and reported by the Polish Press Agency (PAP) on 10 February 1994.

not need visas for ninety-day visits: the only document they must present is a letter of invitation, which can be readily forged.

If political and economic reforms in the former Soviet Union fail, the region may experience wrenching social disorders even if these fall short of anarchy and chaos. Ethnic and religious conflicts, nationalist clashes, poverty, and politically chaotic situations might well trigger an avalanche of refugees.

But even if the reforms in the CIS succeed, it will mean thousands of factories closed down and millions pushed out of work. Increased unemployment, inequality of incomes, and poverty—the unavoidable short-term effects of marketization and privatization—will increase the pressure on individuals to search for better opportunities abroad. Massive and uncontrolled migrations from the former USSR thus might destabilize the Polish labor market and exacerbate social tensions.[57]

Adjustments in Poland's Migration Policy

The absence of a comprehensive Polish migration policy has considerably magnified the impact of changes in Western European and German migration policies. Since 1989 the Polish government has taken a number of steps to bring its migration policy in line with the legal standards that have been in force internationally for a long time, as well as with those newer standards that have only recently emerged in Western Europe.

Poland has become increasingly active in various forms of international cooperation on migration-related issues. Since 1991 Poland has participated in the Vienna-process (concentrating on the East-West movements of people), and the Berlin/Budapest-process (concentrating on illegal migration problems). Poland's membership in the Council of Europe (since 1991) and the International Organization for Migration (since 1992) favor a further intensification of interstate contacts. Polish representatives also take part in consultations of experts from other international organizations.

In view of Poland's expected integration into the EU, the Schengen migration regime is of particular significance. Created by the signatories (Belgium, France, Germany, Luxemburg and the Netherlands) of the 1985 Agreement on the Abolition of Internal Borders, "Schengenland" was subsequently joined by Italy (in 1990), Spain and Portugal (in 1991), and Greece (in 1992); Austria has

---

57. See Wlodek Aniol, "Poland: From Emigration to Immigration?" *Refugees* 76 (June 1990): 35–36.

been an observer since 1994. Schengen activities run parallel to the work of all the EU countries in relation to asylum and border control issues, but they have a more elaborate character. On 26 March 1995 the Schengen Convention abolishing internal border controls between Belgium, France, Germany, Luxembourg, the Netherlands, Portugal, and Spain came into force. Individuals traveling between these countries no longer need to present their passports. The elimination of internal border checks between the Schengen group countries is accompanied by a reinforcement of external borders in order to restrict illegal immigration and inhibit international crime.[58] Although Polish authorities are in the process of adapting their migration policy to the EU approach, it will inevitably take time to harmonize Poland's visa, entry, border control, readmission, and asylum policies with a migration regime that the Western European states developed over more than a decade and with considerable acrimony.

Some of the most important legal and institutional adjustments made in the field of migration after 1989 include the following measures:

1. On 22 November 1990 the government created the position of the Plenipotentiary of the Minister of Interior for Refugees. A month later the Office of the Plenipotentiary for Refugees was established and then transformed into the Office for Migration and Refugee Affairs in February 1993.
2. On 29 March 1991 Poland concluded an agreement with the members of the Schengen Agreement on lifting visa requirements and the readmission of migrants in irregular situations. This accord was a package deal: Poland was removed from the Schengen visa list at the cost of accepting the return of illegal Polish immigrants staying in "Schengenland."[59]
3. On 15 May 1991 a newly created Border Guard replaced the old Border Protecting Army Units. While the former is a de facto border police, the latter were part of the Polish Army.
4. On 2 September 1991 the Polish parliament ratified the United Nations Convention measure relating to the Status of Refugees

58. Italy, Greece, and Austria will implement the Convention once their national parliaments have ratified the accession instruments and their national computer systems are in place. See United Nations/ECE, *International Migration Bulletin* 6 (Geneva: United Nations/ECE, May 1995), p. 11.

59. It is worth noting that the resolution adopted at the Budapest Conference of 1993 refers to this accord as a valid basis for a broader multilateral agreement.

of 1951 together with the Protocol of 1967. In April 1992 the first refugee camp was established in Nadarzyn near Warsaw.

5. In 1990–92 the first bilateral agreements were negotiated and signed with Germany, France, and Belgium dealing with on contract-employment, vocational training, and seasonal workers. However, Poland is not yet a party of any international convention on the rights of migrant workers.[60]

6. On 19 September 1991 the Law on Foreigners of 1963 was amended. In the following month, on 18 October, the parliament amended Article 88 of the constitution concerning the right of asylum. Yet because these amendments still remain too vague, these modifications will continue to fail to meet current needs.[61]

A serious shortcoming of Polish policy is that the authorities do not yet have at their disposal the technical means to implement entry control policies along the same lines as do the states in Western Europe. Hence the data on the number of foreigners currently staying in Poland are vague and rarely available. The same is also true for data on the nationality of people entering Poland or those entrants who have received so-called administrative visas (which means that they have been expelled) or who have illegally prolonged their stay in Poland. All that is available are estimates that vary considerably depending on the source they come from.

Since 1989 a new philosophy and policy towards immigration and refugees has taken shape in Poland. Under the impact of Western European policies, Poland has moved from a liberal to a more restrictive approach.[62]

After 1989 Polish authorities tried to solve refugee problems in a humanitarian way. For example, in the summer of 1989 Poland lent considerable support to refugees from East Germany who were making their way to West Germany. In March 1990 the prime

60. At the top of the list are convention No. 97 of the ILO on migration for employment and the European Social Charter, a convention of the Council of Europe.

61. Article 6 of the amended Law on Foreigners inserts the general rules of the UN Convention on Refugees into Polish domestic law. However, the Constitutional Tribunal declared newly adopted regulations (which provided for the detention in special centers, for up to ninety days, of illegal migrants) to be incompatible with existing Polish legislation protecting civil rights. As a result, foreigners without proper papers can now be detained only up to forty-eight hours and are then released with the warning that they must leave the country. At present, a new Act on Foreigners, more fully compatible with European standards, is being prepared.

62. For the last several years, public opinion in Poland also appears to have shifted in favor of immigration controls.

minister announced Poland's readiness to help Jewish emigrants from the Soviet Union who were making their way to Israel. In March 1990 the issue of the so-called "Baltic boat people" came to the attention of the Polish authorities, as well as to that of the Polish Red Cross.

This case is particularly illustrative, as it reveals how increasingly restrictive asylum and refugee regulations in the West have influenced Poland. Due to the large increase in the number of asylum seekers, the Swedish government changed its asylum policy and modified its relevant administrative procedures in December 1989. Only new arrivals qualifying as political refugees under the 1951 UN Refugee Convention measure would be allowed to remain in the country; people in "refugee-like" situations would no longer qualify for a stay in Sweden.

As a result, on 22 March 1990 the Swedish authorities decided to deport a group of ninety-four Arab and African asylum seekers back to Poland. Some of them had fake Swedish visas. Other deportations followed. Some time after that, about one thousand Lebanese, Syrians, Somalis, Eritreans, Ethiopians, and Iranians found themselves in Świnoujście, a small port town in the northwest of Poland, having been deported from Sweden or having tried unsuccessfully to get there in order to seek political asylum or to receive international travel documents.

Although Poland was not a party to the UN Convention at the time, the government nonetheless granted permission to the refugees to remain in Poland and provided them with all humanitarian aid. In an effort to resolve the problem, Poland also appealed to the UNHCR. These developments helped to speed up the process of adapting Polish policy to international refugee standards considerably. In particular, they compelled the Polish government to elaborate the procedure for defining the status of refugees.[63] The establishment of the Office for Migration and Refugee Affairs and the revision of the old Law on Foreigners and relevant constitutional provisions illustrate this development. Polish refugee and asylum policy became open, liberal, and generous. Soon thereafter, however, the influence of restrictive measures in Western Europe on Polish regulations and practices became readily apparent.

63. See also Wlodek Aniol, "Poland's Response to the Refugee Phenomenon," in Raymond J. Smyke. ed., *Coming, Going and Developing: The Significance of Refugees, Migrants and Returnees* (Geneva: Working Group on Refugees of the European Association of Development Institute, 1992), pp. 44–55.

An illustration of this impact is the draft Law on Foreigners submitted to the parliament in 1995, which refers in detail to the provisions of a refugee-asylum procedure. In particular, it broadens the requirements on place and time, as well as the formalities involved in asylum applications. However, the draft also introduces the concept of "safe countries" to Polish legislation. Article 32 of the draft law states that refugee status may be granted only to foreigners who have arrived in Poland from "a country that is not a safe country of origin or a safe third country."[64] This opens up the possibility to reject an application on administrative grounds without fully processing it or without implementing a simplified procedure in the case of "legitimate" asylum seekers.

Although the draft law provides for the basic rights of refugees, several of the proposed provisions have given rise to serious concerns on the part of the UNHCR, which finds that they are "in contravention of international refugee law." In its present form, for example, the draft law may not be compatible with the principle of non-refoulement. The draft does not identify a central, qualified, and impartial decision-making body responsible for the determination of refugee status. The establishment of a fair procedure is therefore not guaranteed.[65]

Another good example of the "ripple effect" by which the changes in Western European immigration policies have affected relevant Polish regulations is the introduction of visas for Bosnians and citizens of the Federal Republic of Yugoslavia. In this case, restrictive decisions undertaken in Scandinavian countries have brought about similar restrictive measures in Poland and the Czech Republic.

On 1 June 1993 Denmark and Sweden introduced visas for citizens of the Republic of Bosnia and Herzegovina and the "new" Yugoslavia. Too many visitors from these Balkan states had tried to stay in Scandinavia by ignoring the three-month visit limit. Most immigrants also worked illegally. Because of this and on the grounds of readmission regulations, 412 citizens of the former

---

64. *Draft Act on Foreigners*, September 1995 (manuscript), p. 12.

65. Such a procedure, argues the UNHCR, should include: 1) an initial administrative decision by an organ of the central government; 2) an administrative appeal reviewed by someone other than the initial decision-maker; and 3) the opportunity for judicial review for both substantive and procedural reasons. An asylum-seeker should be given sufficient time to apply for refugee status, and should then have the legal right to remain in Poland until the administrative and judicial review of his claim has been completed. See *Letter by J. Horekens, Director of the UNHCR Regional Bureau for Europe, to J. Zych, Speaker of the Sejm of the Republic of Poland*, 22 September 1995.

Yugoslavia were deported to Poland from Scandinavian countries in the first half of 1993.

Only a month later, as of 1 July 1993, the Polish government introduced similar visa requirements to avoid further irregular flows. The Czech Republic made similar policy changes at the same time as well. The Polish government stressed, however, that it was still ready to provide shelter to refugees from former Yugoslavia who continue to be entitled to apply for asylum. In doing so the Polish government took into account the fact that very few citizens from former Yugoslavia entering Poland have decided to use the available refugee-asylum procedures.[66]

A final example of Western immigration restrictions influencing the evolution of Poland's migration policy is the new sanctions imposed on airlines. Recently introduced in a number of Western European countries, they effectively force airlines to act as unofficial immigration officers. Until now Poland has had no legal sanctions against airlines that bring inadequately documented foreigners to the country, although such regulations are expected to be introduced soon. The Polish Border Guard already provides advice to airlines concerning the preparation and implementation of appropriate measures to prevent them from transporting undocumented passengers. In addition, during 1992–93 Poland introduced a number of measures aimed at substantially limiting the inflow of foreigners from a group of almost thirty Asian and African states, commonly referred to as "countries of increased [emigration] risk." These measures include the demand that visa decisions be made by consular offices abroad in cooperation with relevant bodies in Poland, foremost among them being the Border Guards.[67]

The Role of Germany

Postwar Germany's immigration regime was implicitly based on the presumption of an exit control system in central and Eastern

---

66. For example, between January and May 1993, only about one hundred persons out of over twenty-three citizens of Yugoslavia and nineteen thousand citizens of Bosnia who had entered the territory of Poland applied to be awarded the status of refugee. Most of them were in transit across Poland on their way to Scandinavian countries. See T. K. Kozłowski, *Poland: Between Transit, Asylum Seeking and Immigration. Legal and Institutional Consequences of the Phenomenon of Involuntary Migration*, paper prepared for the Seminar on Protection of Refugees in Central and Eastern Europe, Sofia, 21–23 June 1994, pp. 5–6.

67. See Kozłowski, *Poland*, p. 8.

Europe. Since 1989 revolutionary changes in this region have brought about new regulations allowing for easy exit from these countries. Citizens of the post-Communist states now have the option of leaving freely and settling elsewhere. For many of them, Germany is the most attractive destination country.

Faced with waves of immigrants and asylum seekers, Germany has looked to the European Community for help—partly in the sincere belief that this is a European problem, but partly out of expediency. During the negotiations of the Maastricht Treaty, Germany insisted on more EC involvement in asylum and immigration issues. The German government wanted to tighten its liberal asylum policy and hoped that a stiffer Community-wide policy would do the job. Such a EC policy inevitably would be less generous than the German one and—due to EC primacy over national law—would override the German constitution.

However, because of Britain's refusal to accept any larger role for the EC on questions of "internal security," including issues like political asylum and immigration, the Maastricht Treaty does not provide for specific EU rules on these issues. The United Kingdom insists it has to maintain national border controls and argues that migration problems can be managed through more cooperation among states. Hence Germany has been compelled to adapt its migration policy domestically.

In February 1992 the ruling coalition of CDU/CSU-FDP introduced a bill amending the constitutional guarantee of the right of asylum. The draft bill maintained the individual right of asylum for political refugees but provided, in addition, that asylum seekers would have no right to be recognized as refugees once they had entered from a country in which there was no danger of political persecution. Asylum seekers falling under this clause would be refused entry at the border or else deported after illegal entry.

Initially, the Social Democratic Party (SPD) strongly opposed any constitutional amendment of the asylum clause, causing the government to lack the two-thirds majority in the Bundestag necessary to change the Basic Law. Over time, however, the SPD has changed its stance, with the stipulation that its support of constitutional revision is conditional on reaching an agreement with Germany's neighbors: the Czech Republic, Austria, and, foremost, Poland.

Specifically, the SPD has insisted that Germany seek assurances that asylum seekers would be admitted to these neighboring countries and given an opportunity to apply for asylum there. It has also argued that the proposed changes in German legislation would shift the burden of solving the refugee problem to other states, including those which only recently had acceded to the UN Convention on Refugees. Any changes in Germany's domestic laws should therefore be accompanied by international arrangements providing economic assistance to countries like Poland and the Czech Republic. As it turned out, however, only one bilateral agreement with Poland, regarding cooperation on the effects of migratory flows, was enough to win SPD support for a tightening of Germany's asylum policy. On 26–28 May 1993 the German parliament adopted a constitutional change allowing for new measures concerning asylum.

The change involves amendments to Article 16 of the constitution. Under its original version, the right to apply for political asylum was virtually without qualification, allowing for extremely liberal entry policies. Every asylum request, furthermore, had to be examined in accordance with a complex and time-consuming asylum procedure. In the meantime the person requesting asylum was granted the right of entry and a residence permit valid until the asylum procedure was concluded.

The new Article 16a contains qualifications and exceptions to the provision that "the politically persecuted have the right to asylum." The main qualification is that if a person arrives from any country of the EU or from another country where the UN Convention on the Status of Refugees of 1951 is applied, and where the rights of refugees and basic human rights appear to be guaranteed, then that person cannot apply for political asylum in Germany. All of Germany's immediate neighbors, including Poland, as well as all Western European and Scandinavian countries, are currently considered to be "safe third countries."

An agreement between Germany and Poland on cooperation regarding the effects of migratory flows was signed in Bonn on 7 May 1993. It went into effect on 1 July of the same year, together with the German laws amending asylum procedure. The Polish-German agreement includes the following provisions:

1. Applicants for asylum who enter Germany illegally from Poland as a transit country will be sent back within six months of their arrival or after their stay has come to the attention of German authorities. No one who has entered Germany via Poland before the new German asylum law

went into effect and submitted an application for asylum will be returned.

2. The agreement allows Germany to deport to Poland in 1993 up to ten thousand rejected applicants for asylum. After 1993 the Germans will be allowed to deport unlimited numbers of rejected applicants arriving from Poland, but only within six months of their arrival.

3. In the event of exceptional circumstances resulting in sudden or massive influxes of immigrants into the territory of Poland, Germany will authorize entry for certain categories of such persons.

4. The agreement provides for financial assistance for Poland, which amounts to a total of DM 120 million for 1993 and 1994. It is intended to help implement the agreed measures focusing on three areas in particular: the creation of a proper administrative infrastructure for refugees and asylum seekers; the strengthening of border protection; and increased protection of public safety.

The bilateral negotiations for this agreement took six months, and the difficulty of reaching an acceptable compromise was compounded by the fact that immigration had become a highly sensitive issue in both German and Polish politics.

At the outset of the negotiations the German government argued that the amended German law on granting asylum should apply retroactively. The number of asylum seekers that Poland would have to receive in 1993 and the scope of the financial assistance to be supplied by Germany were also bones of contention.

The agreement of May 1993 de facto modifies some points of the former agreement on readmission of April 1991 signed with Germany as a member of the Schengen Group. In 1993 Germany was trying to include under the provisions of the former agreement all unwanted foreigners who arrived from Poland. At issue in the negotiations was whether Poland should be obliged to take back only Polish citizens (staying as guest workers in Germany beyond the permitted three-month period) or all illegal migrants who had traveled through Poland to enter Germany.

By signing the agreement of May 1993, Poland was the first of the central and eastern European states to accept the principle of the "safe third state." The essence of this concept is that applicants for asylum are coming from a country in which they were safe from persecution and to which they may therefore be returned without jeopardizing their safety. This principle was an essential part of the efforts to devise more expedient asylum procedures in Germany. For many reasons, however, the concept of the "safe third state" poses a number of questions and seems to be of limited use in the present situation in Europe.

First of all, that an asylum seeker could have found protection elsewhere does not necessarily mean that his or her application is unfounded in terms of the 1951 UN Convention measures. As the UNHCR has stated in a paper on this topic, "There is no international rule or principle whereby a person who has left his country in order to escape persecution must apply for recognition of refugee status or asylum in the first safe country he has been able to reach."[68]

Furthermore, in accordance with the letter and spirit of the 1951 UN Convention measures, the principle of the "safe third country" can be applied only with regard to the individuals whose status as refugees has already been determined. Only in these cases may a state count on the support of international organizations (such as UNHCR or IOM) for arranging the settlement of such people in third countries.

The implementation of the concept of the "safe third country" with regard to Poland is likely to put additional pressures on the still fragile state of its system of refugee protection, for it will almost certainly be difficult to assure the effective and durable protection of asylum seekers in Poland if large numbers of them are sent back from Germany. It will take time to develop the necessary infrastructure capable in practice of dealing with returned asylum seekers. Furthermore, Poland has itself become the destination of an increasing number of illegal migrants who are trying to settle in Western Europe. Almost all of the people sent back from Germany are third-country nationals without any established right of residence in Poland. Therefore, the vital question is how to facilitate returns directly to the countries of origin, through joint negotiations and multilateral agreements between all states concerned.

Afraid of negative aspects of the new German solutions and bilateral agreement and under pressure from Germany, Poland succeeded in signing in 1995 readmission agreements with the Czech Republic (10 May), Ukraine (24 May), Slovakia (8 July),

68. "The 'Safe Third Country' Policy in the Light of the International Obligations of Countries vis-à-vis Refugees and Asylum-Seekers," paper issued by the UNHCR Branch Office, London, July 1993.

Romania (24 July), and Bulgaria (25 August). In addition, the agreements on repealing visas with Lithuania, Latvia, and Estonia include readmission clauses. Similar readmission agreements with two other states (Russia and Belarus) are under negotiation.

Because of the current trend towards an increase in the irregular movements of people in the region and the lack of effective multilateral cooperation mechanisms to deal with them, the Polish Ministry of the Interior has also considered the introduction of entry visas for the citizens of Romania, Bulgaria, and the CIS. Some political parties have strongly supported this approach, arguing that the flow of migrants from these countries undermines small business and agriculture in many Polish regions. So far, however, these demands have failed to alter the government's policies.

Conclusion

The current thrust of Western European asylum policies can be interpreted as an attempt to transfer the "burden of asylum seekers" eastward by limiting the number of refugees reaching Western Europe through extending the system for taking in asylum-seekers to central and east European countries.[69] This has only resulted, however, in a domino effect of tighter asylum laws and stricter border controls that is now spreading to central and eastern Europe.

Specifically, Germany has tried to solve its problems with refugees and illegal immigrants by deporting them back to Poland. In this view, Poland is assigned the role of a filter for migrants coming to Germany from the east. Put differently, Poland plays the role of cop at Germany and Western Europe's extended eastern border, thus ensuring that illegal immigration does not grow out of control.

The case of Poland's immigration policy specifically shows that a previously liberal, national approach, adopted soon after the political revolution of 1989, is now being slowly replaced by a more restrictive stance reflecting European and German policies. Germany's new asylum law, with its introduction of the safe country principle, has affected this evolution most directly. The concept of "safe country," controversial in the light of international law, has been embodied in Poland's 1995 draft Law on Foreigners.

69. See *Preliminary Draft Report on Refugees and Asylum-seekers in Central and Eastern Europe. (Rapporteur: Mr Iwinski)*, Parliamentary Assembly, Council of Europe, Strasbourg (April 1995), p. 10.

The Protection of the German Ethnic Minority

Poland's policy towards national minorities changed dramatically between 1989 and 1995. The new policy aims at strengthening the development of the cultural identity of minorities, as well as at their integration with local communities and their participation in public affairs. These changes were made possible by the democratic revolution of 1989. Besides the domestic sources of this change in policy, international influences have also had a strong effect on the position of Poland's national minorities.

First, Poland has new neighbors who take a strong interest in the treatment of "their" national minorities.[70] With the emergence of these new states, the importance of the national minorities issue in Poland has grown a great deal. Second, the country's efforts to integrate with Western Europe means that Poland has to accept and respect specific standards of protecting the rights of national minorities, which have evolved in European institutions, particularly in the Organization for Security and Cooperation in Europe (OSCE) and the Council of Europe. During the last four years many provisions of OSCE documents have become legally binding as part of bilateral treaties negotiated by Poland with all of its new neighbors. All of these accords contain provisions for the protection of the rights of persons belonging to national minorities.[71]

For many reasons, the situation of the German minority in Poland is unique. First of all, it is Poland's biggest national minority. And in comparison with other minorities, its situation has changed most dramatically in the 1990s. Last but not least, it appears that international factors have in this case had the largest effect.

Historical Background

For a major part of its history, Poland was a country of many nations. Up to the twelfth century it was inhabited almost exclusively by the native Slav population, descendants of the Lechite

---

70. All the neighbors of Poland changed in 1990–1993. Instead of the former three (the Soviet Union, Czechoslovakia, and the GDR), there are seven new neighbors: Russia, Lithuania, Belarus, the Ukraine, Slovakia, the Czech Republic, and the FRG.

71. The first treaty was signed with Germany (17 June 1991), followed by treaties with the Czech and Slovak Republic (6 October 1991), Ukraine (18 May 1992), Russia (22 May 1992), Belarus (23 June 1992), and Lithuania (24 April 1994). See "Poland's International Obligations with Regard to National Minorities (selected by Łucja Wierzycka)," *The Polish Quarterly of International Affairs*, 1,

tribes of the pre-state period. From the thirteenth century onwards, however, the German and Jewish population grew, especially in the towns. A completely new ethnic situation arose once the Union with Lithuania was concluded in 1385, a union that endured for more than four hundred years. The state was then inhabited not only by Poles and Lithuanians but also by various other ethnic groups, including Ruthenians, Armenians, Tartars, and Germans, who professed a variety of religions: Catholic, Protestant, Orthodox, Jewish, and Muslim among others. The polyglot ethnic composition of the population and the tradition of a powerful federal state, in which Poles enjoyed a dominant political and cultural position, had a strong influence on popular attitudes during the First Polish Republic.

Conquered and ruled in the nineteenth century by three great empires—Russian, Austro-Hungarian, and Prussian/German—Poland avoided a form of natural evolution towards the nation-state based on the classic Western model. This also explains the relatively strong attachment of the Polish nation to its own identity, as well as its distrust and suspicion towards other ethnic groups and neighbors. Throughout this period Polish nationalism had a defensive character and was sustained by the feeling of an endangered national identity.

Although the Polish state, rebuilt in 1918 after 123 years of captivity, did not restore its pre-partition borders, it remained multinational in character. According to the census of 1921, its population was twenty-seven million, with Poles amounting to 69 percent; the Ukrainians, 14 percent; "Jews, eight percent"; Belarussians, 4 percent; and Germans, 4 percent of the total.[72] There were also some Lithuanians, Russians, and Czechs.[73] Xenophobia, national and religious tensions, and conflicts marked the interwar period.

After World War II, the Potsdam Conference defined Poland's western border as lying along the Oder (Odra) and Lusatian Neisse (Nysa Łużycka) Rivers. At the same time, its eastern border was established along the Curzon Line. The shifting of the state

---

1–2 (Summer/Autumn 1992): 171–98; *Synopsis of Provisions for Respect of Frontiers and Territorial Integrity and the Rights of National Minorities Contained in the Treaties Concluded by the Republic of Poland with its Neighbours*. Presented to the Inaugural Conference for the Pact on Stability in Europe, Paris (26–27 May 1994).

72. Historically in Poland, as throughout central-eastern Europe, Jews were considered both a religious as well as an ethnic group.

73. Józef Buszko, *Historia Polski 1864–1948* [*History of Poland, 1864–1948*] (Warsaw: Polish Scientific Publishers, 1978), p. 267.

westward was accompanied by the expulsion of the German population, also legitimated at Potsdam by the fact that almost all the
Polish Jews (some three million) lost their lives in Nazi Germany's
death camps. Millions of Poles from the lost eastern territories
were resettled into new areas acquired by Poland in the west and
north, including the major part of former East Prussia and the former free city of Gdańsk.

In terms of ethnicity, religion, and language, Poland today is
one of the most homogenous states in Europe. This does not
mean, however, that Polish society is monocultural. Between one
and one and a half million Polish citizens of non-Polish nationality are estimated to live within the borders of the Republic of
Poland. That is about 2 to 4 percent of all citizens.

Minorities live in all parts of Poland, some partly concentrated
in specific regions, others dispersed throughout. According to the
best estimates available there are about three hundred to five
hundred thousand ethnic Germans (mostly concentrated in Silesia, but also in the Warmia and Mazury regions), three hundred
thousand Ukrainians (scattered around the country), two hundred
to two hundred fifty thousand Belarussians (living mainly in the
Podlasie region in the East of Poland), twenty to thirty thousand
Gypsies, twenty to twenty-five thousand Lithuanians (in the
Punsk and Sejny districts in the northeast), twenty thousand Slovaks (in southern Poland), "and 10,000–15,000 Jews." This ethnic
mosaic is completed by small communities of Russians, Greeks,
Armenians, Czechs, and Tartars.[74]

The Potsdam Conference decided to deport the German population from the areas acquired by Poland. It is estimated that
between 1945 and 1950 around three million Germans left or were
expelled from territories east of the Oder and the Lusatian Neisse.
However, a group of about one million people, mostly lacking a
clear national identity, stayed and became Polish citizens. The
majority of these were "locals"—regional groups with vague and
ambiguous national identities, such as the Silesians, Mazurians,
Warmians, or Kashubes. The Silesian, for example, most often felt
himself a Silesian first, and a Pole or German only second. Under

---

74. *Mniejszošci narodowe w Polsce i polityka państwa polskiego wobec nich* [*National
Minorities in Poland and Polish Minority Policy*] (Warsaw: Ministry of Culture and
Art, Office for the Culture of National Minorities, 15 September 1995), p. 1. Com-
pare with Ryszard Walicki, *Mniejszošci narodowe w Polsce w 1992 r. w świetle badań
empirycznych* [*National Minorities in Poland in 1992 in the Light of Empirical Studies*]
(Warsaw: Chancellery of the Sejm, Office for Studies and Expertises, 1993), pp. 1–4.

German administration many of them had acquired Polish surnames, cultural and religious traditions, and the Polish language.
Others spoke German at home and their predominant feeling was
that they belonged to the German community. There were also
mixed families having roots in both cultures.

Poland's lack of tolerance towards the retention of a separate
cultural identity was a major reason for emigration. The postwar
policy of "enforced polonization" tended to have the opposite
effect: many people suddenly remembered the German ancestry
they had once rejected. One can fairly assume, however, that a
major factor behind their decision to leave was the growing difference in living standards between Poland and the Federal Republic
of Germany. Many chose to live in the FRG because it was a wealthy
and democratic country. Citizenship in the German welfare state
was perceived as a precious and desirable thing that assured reasonable standards of living and social security in old age.

It is estimated that some 424,000 people emigrated from Poland
to the FRG between 1955 and 1974; in addition, about two hundred thousand persons left the country under the Gierek-Schmidt
Family Reunification Agreement of 1975.[75] This exodus resulted in
the disappearance of German-language education and the demise
of German newspapers and magazines. After several waves of
postwar emigration to the FRG, the Polish authorities stated that
a German minority problem no longer existed in Poland.[76] But
people cultivating the German language, culture, and tradition

75. The numbers quoted by Jacek Kosiarski, "The German Minority in Poland,"
The Polish Quarterly of International Affairs, 1, 1–2 (Summer/Autumn 1992): 48–49.
The package deal, made by Polish Communist Party First Secretary Edward Gierek
and Chancellor Helmut Schmidt during the final CSCE conference in Helsinki,
resulted in three agreements signed in Warsaw on 9 October 1975. Under the first
one, Poland permitted one hundred twenty to one hundred twenty-five thousand
Polish citizens of German origin to leave for the FRG within the next four years (in
1976 the Polish government agreed to extend this period). The second one concerned
the global sum of compensation (DM 1.3 billion) for those inhabitants of Poland who
had the right to pensions in the FRG. And according to the third one, the FRG
granted economic development credits to Poland, amounting to DM two billion.

76. General Wojciech Jaruzelski said in Wroclaw on 7 May 1985: "We have done
more than was required of us in discharging all our international obligations
regarding the repatriation and reunification of families separated by the war. The
problem of a German national minority in Poland has thereby ceased to exist once
and for all." See Jan Barcz (ed.), *Historyczne, polityczne i prawne aspekty tez RFN o
niemieckich mniejszościach narodowych w Polsce (wybór dokumentów)* [*Historical, Political and Legal Aspects of FRG Theses on German Ethnic Minorities in Poland (Selected Documents)*] (Warsaw: Polish Institute of International Affairs, 1988), volume 2, p. 59.

continued to live in the country, mostly in the regions of the former German Reich that after the war had become part of Poland.

Thus, under Communist rule, a kind of "political schizophrenia" prevailed in Poland's ethnic policy, in particular towards the German minority. In the 1970s and 1980s the authorities issued exit permits to persons who could produce incontrovertible proof of ethnic German origin, a practice that was, after all, positive proof of the existence of a German minority. At the same time, however, the authorities did not recognize such persons as constituting a national minority and did not ensure the rights that go with that status as a means of encouraging them to remain in Poland. All in all, Polish authorities simply did not want to fully recognize the existence of national minorities, proclaiming instead the existence of a nationally uniform state.[77]

The Incorporation of International Standards into Polish Policy

The political and legal standards of the OSCE and Council of Europe for the protection of minorities are becoming a reference point for the solution of minority problems in bilateral relations and are finding their way into bilateral declarations and treaties.

This also applies to Poland and its relations with seven new neighbors: the united Germany, the Czech Republic, Slovakia, Ukraine, Belarus, Lithuania, and the Russian Federation. In all of Poland's treaties signed with its neighbors in 1991–94, and in the political declarations preceding them, provisions relating to national minorities have occupied a prominent place. The question of the rights of minorities has been resolved there on the basis of European standards and OSCE commitments in particular. During the negotiations the treaty parties agreed not to look for "special solutions" or separate provisions modeled on pre-war ideas, but to make international standards a foundation for resolving minority issues in bilateral relations.

The most extensive and detailed provisions pertaining to minorities were included in the Treaty on Good-Neighbourly Relations and Friendly Cooperation concluded (on 17 June 1991) between the

---

77. For a more comprehensive treatment of this issue, see Cezary Żołędowski, "Mniejszości narodowe w Polsce" ["National Minorities in Poland"], in Anton Rajkiewicz, ed., *Społeczeństwo polskie w latach 1989–93. Wybrane zagadnienia i dane z zakresu polityki społecznej* [*Polish Society 1989–93: Selected Issues and Data on Social Policy*] (Warsaw: Friedrich Ebert Foundation, 1994).

Republic of Poland and the Federal Republic of Germany. The rights of persons belonging to the German minority in Poland and the Polish group in Germany were given a legal form in three articles of the Treaty (Articles 20–22), which were based on the document that the Copenhagen Meeting on the Human Dimension of the CSCE adopted on 29 June 1990. In many instances the Copenhagen formulas were quoted explicitly or referred to.[78]

The most important congruence between both documents relates to the definition of what constitutes a national minority and how its members can exercise their rights. According to the Treaty, as in the Copenhagen Document, the determination of minority membership is made not only by taking into consideration the origins of a person, but also by "a person's individual choice." This is a point of crucial significance, as it restricts the possibility of denying members of a minority their rights through the simple negation of the very existence of such a minority in the country in question.

Both the Treaty and the Copenhagen Document clearly prefer the concept of individualized rights and reject the treatment of minority rights as group rights. This does not mean, however, that the specific rights to which members of a minority are entitled cannot be exercised collectively.[79] In general, instead of concentrating on the long-standing controversy and deliberations of "individual versus collective rights," the Treaty emphasizes the obligations of the states to protect the minorities in question.

Numerous further provisions of the Treaty and the Copenhagen Document are very similar, touching on such specific matters as the protection of minorities' identities; their rights to education, association, and participation in public affairs; and their freedom of religious association. In the latter case, for example, the relevant provision of the Treaty quotes exactly from the Copenhagen Document (para. 32.4).

Other provisions of the Treaty were added or developed further. For example, unlike the Copenhagen Document, the Treaty includes the right to enjoy, on equal terms with other citizens, effective legal means (remedy) of asserting one's rights, in conformity

---

78. For a more detailed comparison of the provisions included in both documents, see *Joint Polish-German Report on the Implementation of the Bilateral Treaty of 17 June 1991 regarding the German Minority in Poland and the Polish Group in Germany*, presented at the "CSCE Human Dimension Seminar on Case Studies on National Minorities Issues: Positive Results," Warsaw, 24–28 May 1993.

79. This possibility is provided for by the use of the expression "... individually or in community with other members of their group" (Article 20.3).

with national legislation. And going beyond the Copenhagen Document, the Treaty also stipulates that both minorities will have equal access to the media in their regions.

Like the CSCE Document, the Treaty affirms the right to use the minority language. Apart from a general clause, the Treaty recognizes, additionally, the right of members of both minorities to use the mother tongue version of given and surnames. This stipulation exceeds the provisions of the Copenhagen Document.

During the negotiations of the Treaty, Germany was interested in allowing official place-names, in traditional locations of German minority settlement, to be designated in German as well. Poland did not agree on this point at the time. A letter of intent from the Polish foreign minister to the German foreign minister, which was appended to the text of the Treaty, promised that the Polish government was willing to examine the question of topographical nomenclature "in due time."

Finally, there is the key question concerning the prohibition of the abuse of rights by persons belonging to national minorities and the obligation of loyalty to the state. Concerning the former issue, para. 37 of the Copenhagen Document was quoted directly in the Treaty. In addition, the Treaty states that any member of either minority shall be required "to behave loyally towards the State concerned, just like any other citizen, and observe the obligations arising out of the legislation of that State" (Article 22.2). Consequently, the country of residence has the right to expect civic loyalty from the members of respective minorities, as it does from all of its citizens.

The "citizenship clause" has been perceived by Poland as a *conditio sine qua non* for the application of European standards on minority protection to the German minority. Bearing in mind the German concept of citizenship, Poland was looking for guarantees of its political stability and security during the negotiations on the Treaty, and the possession of Polish citizenship by persons belonging to the German minority in Poland was seen as a safeguard against possible abuse of their minority rights.

It is worth adding that although there is no such clause in the Copenhagen Document, the principle of loyalty of members of minorities to their country of residence and citizenship constitutes one of the OSCE standards. It was included, among others, in the Report of the Geneva CSCE Meeting of Experts on National Minorities of 19 July 1991 (chapter IV. 4). Such an approach is also in conformity with the trend of the discussions held within the framework of the Council of Europe on the definition and rights of persons belonging to national minorities.

Other bilateral treaties signed by Poland with its neighbors were also inspired by European instruments and provide very similar guarantees with respect to a set of fundamental rights, as well as to the maintenance and development of an ethnic, cultural, linguistic, and religious identity of national minorities.

The year 1989 brought an important change in the situation of Poland's national minorities. The new democratic authorities recognized that membership in these groups is a matter of individual choice, and consequently guaranteed the exercise of special rights to persons who had chosen this option. At the same time, the Polish government has implemented the standards set down in various multilateral and bilateral instruments signed in the 1990s. The implementation of these international obligations has been accomplished through national legislation and appropriate governmental policies.

The legal adjustments to European standards started as early as the spring of 1989 after the Round Table debate. On the basis of the Law on Association of 7 April 1989, members of national minorities, like other Polish citizens, have acquired the right of association. The Law allows associations to possess their own incomes and signifies a break with the traditional way of, organizing nationally social institutions, for example, and of the licensing of their activities.

All minorities have their own associations. There are now about 120 of these, including several umbrella organizations; in Communist times there were only seven. National minorities are also politically active. In the last parliamentary election, held on 19 September 1993, there were candidates representing the German, Belarussian, and Ukrainian minorities. The first political party to be formed by a national minority was the Belarussian Democratic Union.

The more active participation of national minorities in public affairs began earlier, just after the first semi-democratic parliamentary elections of 4 June 1989. In August 1989 the Committee for National and Ethnic Minorities was established in the newly elected Parliament. It was given two ambitious tasks: to create a bill on national minorities and on the constitutional protection of minorities. Because of considerable differences of opinion, the Committee eventually decided on regulating the question of the protection of minority rights by means of the inclusion of the appropriate clauses in specific statutes.

The issue of introducing a separate law on minorities to the Polish legal system reappeared on the agenda of the parliament elected in October 1991. However, the work of the Committee did not lead to the adoption of any final decisions. When the present parliament was elected in September 1993, the Committee recognized that the issue of a law on minorities should be tackled once again, together with the need to insert eventually a specific reference in the new Constitution.[80]

The participation of minorities in political life has been facilitated by an electoral law which provides them with some privileges. The electoral law for the parliamentary elections of October 1991 contained provisions for the preferential treatment of candidates representing national minorities. For example, the number of signatures required for the registration of these candidates was lowered. As a result, representatives of the German minority entered the Sejm (seven deputies) and the senate (one senator). And the German minority set up its own group in parliament.[81]

Under the electoral law enacted on 28 May 1993, before the 19 September parliamentary elections, minorities also enjoy certain privileges designed to equalize their election chances and help them to secure representation in parliament. Apart from being granted some privileges with respect to putting forward their candidates, minority associations could now also apply to be relieved from the parliamentary threshold of receiving a minimum of 5 percent of all votes nation-wide (for political parties) and of 8 percent (for party coalitions). Yet interest among the minorities to put forward their own tickets was not that high. Some of them preferred to place their candidates on the tickets of larger parties.[82]

Within the structures of Poland's central administration the problems of national minorities were removed from the competence of the Ministry of Internal Affairs and handed over to the Ministry of Culture and Art. In the autumn of 1990 a permanent Group for National Minorities was created within the latter ministry. In April 1992 it was transformed into a separate department, the Office for National Minorities, which in April 1995 was

80. It is widely expected that the new constitution, now being drafted, will contain a clause defining the rights of Polish citizens belonging to national minorities. See Stanisław Podemski, "Prawo mniejszości" ["Minority Rights"], *Polityka* (23 October 1993): 8.

81. At present the German minority has four deputies in the Sejm and one senator. The Ukrainian minority has one representative in the Sejm.

82. See an interview with Łucja Wierzycka of the Helsinki Human Rights Foundation in *The Warsaw Voice* (5 September 1993).

renamed the Office for Culture of National Minorities. Its responsibilities include providing national minorities with financial support for cultural and publishing activities, legal and administrative assistance, and for counteracting infringements on the rights of minorities.[83]

To summarize, by and large there are now no political or legal barriers in Poland standing in the way of the development of the ethnic, cultural, linguistic, or religious identities of its national minorities. However, despite many positive developments the extent of the protection of the rights of national minorities in Poland can still be criticized.[84]

In particular, one can argue that the linguistic rights of minorities do not yet receive proper protection. A still binding decree (of 30 November 1945) on the official and working languages of the central and local administrations provides for no exceptions to the general rule of the exclusive use of the Polish language in this sphere. This is a particularly difficult problem for local governments where members of a national minority constitute a decisive majority of the population, such as Punsk where 90 percent of the population is Lithuanian. Some complaints are also being voiced about the activities of local authorities. Representatives of minority organizations claim that local officials are often too rigid, mistrustful, and reserved in their approach to national minorities. It is also worth noting that at the national level national minorities lack an appropriate partner to negotiate with. In September 1990 the government appointed the Commission for National Minorities, a consultative and advisory governmental agency composed of seven ministers and four heads of provinces. Unfortunately, its activities proved almost non-existent in practice. This body met several times, but no program of actions for national minorities was ever developed.

The Role of Germany

Alongside such fundamental concerns as reunification and a termination of the division of Europe through Polish-German reconciliation, for a long time the question of the German minority in

83. See *Mniejszości narodowe w Polsce w 1993 r. Biuletyn Biura ds. Mniejszości Narodowych przy Ministerstwie Kultury i Sztuki* [*National Minorities in Poland in 1993. Bulletin of the Office for National Minorities of the Ministry of Culture and Arts*] (Warsaw: Ministry of Culture and Arts, 1994).

84. See *Some Remarks on National Minorities in Poland: The Protection of Their Rights, Achievements and Failures* (Warsaw: Helsinki Foundation for Human Rights, May 1993).

Poland occupied a prominent place not only in bilateral relations between the FRG and Poland, but also in the Federal Republic's *"Ostpolitik."* This became the case especially in the late 1980s and early 1990s, in the wake of the fall of communism and during the first period of the democratic transformation in Poland.[85]

During the 1980s West Germany demonstrated its mounting concern for the fate and status of persons of ethnic German origin living in Poland. It pressed for a number of policy changes including easier emigration, and access to school instruction and religious services in German. West German politicians demanded, first of all, an official recognition by the Polish government that a German minority did exist and moreover had the right to cultivate its own identity.[86]

The issue also became one of the main demands of the organizations of German expellees in the Federal Republic. They stood by the highly debatable estimate of 1.1 million Germans living in Poland and stressed the need to make German economic aid to Poland contingent on the protection of minority rights. This was often linked to slogans that negated the borders established after World War II. The fact that the Federal Republic perpetuated the fiction of the Reich as still existing de jure within its 1937 borders enhanced Polish suspicions.[87]

85. In a statement to the *Bundestag* on 15 November 1990, Chancellor Helmut Kohl called the question of the German minority in Poland the "core" of the prospective treaty on good-neighborly relations between the two countries. Much earlier, in 1986, in a speech made by Internal Minister Friedrich Zimmerman, a frank airing of this problem was made a condition for financial aid and, subsequently, even for a possible visit of Chancellor Kohl to Poland. See Kosiarski, "The German Minority," pp. 47–68.

86. Chancellor Helmut Kohl, at a gathering of the Silesian *Landsmannschaft* in Hanover, said on 16 June 1985: "I assure you that the Federal Government will continue to insist on our compatriots being given the opportunity to emigrate and to be reunited with their families if they so wish. Those who wish to remain in their homeland have a right to their cultural distinctiveness and to develop and foster our language and our customs." See Witold Góralski and Jan Barcz, *Dylematy polityki wschodniej Republiki Federalnej Niemiec 1982–1985* [*Dilemmas of the FRG's Eastern Policy 1982–1985*] (Warsaw: Polish Institute of International Affairs, 1987), p. 171.

87. The FRG's legal and political position on the Polish-German boundary has evolved slowly during the whole postwar period. In the 1950s and 1960s the West German authorities did not recognize it openly. For example, Chancellor Konrad Adenauer stated before the *Bundestag* on 20 October 1953: "The German nation will never acknowledge the so-called border on the Oder and Neisse," *The Warsaw Voice* (12 November 1989): 10. In the Treaty on the Bases of Normalization of Relations between the Polish People's Republic and the FRG, signed on 7 December 1970, both countries decided to "confirm the inviolability of their existing borders, now and in the future,

The Polish authorities consistently refused to grant national minority rights to those claiming to be of German descent. West German claims that a German minority existed were dismissed as part of a political ploy aimed at destabilizing Polish society and justifying the idea of the character of Poland's western border as being provisional. Poland also emphasized that West German claims stemmed from the Federal Republic's particular concept of nationality and citizenship.

In the meantime, a position differing from the official line was adopted by some representatives of the Polish democratic opposition, who accused the government of failing to use diplomatic channels to clarify Bonn's intentions. But the attitude of the Polish Catholic Church towards the question of the German minority was mostly not to the liking of West Germany. Cardinal Józef Glemp, for example, the primate of Poland, opposed the idea of organizing services in German for "artificial foreigners" in Silesia.

In the 1980s the attempts of West German politicians to elevate the German minority problem into a contentious issue in bilateral relations was paralleled by the rise of a movement for national emancipation among the minority itself, chiefly in Silesia. A variety of initiatives were developed with the aim of drawing attention to the need for recognition and protection of minority rights.

The Federal Republic supported this ethnic revival and its pro-German sentiments, but in the late 1980s it decided to stem the rising tide of immigrants from Poland who used national or territorial justifications for getting West German citizenship. Between 1980 and 1988, about 382,000 immigrants from Poland obtained German citizenship under Article 116 of the Basic Law of the Federal Republic, which states that "a German is anyone possessing German nationality." In practice, this applies to the entire indigenous Polish population of the western and northern territories transferred from Germany to Poland in 1945. At the end of the 1980s this movement of people grew even stronger.[88]

---

and mutually commit themselves to unconditionally respect their territorial integrity," ibid. However, doubts and controversies persisted. For instance, a statement by the Federal Constitutional Court on 7 July 1975 limited the decisions of the treaty to abstaining from resorting to force in relation to the border. An end to all doubts about its legal status was eventually established in the Treaty between the Republic of Poland and the FRG on the Confirmation of the Existing Border of 14 November 1990.

88. In the 1970s citizens of German origin left Poland at a rate of more than ten thousand a year. In the 1980s a true exodus took place with annual emigration figures varying between fifty thousand and one hundred thousand. In 1989, twenty-five hundred thousand ethnic Germans left the country. In 1991, the figure stood at

Numerous internal difficulties connected with the increasing exodus of ethnic Germans from Poland and other central and East European countries, later on also including East Germany, modified the position of the West German authorities. Their attitude towards re-settlers changed. The necessity of providing the newcomers with housing, employment, and special welfare benefits led to promises by the German government to help improve the conditions for Germans living in Poland along with pledges of financial support for various attempts to revive German culture in Silesia.

Although controversy over the legal definition of its status did not subside, the German minority found that beginning in the autumn of 1989 the Polish government no longer questioned the fact that it existed. The breakthrough came during Chancellor Helmut Kohl's visit to Poland in November 1989, when a Joint Declaration was adopted.[89] The de facto recognition of a German minority in Poland acted as a spur to the activism of its representatives. The first minority organization, the Socio-Cultural Society of the Population of German Stock of Katowice Voivodship, based in Gliwice, was legally registered in court in January 1990. By 1996 there were some sixty such associations.

Poland deprecated all attempts at linkage between guarantees of German minority rights and a treaty on borders, but many German politicians tied the conclusion of a frontier accord to treaty-based guarantees of the rights of the German minority. Poland and Germany eventually removed any lingering ambiguities about the Oder-Neisse frontier through the conclusion of a treaty on 14 November 1990 expressly confirming its definitive status. Only after this date were the relevant provisions on the rights of national minorities included in the Treaty on Good-Neighbourly Relations and Friendly Cooperation of June 1991.

It is worth noting, however, that the term "national minority" is used in the Treaty only with respect to the German minority in Poland. The Polish group in Germany is referred to as "persons living in the Federal Republic of Germany, holders of German citizenship, who are of Polish origin or identify with the Polish language,

---

forty thousand, and in 1992 it fell to under twenty thousand. *The Warsaw Voice* (20–27 December 1992): 4.

89. Paragraph 45 of the Declaration stated: "Both Parties will make it possible for persons and population groups of Polish and German extraction or persons identifying with the language, culture or tradition of the other Party to preserve and develop their cultural identity." *Gazeta Wyborcza* (15 November 1989).

culture or tradition."[90] This terminological asymmetry has given rise to concerns about the alleged lack of symmetry in the rights, duties, and obligations concerning Poles in Germany and Germans in Poland.[91] Doubts have been voiced that one of the consequences might be that only Poland is bound by other instruments on the protection of national minorities in the treatment of the German minority, whereas Germany, in the treatment of the Polish group, is bound only by the Treaty.[92] During the ratification debate on the Treaty in the Polish parliament in December 1991, some politicians tried to point out that it favors the German minority.[93] The prevailing interpretation is, however, that according to the Treaty, both minorities and "equivalent groups" do enjoy the same rights. Thus, in spite of the lack of an explicit qualification of the Polish group in Germany in the Treaty as a national minority, it should be protected as such.[94]

90. Thus the formal acknowledgment of the existence of a German minority in Poland has no parallel as far as the acknowledgment of the existence of a Polish minority in Germany goes. In the Federal Republic of Germany only Danish, Sorbian, and Frisian ethnic groups have the legal status of recognized national minorities. Each of them is estimated at approximately fifty thousand people. Other ethnic groups living in Germany, for shorter periods of time and much more dispersed throughout the country, including the 4.5 million "guest workers" and their dependents, are treated as foreigners. According to official German statistics, there are around two hundred ninety thousand Poles living in the Federal Republic. It is estimated, however, that the Polish-speaking population in Germany amounts to as many as one and a half to two million people. This group is very differentiated in terms of both its legal and social status.

91. For example, see Edward Cziomer, "Uwarunkowania i nowe problemy stosunków polsko-niemieckich w latach 90-tych (ekspertyza)" ["Determinants and New Problems of Polish-German Relations in the 1990s (Analysis)"], unpublished manuscript, 1994, pp. 16–17.

92. See R. Jasica, "Polish-German Treaties of 1990 and 1991 on the Confirmation of their Mutual Border and on Good Neighbourliness and Friendly Co-operation," *Polish Yearbook of International Law* 1991–1992, vol. XIX (Warsaw: Polish Academy of Sciences, 1991–92), pp. 81–82.

93. Replying to these complaints, Foreign Minister Krzystof Skubiszewski argued that the Treaty had been formulated as a compromise between legal possibilities and practical requirements. Senator Andrzej Szczypiorski commented that Poles now living in Germany do not consider themselves to be a minority.

94. Moreover, one can argue that if the notion of the Polish minority had been introduced into the Treaty, the protection would have probably been restricted to only the small group of so-called Ruhr-Polen, sometimes recognized in Germany as a "linguistic minority." Other, more significant groups of persons of Polish extraction living in Germany would have lacked any protection. According to its present provisions, the Treaty guarantees protection to all categories of Poles, including, to some extent, migrant workers who do not have German citizenship. See Jan Barcz, "Poland and its Bilateral Treaties," (Warsaw, unpublished manuscript, 1995).

Since 1990 the government of the Federal Republic has been financially supporting the German minority in Poland in various spheres including community building (equipment and support of meeting centers, clubs, and associations), culture and media (language training, assignment of German teachers of German-as-a-native-language to Polish schools, scholarships, assistance in the development of media), and economic and social affairs (provision of medical and other equipment, as well as urgently needed supplies for hospitals, and the creation of welfare centers for old and sick people).

The German government informs the Polish government about the various programs of assistance.[95] It is worth stressing that these projects, as a rule, benefit not only members of the German minority and are in fact intended to help improve the infrastructure throughout whole regions. However, there are also some forms of financial and technical assistance which have been offered exclusively to persons belonging to the German minority. These include social benefits for the aged and the disabled, and salaries for functionaries of the minority organizations.

The new situation of the German minority in Poland has also created some problems and tensions. No doubt the vast majority of people belonging to this minority behaves with civic loyalty towards the Polish state. And the German caucus in parliament has acted with great responsibility in many situations.[96] However, the influence of radical tendencies and of nationalistic attitudes among some segments of the German minority continues to give rise to concern.

Particularly with regard to Silesia, many Poles remain distrustful of the German community, who they say are claiming German origin en masse in hopes of receiving economic benefits. From time to time fears surface among the Polish public that the recognition of the existence of the German minority may open the way for the birth of a new "fifth column." Leaders of the German associations are criticized for not being sufficiently decisive in distancing themselves from extremists, including those acting in the expellees' organizations in Germany.

This was particularly apparent during 1990–91, when both Polish-German treaties were negotiated. The situation was aggravated

95. All in all, according to information received by the Polish Foreign Ministry, this aid amounted to about DM 46 million in 1993. While the German Foreign Ministry covers expenses for culture and education, the Ministry of Interior deals with social assistance programs.

96. Though, according to Bogvmiła Berdychowska, director of the Office for National Minorities, "the German deputies do a lot better in the Sejm than back in Opole." See an interview with her as reported in *The Warsaw Voice* (27 June 1993): 9.

by some Silesians in Germany who still hoped Silesia would become part of Germany and whose organizations, like the Union of
Expellees (BdV), are subsidized by German authorities. In 1990,
for example, Hartmut Koschyk, the secretary-general of the Union,
called on the Federal Republic to secure a clearly privileged status
and special rights for the Germans in Opole, Silesia. He demanded
facilitation of property settlements in this region by descendants
of its former inhabitants. He wanted the Silesia question to be
internationalized and the territories along the Oder and Neisse
rivers incorporated into the EEC economic area.

Some of these radical claims have strongly influenced the out-
looks of many representatives of the German minority in Poland.
For example, the Central Council of German Associations in the
Republic of Poland, established on 15 September 1990, asked both
governments to confer dual nationality on Germans domiciled in
Poland. In a special memorandum it demanded, among other
things, legal protection by the Federal Republic and closer cooperation between German organizations in Poland and the refugee
associations in Germany.

Despite the many measures taken by the Polish authorities in
recent years, representatives of the German minority have put forward a number of claims which still need to be satisfied. Their major
complaints focus on the ill will at the level of local government.[97]
They also demand the right of former Polish citizens of German origin to return to Poland and purchase real estate, the right to form
minority-based political parties, the introduction of the use of bilin-
gual versions of the names of localities in which the German minority predominates, the right to use the mother tongue in official
contacts or even the recognition of German as a second official language in areas with a minority population, a petition that persons
forcibly drafted into the Wehrmacht be entitled to include these
years of service in their entitlement to retirement pension rights, the
claims that some provisions of the Polish-German Treaty are inadequate and require revision, and a call for changes in the status of
Opole, Silesia, as well as agitation for a plebiscite and autonomy.[98]

97. Henryk Kroll, chairman of the German Minority's Parliamentary Caucus,
stated in an interview: "We have particularly painful relations with the authorities
in Opole province. Starting with general matters, this shows itself in the one-sided
interpretation of the Polish-German Treaty: not respecting our right to tradition, to
have our own schools, and so on." See *The Warsaw Voice* (18 July 1993): 9.

98. As an example one may note demands presented by the National Offensive,
a German revisionist organization, whose members are settled in the village of

The question of dual citizenship for Poles of German origin has also been raised and remains one of the most sensitive issues. It proved to be the biggest sticking point in the negotiation of the Polish-German Treaty of June 1991. The issue was finally passed over in the accord, although the refugee organizations in Germany had tried to alter the results of the negotiations on this point. Like some representatives of the German minority, they were in favor of granting members of the minority dual citizenship.

Poland has not formally recognized any claim to dual citizenship by ethnic Germans as provided by German law on nationality. In practice, however, such persons can be treated in the Federal Republic as German nationals and are entitled to apply to the German Embassy in Warsaw for a German passport. Consequently, they enjoy a special situation which clearly distinguishes them from other minority groups in Poland. It is estimated that in Opole, Silesia, around sixty thousand inhabitants have dual Polish and German citizenship.[99]

There are also some other issues which generate, among the Poles, much emotion and even some suspicion that the German minority desires to break away from Poland and join Germany. One of the objections is that young male members of the minority avoid military service in the Polish army and travel instead to the Federal Republic for prolonged periods of time.[100] The renovation of existing memorials and the construction of new memorials to Germans fallen in both world wars led to tensions between the central authorities and the German minority in 1992–93. Some radical declarations and actions at that time provoked even President Lech Wałesa to issue a special statement which called on the German minority to respect Polish law and warning them that signs of national chauvinism would not be tolerated.[101]

On the other hand, some of the organizations of the German minority define their principal objective specifically as the building of a bridge between the Polish and the German nations. An

Dziewkowice in the Opole region. According to this organization, Silesia should gain autonomy and this would be its first step toward incorporation into Germany. See *The Warsaw Voice* (15 November 1992): 3.

99. See *Rzeczpospolita* (19 June 1995): 2.

100. According to the local authorities of the Opole region, in the places inhabited by holders of German passports only 15 percent of young males appear before local commissions registering for the draft, compared to 98 percent, on average, in other *voivodships*. See *Gazeta Wyborcza* (13 July 1995): 31.

101. See *The Warsaw Voice* (20–27 December 1992): 4; Gerhard Bartodziej, "Pytania bez odpowiedzi" ["Questions Without Answers"], *Polityka* (9 January 1993): 17.

example of such an organization is the German "Reconciliation and Future" Working Community operating mainly in the Katowice *voivodship*; in its efforts it stresses a non-conflicting co-existence with the Polish majority. "Our primary political goal is to further reconciliation between both nations," said its chairman, Dietmar Brehmer.[102]

This way of thinking is also shared and supported by various non-governmental German organizations operating in Poland, charitable and political foundations among others. For instance, the Konrad Adenauer Foundation (KAS), which was established in Poland in 1989, defines its threefold tasks as being helping Poland with European integration, intensifying contacts in bilateral areas, and creating possibilities for the German minority in the country. From the Foundation's perspective, the German minority is perceived as acting as a "translator" for the Federal Republic in the development of mutual relations and as a "catalyst" that can help in speeding up the Europeanization of Poland.[103] On balance, from the perspective of the mid-1990s, such hope does not appear to be misplaced.

Just two days before Lech Wałesa left office in December 1996, the ex-Communist Prime Minister Józef Olesky was charged with spying for Russia, an event that prompted his resignation a month later. This scandal fueled old animosities between Solidarity and former Communists. But it also reflects new tensions between cosmopolitans and true Poles. To some extent it undermined the credibility of President Aleksander Kwaśniewski's express commitment to Poland's joining NATO and the EU at an early date.

Such political crises are probably unavoidable during the establishment of new democratic regimes. And they are mitigated by Poland's economic performance, which is much stronger than many observers had projected only a few years ago. Economic growth amounted to 6.5 percent in 1995; inflation dropped to an

---

102. See an interview given by him to *The Warsaw Voice* (4 April 1993): 7. It is interesting that in the same interview Brehmer criticized the Polish-German Treaty of 1991 as being discriminatory against Poland because "it overlooks the status of Poles in Germany."

103. See an interview with Gösta Thiemer, head of the KAS in Warsaw, in *The Warsaw Voice* (4 July 1993): 7.

unexpectedly low 21.6 percent; unemployment was at 14.6 percent; and foreign investment topped $2.5 billion in 1995, a 60 percent increase over the 1994 figure; it is projected to run between $2.5 and 3.0 billion in 1996.[104]

While the four case studies in this chapter show that Poland's return to Europe is hardly inevitable, these studies to illustrate how less than a decade after a revolution swept away the Soviet empire from central Europe, such a return is being attempted in a number of areas fraught with difficult political problems that touch on issues of security (migration) and identity (the treatment of minorities). Returning to Europe can mean importing liberal European norms, as in the case of ethnic minorities, or adopting more restrictive practices, as in the case of migration. But in all cases it means choosing a multilateral approach to international problems. In a related way, Poland's transformative corporatism has some important affinities with forms of governance that in prior decades have evolved, if in very different circumstances, in Western and southern Europe.

Not all issues are distinguished by the adoption of European norms and governance mechanisms. The Catholic Church, with its grandiose vision of altering the basic nature of a secular Europe, cannot help but advocate a unilateral approach that is predicated on Polish uniqueness. Thus the emerging division in Polish domestic politics that separates "cosmopolitans" from "true Poles" may eventually have a strong impact on the extent to which Poland's return to Europe will be a smooth one for both Poland and Europe.

---

104. In December 1996 the stock of total foreign investment was $12.0 billion (equity and loans) plus $7.9 billion (commitments).

3. HUNGARY
German and European Influences on the Post-Socialist Transition

Péter Gedeon

Europe has always been central to the thinking of the Hungarian political elites, and Hungary has joined or tried to join Europe several times.[1] The prospect of joining Europe created political cleavages between those political forces that opted for it and those political forces that did not want to make Hungary similar to Europe. However, both parties acknowledged the presumption behind either the acceptance or the refusal of the imperative to join Europe. The difference between them lay in the antithetical consequences they drew from the same presumption. This presumption concerned the difference between European and Hungarian social structures and historical developments. For those who favored joining Europe, it was imperative to stay abreast of the mainstream of European history.

The mainstream of European history produced the structures of modern Europe. These structures were based on the emergence in Western Europe of a civil society as distinguished from the political state. In other words, mainstream Europe was created in Western Europe. Europe as a geographical entity was split into Western and Eastern Europe. Western Europe, based on the emergence of a civil society and civil liberties started down the road of capitalist modernization. Eastern Europe, based on the preponderance of the state started down the road of late feudalism.[2]

1. The emergence of the Hungarian state itself was connected with the process of joining Europe: the first Hungarian king integrated Hungary into Europe, forming a Christian state after 1000 A.D.

2. "... in the West, where absolutism remained a historical episode, although a decisive episode: it was one among those 'cumulative' changes that were preparing

Between Western and Eastern Europe the region of central Europe exemplified a mixed pattern of development. Hungary belonged to central Europe in this sense. In the framework of the Habsburg empire, Hungary maintained the economic and political structures of second serfdom and political absolutism but still preserved certain autonomies befitting a civil society that before the nineteenth century took the form of an aristocratic society. The central European element of Hungarian history led to the 1848–49 revolution and war of independence that was an attempt to catch up with capitalist modernization, to return to the West—that is, to Europe. Although the revolution was crushed, the compromise with Austria in 1867 opened up a peaceful road to modernization for Hungary.

The price for this solution was paid during and after World War I. The Austro-Hungarian Empire collapsed. Hungary lost 71 percent of its territory and 58 percent of its population. The defeat, among other factors, resulted in the slowing down of Hungarian modernization and led to the close cooperation between Hungary and Nazi Germany against the new world order. Hungary's hopes for the revival of Great Hungary on the side of Germany were ruined in World War II. As a result of the war, Hungary had to exchange German domination for Russian domination. This brought a new and comprehensive East-Europeanization of Hungary.

After World War II Central Europe disappeared, part of it becoming integrated into Western Europe—that is, into Europe—the rest moving away from it.[3] To put it in economic terms, between 1913 and 1950 the relative position of the East and central European region worsened as compared to the period of 1870 to 1913. Between 1870 and 1913 the average level of GDP in the region reached 44 to 45 percent of the GDP in Western Europe. Between 1913 and 1950 the average level of GDP in the region sank to 41 percent of the GDP in Western Europe. Soviet-type

---

a new structural change. Contrary to this in the East Russian absolutism was the very structure that served as a framework for any cumulative changes." Jenő Szűcs, *Vázlat Eurpa három történeti régiójáról [Draft on the Three Historical Regions of Europe]*, (Budapest: Magvető, 1983), pp. 82–83.

3. Although the reality of Central Europe was gone, the concept of Central Europe was revived in the 1970s and 1980s. The concept of Central Europe represented the "otherness" of Hungary, Poland, Czechoslovakia, etc. in respect to the Soviet Union. Central Europe meant a historical and cultural entity with a development potential rooted in history that may put these countries on the path toward (Western) Europe.

industrialization has had controversial results. In 1973 the region again reached 45 percent of the level of GDP in Western Europe. However, the stagnation and decline that followed brought down the level of GDP in the central and East European region to roughly 25 percent of the GDP in Western Europe. The gap grew from 1:2 to almost 1:4.[4]

The collapse of the Austro-Hungarian Empire and the peace treaties after World War I drove Hungary into the arms of Germany. Between the two world wars the ruling elite of Hungary could expect support for the revival of Great Hungary and the revision of the existing borders only from the losers of World War I. Germany, in turn, could extend its political influence through Hungary. This political influence was coupled with the revival of economic relationships between the two countries. By the end of the 1930s Germany dominated the foreign trade of Hungary. In 1939 52.4 percent of Hungarian exports was directed to Germany and 52.5 percent of Hungarian imports was coming from Germany.[5]

The political course of alliance with Germany bore fruit for the Hungarian political elite when Hitler partially fulfilled their revisionist dreams. By 1940 the southern part of Slovakia, northern Transylvania, and certain parts of Yugoslavia were given or returned to Hungary by Nazi Germany. In exchange, Hungarian politicians had no choice but to join World War II on the side of Germany. Although subsequent Hungarian governments made certain efforts to pull out of the war, these attempts were aborted. Hungary was occupied by German troops in March 1944. Governor Horthy, after failing to break with Germany, resigned but nevertheless legitimated even the last Hungarian Nazi government. Hungary ended the war as an ally of Germany and lost all hope for a revision of the Versailles Treaty of 1920.

After World War II the relationship between Hungary and the two Germanies was determined by Soviet interests, but things started changing at the time of Brandt's *Ostpolitik*. Hungary expanded its political and economic connections with West Germany. Moreover, the Hungarian-German relationship acquired a specific flavor through the role played by the Hungarian government in German unification. For it was the last reform-Communist government, the Németh government in Hungary, that contributed to the

4. Iván T. Berend, "Európa! De miért?" ["Europe! But why?"], *Népszabadság*, 28 January 1995, p. 17.

5. György Ránki, *Gazdaság és külpolitika* [*Economy and Foreign Policy*], (Budapest: Magvető Kiadó, 1981), p. 346.

collapse of East Germany by letting out East German citizens from Hungary to West Germany in 1989.

After the collapse of the Soviet regime Europe gained special political importance for all the important political parties in Hungary, that were using the slogan of "joining Europe" in their electoral campaigns. Europe was seen as a successful model of modernization with its institutionalization of political democracy, market economy, and social welfare. Joining the European Union is now considered to be an indispensable means of catching up with the developed world, and staying out of the European integration process synonymous with the danger of preserving backwardness.[6]

The starting point of the post-socialist transition in Hungary coincided with the emergence of unified Germany. Germany is a key political and economic actor for Hungary in transition. In the eyes of the Hungarian political parties, with the exception of the populist and radical leftist ones, Germany seems to be a natural source of influence, both as a model for institutions and as a pool of resources.[7] Germany has become the most important economic partner for Hungary so far. Germany's share in Hungary's exports reached 27 percent; in imports it reached 22 percent in 1993.[8]

For the political elite in Hungary the road to the EU seems to lead through Germany. Hungarian politicians consider the close relationship with Germany to be instrumental in gaining membership in the EU; German support for the Hungarian effort to shorten the period of the integration process is extremely important, especially if there are signs of reluctance on the part of a number of member states of the EU to let the east and central European countries into the Union.

6. A survey conducted in 1992 showed that 83 percent of the Hungarian population was in favor of joining the EU. See Emöke Lengyel and Antal Tóth, "Közép és kelet-európai lakossági vélemények a térség gazdaságáról és az európai együtt-működésről" ["Opinions of Central and East European Inhabitants on the Economy of the Region and European Cooperation"], in: Sándor Kurtán, Péter Sándor, and László Vass, eds., *Magyarország politikai évkönyve* [*Political Yearbook of Hungary*], (Demokrácia Kutatások Magyar Központja Alapítvány, 1994), p. 638.

7. Although the tremendous costs of German unification and the worldwide importance of the Russian transition significantly diminish German resources that can be allotted to the small states of eastern central Europe.

8. See *Külkereskedelmi Statisztikai Évkönyv 1993* [*Statistical Yearbook of Foreign Trade 1993*], (Budapest: Központi Statisztikai Hivatal, 1994). In 1982 the share of West Germany in Hungarian exports was 7.2 percent, and in imports 11.2 percent. The share of East Germany in Hungarian exports was 6.1 percent, in imports 6.8 percent. See Ferencné Nyitrai, *A magyar gazdaság negyven éve* [*Forty Years of the Hungarian Economy*], (Kossuth Könyvkiadó, 1985), p. 305.

In Hungary there is no public expression of any kind of fear of new German domination or one-sided dependence on Germany.[9] A survey in 1992 asked people which foreign country's firms they would choose to be present in Hungary. Japan and Germany got almost the same number of points, while the U.S. placed third.[10] The same survey asked about the popularity of certain politicians. After George Bush, Helmuth Kohl proved to be the second most popular politician on the list.[11]

The relationship with Germany was not influenced by the results of the Hungarian election in 1994. The new socialist-liberal government does not intend to change the political course toward Germany. The relationship between the two governments is colored by the fact that the new prime minister, Gyula Horn, was minister of foreign affairs in the Németh government and played an important role in the decision to open Hungarian borders to East German citizens.

With the economic and social failure of Soviet-type modernization, Europe—that is, Western Europe—became a source of orientation and reorientation for the political and cultural elites in Hungary. This process was supported by the economic reforms of 1968 that paved the way for a creeping economic, cultural, and even political liberalization in Hungary.

The Argument

The post-socialist transition in Hungary is based on the structural change in international politics brought about by the demise of the Soviet empire. In this respect international politics have directly informed domestic policies: the withdrawal of the Soviet Union from east and central Europe has been a precondition for domestic institutional change. The dual and intertwined process of getting rid of external Soviet domination and internal Soviet-type

9. Again, not mentioning the parties of the radical Right and Left. However, during the first four or five years of the transition these political forces were more or less at the margin of political life.

10. See András Fischer and Ádám Levendel, eds., *Átépítés alatt* [*Under Reconstruction*], (Budapest: Magyar Hitelbank - Századvég Kiadó - Szonda Ipsos, 1992), p. 133.

11. The question asked was: How sympathetic or antipathetic are the following politicians for you? (0=very antipathetic, 100=very sympathetic): George Bush, 74; Helmuth Kohl, 70; Mikhail Gorbachev, 66; François Mitterand, 65; Borisz Jelzin, 45; József Antall, 42. Quoted in Fischer and Levendel, *Átépítés alatt* [*Under Reconstruction*], p. 140.

economic and political structures has set the direction of the transformation process: the post-socialist road out of state socialism has been seen by all the important political actors as a transition to modern capitalism. However, this transition is not an emulation of Western modernization.

The post-socialist countries do not need external pressures, the direct intervention of international political actors, to turn to the Western model of democracy and a market economy. The drive toward these structures comes from within the post-socialist countries. First, Western capitalism offers an institutional model for the desired goal of the transition. Second, the Western world possesses the resources, capital, technology, knowledge, etc. that are the necessary means of this transition but are scarce in the post-socialist states. The tension created by scarce resources and the lack of certain conditions of modern capitalism on the one hand and the goal of the transition on the other, ensures that the process of post-socialist transformation aiming to emulate the existing model of Western modernity will take an idiosyncratic historical form.

Hungary is a small state, but its transition toward capitalism is driven by domestic needs and interests. There is no direct European or German interference in this process of transition. However, it does not mean that European influence, German or otherwise, is absent. It only means that this influence is mediated through the way domestic actors internalize institutional patterns that have emerged in modern capitalism and through their reactions to the external constraints of international economic and political exigencies. The dominant tenor of domestic politics is emerging out of a complex process of interaction between domestic and international actors, institutions and policies. European and German institutions are playing a dual role in the transition. They act as both constraints on domestic actors as well as enabling conditions providing models and patterns of actions that are internalized by domestic actors.[12]

The three cases examined here show varying combinations of these factors. Privatization in Hungary is weakly constrained by international institutions and actors, weakly influenced by German ones, and not at all influenced by European models. Social policy in Hungary is constrained not by German or European institutions but by the international business and financial community (that

12. The important distinction between the two institutional logics (institutions as constraints on action versus institutions enabling action) was proposed to me by Peter Katzenstein.

TABLE 3.1 THE RELATIVE INFLUENCE OF INTERNATIONAL ACTORS AND
INSTITUTIONS ACROSS CASES

Cases	Enabling Conditions of Institutions			Constraints of Institutions and Actors		
	German	European	Other (IMF, World Bank, etc.)	German	European	Other (IMF World Bank, etc.)
Privatization	weak	—	—	weak	—	weak
Social policy	medium	weak	mixed	—	weak	mixed
Central Bank	strong	strong	—	—	—	—
Monetary policy	—	—	—	weak	weak	strong

has provided loans for the Hungarian economy) and by the IMF
and the World Bank. In the case of social policy the enabling
power of institutions makes itself felt through the influence of the
German model of social market economy. However, this influence
is weakened and transformed by domestic and international constraints. In the three cases examined here the influence of German
and European models is relatively the strongest in the case of the
institutionalization of the National Bank of Hungary. However,
the outcome of this process is also being shaped by domestic
actors and domestic constraints on democratic politics and does
not lend itself to a direct emulation of German or European institutions. Monetary policy in Hungary is strongly constrained by
domestic and international institutions and, until the transformational recession ends, is unable to follow the German and European pattern. Table 3.1 summarizes the argument of this chapter.

The Politics of Privatization in Hungary

The concept of privatization can be defined both broadly and nar-
rowly.[13] In the broader context privatization means two different
things: 1) transforming the state-owned economy by putting
state owned-assets into private hands; 2) the emergence of private enterprises outside the sphere of the state-owned economy.
Here, however, I will restrict myself to the narrower definition of

13. See János Kornai, "A privatizáció elvei Kelet-Európában" ["The Principles of
Privatization in Eastern Europe"], *Közgazdasági Szemle*, No. 11 (1991): 1021–40.

privatization—that is, I will focus on the problems attached to the process of transforming state-owned assets into private ones.

For politicians the direct aim of privatization is to create and maintain their legitimacy.[14] The urge to privatize is based on the expectation that an economy built on private ownership will generate economic benefits for the voters which will in turn increase the number of votes in favor of those in power. Politicians consider economic efficiency originating from institutional change to be instrumental to political legitimacy.

However, privatization, especially if it is fast and thoroughgoing, is creating negative economic outcomes. Growing efficiency stemming from successful privatization may lead to mass lay-offs and growing inequality. In Hungary privatization was not comprehensive enough to lead to these outcomes. Marketization and not privatization was causing unemployment via bankruptcies, import liberalization, deregulation, etc. As a result privatization and marketization became separated in the eyes of the voters. It is advantageous for the government if the economic costs of the transition are perceived as being attached not to privatization but to marketization, with the precondition that marketization itself does not also come to be perceived as illegitimate by voters. Up to this point marketization may reduce the legitimation overload of the government, especially if it is coupled with social policy compensation.[15]

The Pattern of Privatization

Privatization in Hungary is a process driven by the logic of domestic political struggles. The privatization that is taking place on the basis of extrication from state socialism is a unique historical process.[16] Although the aim of privatization is to restore or to

14. The interrelationship between the various privatization techniques or patterns and legitimation was analyzed within a comparative framework by David Stark. See David Stark, "Path Dependence and Privatization Strategies in East Central Europe," *East European Politics and Societies*, 6, 1 (Winter, 1992): 17–54. However, in this paper I use the term of legitimation in a broader context than he does. In Stark's essay legitimation was important first of all for the privatization process itself.

15. In the Hungarian case the former conservative government lost the elections even because the outcomes of the policy of marketization were not accepted by the majority of voters. See András Körösényi, "A jobboldal vereségének okai" ["The Causes of the Defeat of the Right"], *Valóság*, No. 12 (1994). Offe discussed the relationship between marketization and social policy in the case of the capitalist welfare state. See Claus Offe, *Contradictions of the Welfare State*, (Cambridge: The MIT Press, 1984).

16. See Stark, "Path Dependence."

create the basis for a modern capitalist economy resembling those found in Western countries, the means and the road that may lead to this outcome cannot be identical to the Western forms of privatization because Western privatization is taking place within the framework of an economy that has already been established on the firm foundation of private ownership. Nevertheless, certain elements or techniques can be borrowed, although these must be inserted into a different setting.

Foreign influence and foreign capital are playing a minor role in Hungary's privatization process. International consulting firms have been involved in the privatization process, advising the government agencies of privatization on solving the problem of asset evaluation and finding the proper buyers for state-owned assets. Because foreign capital may be instrumental for foreign influence, the issue of the participation of foreign capital in privatization is a politically sensitive question for policy makers.

Actors and Transactions

The actors in the privatization process may appear either on the supply side or on the demand side of the transactions. The characteristics of privatization are largely influenced by the characteristics of the demand and supply side of the transactions and by the characteristics of the actors representing either the demand or the supply side. The possible combinations of actors and transactions within the privatization process are summarized in Table 3.2.

Within the framework of centralized market transactions of privatization, state-owned assets are sold by governmental agencies to foreign and domestic private companies. The firms privatized are of relatively great size and economic importance. The price is set through bargains struck between central governmental agencies and the possible buyers.

Within the framework of decentralized privatization, state-owned assets are sold by the managers of state-owned firms to domestic or foreign private persons and companies. The firms privatized are relatively small or consist of smaller parts of former big companies. The price is set through bargains struck between the managers of the firms and the possible buyers. The central governmental agencies have a final say about the transactions, but they relinquish or do not exercise effective control over the transactions.

Hidden or spontaneous privatization takes place when state-owned firms and parts of firms are sold or given away by the

TABLE 3.2 ACTORS AND TRANSACTIONS IN THE PRIVATIZATION PROCESS

Demand Side		Supply Side		
		Government Agencies	**Managers of State-Owned Companies**	**Government Agencies & Managers**
Private owners	private domestic companies	market transaction: centralized	market transaction: hidden	market transaction: decentralized
	private persons	1.market transaction: decentralized 2. compensation	market transaction: hidden	
	managers	market transaction: buyout	market transaction: hidden	market transaction: buyout
	employees	ESOP		ESOP
	foreign investors	market transaction: centralized	market transaction: hidden, spontaneous	market transaction: decentralized
Public institutions	state-owned companies		market transaction: spontaneous	
	institutions (local governments, social insurance funds, non-profit organizations, churches, etc.)	1. gift 2. restitution		
Citizens		Gift		

managers of state-owned firms partly to themselves and other domestic or foreign private persons or companies, and partly to other state-owned firms. The price is set through deals struck between the managers of the firms and the possible buyers.[17] In the managerial buyout transactions, state-owned firms and parts of the firms are sold to the managers of state-owned firms. The price is at a level advantageous to the managers. In the ESOP-scheme, state-owned firms and parts of these firms are sold to the employees of state-owned firms. The price is set at a level advantageous to the employees. Non-market transactions may take the form of gifts and restitution. State-owned assets may be given gratis to citizens by the government, or state-owned assets may be returned to the original

17. The hidden or informal privatization is estimated to reach the magnitude of official privatization. Éva Voszka, "A tulajdonosi szerkezet átalakulásának fél évtizede Magyarországon" ["Five Years of the Transformation of Ownership Structure in Hungary"], unpublished manuscript, 1993, p. 4.

owners. Restitution can be full or partial. The Hungarian pattern of privatization is thus a mixed one.[18] It comprises different types of transactions at different times. The only form of privatization missing is that of mass-scale voucher privatization targeted at citizens.

Privatization in Hungary is structurally determined by the relative strength of social and political actors and by existing economic and political constraints: a disequilibrium in supply and demand, and legitimacy deficits. The main actors are the political elite, the bureaucrats, and the managers of state-owned firms. The varying forms of privatization have emerged as a result of the influence of these forces.[19]

Although foreign influence on the institutional pattern of privatization has not been substantial, foreign participation in investment has not been insignificant. The scarcity of capital on the demand side invites direct foreign investment in privatization, but this effect is counterbalanced by the scarcity of profitable investment opportunities on the supply side, as well as by political fears fueled by legitimacy deficits: the country should not be sold to foreigners.

The Privatization Strategy of the Antall Government

Privatization was seen by all six parties in the new parliament as the basic means to create the basis for a market economy, to generate the necessary economic incentives for the economic actors, and to separate the economy from the polity—that is, to delimit the intervention of the state in the economy and to bring about and maintain ownership control over managers of the firms.[20]

Between 1990 and 1991 the government tried to centralize the decision-making process of privatization.[21] The new political elite justified this centralization with the argument that the old elite is quite capable of transforming its political power into economic power. According to the new elite, this possibility should and could be stopped through state control of privatization. The state

18. See Éva Voszka, "Enyém a vár... Privatizáció 1990–1993" ["My Castle... Privatization 1990–1993"], *Társadalmi Szemle*, 49, 8–9 (1994): 1–9.

19. On the history of privatization in Hungary, see David Bartlett, "The Political Economy of Privatization: Property Reform and Democracy in Hungary," *East European Politics and Societies*, 6, 1 (Winter, 1992): 73–118. On the so-called "spontaneous privatization," see Mária Móra, "Az állami vállalatok (ál)privatizációja" ["The (Pseudo)Privatization of State-Owned Enterprises"], *Közgazdasági Szemle*, 38, 6 (1991).

20. See Voszka, "A tulajdonosi szerkezet" ["Five Years of the Transformation"].

21. See Bartlett, "The Political Economy of Privatization."

bureaucracy also wanted to expand its power and to gain control over the privatization process.

In 1990 the State Property Agency (SPA) was given the right to rule over every transformation of state-owned firms and—above a relatively low value limit—over company foundations of state-owned firms.[22] The SPA was taken out from under the control of parliament and put under the supervision of the government. This change in the legal status of the SPA signaled the efforts of the government to shelter privatization from public debate. In practice it has also meant sheltering privatization from the parliamentary parties in opposition. Originally the representatives of the parliamentary parties in opposition had sat on the board of directors of the SPA, but over time they were gradually replaced by politically loyal delegates of the governing parties. The SPA grew to a non-transparent institution unaccountable to all the parties in parliament as well as the public, provoking attacks from the parties of opposition during the coming years.

Originally the centralization of privatization covered state-owned assets in the value of 127 billion Hungarian Forint (HUF).[23] Within the centralized programs of privatization, foreign consulting firms were assigned an important role in preparing the sale of state-owned assets. In the first program there were only two Hungarian consulting firms out of a total of eighteen. The majority of the participating foreign consulting firms were Anglo-Saxon firms. German consulting firms played only a marginal role.[24]

The program proved to be slow-going and only partially successful. Only a few state-owned firms were truly privatized and not merely transformed into companies. On the other hand the SPA bureaucrats failed to gain effective control over the process: the overwhelming majority of the projects handed to management were approved by an SPA bureaucracy that was lacking administrative capacity to exercise real control.[25]

22. Voszka, "A tulajdonosi szerkezet" ["Five Years of the Transformation"].

23. György Matolcsy, *Lábadozásunk évei* [*The Years of Our Convalescence*] (Budapest: Privatizációs Kutatóintézet, 1991), p. 226.

24. The list of the consulting firms consisted of Swissbank Corp., CCF Corp., E. Rotsch. (Paris), Landerbank, Wricor Grp, Hydec-Agrocons., Co-Nexus, Ernst a. Young, Rotschild (London), Daiwa Europ. Ltd., DRT Touche Rosse, KPMG Peat Marwick, Nesbitt Thomson G., Pénzügykutató Rt., Credit S. First Boston, J.P. Morgan, Nomura, Barclays de Zoette Wedd/coop. See Matolcsy, *Lábadozásunk évei* [*The Years of Our Convalescence*], pp. 211–12.

25. See Bartlett, "The Political Economy of Privatization," and Stark, "Path Dependence and Privatization Strategies."

After 1991 the privatization strategy of the government was changed. The partial success or failure of the earlier privatization program, together with the rivalry between the SPA and the Ministry of Finance, led the SPA to abandon its former strategy and launch a new program of self-privatization. Self-privatization gave the initiative back to the firms, to the managers of the firms. The SPA exercised only the right of final approval. Four hundred twenty-three firms with fewer than three hundred employees and less than three hundred million HUF of capital value were involved in the first wave. Two hundred seventy-seven firms with assets less than one billion HUF took part in the second wave. In the first wave, which ended in March 1993, 147 firms were sold for 5.5 billion HUF. The majority of the buyers were domestic investors. Employee buyout was important: out of the first 147 firms, sixty-five were bought by employees.[26]

In 1992 a new governmental agency, the State Holding Company (SHC), was formed. The SHC was charged with the task of overseeing those state-owned firms that remained under state ownership, although it carried out privatization operations as well. The SHC exercised property rights over 163 firms with capital of fifteen hundred billion HUF.

The centralization of property rights in the hands of the SPA and SHC changed the position of managers: their dependence on the state was growing, and their incentives to bargain with the state on the conditions of privatization and survival of the firm were greatly increased.

Between 1989 and 1993 33 percent of state assets held by the State Privatization Agency were sold for a total of 520 billion HUF, an amount that constitutes one quarter of the total value of state assets to be privatized. A large number of enterprises remained under state ownership: 160 firms under the State Holding Company, and sixty companies under branch ministries. About seven hundred firms were still waiting for privatization. At the end of 1992 there were six thousand companies that were partially state-owned, and this number continued to grow during the following years of privatization.[27]

---

26. Voszka, "A tulajdonosi szerkezet" ["Five Years of the Transformation"], p. 11.
27. That is an important characteristic of Hungary's privatization process: firms are not entirely privatized, and mixed forms of ownership emerge that blur the distinction between public and private. Stark calls this form of ownership recombinant property. See Stark, "Recombinant Property in East European Capitalism," *American Journal of Sociology* 101, 4 (January 1996): 993–1027. However, these mixed

In 1993 and 1994, as the elections grew nearer, the issue of privatization gained in political significance. The ruling coalition initiated inclusive privatization programs with the aim of involving a larger number of people in the privatization process. To give away state-owned assets gratis or at a discounted price was seen as a means of increasing the number of votes for the parties of the ruling coalition, primarily the Hungarian Democratic Forum (HDF). For this reason reprivatization turned out to be the Hungarian method of voucher privatization. The reprivatization program took the form of compensation. Those entitled to reprivatization were given compensation vouchers that could be exchanged for real property titles and shares. Up to 1994 the government agency for compensation handled 1,870,291 cases involving a total value of 113,687,004,000 HUF.[28] The program generated unrealistic expectations and not only because restitution could not be achieved, as the majority of the former owners received only a fragment of their assets, but also because compensation vouchers were not counterbalanced by a sufficient supply of assets. The vouchers were losing their original value, and by 1995 the price of a compensation voucher sank 30 to 40 percent of its nominal value.

The Privatization Strategy of the Horn Government

By April 1994, before the new elections, state-owned assets valued at 421.5 billion HUF were privatized (SPA 205 billion, SHC ninety-nine billion, firms 117.5 billion).

Still, the majority of state-owned wealth had yet to be privatized. In 31 March 1994 the SPA held assets valued at 378 billion HUF, and the SHC held assets valued at 976 billion. The value of the assets to be privatized after four years of the Antall government constituted 60 percent of the assets held by the two governmental agencies.[29]

In the first four years of privatization the initial imbalance between supply and demand of state-owned assets may have

forms of ownership can also be seen as transitory forms toward full private ownership. Another tendency of privatization is the phenomenon of "renationalization." Privatization is not a one-way road. Newly privatized companies lacking capital and heavily indebted to state-owned banks may go bankrupt or may be renationalized. See Voszka, "Enyém a vár" ["My Castle"].

28. *Figyelő* (10 November 1994): 14.

29. According to the prime minister Gyula Horn, 50 percent of state-owned assets have already been privatized. See *Népszabadság* (1 January 1995).

disappeared. The supply of state-owned assets has been steadily diminishing. First of all, assets have been sold. Second, companies have been privatized through liquidation. By 1994 more than fifteen hundred firms have disappeared from the supply side as a result of liquidation. Third, even the value of the firms kept by the state has been steadily diminishing.[30] On the demand side private domestic savings have been growing and have reached the magnitude of state-owned assets. By 1994 the problem was less that of global disequilibrium and more that of structural incongruity: a great number of state-owned firms were not profitable enough to attract demand.[31]

The new socialist-liberal government promised to finish privatization in three years.[32] However, during the election year privatization through governmental agencies slowed down. Before the elections the former government, with the consent of the opposition, did not want to conclude any major transactions; after the elections the new government did not proceed with privatization.

The socialist-liberal government sought to avoid the distribution and donation of state-owned property, preferring selling to any other kinds of transaction. The enormous budget deficit kept the government under pressure to generate revenues from privatization in order to service the internal state debt.[33] Because selling state-owned assets presumes the existence of purchasing power on the demand side, the government expected foreign investors to play an important role in the coming wave of privatization. According to their plans, half of the assets to be privatized would go into foreign hands,[34] and foreign investors would provide 80 to 90 percent of the privatization incomes.[35]

Radical changes in the privatization strategy cannot be expected in Hungary, and the process of privatization continued to be the mixed pattern that had evolved during the previous years. The state continues to try to maintain administrative control over the privatization process. The government merged the SPA with the SHC under the name of Hungarian Privatization and State Holding

30. According to estimates, the value of unsold state-owned firms was being reduced by six billion HUF every month. See I. Nagy, "A vagyonvesztés 73 milliárd forint" ["The Property Loss Is 73 Billion Forints"], *Figyelő* (30 June 1994): 22.

31. Voszka, "Enyém a vár" ["My Castle"], p. 6.

32. *Népszabadság* (23 November 1994): 15.

33. *Figyelő* (29 September 1994): 18–19.

34. *Népszabadság* (23 November 1994): 15.

35. I. Nagy, "Privatizáció, így, úgy, – sehogy?" ["Privatization This Way, That Way—No Way?"], *Figyelő* (17 November 1994): 23.

Company (HPSHC). The new agency remained responsible to the government and received a socialist MP as its head.[36]

The privatization issue was further complicated by the fact that the parties of the coalition represented different ideas on privatization. The Free Democrats were in favor of fast privatization, even if it created short-term economic losses, even if it hurt the social value of justice or equity. Among the Socialists there was a strong tendency that emphasized the need to find the proper price of state-owned assets and the importance of the social values of justice or equity.[37] Those socialist MPs who were the leaders of unions requested a larger role for unions in the privatization process. Although the Free Democrats may have wanted to minimize the legitimation deficit stemming from privatization, and the Socialists may have wanted to avoid these losses,[38] after a year of hesitation, under serious economic pressure to raise revenues for the state budget, the socialist-liberal government speeded up the privatization process. In 1996 the minister in charge of privatization announced that by the end of the year 70 percent of former state-owned assets would be privatized. In 1997 the privatization

36. In spite of the resistance of the Free Democrats, who did not want to maintain a post that they considered to be a negative heritage of the Antall government, Tamás Suchman became the new head of the HPSHC as a minister without portfolio.

37. In the election campaign the Socialist Party promised to investigate the doubtful privatization cases and to draw legal consequences. However, in the ensuing six months, the new government was able to come up with no more than five or six cases that might have broken the law and could be subjected to criminal charges.

38. The affair of the HungarHotels privatization exemplified these differences and the way in which privatization could be politicized by the politicians of the ruling coalition. In the case of the HungarHotels privatization, it was the prime minister who questioned the deal—after it had been concluded. The American General Hospitality (AGH) won a tender announced by the SPA for 51 percent of the shares of the HungarHotels, comprising fourteen hotels. Prime Minister Horn ordered an investigation into the privatization procedure, arguing that state-owned assets should not be squandered. This move by the prime minister was not coordinated with the government and the coalition partner, and created public controversy. The Free Democrats and the Socialist minister of finance publicly criticized the decision of the prime minister. The investigation did not find legal injury but found the agreed price of the hotels was indeed too low. The AGH promised to pay $57.5 million for the hotels, but earlier the Hotel Duna Intercontinental by itself had been sold for $53 million. The government instructed the SPA to renegotiate certain elements of the package with the American party. The SPA raised the price to $67 million, with the condition that one more hotel would be added to the package and the AGH would be asked to spend about $29 million instead of $19 million for the reconstruction of the hotels. As a result, the American investors dropped the deal. This affair led to the resignation of the person in charge for privatization and played a part in the resignation of the minister of finance a few weeks later.

process will come to an end, with only 109 assets valued at 350 billion HUF remaining under long-term state ownership.[39]

The Role of Foreign Capital in Privatization

Foreign investors were present in the privatization process, but fears of an overwhelming influence of foreign capital turned out to be unfounded—at least on the basis of available data. In 1993 the ratio of private domestic investors in the privatization revenue of the SPA jumped from an earlier 20 percent up to 66 percent. The share of foreign capital in joint ventures reached 66.16 percent, but in the total scheme of things remained 9.05 percent.[40] In 1994 companies partly owned by the SPA foreign investors reached a 10.87 percent share.[41] The privatization of large state-owned enterprises of the energy sector at the end of 1995 increased the share of foreign ownership. The minister in charge of privatization expected that by 1997, when the privatization process comes to an end, the share of foreign ownership in the Hungarian economy would reach 25 to 30 percent.[42]

Data on the share of foreign investments in the revenues of the SPA showed a constant decline until 1995. Hard currency sales made up 79 percent of cash revenues and total revenues of the SPA in 1990; this number sank to 28 percent of cash revenues and 6 percent of total revenues by 1994, but rose to 68 percent and 66 percent respectively by 1996.[43] The share of foreign direct investment not targeted at state-owned assets was growing. The share of foreign capital used for buying state-owned assets was between 25 and 35 percent of total foreign capital flowing into Hungary between 1990 and 1993.[44]

39. See *Népszabadság* (25 May 1996): 1. In 1994 the new government wanted to keep in state ownership only assets valued at 200 billion HUF. See *Figyelő* (17 November 1994): 22.

40. Bertalan Dicházi, "Tények és adatok a magyar privatizációról—1993" ["Facts and Data about Hungarian Privatization—1993"], in Kurtán, Sándor, and Vass, *Magyarország politikai évkönyve* [*Political Yearbook of Hungary*], p. 847.

41. Ibid.

42. See *Népszabadság* (6 April 1996): 5.

43. Source: *SPA Privatization Monitor* (March 1995): 6. *HPSHC Privatization Monitor* (March 1996): 5.

44. Andrea Szalavetz, "A külföldi tőkebefektetők részvétele a magyarországi privatizációs folyamatban" ["The Participation of foreign investors in the privatization process in Hungary"], unpublished manuscript, 1994, p. 5. The share of direct foreign sales of state-owned assets must have increased at the end of 1995.

Foreign investments are not dominated by any single country. Between 1992 and 1995 German, American, and Austrian capital took the lead in buying Hungarian state-owned assets. By 1995 Austria went from first to third place. U.S. foreign investment once approached that of Germany, but as a result of the privatization wave at the end of 1995 Germans are now clearly the number one foreign investors. German investments reached 37 percent of the total, almost double the share of U.S. investments (19 percent). French capital (13 percent) has overtaken Austrian investments (6 percent).[45]

This picture is modified if greenfield investments are also taken into account. Within the total of direct foreign investment in 1993 the U.S. took the lead with 29 percent, with Germany second at 25 percent. Japanese investors especially preferred greenfield investments to buying state-owned firms. By 1995 within the total of direct foreign investment Germany was first with 29 percent, followed by the U.S. with 24 percent, Austria with 10 percent, and France with 9 percent.[46]

Fifty-eight percent of foreign investments went into industry, led by engineering and food processing, telecommunications (16 percent), the hotel, office building and real estate sector (7.5 percent), and the financial and trade sectors (7.7 percent).[47]

Conclusion

Privatization in Hungary follows a mixed pattern, avoiding comprehensive voucher privatization schemes and leaning on restricted administrative state capacity. The process of privatization does not lend itself to, and is not shaped by, direct European or German influence. The German pattern of privatization did not inform, as a model, the Hungarian one. Although privatization in Hungary was also led by a central government agency, as in Germany, the two processes remained quite different. In Germany West German capital provided for the demand side of privatization transactions; and a strong state, without legitimation deficits and backed up by a strong private economy, was pursuing a privatization policy that was not compelled to seek revenues from

45. Source: *SPA Privatization Monitor* (May 1993, March 1994, and March 1995), and *HPSHC Privatization Monitor* (March 1996): 4.

46. *Népszabadság* (15 May 1996): 32.

47. Dicházi, "Tények és adatok a magyar privatizációról" ["Facts and Data about Hungarian Privatization"], p. 843.

selling state-owned assets and was moreover able to mobilize economic resources for a rapid, costly, and at the same time centralized privatization program. In Hungary none of these conditions was present.

The available data on foreign participation in Hungarian privatization show a relatively balanced and diversified presence of international capital and does not prove the existence of German or other domination in the process of direct foreign investment.

The existing pattern of privatization in Hungary provides a certain domain for international influence in the form of foreign investment and through the presence of foreign consulting firms. The scarcity of capital and the lack of technical expertise generates economic incentives on the part of politicians for demanding foreign involvement in the process of privatization. Yet these economic incentives are counterbalanced or constrained by the fear of legitimation deficits stemming from foreign participation in Hungarian privatization. If privatization is based on the market, as in the case of mass voucher privatization, the problem of foreign ownership remains more or less depersonalized and does not raise the danger of delegitimation. However, in Hungary government agencies and politicians are and probably will be active in privatization, and thus the question of foreign ownership is and will be a target of political debates. Hungarian politicians have to maneuver between the Scylla of economic rationality demanding foreign capital for Hungarian privatization and the Charybdis of political legitimation with its inclination to limit foreign penetration of Hungarian property rights.

Social Policy in Transition

The post-socialist transition in Hungary has opened up new possibilities and encountered old and new necessities in the field of social policy. The new possibilities include the task of creating a separate, sui generis social policy that did not exist under state socialism.

After the elections in 1990 the new government and the parliament put together a reform program, but this program as a whole was not realized. The delay may have to do with the consequences of a radical reform of social policy: these consequences would combine growing financial burdens with changing or even diminishing social services for large segments of the population. A radical turn of social policy would be very unpopular and would create political dissatisfaction, seeing as the population has grown used to the existing level of social services and the majority of people would resist giving it up.[48] So it is not a surprise that the Hungarian government, in the circumstances of economic recession that resulted in a declining standard of living for the majority of the population, was inclined to postpone the comprehensive reform of social policy. The government refrained from following the proposals of the IMF and the World Bank to carry out a comprehensive reform of social expenditure. Politicians were hoping for an upswing in the economy that would make it easier to change the course and structure of social policy. But these hopes proved to be unjustified. The recession lasted longer than it was expected by political actors.

As a result of the transformational recession[49] the growing deficit of the state budget reinforced the necessity of changing the course of social policy, but under even worse and not better economic conditions. This creates a trap for social policy reforms: the reform is being enforced by those circumstances that make its success less likely, and reforms with long-lasting consequences may be once again created by short-term political pressures and incentives.

The Legacy of State Socialism

Under state socialism, social policy was not separated from economic policy or other specific policies. Under this system, social policy—as was true of all other policies—was dominated by political considerations: social policy, like economic policy, was overdetermined by macropolitical rationality. For instance, the extension of the rights for social security was not constrained by economic factors, or by economic rationality. Social services provided by the state were financed from the state budget, but the magnitude of

48. A survey, conducted in 1991, found that 31 percent of those asked endorsed the statement that "everybody should look after his or her children without state or other external assistance," but only 22 percent did not agree with the statement that "family allowance should be so high that it could cover all the costs of bringing up a child." Similarly, more than 70 percent thought that purchasing the services of a physician should be permitted, but more than 80 percent denied that "patients should pay for the treatment." Gábor Tóka, "A szociális védőháló felbomlása és a közvélemény" ["The Decomposition of Social Safety Net and the Public Opinion"], *Európa Fórum*, No. 2 (1992): 26.

49. János Kornai, "Transzformációs visszaesés" ["Transformational Recession"], *Közgazdasági Szemle*, 40, 7–8 (1993): 569–99.

these services was not dependent on revenues. Revenues and benefits were simply not connected to each other.[50]

The state provided free health care and education, family allowances, earnings-related pensions and sick pay to its citizens. In exchange, wages were kept low. Because employment was full, there was no need to create a social security net against unemployment. Citizens' eligibility for benefits was tied to their employment status. Under full employment social benefits thus were provided on a quasi-universal basis. In Hungary these benefits became truly universal in the 1970s and 1980s when the right for certain social benefits became a citizen's right.

Social policy was a means for socialist industrialization. The rapid and enforced policy of industrialization had to be financed at the expense of the living standard of the employed. On the other hand, the maintenance of the value of human capital and the effort to avoid the discontent of the population required from the state a certain amount of social spending.

This kind of regime works well if industrialization is able to provide the necessary material resources. However, it was one of the main characteristics of socialist industrialization that in the long run it did not create, but rather depleted, the available resources. The result in the field of social policy was that the system acknowledged as legitimate the citizens' need for social services and at the same time exhausted the financial resources necessary to meet these needs.

Hungary's social expenditures by the 1980s became more and more similar to those of the "social welfare" states of Western Europe. In the 1980s Hungary's overall ratio of social income transfers to GDP got close to that of the social welfare states[51]—it was well above what would have been expected for its income level.[52]

50. See Júlia Szalai, "A társadalombiztosítás érdekviszonyairól" ["On the Structure of Interests of Social Security"], *Szociolgiai Szemle*, No. 2 (1992).

51. The World Bank Report on Hungarian social policy names Belgium, Denmark, Finland, France, the Netherlands, Norway and Sweden as the social welfare states. *A Világbank szociálpolitikai jelentése Magyarországról* [*The Report of the World Bank on Social Policy in Hungary*], (Budapest, 1992), p. 34.

52. This figure was questioned by prominent sociologists who argued that we should take into consideration the existence of the informal economy that produces an estimated 25 percent of the GDP. If we adjust the magnitude of the GDP by including the contribution of the informal economy, the overall ratio of social income to the GDP will be close to that of the lower income states. Others thought that the share of the informal economy did not exceed 10 to 15 percent of the GDP. This ratio is not dissimilar to that in the Western states, and thus the informal economy does not modify the overall picture on social policy expenditure.

The internal structure of social services in Hungary showed a diversified picture. Hungary surpassed the lower income states[53] in expenditures on pensions and "other" expenditures (mainly sick pay and family benefits), but fell short on health services and had no unemployment assistance. In education spending, Hungary roughly matched the lower income states but remained well below the social welfare states.[54]

Institutional Models of the Welfare State

The contemporary social policy regime in Europe is based on a mix of two traditions of social protection. The first is rooted in the Bismarckian tradition that connects social protection to the rights acquired through work. The other is based on the Beveridge concept that considers the right to social protection to be a right of citizenship. The first system tailors the benefits it provides to the position of the individuals, while the second one guarantees a basic minimum, independent of the individuals' situation.

> In Beveridge-type systems, the purpose of social security is to cover all residents: in exchange for contributions, a general insurance scheme provides standard benefits, considered as a right and normally paid with no means-testing element; those who, for one reason or another, have paid insufficient contributions may receive "safety net" benefits which are subject to means testing. In Bismarckian systems, "social insurance schemes" pay benefits, which vary according to the wage, to workers (and their dependents) who have acquired rights through their contributions. People who have not acquired sufficient rights may receive "social assistance," granted initially on a discretionary basis and means-tested; it is thus social insurance and social assistance which together comprise social protection.[55]

The last forty years saw the convergence of the two systems. The Bismarckian model extended medical benefits and family allowances for those not employed, so that it now served the entire population. The Beveridge-type social policy created supplementary,

53. The World Bank Report names Greece, Ireland, Portugal, Spain and Turkey as the lower income states. See *A Világbank szociálpolitikai jelentése Magyarországról* [*The Report of the World Bank on Social Policy in Hungary*], p. 34.

54. Ibid., p. 53.

55. Yves Chassard, "The Convergence of Social Protection Objectives and Policies: A New Approach," *Social Europe: The Convergence of Social Protection Objectives and Policies*, Supplement 5 (Commission of the European Communities, 1992), p. 14.

income-related schemes on the basis of agreement between employers and employees.[56]

What is the institutional model of the welfare state that the post-socialist transition in Hungary is now heading for? Economic necessities exert a pressure on the post-socialist states to cut welfare spending and move toward targeted social services. Economic constraints thus make it unlikely that the post-socialist state can turn to the model of the Scandinavian welfare regimes. On the other hand, political constraints may prevent the post-socialist state from giving up the achieved level of social spending that is either universal or tied to the occupational system of society. Political pressures make it difficult for these countries to turn toward emulating the American system. These tensions inform the emergence of the post-socialist welfare state. The political exigencies rooted in citizens' expectations generated by the state socialist system may push the state toward a social policy mix that maintains the corporatist regime of social security and supplements it with targeted social services. The economic exigencies rooted in the transformational crisis may push the state toward the liberal, universal welfare regime that is supplemented by corporatist-like social services tied to the occupational system.[57]

56. Ibid. Another typology, proposed by Esping-Andersen, distinguishes three types of welfare systems. See Gösta Esping-Andersen, *The Three Worlds of Welfare Capitalism*, (Princeton: Princeton University Press, 1990). Both typologies grasp certain social policy regimes but ignore some others. The historically rooted typology concentrates on Europe and dismisses the American case. Esping-Andersen focuses on the dichotomy of the universalistic Scandinavian and the residual American welfare state; he can incorporate in this model the German case as a corporatist welfare regime, but has difficulty fitting into his reasoning the British welfare state that represents a variant of universalistic but liberal and non-socialist welfare regime.

57. Deacon expects the social policy regime in Hungary to turn toward the liberal welfare state. He argues that the weakness of leftist parties from inside and the strength of international organizations (IMF, World Bank) from outside, due to the indebtedness of the Hungarian economy, will push Hungary toward the liberal welfare state. See Robert Deacon, "Developments in East European Social Policy," in Catherine Jones, ed., *New Perspectives on the Welfare State in Europe* (London and New York: Routledge, 1993). However, the first four years of post-socialist transition showed that the internal pressure stemming from democratic politics can counterbalance the external pressure of international organizations. The irony of the situation is that a new government dominated by Socialists may move toward liberal reforms of the social policy regime. In March 1995 the Hungarian government, on the initiative of the new minister of finance, announced an austerity program that contained proposals aimed at cutting back on social expenditures. The program foresaw the abolishment of the universality of family benefits. Liberal reforms inserted into the framework of a socialist welfare state that is being overhauled produce an outcome that may be closer to corporatist rather than liberal models of the welfare state.

The Social Policy Regime in Hungary

In the 1980s Hungary was already mixing elements from both the corporatist and the social-democratic models.[58] Originally all services were financed by the state budget. In 1989 the Social Insurance Fund (SIF) was created to take over the financing of pensions, sick pay, maternity and child care allowances, unemployment compensation, and health care. General tax revenues financed universal family benefits and other social benefits in kind. Only a few minor transfer programs (e.g., social assistance) were means-tested. During the 1980s as real wages of employees were declining, the ratio of social transfers within the income of employees was growing. Social transfers constituted 23.1 percent of the monetary income of the population in 1980. In 1985 it was 24 percent; in 1990, 28.3 percent.[59] Hungarian social policy was getting closer to the social democratic model based on the principle of inclusive universality.

The post-socialist transition has revealed the tensions of social policy. The transition to a market economy has meant the liberalization of prices and foreign trade, the bankruptcy of inefficient firms, the restructuring of the economy, etc. The first symptoms of transition are thus inflation and unemployment. Inflation devaluates pensions, and the pressure on firms to be profitable transforms unemployment on the job into real unemployment. Thus the postsocialist transition increases the financial burdens of social policy, and due to the long recession, when the tasks of social policy are growing but the financial resources are shrinking, the state must deal with growing difficulties in providing the necessary means for financing social policy expenditures.[60]

58. I do not imply that the state socialist welfare regime can be completely fitted into any typology rooted in the Western capitalist development. I fully agree with Tóth that the state socialist welfare state was independent of capitalist models. Tóth calls it a communist-conservative welfare state, a mix of corporatist and universalistic elements. See István Gy. Tóth, "A jóléti rendszer az átmenet idöszakában" ["The System of Social Welfare in the Period of Transition"], *Közgazdasági Szemle*, No. 3 (1994): 327–28.

59. *Népszabadság* (21 October 1993): 10. The ratio of social benefits within the monetary income of the population was growing further in the post-socialist period; in 1993 it reached 31.2 percent.

60. In order to be able to finance social expenditures the state imposed greater and greater burdens on the taxpayers and on employers and employees. In 1990 direct taxes and social security contributions in Hungary made up 36.9 percent of the GDP, while in countries like Spain, Greece, or Portugal the same number was between 15 and 21 percent. See András Körösényi, "Demobilization and Gradualism. The Hungarian Transition, 1987–92," unpublished manuscript (1992), p. 18. In 1992 the employers' contribution rate to the SIF reached 44 percent (as a percentage

All these characteristics of the transition put a hard constraint on social policy making from the aspect of financing. Economic recession leads to growing tasks and diminishing resources. It compels policy makers to adopt a course based on the belief that the universality principle of social policy cannot be maintained. This belief is reinforced by the process of the post-socialist transition that is creating a new poverty and a growing social inequality requiring targeted social services.

The post-socialist transition opens up a path of development that is characterized by a turn in social policy away from the state socialist mix of the corporatist-universalistic welfare state, a change in social policy that is determined by inner constraints and internal political coalitions within an international setting.

The Program of Social Policy

After 1989 the official Hungarian programs to reform social policy insisted on a mix of social policies that corresponded to the European model, were built upon the principle of solidarity, and showed within this framework a certain affinity to the German system. These characteristics of the social policy regime in Hungary are explained by the domestic factors of democratic politics and the initial conditions of the state socialist welfare state. There were no direct EU or German actions to shape the Hungarian social policy regime. The moderate changes that were initiated by the government were dictated by the requirements of economic rationality. The puzzle that the government tried to solve was how to save money on social provisions and at the same time maintain the achieved level of social services. The model of the social market economy seemed suitable for this task, seeing as its emphasis on the principle of subsidiarity tied the importance of social provisions to the requirements of economic rationality.

---

of total wages), the employees' contribution rate was 10 percent. The total contribution rate of 54 percent is very high by international standards (in 1987 the contribution rate of employers as a percentage of gross earnings was 17.1 percent in Germany, 10.5 percent in the UK, and 30.9 percent in Spain; the unweighted average for OECD lower income states was 22 percent, for OECD social welfare states it was 20.7 percent. The contribution rate of employees in the same year was 17.1 percent in Germany, 9 percent in the UK, 6 percent in Spain, 10.4 percent for OECD lower income states, and 10.1 percent for OECD social welfare states. See *A Világbank szociálpolitikai jelentése Magyarországról* [*The Report of the World Bank on Social Policy in Hungary*], p. 171. The high level of the contribution rate may weaken the incentives for economic growth and the enduring recession, again, may add to the burdens of social services.

In 1990 the official program of the new government of Hungary delineated the process of the post-socialist transition. According to the program, the economic transition from a state socialist system should lead to a social market economy.[61] The allusion to the German model was quite obvious and deliberate.

There is a parallelism in the historical situation of the two countries that may have supported this choice by the Hungarian government. In both cases the model of a social market economy was contrasted to a totalitarian and planned economy. The social market economy was seen as a solution to the collapse and failure of a centrally planned economy. And, in the case of Hungary, this contrast involved the comparison of a successful and an unsuccessful model. History has confirmed for Hungarian policy makers that the German pattern is not only desirable but viable.

The concept of a social market economy in the context of the post-socialist transition represented a break with the notion of a planned economy and a turn toward a market economy based on private property. The adjective "social" expressed the government's concern about maintaining the system of social protection. The program confirmed the belief that the transition to a market economy should not lead to the reduction of government responsibility in safeguarding the social security of the community.

In the field of social policy the concept of a social market economy meant that the government acknowledged as a right of citizenship the right of individuals to a socially determined minimum level of subsistence. In this respect the government endorsed the basic liberal principle of social protection. The program would deploy the resources of social policy toward achieving a socially acceptable level of social provisions with the intention of widening the scope of targeted and means-tested schemes.[62] The program supported voluntary organizations providing social services and civil initiatives based on the principle of self-help. The program emphasized the importance of family in meeting the guidelines of a new social policy. These guidelines showed the influence of the conservative tradition and similarities to the German model.

The resolution of parliament on the modernization of the social security system, passed in 1991, foresaw a compulsory social insurance system guaranteed by the state. According to the resolution,

61. *A nemzeti megújhodás programja* [*The Program of National Revival*] (Budapest, 1990), p. 13.
62. Ibid. p. 120.

social assistance should be separated from social insurance, the latter to be financed mainly from employer and employee contributions.

The Pattern of Social Policy

The inherited pattern of social policy that combined a relatively high level of welfare spending with unsound financing threatened the collapse of the social policy regime. The task of matching contributions and benefits was of eminent importance for the reform of social policy, an importance that is being reinforced by the fiscal crisis of the state. As a result, the government faced the growing necessity of either reducing or restructuring state involvement in the financing of social policy.

The new democratically elected government in Hungary started the reform of the welfare system very cautiously, postponing the major structural reforms for the next government. The most important reform that the government introduced was the establishment of a social policy regime charged with tackling the problems of unemployment and poverty. This was a step that could not have been avoided for political reasons. In the field of health care the government has changed the pattern of provision by changing the criteria for eligibility. The universality of health care provision was withdrawn, and eligibility has been tied to employment status. However, health care remains a big issue that may see further adjustment. Minor changes were made in pension policy, but structural reforms have been avoided in this field, as well as in that of family allowances. The redistributive effects of inflation have in fact partly substituted for structural reforms. The losers in the social policy game were the unemployed, families with children, and small pensioners.[63]

The new pattern of social policy in Hungary is about combining the reduction of state involvement in the financing of social policy with the withdrawal of certain universal rights. The former step has continued to be more or less avoided. After 1989 social spending was growing faster than the measured GDP in Hungary, partly because the GDP was shrinking. Social spending was growing from 38 percent to 54 percent in the state budget between 1985 and 1992.[64] The preservation of social protection, the reduction of the number of

63. Zsuzsa Ferge, "A szociális polgáriság feltámasztásának nehézségei" ["The Difficulties of Resurrection of Social Citizenship"], *Esély* No. 6 (1993): 20.

64. This growth is partly due to the reduction of subsidies and other direct economic expenditures in the state budget. See Tóth, "A jóléti rendszer az átmenet

universal social services, was coupled with the strengthening of the contributory nature of social policy, placing a great financial burden on the shoulders of employers and employees. In 1994 the government slightly reduced for the first time the amount that employers contributed to the social security system. This was made possible by the stagnating or declining number of unemployed people who were being financed by employers' contributions.

This pattern of change in social policy is different from the pattern that emerged during the south European transition from dictatorship to democracy. For instance, as Jimenez Fernandes argues, the task of social policy in Spain was to establish a comprehensive welfare network that paid particular attention to the least well off and made social security available to groups not previously entitled to it, thus achieving a virtually universal application of certain benefits (e.g., health care benefits, family allowance).[65] In the 1980s the first reform adopted in Spain was designed to match contributions and benefits, strengthening the contributory nature of the system. Subsequently, a new program of non-contributory protection with a tax-based funding emerged. Accordingly, employee and employer contributions funded 89 percent of the social security budget in 1980 but only 69 percent in 1991, whereas state funding and other contributions rose from 11 percent in 1980 to 31 percent in 1991.[66]

Hungarian social policy faces similar problems of matching the costs and benefits of social protection. And yet in Hungary it is not the lack but the existence or the extent of certain benefits (e.g., maternity leave, sick pay, earnings-related pensions, etc.) that are causing problems. In Hungary, unlike in Spain, the reform of social policy aims at diminishing, not increasing, the role of the state in the financing of social protection. In Hungary it is not the absence but the existence of universalistic rights and expectations that is causing difficulties from an economic point of view. These different outcomes can be attributed to the same cause—to the nature of democratic politics. In Spain democratic politics was driving the change of the social policy regime. In Hungary democratic politics was preventing structural changes in the social policy regime.

---

időszakában" ["The System of Social Welfare in the Period of Transition"], pp. 316–18.

65. A. Jimenez Fernandes, "Closing Address," in *Social Europe. The Convergence of Social Protection Objectives and Policies* (Supplement 5/1992), p. 55.

66. Ibid. p. 56.

Social Policy after the 1994 Elections

The direction of future social policy has been determined by the protracted economic crisis and the previous avoidance of radical reforms of social policy. The growing budget deficit exerted growing pressures on policy makers to limit the financial sources of social policy, pressures that added to the inclination of politicians and bureaucrats to accept the principle of selective or targeted[67] social services. However, the political cycle caused further delays of possible reforms. 1994 was an election year in Hungary, and no government would have taken the risk of implementing such reforms before the elections.[68] These were left to the next, socialist-liberal government.

The first government did not have the determination to follow a more radical path of social policy reform, although it may have had greater room to maneuver—not only from an economic point of view but also because trade unions were divided and did not represent a counterweight to the policy of the government. Under the economic pressures of the transformational recession the Horn government has been compelled to be more resolute about the reform of social policy, although it will encounter a stronger and more united front from the trade unions.

Between 1990 and 1994 unions proved to be too weak to play an important role in politics for a variety of reasons. This gave the first government a free hand in the field of economic and social policy. In the case of social policy the bargaining power of strong unions was replaced by the fears of the government regarding a deficit of legitimation. The state socialist system created strong expectations for social stability and for comprehensive social services provided by the state, and the government internalized these expectations.[69] Democratic politics may make the political elites

67. The fact that social services are targeted in itself does not reveal the nature of the welfare regime. Targeted social services can be built on both means-tested and universalistic provisions.

68. However, even the avoidance of drastic changes in the social policy regime could not save the conservative government. The majority of voters was not grateful for the efforts of the government to maintain the existing system of social provisions, partly because even these efforts could not guarantee the achieved level and standards of social services for citizens.

69. Let me give just two examples. The minister of social welfare, Mr. Surján, talking about the planned rise of the pension age limit, said the following: "As the society opposed the raising of the age limit, and in the Council of Interest Mediation both the employers' and the employees' representatives rejected its introduction in 1993, the government proposes an adjournment." A. Rádi, "Nyugdíj, kor,

responsive to the demands for social protection, even in the absence of strong interest representation and the interest mediation of a civil society.[70] The structural constraints of democratic politics, with its symptoms of general associational weakness, may counterbalance the effects caused by the coincidence of liberal-conservative political predominance.[71] However, contrary to Offe's expectation, the interplay of these factors resulted not in a lack of social policy and social provisions, but rather in the avoidance of those comprehensive structural reforms of the existing social policy regime that would have brought about the withdrawal of the state from the provision of social services. It is the irony of postsocialist transition that a government dominated by the Socialists, in circumstances of stronger interest representation of unions, is compelled to initiate social policy reforms that aim at easing the burden of the state in financing social policy. In March 1995 the government announced a new program of austerity that foresees the reform of social policy through the substitution of means-tested provisions for existing citizenship rights on family benefits. In this limited field the Socialist-dominated government took a step towards the residual welfare state. However, reforms of this kind will have to confront new political constraints. First, the

határ" ["Pension, Age, Limit"], *Népszabadság* (8 March 1994): 7. The minister of finance, Mr. Szabó, said in an interview: "The budget deficit can really be balanced only by economic growth, because I do not think that the level of the social-cultural provision of society could be radically lowered. To take away acquired rights from the people can be perilous because it threatens to overturn social trust and stability—that may deter the capital coming into the country, too." Anikó Szántó, "Nem a pénz beszél" ["It Is Not Money That Talks"], *Heti Világgazdaság* 13, 40 (10 May 1991): 45.

70. "Both looking back and looking to the West will generate a social demand for protection and security that is not easily met by the newly emerging economic and institutional structures and resources.... Thus, political elites of the new regime appear to be largely aware of the need to respond to demands for social justice that arise in the process of transition. Such responsiveness is all the more called for as societies of the newly democratizing countries of Central and Eastern Europe have acquired the political resources to vote those elites out of office who are seen as frustrating demands for social justice. People in these societies are not used to coping with insecurity." Claus Offe, "The Politics of Social Policy in East European Transitions: Antecedents, Agents, and Agenda of Reform," *Social Research*, 60, 4 (Winter 1993): 660.

71. "... the coincidence of liberal-conservative political predominance with the symptoms of general associational weakness is the worst possible structural background for the emergence of social policy institutions. Associational weakness may well be a stronger impediment to the evolution of social policy institutions than it is for any other policy area." Ibid., pp. 672–73.

socialist-liberal government has to face stronger unions. Second, another political constraint on the reform of social policy may come from the behavior of the socialist MPs who may be reluctant to vote against their social values in favor of a social policy reform that reduces the role of redistribution in social policy. In any case, the economic exigencies of a very large budget deficit and very high level of employer contribution to the social policy regime hardly allow for an increase in revenues, or the growth or even the maintenance of social policy expenditures. If structural reforms are further delayed, expenditures may still be controlled with or without the use of inflation. Although social policy outcomes can be regulated even if structural reforms are not brought about,[72] economic exigencies would seem to be forcing the government to opt for radical reforms that will internalize, and in certain respects, as in the case of family benefits, may even overshoot the earlier propositions of the IMF and the World Bank.

The Role of International Actors

The international organizations that may have an influence on Hungarian social policy are the IMF, the World Bank, and the EU. The EU has extended its financial support to the field of social policy within the framework of the PHARE program. Since 1990 PHARE has helped, with a three million ECU grant, in launching a new foundation for the development of local social welfare networks that aim at stimulating local self-help initiatives. Then too, PHARE gave fifteen million ECU for the creation of an employment and social policy development program. The content of the program has been negotiated by the Hungarian ministries in charge and EU representatives. The EU provides experts and studies that introduce Western European patterns to its Hungarian partner.

72. Pension regime exemplifies the first, social assistance the second case. In the absence of comprehensive structural reforms of the pension regime, the level of new pensions was declining. 1990 was the last year when the level of the new pensions was higher than the average level of pensions. "The policy choice has been made in Hungary that a lot of people are given less and less pensions with a relatively satisfactory guarantee of value maintenance of pensions." István Gy. Tóth, "A postás még hányszor csenget?" ["How Many Times Does the Postman Still Ring the Bell?"], *Figyelő* (10 November 1994): 19. The support given to local governments by the central state for the purposes of social assistance does not keep up with the rate of inflation. In 1994 32.4 billion HUF was allocated for this purpose; in 1995 the amount given was 36.2 billion HUF, while the estimated rate of inflation for 1995 ran at about 20 percent. Sándor Rege, "Széteshetnek a szociális rendszerek" ["Social Policy Schemes May Collapse"], *Népszabadság* (30 December 1994): 12.

The World Bank has been providing loans targeted at the modernization of the Hungarian social security system. In 1993 the World Bank gave a 223 million dollar credit to the government for fifteen years that must be spent on the development of social security. Health care institutions have been given ninety-one million dollars to help towards increasing the capacity of health care institutions, for educational programs, and for the development of computer-based data files. The system of social insurance received 132 million dollars for the upgrading of its computer system. In exchange the government and the social insurance funds promised that they will not initiate the increase of the social insurance contribution before 30 June 1998.[73]

The EU, the IMF, and the World Bank have built up different channels for the flow of money and information to different actors and institutions within the Hungarian state administration. The EU primarily has connections with those ministries and institutions that are responsible for the various aspects of social policy. The IMF and the World Bank have close connections with the Ministry of Finance, the ministry with the greatest power over Hungary's economics. This means that the influence of the EU may spread throughout the institutional structure from below in dispersed form. On the other hand, the influence of the IMF and the World Bank may spread in a concentrated form from the top down. But it does not necessarily mean that the IMF and the World Bank will always exert far greater influence over Hungarian social policy than the EU. Because the Antall government chose the tactics of piecemeal engineering in the field of social policy, until 1994 the effect of the dispersed influence of the EU might have been equal to the influence of the IMF and the World Bank, whose aims have been to bring comprehensive reform to Hungarian social policy. This situation changed in March 1995 when the Horn government decided to embark on a course of radically austere economic reforms and set in motion the postponed reforms in restructuring and the cutting of social expenditures.

The IMF and the World Bank insist on the restructuring of social policy, on introducing the insurance principle in health care, pensions, and unemployment, on putting an end to the growth of state involvement in the financing of social services, and on redirecting the resources from universal social services to targeted

73. *Népszabadság* (24 April 1993): 5.

social assistance.[74] The EU, with its norms and requirements for social policy, may be a point of orientation for Hungarian policy makers who are eager to join the EU.

Because the indebtedness of the Hungarian economy is rather significant (see the case on monetary policy), the IMF and the World Bank may have a more direct influence over Hungarian social policy reform in the future. The critical magnitude of the budget deficit exerts a real pressure and may reinforce the influence of these international actors on the government to do something about the structure and the size of state expenditures.[75]

The influence of the EU is partly tied to the integration process, through which Hungary may acquire full membership in the Community. However, there are no strict and compulsory EU requirements in the field of social policy that the Hungarian government is forced to observe. The change of the social policy regime in Hungary is not directly constrained by the EU.

In theory, the advice and requirements of the IMF, the World Bank, and the EU do not exclude one other. The suggestions of the IMF and the World Bank are not intended to expel from social policy the principle of universality and solidarity.[76] The EU norms do not require the maintenance of the existing social policy regime

74. The deputy director of the IMF, Gerard Belanger, in an interview given to the Hungarian newspaper *Magyar Hírlap*, saw the problem of social security as being that in Hungary, as in other post-socialist countries, the only mechanism of social insurance is the old system of social redistribution—the safety net is simply put on top of it. Belanger emphasized that the resources available for social insurance are universally distributed in a situation where social policy is lacking resources. As he remarked, Hungary was spending too much on social insurance, so the amount spent on this purpose cannot be increased. The solution is the targeted redirection of this money to those in need. People with higher incomes should not receive the same support as the poor. Zsuzsa N. Vadász, "Belanger: az ígéreteknek ára van" ["Belanger: Promises have a Price"], *Magyar Hírlap* (9 October 1993): 8.

75. This point is emphasized in Deacon, "Developments in East European Social Policy."

76. Deacon expresses another view. He thinks that the IMF and the World Bank simply represent a neo-liberal set of social policy proposals and are incapable of learning or adapting to the specific east European circumstances. See Robert Deacon, "A nemzetek fölötti és globális szervezetek hatása a közép-eurpai nemzeti szociálpolitikára" ["The Impact of Supra-National and Global Organizations on the Social Policy of Central European Nations"], *Esély*, No. 6 (1992); and Deacon, "Developments in East European Social Policy," p. 192. However, the liberal proposals of these international organizations do not necessarily lead to a residual welfare state. To give one example, when the World Bank proposed to transform the regime of family allowances into a more targeted system, it did not imply abolishing the universality of this provision. See *A Világbank szociálpolitikai jelentése Magyarországról* [*The Report of the World Bank on Social Policy in Hungary*].

that is judged by the IMF and the World Bank to be unsound and not viable in the long run. All these institutions contribute to the strengthening of private actors within the field of social policy. Domestic policy makers seem too inclined to follow the suggestions of the IMF and the World Bank, not because they are under external pressure, but because a great number of them have internalized the pattern that dominates the direction of problem solving in this field. However, important elements of the policy reform, as I mentioned earlier, have yet to be realized. Governments risk losing the support of voters by implementing unpopular reforms in a radical way only if they feel that they are acting under circumstances of economic emergency.

Conclusion

The social policy of the first democratically elected government has brought about a few inconclusive steps toward a new social policy regime. The former system of universal or quasi-universal social services was partly abandoned, although a new policy regime of targeted social services that would seem to be desirable from an economic point of view has yet to be reached. This option has been made inviable by democratic politics. Consequently, the measures taken were not able to relieve the financial pressure of social policy on the state budget.

The evolution of the social policy regime in Hungary is going on within two contradicting constraints. There are economic constraints rooted in the transformational crisis that put the government under pressure to make partial spending cuts, and partially restructure welfare spending. There are political constraints rooted in the nature of democratic politics that put the government under pressure to maintain the achieved level of social services and to compensate the losers of the economic game. The character of the future social policy regime in Hungary will be determined by the outcomes of the political struggle going on among the various political actors and of the efforts of the successive governments to make compatible those incompatible demands of market economy and political democracy.

The influence of international actors is mediated through the structural contradictions of domestic politics. To a certain extent the German social policy regime has served as an institutional model that can be used as a point of orientation by policy makers. The influence of the EU, however, may take the form of an institutional constraint. But in the short run the aim to join the EU may not serve as an effective constraint on the formation of social policy in Hungary. Among the international actors, the IMF and the World Bank may very well exert a direct influence on Hungarian social policy in the future. The more serious the economic problems of Hungary are, the more effective the constraints set by the IMF and the World Bank will almost certainly be. Finally, the influence of the EU, the IMF, and the World Bank may not necessarily exclude one another.

The Central Bank and Monetary Policy in the Post-Socialist Transition

The Legacy of State Socialism

Although the socialist economy was formally a monetized economy, money played a passive role in comparison with the role of money in a market economy. In the classical socialist economy, planning in kind dominated planning in monetary categories, and the institutions of planning dominated monetary institutions. Under classical socialism the banking system was state-owned. Banks became a branch of the party-state bureaucracy, and the central bank lacked any kind of institutional or even informal autonomy and was subordinated to the government. The other specialized banks were subordinated to the central bank in the same way as the central bank was subordinated to the government. As a result, the banking system behaved like a monobank.[77]

The central bank under classical socialism performed the function of a central bank under capitalism: the emission of money. It also had a function that was fulfilled in a market economy by the commercial banks: handling the short-term credit supply of state-owned firms. Each state-owned firm had to keep an account at the central bank.

Within the framework of the reformed economy in Hungary, the modernization of the banking system began at the beginning of the 1980s.[78] The centralized system of capital allocation was

---

77. János Kornai, *The Socialist System: The Political Economy of Communism* (Princeton: Princeton University Press), pp. 132–33.

78. David Bartlett, "Banking and Financial Reform in a Mixed Economy: The Case of Hungary," in Perry Patterson, ed., *Capitalist Goals, Socialist Past: The Rise of the Private Sector in Command Economies* (Boulder: Westview Press, 1993).

eased by the emergence of monetary funds created from the various funds the state-owned firms were obliged to keep, and from centralized governmental money. These funds were the origin of specialized monetary institutions that came into existence during the middle of the 1980s and now constitute the small and middle-sized commercial banks.[79]

The other important institutional change was the formation of the two-tier banking system. Since 1 January 1987 the central bank has been separated from the new system of commercial banks.

However, these reforms did not change the logic of economic coordination. The central bank was not given real autonomy, and remained under the sway of political and fiscal interests.[80] The new commercial banks could not base their activities on the market principle, as firms were still under the power of bureaucratic coordination. As a result, commercial banks accumulated a significant amount of bad debt originating from the sector of state-owned firms and cooperatives.

The modernization of the banking system reached a new level after 1990. The parliament passed bills on the central bank, on banks and banking activities, on accounting, and on securities. These acts have created a new legal framework for the market economy in Hungary.

The Status of the Central Bank

The Act on the National Bank of Hungary (NBH) was passed as early as 1991. There was a consensus among the political parties in the parliament that a relatively independent central bank would be an important condition of a functioning market economy. This consensus was rooted in the negation of the state socialist past of the monobank under the surveillance of the central planners. To create an autonomous central bank meant—for the reform economists, who became part of the new political elite—the completion of the separation of economic powers, the creation of a countervailing power to fiscal interests, and the safeguarding of the normal functioning of market economy.

The central bank itself played a decisive role in the process of devising the new status of the bank. In Hungary the central bank

79. Éva Várhegyi, "A monetáris politika és közvetítő rendszere a piacgazdasági átmenet útján" ["Monetary Policy and Its System of Mediation on the Way of Transformation toward Market Economy"], unpublished manuscript, Budapest, 1993.

80. Bartlett, "Banking and Financial Reform."

already occupied a special position before 1989. Due to earlier reforms, the president of the NBH was responsible not to the minister of finance, but directly responsible to the prime minister. This arrangement gave the bank more room to maneuver and may very well have served as a basis for future attempts to institutionalize an independent central bank.

The new bill regarding the status of the NBH after 1989 was prepared by the bank and reflected the influence of the German model both directly and indirectly. Those who prepared the bill on the NBH did not need German advisors or direct German influence to arrive at a proposal for the Hungarian parliament that was similar to respective German legal regulations. Because the bank sought an autonomous status for itself, an obvious model was the most independent central bank in Europe. The institutional setting of the Bundesbank could and did provide a model for the NBH in devising a proper central bank for a proper market economy in Hungary. This direct effect of the German model without direct interference of the Germans was reinforced by the preparations of the Maastricht Treaty that foresaw the setting up of a European central bank. The new political elite in Hungary was more or less united in its intention to join the EU. The NBH could confirm its intentions to form an independent central bank by pointing out the European efforts to set up a European central bank, the status of which also reflected the German model. This indirect effect of the German pattern, mediated through the EU, reinforced the more direct effects of the German model on the preparation of the new act regarding the role of the NBH.

Although the proposal on the new status of the central bank was backed up by a general consensus on the necessity of an autonomous central bank, it did not mean that there were no debates or conflicts of interest regarding the proposed extent of this autonomy. On the bureaucratic level the Ministry of Finance, which represented fiscal interests, had a stake in limiting the autonomy of the central bank, as this autonomy put a constraint on financing the budget deficit. The clash of different interests was resolved on the political level in parliament.

The parties of parliamentary opposition, especially the liberal parties, argued in parliament for a more autonomous central bank that would constrain the power of the government. The government supported a version of the original draft that maintained the autonomy of the central bank but also included modifications favoring the government.

Influential members of parliament from the parties of the ruling coalition argued for a more limited autonomy for the central bank. The bill was criticized in parliament by István Csurka, the leader of populist MPs within the biggest party of the ruling coalition, the Hungarian Democratic Forum (HDF), and by Iván Szabó, who belonged to the center of the HDF and was the leading politician in the field of economic policy for the HDF.

Iván Szabó proposed to parliament that the paragraph prohibiting the government from giving orders to the bank be deleted from the bill; that the president of the bank be appointed to a term limited to four years; that the bank be requested to report to parliament more than just once a year, etc.[81] However, the attempts at significantly limiting the independence of the central bank were squelched by the prime minister, who already had a gentlemen's agreement with the president of the NBH in which the prime minister agreed to acknowledge the de facto autonomy of the NBH prior to passing the new Act on the NBH in 1991.

The outcome of the political debate was close to the position advocated by the government: a compromise that guaranteed the relative autonomy of the NBH. The paragraph safeguarding the independence of the bank from the government was saved. In the bill passed by parliament, only minor limitations on the autonomy of the bank were introduced as modifications to the original draft. In the bill proposal the president of Hungary would have had the right to appoint the president of the NBH, the vice presidents would have been appointed from among candidates proposed by the president of the NBH, and the number of outer members of the Central Bank Council would have been smaller than the number of bank managers. In the bill passed it is the prime minister who has the power to nominate the president and the vice presidents of the bank, and the number of external members is identical to that of the vice presidents.[82]

81. The argument of Iván Szabó in favor of a moderate autonomy for the NBH was based on the requirement that the primacy of the government in matters of economic policy be maintained. He writes: "I believe there is no responsible political force in this country that would dare to say that in a transitional period like this the legitimately elected government should pull out from the governance of the economy to the extent that it would not want to influence monetary policy." See Anikó Szántó, "Nem a pénz beszél" ["It Is Not Money That Talks"], *Heti Világgazdaság*, 13, 40 (10 May 1991): 6.

82. Parliament passed the bill on the central bank with a 68 percent majority. All the MPs of the HDF present voted yes, Iván Szabó included. The biggest party of the opposition, The Alliance of Free Democrats, voted against the bill. The rejection expressed its dissatisfaction with the deviation from the original draft.

TABLE 3.3 THE INSITITUTIONALIZATION OF THE HUNGARIAN AND THE GERMAN CENTRAL BANK[a]

Hungary	Germany
The president of the National Bank of Hungary (NBH) is accountable to parliament.	The *Bundesbank* is not accountable to the *Bundestag*.
The NBH is not subject to the supervision of any ministries.	The *Bundesbank* is not subject to the supervision of any federal ministries.
The president of Hungary appoints to three-year terms the members of the Central Bank Council recommended by the prime minister. The members of the directorate are elected at the annual meeting of shareholders recommended by the president.	The president appoints to eight-year terms the candidates for membership of the directorate recommended by the federal government.
The president of the NBH is appointed for six-year term by the president of the Republic on the recommendation of the prime minister.	The president of the *Bundesbank* is appointed by the chancellor.
The NBH must support the government's overall economic policy. The bank's main task is the defense of the national currency. The bank pursues its policy independently.	The *Bundesbank* must support the government's overall economic policy as long as it does not interfere with the aim of safeguarding the currency.
The representatives of the government must be invited to the meetings of the Central Bank Council.	Cabinet members have the right to attend the meetings of the Central Bank Council.
The president of the NBH has the right to attend cabinet meetings dealing with important monetary issues.	The president of the *Bundesbank* has the right to attend cabinet meetings dealing with important monetary issues.
The NBH may give loans to the state budget of up to 3% of the annual revenues of the state budget.[b]	The *Bundesbank* cannot be obliged to finance the state budget deficit.

[a]Source: Peter J. Katzenstein, *Policy and Politics in West Germany* (Philadelphia: Temple University Press, 1987), pp. 61–62; and the *Act on the National Bank of Hungary*.

[b]Before taking effect, the 3 percent limit was changed to 5 percent in 1993 by parliament and then abolished in 1994.

The 1991 Act on the Central Bank of Hungary institutionalized, even in international comparison, a relatively great autonomy for the NBH. From a legal point of view, on the basis of the Goodman indicators of central bank independence,[83] the NBH stood somewhere in between Germany on the one hand, and France and Italy on the other hand. Legal regulations bestowed a relatively high degree of independence on the NBH and showed similarities to the status of the Bundesbank. However, this autonomy has not reached that of the Bundesbank (see Table 3.3).

The NBH is responsible to parliament, and must submit an annual report on the activity of the bank and on the annual guidelines of monetary policy to parliament. The government takes a

83. See John B. Goodman, *Monetary Sovereignty: The Politics of Central Banking in Western Europe* (Ithaca and London: Cornell University Press, 1992), p. 11.

stand on any matter that might arise before any discussion in parliament, although it may not give orders to the bank. The president and other chief executives serve a shorter term than their colleagues at the Bundesbank. In these respects the NBH's autonomy is more circumscribed than that of the Bundesbank.

The NBH has a legal right to express publicly its position on the decisions of the government and ministries, although it cannot otherwise assert its own views during the process of policy making.

The Act kept the deficit financing activity of the central bank within reasonable limits. According to the original regulations after 1993 the loans given to the state budget by the central bank may not exceed 3 percent of the planned annual revenue of the state budget.[84]

The bank is sheltered from political influence by the regulation that the president and vice-presidents of the bank, along with the members of the Directorate and the Central Bank Council, cannot hold any position in political parties and are prohibited from pursuing any public activity in the interest or in the name of a party.

The Act on the National Bank has set high standards of autonomy in favor of the bank. The relatively early institutionalization of the status of the National Bank made it easier to arrive at such a regulation. At the beginning of the post-socialist transition, the German model of central bank autonomy that seemed such a desirable example of market economy and seemed to be in accordance with the European trend could have a higher influence on the actual institution-building policy of the Hungarian government than in a subsequent period when the accumulated experience of governing reinforced the interests of the government to avoid self-imposed limitations on its authority. The government was looking for substitutes in order to push farther away the self-imposed limits on its authority.

The prime minister sought to circumvent the institutional barriers of the autonomy of the NBH by proposing Péter Ákos Bod for the post of president of the NBH, after parliament had passed the Act on the NBH.[85] Mr. Bod belonged to the inner circle of the prime

84. The Amendment to the Act on the NBH passed in 1993 stipulates that the amount of the loans given to the state budget is unlimited in 1992, is 5 percent instead of 3 percent in 1993, and will be eighty billion HUF in 1994.

85. Originally the president in office, György Surányi, was expected to remain the president of the NBH. Surányi was a protagonist in the struggle for the largest possible autonomy for the central bank. However, the official explanation for why Mr. Bod was proposed for the post of president by the prime minister was referring to something else. Mr. Surányi signed the so-called Democratic Charta that was

minister in the Hungarian Democratic Forum (HDF). He played an important part in preparing the economic program of the HDF and was minister of industry in the Antall government. He was expected to be loyal to the prime minister and to represent a personal guarantee that the authority of the government in the field of economic policy would be preserved. However, after having been appointed, Mr. Bod, following the requirements of the law, resigned from his membership in the parliament and suspended his membership in the HDF. In any case, the government simultaneously imposed formal limits on its own authority in the field of monetary policy while seeking to circumvent the institutional guarantees of central bank autonomy with informal, personal guarantees.

After the elections in 1994 the issue of the personal integrity of the president of the NBH was again coming to the fore of public discussions. The new ruling coalition of socialists and liberals, referring to the circumstances under which Mr. Bod became president, publicly announced that a change in the post of the president of the NBH would be desirable.[86] Because the president was appointed for six years, the new government had no legal grounds for dismissing Mr. Bod. Six months after the elections Péter Bod yielded to pressure and resigned from the presidency.[87] The new president of the NBH came to be the former one, György Surányi.

The government also had its way in changing certain legal regulations that it felt were necessary from the point of view of fiscal policy. In 1993, under the burden of financing the growing budget deficit, parliament modified the Act on the Central Bank on the initiative of the government and publicly provided a lump sum loan valued at eighty billion HUF to finance the budget deficit by the central bank for the year of 1994. The NBH was protesting against this amendment of the Act but did not have the power to prevent

---

launched in defense of Hungarian democracy by intellectuals from the circles of the Free Democrats and Socialists. In the opinion of the prime minister, Mr. Surányi lost his political independence by joining a movement that was led by politicians and intellectuals of the parties of the opposition, and this fact disqualified him from being considered for the presidency of the central bank. However, this argument about the undesirable political influence on the person of the president of the NBH did not prevent the prime minister from nominating for this post someone who was a member of his own party.

86. The socialists and the liberals argued that because Mr. Bod assumed the presidency of the NBH as a politician, he was no longer suitable for this position and should resign.

87. In exchange he became the Hungarian representative at the European Bank of Development and Reconstruction.

the government from changing this legal regulation. In this case policy considerations had an effect on the institutionalized autonomy of the central bank and led to the curbing of this autonomy in favor of greater government control that increased its room to maneuver in policy making. Because the government avoided the reform of the budget mainly for political reasons, in order to avoid legitimation deficits,[88] it was inevitable that the politicians in power would lift the legal constraints that might have prevented them from financing the inescapably growing budget deficits.

Monetary Policy

In the classical socialist economy, money did not integrate the economy, economic actors were not sensitive to changes in prices, and interest rates, etc. Under these circumstances monetary policy was rather ineffective and was dominated by planning in kind.[89]

In Hungary after the economic reform in 1968 monetary regulators replaced the production quotas of target planning and administrative restrictions. The result was the emergence of macro tensions in the economy.[90] An important form of these macro tensions was the growing foreign indebtedness of the country.

The macroeconomic conditions of monetary policy At the end of the 1980s monetary policy was emancipated from fiscal policy, but as a result of growing macro tensions the room to maneuver in monetary policy was very limited. Monetary policy had to follow the goal of putting an end to the growth of indebtedness, an aim that required a restriction on internal demand that it was hoped would lead to declining imports and rising exports.

In 1989, under the Németh government, restrictive monetary policy was thought to counterbalance inflation resulting from price and wage liberalization. In fact, monetary policy, under the pressure of big state-owned firms, proved to be restrictive only in relation to individual households.[91]

Monetary policy under the Antall government After the elections in 1990 the Antall government faced the contradictory task of fighting inflation and reducing foreign indebtedness.[92] Fighting

88. On this problem, see the section on social policy.
89. János Kornai, *The Socialist System*.
90. Ibid.
91. Várhegyi, "A monetáris politika" ["Monetary Policy"], p. 398.
92. In 1991 the rate of inflation reached 35 percent, the balance of payments was positive (with a surplus of $267 million), the budget deficit was 1.4 billion HUF. In

inflation creates negative incentives for firms to invest or raise output. Reducing the extent of foreign indebtedness under the circumstances of import liberalization requires growing exports and positive incentives for the firms to raise output.

The NBH was using the real revaluation of the currency as the basic means of anti-inflationary policy, although this conflicted with the interests of the export sector of the country. This policy led to trouble in 1993 because of the growing negative balance of trade caused by the radical decline of exports in relationship to the growth of imports.[93]

Another constraint on monetary policy was set in motion by the growing budget deficit: monetary policy had to create the means for deficit financing and for counterbalancing the inflationary effects of this policy. It meant that in spite of the formal autonomy of the central bank, the necessary room to maneuver for autonomous and effective monetary regulation could not come into existence: the processes in money and capital markets were influenced by the economic behavior of the state through the effects of the growing budget deficit on these markets. In order to finance the budget deficit the state was compelled to issue state bonds and treasury bills that, as a consequence of being the dominating security on the supply side, could dominate prices in an underdeveloped financial market. As a result, fiscal policy could dominate monetary policy in the formation of interest rates.[94]

Financing the budget deficit without direct inflationary consequences meant giving loans to the budget—that is, it meant crowding out private investment. Financing the budget deficit this way without direct inflationary consequences means contributing

---

1992 the rate of inflation declined to 23 percent, the balance of payments was still positive ($325 million), but the budget deficit was growing to 114.2 billion HUF. In 1993 the rate of inflation was about 23 percent, the balance of payments became negative ($3 billion) and the budget deficit was 214.7 billion HUF, around 7 percent of the GDP. See Zita M. Petschnig, *Jelentések az alagútból. Jelentés a gazdasági átalakulás 1990–1993 közötti folyamatairól* [*Reports from the Tunnel. Report on the Processes of Economic Transformation Between 1990–1993*] (Budapest: Pénzügykutató Részvénytársaság, 1994). These data show both the constraints and at the same time the outcomes of the monetary policy pursued.

93. In 1993 exports declined to 87 percent of the exports of 1992, while imports increased by 21 percent over imports in 1992. Petschnig, *Jelentések az alagútból* [*Reports from the Tunnel*], pp. 137–41.

94. Várhegyi, "A monetáris politika" ["Monetary Policy"], p. 48. Várhegyi, "Monetáris és bankpolitika: a rendszerváltozás első kormányának mérlege" ["Monetary and Banking Policy: The Balance of the First Government of System Change"], *Külgazdaság*, No. 4 (1994): 39–52.

to long-lasting recession. Consequently, there was the constant danger that the continuing recession would lead to the repoliticization of monetary policy if politicians, under the burden of the long recession, started thinking about using monetary policy to promote economic growth.

This was the case in 1992, when the government, underestimating the depth of the transformational recession, found itself trying to create incentives for a new phase of economic growth. This endeavor was triggered by political calculation: the government was already looking toward the 1994 elections.

In December 1991 the prime minister formed a special committee with the aim of designing a new economic policy that would lead the economy out of the depression. In 1992 the government embarked on a new course in economic policy that foresaw the stimulation of the economy on the basis of the existing surplus in the balance of payments. A non-restrictive monetary policy was part of the policy package.[95] The central bank also thought that economic stimulation was a possible way out of the recession and supported the change in economic policy. In 1992–93 the NBH was using credit policy to create relatively cheap money in order to encourage new investments. The NBH did its part by reducing interest rates. On the other hand, as a countermeasure, the central bank tried to maintain its foreign exchange rate policy in order to avoid an increase in inflation. In the end the positive effects it was hoped the economic policy would achieve did not come about, while the negative effects were making themselves felt.

Stagnation continued, and the positive balance of payments disappeared. The negative balance of payments was due to the growing gap between exports and imports. The fall in interest rates did not lead to growing investments, but rather to falling domestic savings that even had a painful effect on the budget, since budget deficits were earlier financed from growing domestic savings.

At the end of both 1993 and 1994 the government was forced to change course regarding its economic policy. Although the economy started growing in 1994, the price paid was very high. The danger once again of growing indebtedness, the large negative balance of trade, and the high level of budget deficit created constraints that forced the government to abandon the policy of stimulation. The NBH again raised interest rates and at the same time had to change its foreign exchange policy. The Ministry of Trade

95. Zita M. Petschnig, *Örökségtől örökségig* [*From Legacy to Legacy*] (Budapest: Századvég Kiadó, 1994), pp. 69–76.

and the business interest groups had earlier argued for currency depreciation in order to boost exports. The deteriorating balance of trade now gave weight to these arguments. The national currency was depreciated several times during 1994.

Monetary policy under the Horn government In 1994 the growth rate of the economy reached 3 percent. However, the growth of the economy was accompanied by a further worsening of monetary indicators. Under the pressure of these imbalances the socialist-liberal government opted to pursue a policy of monetary restriction. The NBH also favored a strict monetary policy that would raise the interest rate and contract the quantity of money. The deficit in the balance of trade forced the Horn government into a major, 10 percent depreciation of the currency that was followed by smaller depreciations made by the NBH. A course of economic policy is subject not only to economic but also to political pressures, seeing as the restrictive monetary and fiscal policy inevitably encounters legitimation constraints rooted in democratic politics.[96] These internal tensions were expressed in public debates between the members of the coalition. The smaller coalition partner, the Free Democrats, was pressing the government for a restrictive economic policy. Within the Socialist Party, however, the primacy of a stabilization policy was debated. The lack of determination on the part of the Socialist Party and the prime minister to stand behind this program led to the resignation of the Socialist minister of finance. However, the pressure of economic exigencies (internal and external imbalances) and growing criticism from the international financial and business community, organizations, and the press forced the prime minister to opt for an economic policy of austerity. The newly appointed minister of finance, together with the new president of the NBH, announced a strict new monetary policy, radical fiscal reforms, and successive devaluations of the Forint.

The influence of the EU and Germany on monetary policy The political program of aiming toward joining the EU will create economic constraints on monetary policy. However, the existing deficits in the balance of trade and payments, as well as the rate of inflation, are higher than the targets set by the EU. Under these circumstances there is no chance for a stable exchange rate policy.

The president of the Bundesbank, Helmut Schlesinger, has already suggested to Hungarian policy makers that they should link the exchange rate of the Forint to that of the German Mark in

96. On this problem, see the section on social policy.

order to maintain the stability of the currency.[97] However, the conditions have not yet been ripe for such a move. Similarly, monetary policy in Hungary cannot consider the monetary targets of the EU as guidelines for policy making, although these targets may influence Hungarian policy some time in the future, as a framework for the integration process. These adaptations are dependent on the end of the recession, which would ease the external and internal indebtedness of the country and create more favorable conditions for policy makers to sacrifice certain tools of autonomous economic policy making in exchange for the advantages of joining the EU.[98] For the time being, the economic constraints stemming from the transformational recession and the political constraints stemming from democratic politics have prevented the government from relinquishing some of its autonomy in monetary policy in exchange for a reliable and stable national currency.

Conclusion

The course of the reform of the central bank was shaped by the specific political and economic elites. The institutional setting of the Bundesbank and the idea of a European-style central bank that also reflected the status of the Bundesbank was used by the NBH as a model and justification for assuming the highest possible degree of autonomy. In the final outcome the institutionalization of the role of the NBH followed the German pattern, although there were also important modifications.

Under the pressure of economic exigencies of the post-socialist transition monetary policy showed a different picture from that of Germany. Due to circumstances, monetary policy remained defensive, and was unable to follow the recipe for export stimulation that calls for keeping the national currency stable and relatively undervalued. However, economic growth in Hungary cannot be anything else but export-led growth. This creates pressure to fashion a monetary policy that takes measures in favor of an undervalued currency, although, in contrast to Germany, Hungary must deal with a far less stable national currency.

The Central Bank of Hungary, on the basis of its independence from political actors, is freed from the compulsion of seeking

97. Schlesinger's proposal was made in a lecture held at the Budapest University of Economics in March 1993. *Népszabadság* (2 April 1993): 5.

98. This is the usual trade-off for small West European states. See Paulette Kurzer, "Euromoney and Europol: German Influence in the Low Countries," manuscript, 1994.

legitimation. By contrast, the government cannot help but feel the pressure to defend its legitimacy. This difference may create tensions between the bank and the government. The central bank may try to legitimate the course of its monetary policy by pointing to the requirements of the international financial community, to the standing and policy of the Bundesbank, and to the monetary requirements of the EU. The government may try to resolve the tension by initiating in parliament changes in the legal status of the bank that put limitations on its autonomy. The bank may be able to maintain its autonomy if it is able to mobilize domestic political support in favor of its relative independence, or if the financial crisis is big enough to threaten shattering the confidence of the international business community and especially that of the main foreign creditors.[99] The financial crisis of 1995 reinforced the autonomy of the NBH.

As part of the framework of the integration process, monetary policy in Hungary will have to deal with the requirements and economic constraints set by the EU. This adjustment may be mediated by pegging the Forint to the German Mark. However, under the pressure of fiscal crisis and deficits in the balance of trade and balance of payments, the Hungarian government is not in the position to give up the autonomy of its exchange rate policy. In order to pull itself out of its economic recession and move toward the European economic regime, the Hungarian government must try to lighten the constraints of democratic politics. It looks as though this process has been set in motion.

Hungary has set out on the road that leads toward European structures and policies, but this road will be longer than originally expected. In the transition institutions, policy regimes and policies are constructed that reflect domestic interests, look to external models, and are constrained by internal and external exigencies.

99. For instance, the prime minister of Hungary, Gyula Horn, complained in parliament that if the National Bank raised interest rates it would increase the burden of the state budget, because the interest on the loans given to the state would be higher. According to the prime minister, the independence of the National Bank may be too great. However, it will be very difficult for him to change the status of the bank through the modification of the Act on the National Bank of Hungary if he wants to maintain the coalition with the Free Democrats.

In the first few years of the transition those who had direct access to the decision-making process, the political and the economic elites, had more freedom to set up institutions and pursue policies that served their own interests because the potentially collective actors of broad social coalitions in civil society were still weak or were not organized enough to be able to put politics and politicians under pressure. The constraints on institutional reforms emerged from the effects of state socialist structures, from a lack of resources to help mobilize economic progress, and from the post-socialist policies themselves.

Institution-building has been influenced by the German model, and not only because of Germany's importance to the region, but also as a result of the former historical development and the existing traditions in Hungary. But German influence does not mean Hungarian emulation. Furthermore, in the three cases examined here the EU did not exert a strong influence in terms of either enabling or constraining institution-building in Hungary (with the possible exception of the central bank, although in this case the influence of the EU reflects Germany's institutional pattern). However, in the long run the process of European unification, coupled with the intention of Hungarian policy makers to acquire full membership in the EU, may have a more direct influence on the formation of domestic institutions.

Policies in the post-socialist transition are shaped by the presence or absence of institutional reforms. During the first years of the transition the existing circumstances did not require and did not make possible a direct adaptation to EU policy standards. These EU requirements can be quite different: for instance, they would give more room to maneuver in social policy, but less freedom in monetary policy. However, more thorough adaptation to German and EU policies and policy regimes cannot take place until the end of Hungary's economic recession.

The influence of Germany and the EU is being mediated by domestic structures and interests. In the process of transformation political actors redefine the rules of social action. This constitutional phase of decision making takes place behind a veil of uncertainty but is nonetheless shaped by the interests of the participants. As a result of the effects of domestic structures, the outcome of the application of German or other institutional models will deviate from the original intentions. Emulation, if it occurs, will be at best only partially successful and will introduce unintended institutional structures and policy outcomes.

4. THE CZECH REPUBLIC
Internationalization and Dependency

Hynek Jeřábek and František Zich

The Velvet Revolution of November 1989 and the spectacularly rapid extinction of Leninism in central and Eastern Europe stirred Czechoslovakia to make a rapid transition from socialism to capitalism, from authoritarianism to democracy, and from economic and political isolation to full engagement with Western institutions. A roundtable organization for all political movements backing an agenda favoring a dramatic break with the past, the Civic Forum quickly gave way to more conventional political parties covering the middle ground: the Civic Democratic Party, the Civic Democratic Alliance, the Christian Democratic Party and the Christian Democratic Union on the center-Right, and the Social Democrats on the center-Left. They were opposed by small extremist parties on the Left (the Communist Party) and the Right (Republican Party).

The evolution of the Czechoslovak, and since 1993, the Czech, political economy and civil society has been steered by a coalition of centrist parties. The most important elements of the transformation were crafted and overseen by a small number of economists from the Civic Forum. The political leadership quickly adopted price liberalization and the active encouragement of foreign investment. Furthermore, the government also implemented restrictive monetary and fiscal macro-economic policies, thus seeking to further the objective of stabilizing the currency that is expected to be fully convertible by 1998. Characteristic of the government's strategy was its willingness to temper a strong commitment to economic reform with due respect for the requirements of social stability and political legitimacy; this was illustrated, for example, by the caution with which it approached the slow process of deregulation of the housing market.

Privatization became the prime instrument through which the government established the domestic legitimacy for a new political economy. Privatization has dispersed ownership among Czech citizens who often hold shares of mutual funds. While the forms of privatization have varied, ranging from the direct sale of state assets to coupon privatization, the political consequences were, broadly speaking, similar. Privatization has created a large group of stakeholders in one of central Europe's most promising emerging economies. And privatization has helped to attract sustained foreign investment. In turn, the reorganization of the international links of the Czech economy has had important consequences for both the domestic political economy and the perception of its legitimacy in the eyes of Czech citizens.

Before 1989 the relationships between Czechoslovak institutions and organizations and other states in Europe was severely restricted. After 1989 Czechoslovakia and the Czech Republic have sought to join the full range of international, European, and central European institutions. Within eleven months of its formation, the Czech Republic was elected as a non-permanent member of the UN Security Council. And the Council of Europe was the first European institution to offer the Czech Republic full membership after the split-up of Czechoslovakia.

As the oldest and strongest of all security institutions in Europe, NATO promises to enhance the security of all central European states, including the Czech Republic. President Clinton's "Partnership for Peace" and NATO's Cooperation Council offer the Czech Republic and the other central European states hope for eventual full membership and thus greater security against possible threats looming both from eastern and southeastern Europe, and from its two large neighbors, Germany and Russia.

The European Union (EU) has arguably become central to Czech attempts to reconnect itself back to the Western community of states. The EU is the most important trade and investment partner. The Association Agreement with the EU has opened European markets to Czech goods. But quotas and high tariffs on some products are a barrier to Czech exports. Thus steel, cement, and some other products that are much cheaper to produce in the Czech Republic than in the EU do not enjoy free access to the EU market. And the Common Agricultural Policy (CAP) of the EU opens the Czech market to severe competition. The eastern enlargement of the EU, however, holds forth the promise of the Czech Republic's joining the EU in the near future, perhaps as early as the end of the century. Regional organizations in central Europe, such as the Visegrad Group or the Hexagonal, as Valerie Bunce argues in chapter 6 below, have served no more than instrumental purposes for the Czech government, markers on the road leading to full EU and NATO membership.

In light of Czech history, memberships in multilateral institutions appear to be a promising avenue for living in close proximity with powerful neighbors. The Czech Kingdom was founded in the early middle ages, on the territory of the present Czech Republic. After the Thirty Years War, for centuries it was joined with the Austro-Hungarian Empire. At the end of World War I Czechoslovakia was established as a new state. But the Munich Agreement of 1938 and the aggression of Nazi Germany ended two decades of democratic development in the first Czechoslovak Republic. After the war, democratic order was restored briefly between 1945 and 1948. For after the Communist coup of February 1948, Czechoslovakia experienced forty-one years of Communist rule, under the continuous influence of the Soviet Union. The new democratic regime established after November 1989 formed a federal state made up of the Czech and Slovak republics. When, at the end of 1992, politicians from both republics chose to divide the country into two independent states, the potential threat from larger neighbors, in light of historical experience, grew even stronger.

The Czech Republic has been intimately linked to Germany through numerous economic, cultural, social, and political links. Between 1918 and 1938, 7.4 million Czechs and 3.5 million Germans, concentrated in the Czech regions, lived together in Czechoslovakia with 3 million Slovaks and a Hungarian minority of 0.7 million. The dominant German parties participated in the governing coalitions. However, Nazi Germany's brutal occupation and dismemberment of Czechoslovakia has profoundly shaped collective memories and put a dark cloud over Czech-German relations that, half a century later, remains a powerful political reality. The older generation in particular associates terms like "fascism" and "brutality" with "Germany." The fear of Germany's economic and political power, reinforced by German unification, has a powerful grip over the Czech people.

The strong support which the Germans living in Czechoslovakia lent to Nazi Germany make these memories especially powerful. The expulsion of the Sudeten Germans after 1945, backed by the Potsdam Agreements, have created serious diplomatic difficulties in Czech-German relations in the 1990s that are not easily accounted for by the "objective" conditions on both sides of the border; after all, Germany and the Czech Republic constitute similar political regimes that both seek to position themselves as part of an integrating Europe.

This chapter examines the Czech Republic's relations with Europe and Germany in three areas: the internationalization of the Czech automobile and media industries, which are both marked by large German investments, and the political economy of the Czech borderlands. Until the mid-1990s, VW's acquisition of Skoda in 1990–91 remained the single, largest investment by any Western company in the former Communist bloc. It has been of great practical significance for the Czech economy. As the core of a mature, industrial economy, this case illustrates the degree to which Czech autonomy has been sacrificed in favor of rapid modernization. Mass media are institutions that are central to any democratic polity, and the media case illustrates that German penetration of the Czech economy occurs within a broader international setting which links Czech and global media markets. The nesting of different media markets in the Czech Republic and in European and global communication networks was accomplished with great speed and is likely to help shape relations between state and society and, more generally, the evolution of Czech democracy. Finally, underlining the importance of the legacies of the past and the power of historical memories, this chapter also examines the politics of border areas which the Sudeten Germans inhabited before World War II.

VW and Skoda

VW's extensive investment in Skoda is a distinctive part of the rapid privatization of state-owned assets in the Czech Republic. Because of Skoda's size, domestic privatization simply was not an option. And because Czechoslovakia's public sector had comprised 98 percent of all firms, the reformers were looking for as fast and irrevocable a break with the past as possible. While virtually all reformers agreed on the overall objective, they disagreed about the means. Some favored direct sales and public auctions; others emphasized the advantages of new forms of privatization such as employee buy-outs or management buy-outs; still others argued in favor of a voucher scheme organized by state investment funds. In the end the federal Czechoslovak government settled on a three-step process of privatization. First, within a few years most of the small, state-owned firms were to be auctioned off; in the case of the Czech Republic this meant that more than 90 percent of these small firms would be sold within three years. Second, large companies were either sold directly to the public or joint ventures were formed with foreign companies. Between 1990 and 1995, for example, foreign firms invested $5.8 billion in the Czech economy.[1] Finally, and most important, Czechoslovakia decided on a process of voucher privatization. The five rounds of the first wave were implemented in 1992 prior to the country's breakup. This program aimed at the privatization of large firms valued at 166.5 billion Czechoslovak crowns. The program relied on both direct (12.3 billions crowns in 1992) and indirect sales (through the issuing of individual vouchers). In addition, as part of the small-scale privatization program, 9,306 of 11,420 economic units were successfully auctioned off. This resulted in total sales of 14.1 billion CSK, two billion more than the original offering price. In 1994 the Czech Republic followed through with a second privatization wave. In the first round of voucher privatization each adult citizen had received for a thirty-five dollar fee, coupons nominally worth one thousand dollars which he or she could use to purchase shares in hundreds of former state-owned firms.[2] In all, state-owned companies valued at ten billion dollars, or 70 to 80 percent of the public sector, were thus transferred into private hands within a few years.[3]

Though motivated primarily by economics, VW's acquisition of a large stake in Skoda has had substantial economic and political consequences. In the early 1990s Skoda produced 190,000 to 220,000 cars annually, 100,000 for export markets, about 7 percent of total Czech exports. Employing between 17,000 and 19,000 workers, the main Skoda enterprise is the heart of Czech's formidable industry. Because Skoda is tied to hundreds of subcontractors, German influence in the Czech economy is actually wider than the investment and employment figures, impressive though they are, might

---

1. Hana Písková, "Příme zahranicni investice vzrostly" ["Direct Foreign Investment Increased"], *Hospodářske noviny* [*Economic News*] (1 March 1996): 7.

2. In the second wave, which occurred in the Czech Republic in 1994, citizens received coupons worth nominally seven hundred dollars.

3. Most Czechs placed their coupons with investment funds which received 70 percent of the coupons in the first round, 60 percent in the second.

suggest. VW is one of the leading German corporations with mixed public-private ownership. As Simon Reich's study demonstrates, both before World War II and after, VW was strongly supported by quite different German regimes.[4] Furthermore, the joint venture linking VW to Skoda is one of the biggest investment projects in central Europe. German corporate interests thus have a strong impact on economic developments in the Czech Republic, affecting both specific decisions and broader policies of the Czech government.

In 1990 state-owned Skoda was running an annual deficit in excess of 150 million dollars and lacked the capital to invest in the necessary modernization of its production facilities.[5] For these reasons the government decided to look for a strong foreign partner who would promise to take a long-term perspective.[6] The Czech government insisted that the partner corporation protect the Skoda trademark, retain final assembly of cars in the Czech Republic, employ about 19,000 Czech workers, and transfer technology.[7]

In the late spring of 1990 eight companies were interested in a collaboration with Skoda: BMW, Citroen/Peugeot, Fiat, GM, Mitsubishi, Subaru, Renault/Volvo, and VW.[8] The Czech government hired Price Waterhouse Privatization Services to help choose a foreign corporation that would set up a joint venture operation with Skoda. In the end the choice narrowed down to two firms: VW and Renault-Volvo.

Both companies committed themselves to an annual production of 380,000 to 440,000 cars. They agreed to substantial technology transfer and staff training. And while the total investment figures differed only slightly (16 billion Frs for VW as compared to thirteen billion Frs for Renault), VW was interested in acquiring majority control (51 percent or more) of Skoda while Renault proposed to become a minority partner (40 percent). In some ways the Renault bid was less intimidating. Through the provisions of an

4. Simon Reich, *The Fruits of Fascism: Postwar Prosperity in Historical Perspective* (Ithaca and London: Cornell University Press, 1990), pp. 147–201.

5. Estimates of the deficit vary between a low of about 2.5 billion Czechoslovak crowns (Kčs) and a high of about 7 billion Kčs. For the low-end estimates see Peter Dedek in *Mladá fronta Dnes* (Young Front Today), (16 March 1991) and Zdeněk Kadlec in *Svobodné slovo* (Free Word), (16 November 1991). For the high-end estimate see *Mladá fronta Dnes* (Young Front Today), (23 March 1990). Decisive for the joint venture was the fact that VW promised to pay in three installments a total of about 3.6 billion Kčs. See *Lidové noviny* (People's News), (12 June 1991).

6. A Strategic Profile of Skoda. EIU International Motor Business (October 1990), pp. 31–47.

7. Jaroslav Šimek, *Rudé právo* (Red Right), (22 August 1990 and 24 October 1990).

8. Karel Hrubes, *Signál* (1991).

independent partnership of Skoda, Renault, and Volvo, it promised to insulate the managerial decisions affecting Skoda from the influence of decisions taken in France.

Several factors, however, spoke for VW: a similarity between Czech and German technical norms and the technical similarity between Skoda's Favorit and VW's Golf;[9] a shorter distance between Mlada Boleslav and Wolfsburg (400 km) than Paris (1,100 km); the better reputation of VW among Czech trade unions; more generous provisions for employment and social security of workers; a smaller language barrier, as more Czechs know German than French; and, compared to France, a greater cultural similarity between Germany and the Czech Republic.

Two factors proved decisive in VW's selection. VW's perfectionism and its strong interest in Skoda's operations, evident in many details, was an important factor. From the very beginning of the bidding, the VW team took an active interest in the managerial staff of Skoda company, in talking to trade union leaders, in meeting with suppliers, and in making itself available to Czech journalists. VW's proposal was also more precise than Renault's and changed very little from the first version to the last.

Second, there was the fact that the new Czech leadership, and most of the Czech citizens, did not believe in a self-transformation of Skoda's management and workforce. Forty or fifty years of a deficient and unsuccessful socialist economy had left deep traces in the work processes and in the attitudes of workers. Linked through an invisible net with old allies posted throughout the Czech economy, the old Skoda managers might not have been sufficiently disrupted by the approach that Renault was proposing. The new political elite preferred VW because it planned to shake up Skoda's old corporate structure. To achieve economic success and a far-reaching transformation of the corporation's way of operating, a marked change in Skoda's standard operating procedures was needed in addition to the changes in investment and technology that would be brought about by a change in ownership. In brief, while there were some areas in which the offer made by Renault was superior to that of VW, on balance, VW was more attractive.

In a letter signed by former Czech Prime Minister Petr Pithart the Czechoslovak government committed itself on 28 March 1990 to a number of concessions that were eventually included as an

9. As early as 1988 Czechoslovak managers had started preliminary negotiations with VW about some cooperation between Skoda and VW. See *Road & Track* 39, 9 (May 1988): 120.

appendix to the agreement reached in December 1990.[10] Specifically, the government granted a two-year tax holiday to the company and, thereafter, agreed to a 40 percent ceiling on the tax rate it could charge; it offered a number of investment tax credits (17 percent annually for machinery for the first three years and 6 percent annually for buildings and constructions for the first five years); it committed itself to zero tariffs on the import of automobile parts subsequently re-exported (thus meeting VW's new strategy of relying world-wide on one frame for all cars within the same class produced by VW, Audi, Seat, and Skoda, while using engines and other high-tech parts produced in plants around the world); it granted VW unrestricted powers to set prices for cars and all services (with the only possible exception being the misuse of VW-Skoda's monopoly position); and it agreed to a 19 percent minimum tariff levied for four years on cars imported to Czechoslovakia as well as to additional taxes impairing car imports. Since signing the agreement, the Czech government has met all of these conditions.

VW maintained its end of the bargain only with respect to the purchase price. In a document not available to the public, the Czech government and the VW-Skoda Group agreed in writing to a set of conditions that governed the joint venture.[11] VW committed itself to investing a total of 1.2 billion DM in three separate installments, in 1991, 1994, and 1995. The first installment of 300 million DM bought VW a 31 percent stake of the stocks in the joint venture in 1991. At the same time, VW paid 120 million DM to the Czech state to help cover some of Skoda's outstanding debts. In 1994 VW paid an additional 350 million DM for another 19.5 percent of stock and a 50.5 percent majority ownership of Skoda-VW; it paid another forty million DM to cover additional Skoda debts owed to the government. In the third installment VW paid a final 350 million DM in 1995 to round off its ownership of the Skoda-VW Group at 70 percent. In addition, the new majority owner paid back the final outstanding debt of forty million DM.[12]

But on most issues other than price VW has modified the initial agreement it had signed. A feasibility study frequently mentioned

10. An unofficial version of the agreement was published eventually in 1991. See *Lidové noviny* (31 May 1991).

11. Because publicly available materials about the agreement between VW and Skoda and between the Skoda-VW Group and the Czech Republic are scarce, this research rests on a close reading of newspaper articles. In addition we conducted five interviews with managers of the Skoda-VW Group, and relied on the information provided by two papers written by students of Charles University.

12. *Lidové noviny* (12 June 1991).

in the negotiations by all participants, usually without citation, set VW's anticipated total investment in Skoda by the year 2000 at nine billion DM.[13] That figure was revised downward to seven billion DM in 1992.[14] After Ferdinand Piech had become president of VW in 1993, and José Lopez, with his innovative methods of cost cutting, had moved from Detroit to Wolfsburg, VW's new top management sharply cut back its proposed investment in Skoda. In September 1993, one day before payment was due, VW withdrew a scheduled loan of 1.4 billion DM to Skoda. Some reduction in VW's investment was quite reasonable, as the recession of the early 1990s had lowered the cost of investment by perhaps as much as 30 percent. Then too, VW's profitability had deteriorated greatly by 1993. Hence a new plan, unveiled in the first days of December 1993, revised VW's total investment downward to only about 3.7 billion DM.[15] The chairman of the Foundation of National Ownership, Tomas Jezek, at that time the owner of 69 percent of stocks in the Skoda-VW Group, and Vladimir Dlouhy, secretary of the Ministry for Business and Industry, were not consulted on this decision, provoking each to proclaim in public that the Czech delegation would dispute Piech's interpretation of a clause in the written agreement. It was in fact only in September 1993 that it was made clear to the Czech public that, because VW had never signed any documents mentioning any concrete sums, all of VW's investment plans had never been binding. However, as Czech officials pointed out at the time, this sharp reduction in VW's investment risked endangering critically important parts of Skoda's modernization program. The promise of developing locally a new car and a completely new engine for Skoda and VW cars and the expectation that new factories for the production of cars and engines would be built in the Czech republic could not be met with a 50 percent curtailment in VW's overall investment.[16]

The number of cars that VW-Skoda would produce was also affected by VW's unilateral cutback. Several months after acquiring a majority stake in Skoda, Piech discussed his plans in 1994, mentioning that Skoda would eventually produce "more than 300,000

13. The sum oscillates between 8.3 and 10.0 billion DM. See *Mladá fronta Dnes* (Young Front Today) (24 and 27 October 1990 and 7 July 1991); *Lidove noviny* (12 December 1990); *Hospodarske noviny* (Economic News) (29 November 1991); *Rudé právo* (Red Right) (27 May 1991); *Svobodné slovo* (Free Word) (16 November 1991).

14. *Finance East Europe* (23 September 1993) 3, 18, pp. 2–3.

15. News broadcast by the Czech television show "Deník ČT" (16 December 1993).

16. *Süddeutsche Zeitung* (23 October 1994). *The Financial Times* (17 December 1993). *Handelsblatt* (30 November 1993). *Frankfurter Allgemeine Zeitung* (22 July 1994).

cars in the late nineties."[17] This figure became a new basis for discussion between the Czech government and VW in the fall of 1994. An appendix to the initial VW-Skoda agreement was signed in December 1994. In it the Czech government did not insist on either the development of a new engine or the promised production capacity of 400,000 to 440,000 cars by 1997. The appendix set the production target at about 340,000 cars, and made no promises that a new engine would be developed in the Czech Republic or that a new engine plant would be built. Lower investment figures, lower production capacities, no new engine plants; all of these point to an enhanced structural dependency of Skoda and the Czech Republic on VW.

Between 1990 and 1993 a series of episodes illustrated the asymmetry in the bargaining power of VW-Skoda and the Czech state. A deterioration in the demand for automobiles prompted the company not only to lay off some foreign workers but to win from the government new tax cuts for itself and additional tax increases on imported cars. On the grounds that the company was exploiting its monopoly position, the Federal Office for Economic Competition attempted to contain price increases of Skoda cars sold in Czech markets. But the Skoda-VW Group prevailed in this conflict; compared to 1990, by the end of 1993 prices had more than doubled. For the same reason the Office for Economic Competition attempted to reduce by nearly 50 percent the tariffs levied on imported cars (from 19 to 10 percent). But VW-Skoda prevailed in this conflict as well, arguing that increasing imports might endanger its shrinking investment program and the jobs of thousands of workers. Backed by the relatively strong Czech unions, workers struck unsuccessfully in September 1994 against company policy seeking to reduce staff working outside of the direct production process. Yet no change in personnel policy occurred that honored the company's agreement to guarantee employment for 19,000 Czech workers. And unaffected by the protests of existing distributors both at home and abroad, VW created a brand-new distribution network for Skoda cars. Finally, despite this series of victories, the potential veto power of the Czech minority owner of VW-Skoda, guaranteed until the year 2000, may well be nullified by the German majority owner's option to buy, as it did with Spain's SEAT, the rest of Skoda.[18]

17. *Süddeutsche Zeitung* (23 October 1994).
18. *The Financial Times* (17 December 1993).

The structural dependency of the Czech state in its dealings with VW is also illustrated by the experience of producers of automobile parts. As is true in other states, the Czech automobile industry occupies a central position in industry. Hundreds of suppliers manufacturing parts and components for cars depend on the central automobile producer around which they cluster. Thus VW-Skoda profoundly affects Czech industry in general. As the biggest car producer in the Czech Republic, Skoda had 429 suppliers in September 1993. Of these, 269 (63 percent) were Czech, thirty-nine (9 percent) were Slovak and 121 (28 percent) were foreign. More than 60,000 workers were employed by the more than 300 Czech and Slovak Skoda suppliers, accounting for about 3.5 percent of the work force in the Czech Republic and Slovakia.[19]

Among the foreign firms participating in joint ventures in Czechoslovak industry, German firms accounted for 35 percent of the total in June 1992. In sharp contrast, among Skoda's foreign suppliers, 71 percent (not including Slovak firms) were German in September 1993. Limitations in the available data make it impossible to draw strong inferences from these data. But the great difference between the figure for Czech industry and the Czech automobile industry suggest a strong German influence in the latter (see Table 4.1).

This influence will grow as VW-Skoda moves to a "just-in-time" production system that will come on line with the completion of an industrial park near the central production line in Mlada Boleslav. Suppliers will build (or supply), at their own cost, shops that produce parts for Skoda cars. This rearrangement of the production process is likely to lower somewhat VW's future investment in Skoda. Significantly, strong opposition by German unions has made it impossible for VW to adopt this organization of production in Germany.[20] It is probable that the new system will lead to an increase in the Czech suppliers' dependence on Skoda-VW and also on VW.

In their speeches, VW and Skoda managers frequently mention that they will support Skoda suppliers and that VW-Skoda expects high-quality components and an effective collaboration with strong, high-tech foreign firms. In the attempt to upgrade the quality of production, VW-Skoda puts some of its suppliers in direct contact with foreign firms, many of them German. Closer collaboration between Czech part suppliers and such foreign

19. Press Information Skoda, a.a.s., Public Relations.
20. *Frankfurter Allgemeine Zeitung* (24 March 1994).

Table 4.1 FOREIGN PRESENCE IN CZECH INDUSTRY AND IN THE CZECH
AUTOMOBILE INDUSTRY

Country of Partner	Czechoslovak Joint Ventures		Skoda Foreign Suppliers	
	Frequency	Percent	Frequency	Percent
Germany	29	34.9	86	71.1
Austria	12	14.5	7	5.8
France	8	9.6	5	4.1
Italy	3	3.6	9	7.4
Benelux	3	3.6	3	2.5
EU-other	6	7.2	3	2.5
West Europe	12	14.5	4	3.3
East Europe	1	1.2	4	3.3
USA	8	9.6	0	0.0
Other	1	1.2	0	0.0
Total	**83**	**100.0**	**121**	**100.0**

Source: Czechoslovak Joint Ventures, June 1992; List of Skoda-VW suppliers,
Press Information Skoda, a.a.s., Public Relations (September 1993).

TABLE 4.2 LINKS BETWEEN SKODA SUPPLIERS AND FOREIGN PARTNER
FIRMS (OCTOBER 1993)

Country of Partner Firm	Frequency	Percent
Germany	33	60.0
Austria	4	7.3
France	3	5.5
Italy	2	3.6
Benelux	1	1.8
EU-other	4	7.3
West Europe	2	3.6
East Europe	0	0.0
USA	5	9.1
Other	1	1.8
Total	**55**	**100.0**

Source: Mail questionnaire to all 269 Czech suppliers of the Skoda-VW Group,
with a response rate of about 60 percent (160 Czech suppliers responded).

firms enhances the structural dependence of the Czech automobile industry on foreign and German firms, especially when business conditions are poor. There is some evidence for the growth of
such dependence. About 60 percent of Skoda's part suppliers have
links with foreign and German partner firms (see Table 4.2). Furthermore, in February 1991 the VW-Skoda Group organized a conference in which forty-seven firms, traditionally closely linked to

VW, and 115 Skoda suppliers took part.[21] Among the suppliers operating with German partners, eight of thirty-three (or 24 percent) had established links only after 1991. This figure is larger in both absolute and relative terms than the corresponding figure for suppliers collaborating with non-German foreign firms (four out of twenty-two or 18 percent). VW has committed itself to supporting the Czech suppliers of Skoda. The Czech automobile industry, following the VW-Skoda link-up, is rapidly moving into Germany's economic orbit.

The Privatization and Internationalization of the Media

Before the Velvet Revolution Czechs had only very limited opportunities through which they could deviate from the state-imposed uniformity of the mass media. In early 1988 *Lidové noviny* (People's News)—a samizdat monthly—started its illegal publication. It drew attention to unjust political trials and the imprisonment of Czech and Slovak dissidents. And it provided uncensored commentary on current political events. Even though its editors, writers, and distributors were mercilessly persecuted, the paper's circulation grew steadily. The broadcasts of Radio Free Europe provided a second source of information not controlled by the Czech state. Emigrants and others, some of them drawn from the ranks of domestic dissidents, prepared programs adjusted to the needs of Czech and Slovak listeners. The Voice of America, the BBC, and other foreign radio stations provided important alternative sources of international news, culture, and music, which counteracted the distorted information provided by domestic media. Foreign television broadcasting, and in later years, satellite broadcasts, had an indirect influence. Rather than providing political information, they showed new movies and offered a "window on the West"—images of the evolving way of life on the other side of the Iron Curtain.

But these were exceptions. The rule was a state-controlled Czechoslovak media complex. At the end of 1989 Czech society inherited from its authoritarian past a media structure adapted to the need for politically controlling the information reaching all readers, viewers and listeners. Thus it also inherited a large army

21. *Pravda* (Truth) (21 February 1991); *Zemědělské noviny* (Countryside News) (21 February 1991); *Rudé právo* (19 March 1991).

of producers and censors who, in the name of the Communist Party, subjected all mass media to strict political supervision. In collaboration with other state bodies, the secret police repressed most efforts to implement freedom of speech and freedom of the press. Czech society, for the most part, lived behind an information "Iron Curtain."

The process of transforming the Czech media after 1989 can be described, in its main features, as the composite of two linked processes: democratization and privatization, and commercialization and internationalization. This section offers an overview of these two processes before presenting illustrative evidence drawn from the privatization of television and the print media, including the regional press.

Overview

In the first phase after 1989 press censorship was abolished and so was the leading role of the Communist Party. *Lidové noviny* appeared once, and then twice, weekly, and later in the spring of 1990 it became a daily newspaper. Civic Forum initiated the publication of *Občanský deník* (Civic Daily). The publication of other dailies, weeklies, and monthlies followed in rapid succession with variable commercial success. The influence of democratization and privatization was apparent almost immediately. Dozens of new magazines appeared with the most varied thematic orientations and readerships. Among these, a conspicuous place was taken by erotic magazines, small-ad periodicals, and Czech versions of international magazines. Besides the Czech newspapers and magazines published for Bohemia and Moravia and the Slovak productions for Slovakia, a range of regional periodicals also began to be published.

In 1990 state organizations and established political parties owned the overwhelming majority of newspapers and periodicals published in Czechoslovakia. Private publishers were at a disadvantage. They typically lacked sufficient capital, as well as editorial skills and production facilities to be competitive. Foreign foundations and publishers provided some assistance, but compared to the assets of formerly Communist publishing ventures these were plainly inadequate. Some of the established, formerly Communist papers transformed themselves quickly and successfully. One of the first to do so was *Mladá fronta* (Young Front), the publishing house of the Association of Czechoslovak Youth, a stalwart supporter of the Communist Party. A group of sixty editors founded a joint-stock company and began to publish their own daily *Mladá fronta Dnes* (Young Front Today). As the name *Mladá fronta* in the newspaper's title gradually grew smaller and the name "Dnes" (Today) grew larger, the paper became a reputable news daily read by a wide cross section of Czech society.

Individual dailies created profiles for themselves as either general newspapers with a broad readership or as tabloids: popular-style publications for undemanding readers. *Mladá fronta Dnes* (Young Front Today) is unambiguously a general newspaper but so too is the more critical but respected *Rudé právo* (Red Right) as well as the dailies *Práce* (Work) and *Večerník Praha* (Evening Prague). *Lidové noviny* attracts more educated readers interested in editorials and commentary on political events. Businessmen and economists following in detail changes in the financial market and news of the economy make up a large proportion of the readers of *Hospodářské noviny* (Economic News). *Svobodné slovo* (Free Word) already had an established readership made up of the middle levels of the middle and older generation. The popular tabloid press is divided between indiscriminate critics of the current regime, a category to which two new tabloids *Špígl* (Mirror) and *Český Expres* (Czech Express) clearly belong, and friends of "light" reading, represented by the color-printed *Blesk* (Lightning). Other dailies extend the range of print media offered to Czech consumers. The full-sized *Lidové noviny* (People's News) and *Občanský deník*, which later succeeded as *Český deník*, specialize in criticism of the current government from the Right and provide readers with daring but not always properly verified information about Czech political and social life. *Haló noviny* (Hello News), published by the Communists, fulfills the role of a left-wing, critically oriented paper. *Český sport* (Czech Sport), understandably, has its traditional readership. The autumn of 1994 saw the launching of the brand-new weekly, *Týden* (Week), whose spiritual father, Karel Hvížďala, in exile during the 1980s, was one of the founders of the private *Mladá fronta Dnes* and then one of the journalists writing for the ever-popular *Mladý svět* (Young World).

But dailies also disappeared. *Telegraf* (Telegraph) and *Metropolitan* were two new dailies which later merged into one—*Metropolitní telegraf* (Metropolitan Telegraph), which then failed. After its demise, a new daily—*Denní telegraf* (Daily Telegraph)—made its appearance. The daily *Prostor* (Space) came out in large format for less than a year. In addition, the transformed *Večerník Praha* (Evening

Prague) was challenged in the evening market by *Dobrý večerník* (Good Evening News). Additional casualties have included *Lidová demokracie* (People's Democracy), the traditional paper of the Czechoslovak People's Party that was later sold to the Czech publisher Fidelis Schlée; the large-format dailies *Prostor* (Space) and *Metropolitan;* and, at the end of 1994, *Český deník* (Czech Daily), the paper which had emerged from the transformation of *Občanský deník* with the help of the Czech publisher Josef Kudláček. The weeklies *Reportér, Tvorba* (Creation), and *Kmen* (Tribe), along with the monthly *Přítomnost* (The Present), have also all gone under, while the weekly *Tvar* has become a bi-weekly publication.

While the reorganization of print media was affected by the functioning of markets, the licensing of television and radio stations was politically less simple. An independent "Radio and Television Broadcasting Board" was set up on 21 February 1992 (Czech National Council Law no. 103) as an "independent body" existing outside the government's jurisdiction though under parliamentary control. Parliament elects the ten board members who report annually on the board's activities. Parliament can dissolve the board only under specific conditions. After it had granted the first licenses for national television broadcasting, the Board became the center of a sharp political controversy that had been initiated particularly by those who had backed unsuccessful proposals and who sought to curtail the board's power. Even though the chairman of the board was replaced three times over just a few months, attempts to influence or intimidate the board and to roll back its independence proved to be unsuccessful. After a year's preparation the first private television station with a complete program structure and news service in any post-Communist European state, *Nova*, began operations.

Radio broadcasting was marked by a proliferation of new stations. Several dozen new radio companies started broadcasting and competed for the favor of listeners and advertisers. Most broadcast regionally. Three of them—Radio Alfa, RG Evropa 1, and Radio Echo—were granted national licenses. Because it had previously enjoyed a monopoly status as the state radio station, and because it had very uncertain financial prospects, the board put out of business the established station, *Radiožurnál* (Radiojournal), traditionally listened to by a majority of the older generation.

Achieving competitive conditions in television and radio broadcasting has proved difficult. Changes in legislation and the liberalization of advertising led to a spontaneous process of commercialization in the programming of both private and public television and radio stations. This has been a source of controversy. Financed from concessionary fees, public television has been accused of adjusting its programming to the wishes of advertisers. Critics are demanding a prohibition of advertising on public television, at least during prime viewing times.[22]

The inflow of foreign capital into Czech media markets was slower and occurred on a smaller scale than in automobiles. Nevertheless, foreign firms have shown a growing interest in Czech print media and have also played an important role in the privatization of Czech television. Questions of editorial "independence" have been resolved for the most part by agreements between the owner, who takes care of the commercial side of the newspaper, and an "independent" editor-in-chief and his or her team who are not subject to interference by the newspaper owner. It remains to be seen to what extent this division of responsibilities will be respected in the future during unforeseen or unusual situations.

Besides investment, foreign companies also bring the technical "know-how" that Czech publishers and producers lack. Reuters, for example, has brought not only its capital but its style of work, its high degree of professionalism, its training programs for Czech journalists, its study visits abroad, and other benefits. A long-time owner of *Mladá fronta Dnes* (Young Front Today), the French MAFRA has introduced computer type-setting. The Swiss concern Ringier has offered its wealth of experience in publishing to *Lidové noviny*, *Československý profit* (Czechoslovak Profit), *Blesk* (Lighting), and other papers and magazines. The German concern Passauer Neue Presse is introducing new methods that enhance the national and international content of the Czech regional press while also increasing the regional content of national newspapers. Four companies, Labe in northern Bohemia, Vltava in southern and western Bohemia, and PNP in eastern Bohemia, prepare the common element for several regional papers; district editorial offices then augment their dailies with local news and regional advertising. Thus regional dailies maintain a regional form and content while sharing the cost of foreign and national news reporting.

22. Advertising's share in broadcasting has been smaller than in Western European or American television markets. Until 1993 Czech television viewers were not used to the interruption of films or television productions by advertising breaks. Claiming that advertising is its sole source of revenue, the private television station Nova will begin advertising in the middle of films, although these commercials will be brief.

Privatizing Television

In December 1992 the Czech National Council decided to permit a privatization of one of the two national television channels. The Radio and Television Broadcasting Board immediately announced the procedures it would adopt for assigning the license. In all twenty-six applications were submitted. The supposed front-runners in this lucrative race were companies belonging to Czech "millionaires," such as Art Production K, owned by Michael Kocáb, the former rock star and post-November deputy, and Bonton, belonging to the musician Martin Kratochvíl. Other applicants included a company supported by the Czech film industry, the operators of a successful Prague regional television station *Premiéra*, and a company founded by the new team from the former federal Czechoslovak Television.

The deadline for the acceptance of applications, which were required to provide information on financial backing, program structure, and the anticipated participation of Czech producers in television broadcasting was 20 January 1993. After a week of public hearings in January 1993, the board immediately granted the license to CET 21 (Central European Television for the twenty-first Century) in an attempt to forestall political pressures. The victorious company was backed by Czech-American capital and led by the screen writer and manager Vladimír Železný in addition to a sociologist, a political scientist, an economist, two film-makers, and a successful television journalist. American capital, represented by an international consortium, the Central European Development Corporation, was organized by Mark Palmer, a former diplomat in the Reagan administration.

The decision to grant the license instantaneously became a major political issue. The strongest of the governing political parties—the ODS (The Civic Democratic Party)—declared it politically dangerous. The political significance of this privatization was emphasized by several chairmen of parliamentary clubs and committees, the minister for economic competition, and the minister of foreign affairs. Prime Minister Klaus called the license allocation an "unbelievably strange decision."[23] In contrast, the U.S. Ambassador, Adrian Basora, reacted positively to the decision.[24] President Václav Havel expressed in public his surprise at the criticisms.[25]

23. *Lidová demokracie* (People's Democracy) (5 February 1993).
24. *Lidové noviny* (5 February 1993).
25. *Český deník* (Czech Daily), "Havel o CET21" (Havel on CET21) (9 February 1993).

The Radio and Television Broadcasting Board drew public criticism for a number of reasons. At the time of holding its public hearings on granting the license for a second television channel, the board was incomplete. With the division of Czechoslovakia the mandate of three of its members had expired. Moreover, the board decided on the license almost immediately after the conclusion of the public hearings. While it was within the board's power to do so, none of the interested parties had expected this and expressed strong, public criticisms.

The executive vice-president of the governing Civic Democratic Party (ODS), Petr Čermák, expressed an entirely unambiguous opinion on the political significance of the decision. He said that he could not "... reconcile himself to the fact that the license for national television broadcasting had been given to a foreign company with a management that included a former leading representative of a state that had broken away from the Czech Republic, a representative of Hungarians and a representative of a movement defeated in the elections."[26] He expressed the fear that the station would establish anti-Slovak and anti-Hungarian broadcasting on the territory of the Czech Republic.[27] The other political parties abstained from sharp comments, and a number of deputies, even from the ODS, supported the board's decision.[28] Throughout February, March, and much of April 1993 Czech newspapers were filled with commentary on the entire affair.

Two months after the granting of the license, the second round of the struggle for the control of the media took place. But this time it was not a license that was the focus. Instead, a political war about the integrity of the licensing board broke out. Parliament debated the second version of a previously rejected annual report. The board's very existence was at stake, as were the positions of most of its members. The chairman, Daniel Korte, had to defend the board's activity. Three groups that had bid for the television license unsuccessfully claimed that three members of the board had demanded bribes. Claim was opposed by counter-claim. But the parliamentary hearings did establish that some members of

26. *Lidové noviny*, "Revize televizní license?" (Revision of the Television License?) (4 February 1993).

27. *Rudé právo*, "ODS: Rozhodnutí Rady je politicky nebezpečné" (ODS: Decision of the Board is Politically Dangerous) (2 February 1993).

28. *Mladá fronta Dnes* (Young Front Today), "Přidělení license nelze zpochybnit" (The allocation of the license is beyond reproach) (2 February 1993); *Rudé právo*, "Podle poslanců Rada rozhodla regulérně" (According to deputies board decided by regular methods) (2 February 1993).

the board had repeatedly met with applicants in the licensing proceedings.[29] *Lidové noviny*, in two lengthy articles, presented evidence of attempts to influence members of the board.[30] According to these articles, the board's chairman, Daniel Korte, was invited to a personal meeting with the secretary of then Federal Minister of the Interior, Petr Čermák, and to a short conversation directly with Petr Čermák. The discussion concerned the allocation of the license for regional radio broadcasting in the Liberec area. By coincidence, both of the high civil servants were partners in one of the companies applying—EURO 1. On 27 May 1993 Daniel Korte resigned from the board. By the end of 1994, three chairmen had followed each other in quick succession: Oldřich Tomek, Jindřich Kabát, and Bohuslav Hanuš. In connection with the board's second annual report, the discussion of the need for a "media board" heated up once again in the spring of 1994. The board was dissolved, only to be immediately reelected.

In the end the allocation of the license to CET 21 for twelve years stood. The establishment of the Czech independent television company, which is the founder and operator of TV Nova, took place on 8 July 1993. The Czech Trustee Savings Bank (22 percent) and the Central European Development Corporation (CEDM - CME) (66 percent) became partners of CET 21 (12 percent).[31] Nova launched its transmission on 4 February 1994, little more than a year after it had been granted the broadcasting license. In its very first year it became a powerful competitor to the public station Czech Television. Research undertaken by GfK-AISA, a consortium of independent companies, showed that by October 1994 Nova had emerged as the most popular television channel with a 63.5 percent viewership as compared to Czech Television's 31.5 percent. Nova has its highest ratings among the young and the economically active; among teenage viewers it had three times the share of loyal viewers than that held by Czech Television (39 as compared to 14 percent). The data are

29. *Český deník*, "Korteho Rada bere úplatky?" (Does Korte's Board take bribes?) (14 April 1993); *Mladá fronta Dnes*, "Prokuratura bude šetřit možnou korupci v Korteho radě" (Procurer will investigate possible corruption in Korte's Board) (14 April 1993).

30. *Lidové noviny*, " Česká bramboračka (1) Skandály Rady pro rozhlasové a televizní vysílání: Koubek vs. NTS-TV1" [Czech Potato Soup (1) Scandals of the Board for Radio and TV Broadcasting: Koubek vs. NTS-TV1] (18 June 1993); and *Lidové noviny*, "Česká bramboračka (2) EURO 1" [Czech Potato Soup (2): EURO 1] (22 June 1993).

31. *Hospodářské noviny* (Economic News), "10 měsíců s Novou" (10 Months with Nova) (2 December 1994): 19.

testimony to the unambiguous success of the first commercial national television station in the whole post-Communist world.[32]

So far the television market has been characterized by national broadcasting offering a "complete-format" range of programs. There has also been plenty of interest in licenses for regional broadcasting for which the Radio and Television Broadcasting Board has followed a policy of encouraging "networks" in which all stations follow a joint schedule. For example, the television station FTV Premiéra, until now the regional television for Prague and the surrounding area of central Bohemia, provides the bulk of programming to regional stations which augment it with their own regional three- to four-hour broadcasts. Some regional television companies that are still waiting for licenses have condemned these conditions; they claim that the short regional transmission time will not generate enough revenue from advertisers.[33]

Satellite transmission of television programs offers an additional venue. After public hearings, the board awarded satellite licenses to three of the ten candidates: Art Production K, CET 21 and FTV Premiéra.[34] They are negotiating conditions of transmission with the operators of Astra, Eutelsat, and other satellites. The companies estimate a doubling of the percentage of Czech households (from 15 to 30 percent) that will be able to receive satellite television in the near future and expect to recover their investment in about eight to twelve years.

The political controversy over the competence—indeed the very existence—of the Radio and Television Broadcasting Board, the extensive campaign in the press, the discussion in parliament, the rejection of the board's annual report, the forced resignation of its chairman and subsequent further changes in leadership, have all illustrated the major political importance of the institution of mass media in a democratic polity. The board survived these controversies to act as a watchdog ensuring a plurality of voices in the media.

Internationalizing the Press

The appearance, after 1989, of a whole range of new periodicals, many of which later became dailies, signaled the coming of

---

32. Ibid.

33. *Mladá fronta Dnes*, "Regionální televize uvažují, že odmítnou license" (Regional Television Considers Refusing to Grant License) (26 November 1994): 3.

34. *Telegraf*, "Satelitní license byly přiděleny" (Satellite Licenses Allocated) (30 June 1994).

democracy. The internationalization of the press accelerated between 1992 and 1994. This tendency was expressed in the print media on both the national and the regional levels.

The privatization of print media opened the door to foreign investors as most publishers of dailies reorganized themselves as joint-stock or limited liability companies.[35] For example, *Mladá fronta* (Young Front) transformed itself into *Mladá fronta Dnes* (Young Front Today) and was published first by the Czech joint-stock company MAFRA, later with Czech-French capital participation, and finally with majority ownership belonging to the German company Rheinisch-Bergische Druckerei und Verlagsgesellschaft mbH. Some publications—*Práce* (Work), *Svobodné slovo* (Free Word) and *Čs. sport* (Czechoslovak Sport)—changed only the form of ownership; they are not published by Czech companies. Fidelis Schlée, a Czech businessman, acquired *Večerník Praha* (Evening Prague) and bought the daily *Lidová democracie* (People's Democracy) from the Czechoslovak People's Party. As owner of the Pragoprint company, he bought the evening paper *Večerník Praha*, reorganized it, and hired a new staff. However, in the summer of 1994 he ceased publishing *Lidová democracie* and handed it over, with all its subscribers, to Ringier, a Swiss concern, and the publisher of *Lidové noviny*.

The internationalization of the national press was marked by a high degree of public sensitivity that was illustrated by different scandals. These concerned, among others, the privatization of a printing and publishing house, the sale of shares in a freshly privatized daily, and the acquisition of a majority stake in some of the dailies by a foreign publisher.

The most important and earliest foreign investments came from the Swiss concern Ringier and the French group Hersant. By the autumn of 1992, Ringier already had bought the daily *Blesk* (Lightning) and held a majority share in one of the important Moravian dailies *Moravskoslezský den* (Morava-Silesia Day). Also, by that time, the French company Socpresse, a member of the

35. For example, a joint stock company was formed to publish *Lidové noviny*. The previously Communist *Rudé právo* retained its old name, but gradually changed its editorial staff, publisher, and character as a paper, putting more emphasis on news reporting. Josef Kudláček, who after his return from exile began to publish the very successful small-ad magazine *Annonce*, and transformed the debt-ridden *Občanský deník* into the right-wing *Český deník*. But repeated disputes between him and the staff, a diminishing print-run, a readership that was not very interesting to advertisers, and rising competition and costs made him in late 1994 replace the daily with a twice-weekly publication.

Table 4.3 READERSHIP AND OWNERSHIP OF THE DAILY PRESS IN THE CZECH REPUBLIC

1993 4th Quarter GfK	Readers 1993	Owner			% Foreign Owner-ship
		State 1992	State 1995	Company	
Blesk	22.3	CH	CH	Ringier	100
Mladá fronta Dnes	16.6	F	G	Rheinisch-Bergische	51
Rudé právo	10.7	Cz	Cz	Borgis a.s.	
Zemědělské noviny	6.5	G	G	Mittelrhein Vrlg.	65
Práce	5.0	Cz	Cz	DE DRA a.s.	
Svobodné slovo	4.7	Cz	Cz	Melantrich	
Hospodářské noviny	4.4	F-US-G	F-US-G	Euroexpansion	100
Svoboda	3.8	F	G		40*
Sport	3.6	Cz	Cz	Cs. sport s.r.o.	
Moravskoslezský den	3.2	CH	CH	Ringier	51
Plzeňský deník	3.0	Cz	G	Neue Passauer Presse	100
Expres	2.9	G	G	Mittelrhein Vrlg.	86
Český deník	2.8	Cz	x	Kudláček	
SD severočeský reg.deník	2.8	Cz-F	?	Logos + French capital	
Lidové noviny	2.7	Cz	CH	Ringier	51
Severočeské noviny	2.5	Cz	G	Neue Passauer Presse	100
Špígl	2.4	Cz	Cz	Froněk	
Večerník Praha	2.2	Cz	Cz	Schlée	
RT Rovnost	2.2	F	G	?	42*
Hradecké noviny	2.2	Cz	G	Neue Passauer Presse	100
Jihočeské listy	2.0	Cz	G	Neue Passauer Presse	100
Lidová demokracie	2.0	Cz	x	Schlée	
Haló noviny	1.3	Cz	Cz	Futura a.s.	
Dobrý večerník	1.0	x	G	AGR	51
Denní Telegraf	1.0	Cz	Cz	Dialog s.r.o.	

Source: "Zahraniční kapitál v denním tisku," Telegraf, 15 November 1993; "Prstenec kolem středu Cech," Práce [Work], 30 July 1993; "kdo co ovládal v tisku v roce 1992," esky deník [Czech Daily], 26 March 1993; "nejčtenější deníky: Blesk, MfD a Rudé právo," Rudé právo, 23 December 1993; "Nejčtenější deníky v Ceské republice: Blesk, MFD, RP a ZN noviny," Zemědělské noviny [Countryside News], 28 December 1993.

*The figure is a minimum estimate.

Hersant group, owned 49 percent of the daily *Mladá fronta Dnes* (Young Front Today)—the newspaper with the second largest readership and circulation in the country—and had also acquired three significant minority holdings: in the Ostrava newspaper *Svoboda* (Freedom), the *Brno Rovnost* (Equality), and in northern Bohemia's *SD Severočeský regionální deník* (Northern Bohemian Regional Daily).

In 1992 Czech publishers owned fifteen of the twenty-four papers with the highest circulation, and almost 40 percent of readers regularly read newspapers owned and published exclusively

TABLE 4.4 CHANGES IN THE OWNERSHIP OF CZECH DAILIES, 1992–95

Majority Ownership of Dailies	Czech	German	French	Swiss	Other	Total
1992 no. of titles	15	2	4	2	1	24
1992 % readers	28.1	9.4	25.4	25.5	4.4	
1995 no. of titles	8	10	1	3	1	23
1995 % readers	31.9	41.7	2.8	28.2	4.4	
Change in title nos.	-7	+8	-3	+1	0	-1
95/92 % readers	-16.2	+32.3	-22.6	+2.7	0.0	

Source: "Zahraniční kapitál v denním tisku," Telegraf, 15 November 1993; "Prstenec kolem středu Čech," Práce [Work], 30 July 1993; "Kdo co ovládal v tisku v roce 1992," Český deník [Czech Daily], 26 March 1993; "Nejčtenějsí deníky: Blesk, MfD a Rudé právo," Rudé právo, 23 December 1993; "Nejčtenějsí deníky v České republice: Blesk, MFD, RP a ZN noviny," Zemědělské noviny, 28 December 1993.

by Czech publishers. While German capital was involved in *Zemědělské noviny* (Countryside News) and in the tabloid *Expres* (Express), the readership of these papers accounted for less than 10 percent of the population.

The situation changed rapidly in the following years, as is illustrated by Tables 4.3 and 4.4. The French lost three dailies, among them the prestigious *Mladá fronta Dnes*. Two Czech dailies went under. And five changed ownership—Ringier moved into *Lidové noviny*, and the Bavarian concern Passauer Neue Presse acquired three groups of regional dailies. If we take into account the purchase of *Mladá fronta Dnes* from French owners by the Rheinisch-Bergische Druckerei und Verlagsgesellschaft, and of the *Ostrava Svoboda* and *Brno Rovnost* by German owners, together with the launching of the *Prague Dobrý Večerník* by AGR, a company with German majority holdings, the economic involvement of German investors in the Czech newspaper market rose from two to ten titles and the percentage of readership of these papers increased by more than 30 percent to 42 percent.

In the Czech Republic, the pattern of ownership has developed from the 100 percent Czech share of 1989, the 50 percent share in 1992, to a 33 percent share at the beginning of 1995. The long-term consequences of foreign control of the Czech media are likely to raise in the future difficult issues concerning both sovereignty and democracy.[36] The Czech government has emphasized the need for

36. *Český deník*, "Výprodej českého tisku" (Selling-Off the Czech Press) (3 September 1993).

the Czech Republic to remain attractive to foreign investors and remains, to all appearances, satisfied with the protection offered by an anti-monopoly law which does not make distinctions based on the national origin of capital.[37]

The issue of foreign takeovers is even more apparent in the case of the Czech regional press. Before November 1989, Czechoslovakia's regional press had barely survived. It lacked an adequate news-service base, advertising clientele, and professional management. It had no practical way of competing with the national press. Since 1990, however, foreign investors have introduced modern conceptions of how to publish regional papers that have central editorial offices for the coverage of foreign news and district editorial offices and regional reporters. The German company Passauer Neue Presse in particular has invested substantial amounts of capital to affect such changes. It has founded the publishing houses "Vltava Ltd." (south, west and, in part central Bohemia), "Labe Ltd." (north Bohemia), and "PN Press" (eastern Bohemia), all fully funded with Bavarian capital. It owns four printing presses in the Czech Republic and in some areas has acquired significant shares in distribution systems.[38] It has purchased, largely from urban or district authorities, local, district and regional papers, usually weeklies, which, with a few exceptions, had not been particularly successful. Within a few months it transformed many of these papers into dailies. In the south Bohemian and west Bohemian regions the papers owned by the Passauer Neue Presse encountered practically no competition.[39]

These regional mergers have permitted the Bavarian publisher to introduce the system of a common, basic daily with several local mutations. Currently this corporation owns, via individual companies, twenty regional dailies and weeklies, most of which are published in a few modified forms.

37. *Lidové noviny*, "Vydavatelé ani politici nejsou proti zahraničnímu kapitálu v českém tisku" (Neither Publishers nor Politicians are against Foreign Capital in the Czech Press) (21 July 1993); *Lidové noviny*, "Cizí kapitál v českém tisku" (Foreign Capital in the Czech Press) (22 July 1993); *Lidové noviny*, "Zahraniční kapitál v českém tisku" (Foreign Capital in the Czech Press) (23 July 1993); *Reflex* "Omyly ministra Bělehrádka. Je zahraniční kapitál v tisku opravdu nebezbečny?" [The Mistakes of Minister Bělehrádek. Is Foreign Capital in the Press really Dangerous?], no. 36 (1993).

38. *Mladá fronta Dnes*, "Ministr Bělehrádek chce zastavit expanzi bavorskych vydavatelů " (Minister Bělehrádek wants to stop the expansion of Bavarian publishers) (7 July 1993).

39. Ibid.

On 23 November 1992, an article in *Český deník* launched discussion on the Czech regional press and its Bavarian owners.[40] Subsequent press coverage detailed how the Passauer Neue Presse had obtained nearly 80 percent of the regional press in the Czech Republic.[41] At the beginning of 1993, *Lidové noviny* questioned the ease with which the Bavarian publisher had acquired a dominant share in the regional press in four of the five Czech regions. In defense, the business director of the Bavarian publisher stated in an interview about the original owner, Hans Kapfinger, that "he always wanted to support ordinary people, his readers, and it is in this spirit that his publishing house operates to this day. And this is also why we regarded it as our task to support your Civic Forum immediately after the revolution. I don't like to talk about it, but it should be said here. We supplied election posters for 250,000 deutschmarks for the first democratic elections in Czechoslovakia...."[42]

Because of this public debate, the Ministry for Economic Competition started an investigation in 1993 to determine whether the regional papers were violating provisions of the monopoly law by holding quasi-monopoly positions in their respective regions. The investigation concluded that three companies (Vltava, Labe, and Passauer Neue Presse) had failed to ask the Ministry to approve the merger of eleven of the screened periodicals. The three companies were ordered to fulfill this obligation. However, because the distribution of the publications was not limited to specific Czech regions, the Ministry found that the mergers had not resulted in monopolies. Thus the overall conclusion of the investigation was favorable for the Bavarian firm, and no further corrective measures have been taken.[43] Democratization and privatization have created very competitive conditions in the Czech media markets. This has drawn foreign and especially German investors who now dominate regional and national print media.

40. The article had the title "Tiskovy obchvat" (Press Out-Maneuver) and was signed by "Kateřina Rollová and the regional reporters of D."

41. For example, see the article entitled "Prstenec kolem středu Čech" (Ring around the Center of Bohemia), *Práce* (Work) (30 July 1993).

42. *Plzeňský deník* (Pilsen Daily) (12 January 1993). In an initialed article (pš) entitled "Kudy teče Vltava" (Where is Vltava Flowing?) published in the same paper, a journalist commented: "Is it possible that this part of the answer is an explanation of why "Vltava" so easily sailed past our anti-monopoly legislation in the last election period?" See *Lidové noviny* no. 10 (1993). Quotation according to *Výběr* (Selection) no. 5 (1993).

43. *Rudé právo*, "Fúze PN Press, Vltavy a Labe byly schváleny" (Fusion of PN Press, Vltava and Labe Approved) (19 February 1994).

The entry of foreign investors into the media markets of the post-Communist states in central Europe has followed a similar pattern elsewhere. German and Swiss capital can be found wherever there is a need for it in central and eastern Europe. "The growing power of capital is awakening distrust in Eastern European countries ... critics are now, 55 years after the outbreak of the Second World War, afraid of Germanization."[44]

The Czech Borderlands between Germany and Europe

The end of the Cold War opened frontiers in central Europe and renewed cross-border cooperation. Yet this process also made dormant problems reappear, and created new ones. Within newly-established international and transnational relations the post-Communist polities are experiencing domestic processes of economic transformation (including, in the initial stage, the privatization of public, cooperative, and municipal property and the restitution of illegally seized properties) and the building of democratic political institutions. The Western European states, specifically, adjusted to the rapid breakdown of the Soviet empire through a European integration strategy that was quickly broadened to encompass central-eastern Europe.[45]

Czechoslovakia confronted an acute internal problem after 1989 that illustrated the difficulties created by a relaxation in international tensions. Lacking the will to compromise on long-neglected political issues, the two parts of the federation parted—against the will of the majorities in both parts of the country. A public opinion poll conducted in November 1992 showed that 43 percent of Czech and 49 percent of Slovak respondents believed that the breakup was not inevitable, while 50 percent of the Czech and 40 percent of the Slovak respondents believed that it was

44. *Český deník*, quoting *Der Spiegel* 14/93, "Vydavatelé v Německu žasnou" (Publishers in Germany Astonished) (18 June 1993); *Hospodářské noviny* (Economic News), "Svoboda středoevropského tisku závisí na marce a franku" (The Freedom of the Central European Press Depends on the Mark and the Franc) (16 December 1994): 23.

45. See "Europa Potřebuse Novou Transformační Strategii pro Nové Demokracie" ["Europe Needs a Transformation Strategy for New Democracies"]—interview with Polish Minister for European Integration Krzysztof Bielecky and with Krzysztof Skubiszewsky *Mezinárodní politika* (*International Politics*) no. 4 (1993).

inevitable, with 7 percent of the Czech and 11 percent of the Slovak respondents professing not to know.[46]

Only time will tell whether the applause from international media for a civilized and nonviolent breakup of the country is sufficient compensation for the greater weakness of the two new states. The breakup has allowed the leadership in both countries to avoid complex internal disputes about the methods and forms of economic and social transformation. The partition strengthened the pragmatic right wing faction in the Czech republic, whose political leaders have pushed for a rapid economic transformation and prepared for close cooperation with Western Europe. They have tended to neglect more provisional, international groupings such as the Visegrad Group, discussed in this volume by Valerie Bunce in chapter 6.

In their initial euphoria, Czechoslovakia and the other post-Communist countries of central and eastern Europe looked to the West in hopes of generous assistance and early admission to the EU. They expected an inflow of foreign investments and an influx of new technologies, aid, and ready access to Western markets. But soon these countries came to recognize the harsh reality of market-oriented political economies. Investment occurred only in profitable ventures; technology transfer created unexpected competition; assistance was conditional; and exports encountered protective measures in sectors such as agriculture and steel. The road to Europe turned out to be complex, requiring large domestic changes and prolonged international negotiations.

Along with other post-Communist countries, the Czech Republic obtained associate status with the EU and in this capacity attended the December 1994 session of the European Council. Despite this milestone, the road to full membership, as is illustrated by the resolutions passed at that meeting, requires many compromises and much good will to invest in cooperative ventures. Specifically, countries such as the Czech Republic, kept on the waiting list to join the EU, are open to political pressure from strong EU members such as Germany. Czech observers are extremely sensitive on this score. For example, one sentence in the 1994 Government Policy statement that Chancellor Kohl delivered stated that "... it is in the interest of Germany and Europe to keep in mind first of all Poland in future expansion of the EU...."— without mentioning at the same time other countries. Despite

46. See Research Report of the Public Opinion Research Institute, Prague, November 1992.

diplomatic assurances, this formulation drew public attention and indignation in the Czech Republic. Czechs saw in Kohl's statement a signal that Germany might impose additional conditions before it would support Czech admission to the EU.

Such conditions, it is feared, may be related to the political agenda of Sudeten Germans who possess strong organization and intimate political ties to the CSU and thus to the political coalition governing in Bonn/Berlin. Such fears are not made of thin air. Specifically, the Bavarian Prime Minister, Edmund Stoiber (CSU), wanting to preempt a political challenge to his party from the Bavarian Right, has publicly gone on record that Bavaria will continue to defend the interests of the Sudeten Germans. A political issue that was apparently swept off the European agenda fifty years ago now threatens to create new problems for Czech-German relations and, possibly, Europe's wider international relations as well. Confronted with this prospect President Václav Havel stated in a speech delivered at Charles University on 17 February 1995 that "our republic will not discuss a revision of any of the results of World War II, and it will not tolerate any intervention in our constitutional order or accept any alterations in the course of history that would harm the present generation."[47]

The Sudeten German Issue

The core of the Sudeten German issue reaches deep into the history of the coexistence of Germans and Czechs on Czech territory. It cannot simply be reduced to the issue of the legality or illegality of the transfer of three million Germans from the Bohemian borderlands in the wake of the defeat of Fascist Germany. While it is difficult to cut arbitrarily into any national history, the period of National Revival in the late eighteenth century is an important watershed in modern Czech history.

Czech national liberation efforts did not aim at the liquidation of German influence. Rather, the main goal was to achieve equal linguistic, cultural, and social opportunities within the Habsburg Empire. The Germans, however, did their best to block all attempts at national emancipation and thus helped polarize the relationship between the two ethnic groups. Eventually the national resistance articulated claims for an independent Czech state.

With the defeat of Germany and Austria-Hungary in World War I, the domestic and foreign Czech resistance achieved diplomatic

47. *Rudé právo* (18 February 1995): 4.

recognition of a sovereign Czechoslovak Republic in 1918. Because it was a multi-ethnic state, however, the internal affairs of the new state were not without problems. Accounting for about one-third of the Czechoslovak population, Germans enjoyed the same civil rights as Czechs. They had their own political representatives, and six German political parties stood for parliamentary elections in 1920. The strongest of them, German Social Democracy, won 11.1 percent of the popular vote.[48] Nevertheless, Germans living in the Czechoslovak republic never lost a sense of bitterness and injustice after 1918. In 1920 the Czechoslovak Republic experienced dynamic economic growth, especially in the Czech lands. Despite the global economic crisis of the 1930s, the Czechoslovak Republic became one of the seven top economic powers in the world. Yet despite its economic strength and democratic credentials the first Czechoslovak Republic did not resolve its nationality problem. Germans living in Czech territory longed for their own state and undermined, directly or indirectly, most cooperative ventures with the Czechs. Their explicit goal was to tear off the Sudeten borderlands from Czechoslovakia.

Most Sudeten Germans had not welcomed the birth of the Czechoslovak Republic, and they did not forget the failed attempt to establish their own Deutsch-Böhmen (German-Bohemian) state in 1918. This memory was the main reason why a majority of the Germans accepted nationalist, even chauvinist, ideas spread from and by Germany. The attitudes of Sudeten Germans soured even more once Adolf Hitler and his Nazi Party seized power in Germany. The pro-Germany, Nazi Sudeten-German party won 15.2 percent of the Czechoslovak vote in the 1935 parliamentary elections, while the Social Democrats won only 3.6 percent.[49] The Sudeten-German Party received the support of 67.2 percent of the voters in the border regions which were mostly settled by ethnic Germans. It won forty-four seats in parliament, making it the largest political party in the Czechoslovak Republic at the time.[50] The crisis in Czech-German internal and external relations culminated with the Munich Agreement, in which France and Great Britain abandoned the Czechoslovak Republic to the mercy of Nazi Germany's plans for the creation of a Pan-German empire in Europe.

48. *Malý encyklopedický slovník* [*Small Encyclopedic Dictionary*] (Prague: Academia Praha, 1972), pp. 205–6.

49. Ibid., p. 206.

50. Karel Richter, *Sudety* (Prague: FAJMA, 1994), p. 84.

After the Munich Agreement, most Czech citizens left the borderlands. When the German army seized the remaining Czech
territory on 15 March 1939, the Czechoslovak Republic disintegrated. Nazi Germany created an independent Slovak Republic,
with a nationalistic and pro-German puppet government. A new
era of brutal oppression commenced under Nazi Germany's occupation regime.

Both expatriate and resident Czechs were active in the resistance, and most of the Czech population participated in measures
of passive resistance. The Czech struggle for freedom was paid for
with many lives. The casualties of war and Nazi cruelties, actively
promoted by many Sudeten Germans, generated a Czech hatred
for all things German. Even before Germany was defeated, the
Czechoslovak government-in-exile, headed by E. Beneš, in conjunction with the Allied powers, had concluded that it would be
necessary to transfer the ethnic German populations out of postwar Czechoslovakia, Poland, and Hungary. This plan was the
result of a world-wide mood of anti-fascism directed at Europe,
specifically, against Germany. In Czechoslovakia this plan reflected an anti-fascist hysteria that was grounded in the war experience that had led most Czechs to identify all Germans with
fascism and Nazism. The plan was carried out in many places
immediately and spontaneously at the end of World War II. This
"wild" transfer involved the greatest violence that Germans suffered at the hands of Czechs.

Attended by leaders from the U.S., the USSR, and Britain, the
Potsdam Conference legalized the transfer of the Sudeten Germans on 2 August 1945. The Potsdam Resolution stated that "the
above three governments consulted all possible aspects of this
issue and recognized that the transfer of German population or its
segments who remained in Poland, Czechoslovakia, and Hungary
to Germany must be carried out."[51] Most of the Sudeten German
population was transferred from Czechoslovakia to Germany
between 1945 and 1947. At the same time, the Czech population,
expelled by Germans in 1938, started to return to the borderlands,
where it was joined by new settlers. A new era had begun in the
Bohemian borderlands, and a purely Czech population in former
Sudetenland began forming.

---

51. *Documents of International Law and Politics*, vol. 1 (Prague: Ministry of Foreign
Affairs, Institute of Foreign Relations, 1963), p. 115.

The Bohemian Borderlands after 1945

Sudeten Germans constituted a majority in an area of about 27,000 square kilometers which was occupied and joined to Germany between 1 October 1938 and 8 May 1945. The frontiers of this area did not follow the territorial structure of the Czechoslovak Republic. Communities were affiliated and districts divided by the arbitrary criteria of the German invaders. Thus the Germans occupied 36.3 percent of the original Czechoslovak territory (32 percent of all communities). Depending on how this territory is defined precisely, the 1930 census shows a German population of 3.6 million (or 34.1 percent of the total Czechoslovak population), approximately 25 to 30 percent of which was Czech while about 72 percent was German.[52] In early May 1945, Czechs made up about 18 percent of the approximately 3.3 million inhabitants living in the Bohemian borderlands.[53]

Mass population movements to the borderlands started immediately after the end of World War II. The first to return were the Czechs expelled in 1938. Most of the new settlers (about 90 to 95 percent) arrived between 1945 and 1947 from the inland districts of the Czechoslovak republic. The strongest migration inflow took place between neighboring inland districts and border districts. About 5 percent of the settlers (about 115,000 persons) came from abroad. Most of them—about 40,000 individuals—had lived in Germany and Austria before 1 May 1945. These were mostly Czechs who had been forced to work in the German armaments industry. Over sixty-eight hundred new settlers had served in the Nazi army, and 7,714 persons had been held in concentration camps. The largest group of foreign Czechs was the Volhynia Czechs, who numbered 26,908. Other, smaller groups arrived from Poland, France, Bulgaria, Hungary, Yugoslavia, and the USSR, outside of Volhynia.[54] The new inhabitants brought different life styles, experiences, customs, and values to their new homes. They had to get acquainted with each other, accommodate themselves to the new setting, and create a new civic society.

---

52. See *Population, Economic and National Development in Border Districts of the Czechoslovak Republic from 1930 to 2010.* (Prague: Czechoslovak Ministry of Construction, 1989). Other sources, however, show that in these regions the share of the Czech population was lower.

53. See, for example, Tomáš Staněk, *Transfer of Germans from Czechoslovakia 1945–1947* (Prague: Academia and Nase vojsko, 1991), p. 54.

54. *Population, Economic and National Development,* p. 8.

The settlement of Bohemian borderlands slowed after 1947. Domestic population sources were exhausted, and inland jobs were plentiful. After the spontaneous mass settlement had terminated in late 1952, the borderland population numbered only about 2.3 million people, that is, only two-thirds of the level of 1930. Strong return migration to the inland regions also occurred after 1945. Some of the settlers had come for strictly material reasons, such as to gain property. At the first sign of trouble, however minor, they returned to their original homes. The process of return migration increased after February 1948 when the Communist Party seized power and initiated a nationalization program for agriculture and industry—something that was widely believed to have initiated an early liquidation of the service, trade, and small crafts sectors. The Cold War also adversely affected the formation of newly settled populations in the Bohemian borderlands. After 1948 the frontiers with West Germany and Austria were tightly closed, and the government set up a security border zone area. National security policy required large, new zones for military training and exercises; all this contributed to a reduction in the population and even to the outright destruction of many villages.

Communist attempts to develop the economic potential of the borderlands also contributed to demographic instability. Owing to the government's emphasis on heavy industry and energy, industrially and economically powerful northern and northwestern Bohemia and northern Moravia experienced a population boom. Other, less populated regions suffered from a decline in population, and the whole situation required governmental actions. An organized campaign seeking to complete the settlement of the Bohemian borderlands began in 1953. The government allocated special funding to specific districts and communities, but the results were problematic. The population grew, but much of it was either socially undesirable (for example criminals or the unemployed), or not ethnically Czech.

In spite of these difficulties the population of the borderlands grew. Compared to 1945, it had increased by 16 percent by 1955. However, population in the borderlands remained 29 percent below the level reached in 1930. In the 1960s and 1970s the population stabilized, and conditions for further growth were created in many cities and villages. Nevertheless, in the late 1980s the population in the borderlands was still 20 percent below that of the 1930s. And population settlement and urbanization remain uneven, containing a wider range of nationalities and a larger non-Czech population than in the inland regions. The 1991 census shows that the share of the Czech population in the border regions ranges between 80 to 96 percent, and the share of Slovaks varies between 2 and 10 percent. Approximately one percent are German, and between 0.5 to 1 percent are Gypsies. These regions have a relatively low share of university and secondary school graduates.

In brief, the demographic structure of the population still shows the effects of population changes after 1945. But in the 1990s the borderland population as a whole has remained stable. The inhabitants are mostly third-generation settlers who have developed firm ties with their homes, as illustrated by the wide range of civic activity occurring in towns and villages.[55] The results of municipal and parliamentary elections in the early 1990s, covered by a German-owned regional press that remained politically neutral, have confirmed a political orientation in the borderlands that does not differ significantly from that of the Czech population at large. In the parliamentary elections of 1992, the electoral coalition between ODS (Civic Democratic Party) and KDS (Christian Democrats) won the most votes in the borderlands, taking about 30 percent, close to the national average. The Left Bloc, whose core consists of former Communists, also gained a relatively strong position (15 percent). Adding other leftist parties, a strong leftist bloc gained around 30 percent of the vote. The xenophobic Radical Republican Party (SPR-RSC) won about 10 percent of the vote in northern Bohemia, more than the national average. These voting preferences were reconfirmed during the municipal elections of 1994 and the national elections of 1996. Its electoral victories allowed ODS-KDS to form a strong ruling coalition in parliament and subsequently to form governments in the regions, including the Czech borderlands.

Changes in the Bohemian Borderlands Since 1989

After the Velvet Revolution the transition towards a market economy and the opening of frontiers have altered the future course of events in the borderlands. The privatization of big industrial enterprises has resulted in gradual structural change and a very slow introduction of new production technologies. Economic rationalization affects north and northwest Bohemia especially

55. This contradicts the tendentious and inflammatory characterization of the demographic situation in the Czech borderlands that a leading spokesperson of the German Sudeten organizations is offering when he writes that the Czech government

strongly, in particular its fuel and electric power industry based on brown coal. Coal mining has shrunk, and some mines have been closed. Unemployment has increased especially among the less educated.

Foreign capital is also playing a growing role in the borderlands. Foreign investors are interested only in highly profitable industries such as chemicals, glass, porcelain, and certain raw materials. According to some knowledgeable observers such investment typically takes the form of a silent partnership, particularly when the investors are German. Czech companies commonly perform simple assembly work for German firms.

The reduction of agricultural output and the termination of most agricultural subsidies illustrate the problematical side of economic restructuring in the borderlands. Privatizing agriculture is difficult because of the poor profitability of most agricultural enterprises. Most of the reduction in agricultural output has occurred in small, upland communities where agriculture is often the only source of income. As a result, a further outflow from small and remote villages is very likely.

Labor markets have increasingly become one of the most important areas of cross-border cooperation. Despite undeniable problems, this sector is vitally important for the establishment of normal relations between Czech and German populations. In regions neighboring Germany and Austria, the labor market has begun to span national frontiers. While the north Moravian borderlands report major unemployment (around 6 percent), unemployment is very low (about 2 percent) in the districts neighboring Bavaria. It is clear that here the foreign demand for labor is strong, and a significant number of Czechs work in Germany both legally and illegally. Cheb District, for example, reported less than 2 percent unemployment in July 1991; in fact, this district employs foreign workers from east European countries. Thus the labor market has rapidly internationalized. Data gathered in border districts show that between 5 and 8 percent of Czech labor works in Germany. These are "commuters" who travel daily to their German workplaces. Only 10 percent stated that they commute to Germany because they are unemployed at

---

settled primarily "outrooted rabble, merited Communists, Gypsies, Vietnamese, Cubans and Czechs expelled or returned from Russia in the borderlands. This mixture has not yet become homogeneous and has no social structure deserving the sense of belonging to this home." Quoted in a speech by Frank Neubauer, *Revue Střední Evropa* 41 (1994): 46.

home. Their motivation is higher wages and salaries, a result of the exchange rate differentials between the Czech crown and the deutschmark. Economic cooperation across national borders also occurs in the absence of labor migration, through the "putting out" system by which German firms subcontract the assembly of various simple products or wood components to women working at home in the Bohemian borderlands.

Despite its many positive effects, the new, cross-border labor market also creates problems. The mostly highly skilled workers who commute perform less skilled jobs abroad and receive lower wages than do German workers. The area has suffered a shortage of some types of skilled workers, and young, unskilled workers resent the older workers' abandonment of the local economy. On the German side (mostly Saxony), the labor unions object to the competition from cheap Czech labor. And the regulation of working permits in Germany has many loopholes. The number of Czech employees in Germany and Czechs commuting for work to Germany has recently declined, a consequence of the more stringent registration requirements and higher penalties for the illegal employment of foreigners that Germany has adopted. Alternatively, it is also possible that this decline results from the competitive pressure of even cheaper labor coming from other post-Communist states further to the east.

An unprecedented growth in tourism occurred after the opening of the frontiers. Tourism and the interests of Germans and Austrians in cheap goods and services on the Czech side led to unplanned growth along main traffic arteries linking the three countries. Along with Czech traders, both Vietnamese and Chinese salesmen have been very successful. The growth of street vendors has been accompanied by a spread in prostitution, the buying and selling of stolen goods, and the smuggling of illegal migrants. Although these social developments have heightened the sense of insecurity in the borderlands, local authorities have not found effective tools to suppress them. These activities do substantial harm to normal neighborhood relations, damage the image of the Czech Republic, and lead some Germans to think that virtually everything is permitted on the Czech side of the border. Sex tourism in particular often goes hand in hand with criminal activity. In sum, while most of the economic and social changes in the Bohemian borderlands have enhanced and normalized life according to Western European standards, all of them entail unavoidable foreign influences.

The Politics of Sudeten German Claims

Extending beyond the economic realm, German influence in the border regions also shapes ways of thinking. Specifically, the re-introduction of the Sudeten German agenda has had exceptionally important consequences. Indeed, Sudeten Germans are a forceful reminder of unresolved issues. Sudeten Germans frequently cross the border to visit their former homes and to leave certain historical reminders, and such activities inevitably lead to an increase in anxieties among the Czech population in the Bohemian borderlands. Thus the activities of some Sudeten Germans are a troublesome and important exception to generally good relationships across the German-Czech border.

In early 1995, in particular, the situation deteriorated. The political support of the Bavarian CSU for the Sudeten Germans turned out to be more than an electoral ploy. This political alliance was evidently deployed to put political pressure on the Czech government. The CSU leadership, with its close contacts to the CDU and Chancellor Kohl, insists that the Czech government should open a direct dialogue with the Sudeten German leadership concerning a broad range of issues that, if reopened, would threaten the very basis of the post-World War II settlement. In early 1995 this issue suddenly became highly politicized, with the publication of an appeal, "Reconciliation '95," addressed to the Czech government, and signed by 105 Czech and German intellectuals. In the interest of the future and a "fair" reconciliation between Czechs and Sudeten Germans, the appeal asked the Czech government to open a direct dialogue with the Sudeten Germans. Most Czechs deem this demand to be quite unacceptable and regard the appeal as a serious infraction of Czech national interests. Opinion surveys have recorded that a strong majority of the Czech population refuses to accede to any of the claims made by the Sudeten Germans. It regards the whole issue of the borderlands as resolved once and for all. Nonetheless this issue remains very much present in the background of everyday Czech life and in the contacts between Czechs and Germans.

Some of the representatives of Sudeten German organizations characterize the entire postwar period as one of lawlessness and illegal violence against the German population of Bohemia. They would like to void the Beneš decrees that, together with the Potsdam Agreement, provided the legal basis for expelling the Sudeten Germans. Thus discussions of the Sudeten German issue often focuses on the right to a homeland. F. Neubauer, speaker for the Sudeten German Homeland Society, defines this as "the right to live in our homeland and the right to free advancement in all ways and manners on the basis of guaranteed national minority rights using our mother language and developing our own culture."[56]

But such a change might lead to the revision of the whole postwar settlement in this part of central Europe and raise the entirely unpredictable issue of the transfer of property. The Czech government has therefore consistently insisted that February 1948 constituted the deadline for executable restitutions. When a descendant of a Sudeten German family, now living in the Czech Republic, went to court to claim the property of his parents, the Constitutional Court of the Czech Republic ruled on 8 March 1995 that the Beneš decrees were fully legal and prohibited any political attempt to revise them.

When Václav Havel, now president of the Czech Republic, apologized for the expulsions soon after becoming president of Czechoslovakia in 1990, Sudeten Germans took courage. But in Czechoslovakia left- and nationalist-oriented political forces criticized Havel's speech. While the president was interested in creating some basic pre-conditions for achieving some measure of reconciliation between Sudeten Germans and Czechs, he succeeded in both activating claims on the German side and politicizing the issue in Czech domestic politics. On 17 February 1995 President Havel responded to the increasingly insistent demands of the Sudeten Germans. In an important speech he insisted that, after apologies had been made, the next step was a search for practical solutions to outstanding problems. In Havel's view the solution lies in the Western European principle of citizenship and not in the central European principle of nationality.

A German historian of Sudeten German origin, Professor Rudolf Hilf, criticized Havel's position as "a step backwards." Hilf is a moderate and a proponent of the idea of Euroregions as an instrument of international cooperation. But he remains dissatisfied with Havel's unwillingness to revise any of the consequences of World War II. Indeed, he issued a veiled threat when he wrote that "if the Czech side undertakes the attempt to justify the expulsion

56. See the speech of Frank Neubauer, a prominent spokesperson for the Sudeten German group, *Revue Střední Evropa*, 41 (1994), p. 46. It should be noted that this claim goes beyond the often quoted statement that the Sudeten Germans do not strive for any property restitution but only for moral condemnation of the transfer of the Germans out of Czechoslovakia after World War II.

[of ethnic Germans after World War II], then the demands of the Sudeten Germans will escalate...."[57]

The organizations of Sudeten Germans in Germany responded to Havel's speech by reiterating their demand for a dialogue between the Czech government and the Sudeten German Homeland Society. The Czech government, however, refuses to do so, arguing that a sovereign Czech state can have a dialogue only with the authorities of the German state. The Bavarian government has declared itself to be the patron of the Sudeten Germans, and, during Sudeten German Days, in May 1994, Edmund Stoiber, the Bavarian governor, stated that dialogue between the Sudeten Germans and the Czech government and parliament was currently the only missing and needed thing.[58] This call for dialogue conceals a hidden agenda. Its purpose is to use the recognition of the Sudeten German Homeland Society as a negotiating partner and thus to create a basis for a future settlement of individual property claims.[59]

The claims of the Sudeten Germans are of critical importance to both Czech-German relations and to life in the Bohemian borderlands with their more than two and a half million inhabitants. In national politics an overwhelming majority of the Czech electorate refuses to vote for a political party that is willing to make any concessions to the demands of the Sudeten Germans. Locally, Czechs are beginning to organize politically to counter this German

57. Rudolf Hilf, "Projev Václava Havla a Jeho Dusledky" ("Václav Havel's speech and its implications"), *Rudé právo* (7 April 1995), p. 19.

58. See a report of the 45th Sudeten German Day, Nurnberg, 22 May 1994, as reported in *Revue Střední Evropa*, 41 (1994): 37–47.

59. One of the theoreticians of the Sudeten German organizations and a professor at the University of Munich, Professor Kurt Heissig, has suggested the following formulation of the Sudeten German settlement claims: 1) in return for waiving claims to territorial autonomy, the Sudeten Germans should be granted a liberal measure of personal autonomy on Czech territory; 2) they should be allowed to return and settle in the Czech Republic with the encouragement of the Czech government especially for regions historically settled by Germans; 3) Sudeten Germans should recognize the right of domicile for all social groups currently settled there; 4) property that is now in the hands of the state should be returned *in natura*, and in the case of lost property or property held privately, the affected party should be permitted to choose between a compensatory property or financial compensation; furthermore, the Sudeten Germans should accept that compensation payments will be small and that the recipients will have to pay Czech taxes on the payments they receive; 5) both states should allow double citizenship or, for some time, equality of legal position for Sudeten Germans and Czech natives in certain areas. "Sudetonimecká budoucnost v Èechách a na Moravì" ("Sudeten German Future in Bohemia and Moravia"), *Revue Střední Evropa* 33 (1993): 27–28.

pressure. The Bohemian Borderlands Clubs in particular are a response on the part of social and political groups to the increase in German influence and, in particular, to the settlement claims that certain Sudeten Germans and their organizations are making. Judging from their statutes, the newly established clubs exist to champion the interests of the population in the Czech borderlands against an increasingly strong German influence. Their program requires "… that our Bohemian borderlands are and will always remain a permanent home for all existing inhabitants and that nobody is allowed to question their right of domicile."[60]

The Borderlands and Europe

Even though both Germany and the Czech Republic wish, as they repeat on all occasions, for the best relations possible, problems and misunderstandings continue to exist behind the rhetoric. At this stage, political leaders and basic international documents are playing a decisive role. The treaty signed by the two governments in 1992 contains some debatable points and has left some issues outstanding. This applies primarily to the definition of the invalidity of the Munich Agreement of 1938. In addition, the treaty uses the term "land frontier" instead of "state frontier," does not cover property issues, and does not resolve certain outstanding issues such as the indemnification payments to the Czech victims of German fascism.

The negotiations and the ratification of the treaty were controversial in both parliaments. When the treaty was signed, the foreign ministers exchanged letters containing identical wordings. The letters specifically emphasized that in return for Germany's support for the admission of the (former) Czechoslovak Republic to the EU the Czech (Czechoslovak) state would create a legal framework for German nationals to settle in the Czechoslovak Republic. In short, the treaty left many sensitive issues unaddressed.

Czech-German relations play an important part in the European integration process. Projects financed by the PHARE program in northern Bohemia, for example, provide numerous illustrations of successful cross-border cooperation. These projects enhance business and educational opportunities, address local environmental problems, and improve the infrastructure of

60. "Českomoravský hraničář" ("Patriots Living in the Czech-Moravian Border Area"), *Bulletin of the Preparatory Committee of the Bohemian Borderland Club* 1 (Usti upon Elbe, 1992).

the region on both sides of the border. A similar program has been drawn up in 1995 for the border region linking the Czech Republic and Bavaria. Here, too, the experience has been overwhelmingly positive.

Regional associations of towns and villages span national borders. Cross-border Euroregions have been established in conjunction with German and, to a lesser extent, Polish towns and villages.[61] Euroregions on Western European borders are promoted by the EU, and they have responded by demonstrating their viability and, at the very least, their symbolic usefulness. The initiative to establish Euroregions usually comes from the German side. The first Euroregion, Egrensis, was formed on the frontier separating Bavaria and Saxony. Its founders wanted it to become a tool for cross-border cooperation and for the solution of various, primarily environmental, issues. Ideally, it will also assist in the solution of the Sudeten German issue. Other Euroregions have followed: Nisa (the Neisse), Labe (the Elbe), Krusné Hory (the Ore Mountains), and Sumava (the Bohemian Forest). Their activities differ, and most involve only the establishment of joint bodies and some relatively modest activities that do not significantly affect the life of ordinary citizens. Indeed, most people do not know these Euroregions exist, as a survey of the Czech population of the Egrensis Euroregion showed. The survey of the Cheb district revealed that as little as 13 percent of the respondents were reasonably well informed about the purpose and goals of the Egrensis Euroregion.[62]

Thus, with a few exceptions, the activity of the Euroregions is generally weak. They are held back by a variety of factors: great differences in the economic conditions on both sides of the border, incompatibilities in regional and national legislation, and differences in socio-cultural levels of development. Practical cooperation between communities or cross-border associations turns out to be more effective than Euroregions. Thus Czech governmental authorities have taken a skeptical attitude towards the establishment and activity of Euroregions. The prime minister and the minister of foreign affairs, for example, see Euroregions

61. František Zich, "Euroregions along the Czech/German and Czech/Austrian Borders," Institute of Sociology, Academy of Sciences of the Czech Republic, July 1993.

62. František Zich, Václav Houžvička, *Přeshraniční souvislosti sociálních změn v oblasti české části euroregionu* [*Cross-border relevances of social changes in Czech segment of Euroregion Egrensis*] (Prague: Chebsko Sociologičký Ústav Avčr [Prague: Czech Academy of Sciences, Sociological Institute], 1993).

as redundant. Especially problematic is the fact that the Euroregions set up their own parliaments and other representative bodies and conclude cross-border agreements themselves. There is also the risk that some interests will not be properly represented, and that the integrity of the state may be jeopardized.[63] Indeed, some go so far as to claim that Euroregions are a Trojan horse of the Sudeten Germans.

The Czech political experience is poised precariously between the promises of a European future and the disappointments of a central European past. The promises of the future are marked by economic prosperity and a diversified dependence on numerous states that provide investment and technology (as in the automobile industry), abstain from interfering politically in domestic political affairs (as in the national and regional press), and are committed to Western principles of citizenship (as in the issues that the Sudeten Germans raise). The disappointments are a structural dependency on an economically overbearing and politically suspect Germany, and the resurgence of ethnic principles in the negotiations between states.

The case studies in this chapter are no more than illustrative, but the data suggest that Czech fears of German economic hegemony and consequent Czech dependency are not unfounded. In the 1930s German economic influence was based on a deliberate political strategy of creating asymmetric economic dependencies between Nazi Germany and its smaller central and eastern European neighbors. In the 1990s German government and German business appear to lack a deliberate strategy to dominate the Czech Republic. But the spontaneous expansion of German business and the resulting structural dependency of the Czech political economy on Germany is indisputable. Hence, for the foreseeable future the Czechs, like the Austrians in the late 1950s and 1960s, will debate, and worry over, the "kalte Anschluss"—economic and political annexation by the backdoor. But because Austria has diversified its dependence on other states, because its

---

63. Václav Klaus, "Premiérova Premiéra" ["Prime Minister's First Performance"] (S'93): 23. "Euroregiony ano, či ne?" ["Euroregions yes or no?] *Hospodářské noviny* [*Economic News*] (7 July 1993).

economy is growing and vital, and because it is linked to its German neighbors, together with other European states, in numerous multilateral institutions, such fears no longer count for much in the Austria of the 1990s. Whether developments will turn out equally well for the Czech Republic during the next two or three decades remains to be seen. The outcome will depend in part on European and global developments that the Czech Republic has little chance of controlling directly.

5. THE SLOVAK REPUBLIC
Bridge between East and West?

Daneš Brzica, Zuzana Poláčková, and Ivo Samson

The end of the Cold War brought to Slovakia both a new state and a new political regime. This has led to a high degree of political uncertainty and a bitter power struggle over the future direction of the country. Whether Slovakia will anchor itself firmly to western European models of politics and international institutions remains an open question that is important both for its central European neighbors and for the western European states.

After 1990, politics in Czechoslovakia[1] gradually came to be dominated by differences in foreign and domestic policy orientations that culminated, during 1992, in Slovak demands for a fundamental restructuring of the state. The federalization of Czechoslovakia after 1969 had resulted in three governments that acted simultaneously. Whereas in Communist times the republic's ministries, with the exception of the ministries of culture, played only subordinate and symbolic roles, after the Velvet Revolution the Slovak and Czech governments negotiated most issues as equal partners, while the federal government maintained control over defense and foreign policy.[2] Following the parliamentary elections of June 1992 political divisions became increasingly visible. The Slovak side called for the "sovereignty" of Slovakia while the

1. After 1990 the name of Czechoslovakia—according to a Czech-Slovak Agreement on the change of the Czechoslovak Socialist Republic to Czech and Slovak Federal Republic—was written as Czechoslovakia in the Czechlands and as Czecho-Slovakia in Slovakia.

2. Based upon the December 1990 Czech-Slovak agreement on the division of power.

Czech side sought to preserve only a "functional" federation.[3] On the Slovak side the winners had fought the electoral campaign with strident demands for greater sovereignty. The political forces in the Czech republic that emerged as winners rejected the Slovak demands and began to push for partition.[4]

When Slovakia first showed interest in greater autonomy, Western countries were seriously concerned. Territorial changes in central-eastern Europe had already led to eruptions of violence in the former Yugoslavia and the former Soviet Union. But in this instance, partition was accomplished without any threat of violence. Slovakia remains socially less cohesive than its central European neighbors and thus more vulnerable to nationalist and populist appeals. The ease with which the country had stripped itself of the remnants of communism thus offers no durable guarantee for Slovakia's domestic transformation and international reorientation.

From the vantage point of Berlin/Bonn and Brussels, Slovakia's future appears more uncertain than that of the other central European states. For this reason alone, the country deserves closer attention than it normally receives. This is true even regarding the economic issues that matter to so many of the Western consultants traveling to Prague, Budapest, and Warsaw but who bypass Bratislava, although it lies just beyond the outskirts of Vienna. This is a mistake. A joke in the 1960s held that the real economic miracle after 1945 had occurred not in Germany but in Italy—for the Italians had accomplished theirs without working. The breakup of Czechoslovakia, it was widely assumed, had created an economic basket case in the middle of Europe. Slovakia has disproved these gloomy predictions. It holds its own in many economic comparisons and leads its central European neighbors in several important areas.

Among many complicated reasons for this strong performance, a painful policy of military conversion ranks high. This policy has dwarfed any comparable effort by any other industrial state in recent years. We analyze this policy here in the chapter's first section. Another important aspect is Slovakia's privatization policy

---

3. In Slovakia the Movement for Democratic Slovakia advocating the "international sovereignty" of Slovakia won with about 37 percent of votes; in the Czech Republic the Civic Democratic Party, adhering strictly to federative principles, won about 34 percent of votes.

4. The Civic Democratic Party, the Civic Democratic Alliance, and the Czechoslovak People's Party.

that was shaped by the initial policy of Czechoslovakia before 1993 and which, in contrast to the Czech Republic, has since become a source of acrimonious domestic political debate and conflict. It would be a great irony if, despite great differences between the market preferences of the Czech government and the mercantilist preferences of the Slovak government, privatization would leave the banks in both countries in the pivotal political position that they have traditionally enjoyed in central Europe. Slovakia's privatization is the subject of the chapter's second section.

On another issue, the protection of minority rights on both sides of the Slovak-Hungarian border, the central European past could conceivably threaten peace in the region. Ethnic definitions of national belonging pose complex issues that continue to trouble Slovak-Hungarian relations. These central European definitions are in conflict with the civic definitions that western European institutions such as the European Union (EU) are setting as standards for all of its potential new member states. The chapter's third section explores this complex and volatile issue. Finally, Slovakia's security policy is also steering a course that sets it apart from that of the other three central European states. While the Slovak military appears to be making good progress in matching the military requirements of future membership in NATO, the government's close relations with Russia, and more importantly, the political uncertainties in Slovakia's domestic politics are making it increasingly doubtful that Slovakia will become an early member of NATO. This issue is explored in the last section of the chapter.

These four case studies are illustrative, not definitive. They map a course that shows a radical break with the past, the achievement of statehood and a new political regime, and political squabbling about the domestic and international course that Slovakia should pursue in central Europe in the future.

Conversion of the Armaments Industry

Among the large number of economic and social problems the Slovak Republic faces, the conversion of its armaments industry to civilian production is one of the most crucial and complex.[5] The end of the Cold War in Europe and the attendant reduction in

5. This study cannot fully cover all aspects of the topic. Moreover, the importance and sensitive nature of these policy problems have led us to use publicly presented facts and figures rather than more confidential ones. Sometimes apparent or

defense budgets, the collapse of the Soviet Union, the political and economic transformations in central-eastern Europe, the Gulf War and the loss of export markets in the third world due to the proven inferiority of traditional mechanized forms of warfare, and last but not least, the change in the regime of Czechoslovakia and a new policy of sharply restricted arms exports all conspired to bring about a dramatic reduction in the oversized armaments industry that had been built up in central Slovakia. In a broader perspective, Slovakia's program for the dramatic conversion of its armaments industry is without parallel in the industrial world. Between 1988 and 1992 the production of the thirty-six Slovak weapons manufacturers dropped by an astonishing 89 percent.[6]

Slovakia's arms industry has traditionally dominated the industrial structure of the country, providing a stable flow of revenues to state coffers. Production peaked in 1988 at approximately 19.3 billion ČSK. The growth of Slovakia's modern arms industry dates back to 1928 when the Czechoslovak government decided to relocate certain parts of the biggest arms firms to the Slovak Republic. Škoda, ČKD, and other companies began to establish factories in the eastern part of the country where they were well removed from possible threats from neighboring Germany. Eventually, the area produced heavy weapons like tanks and armored vehicles, while arms production in the Czech lands concentrated on lighter arms. After World War II, as relations with the U.S.S.R. strengthened, the strategic importance of Slovakia became very much evident. This led to further support for the production of heavy arms in Slovakia, buttressed by international licenses and a widening market among the members of the Warsaw Treaty Organization (WTO). In addition, the Council of Mutual Economic Assistance (CMEA) encouraged exports to third world countries.

Policy Change and Its Socio-Economic Consequences

Even before 1989, Slovakia experienced strong pressures to initiate political and economic change. The general aim of transforming a

---

real contradictions in the statements of political parties, government bureaucrats, and business managers are due to their changing ideas concerning different aspects of arms production and conversion over a relatively long period of time, from 1989 to 1993.

6. Brigita Schmögnerová, "Konverzia v podnikoch Slovenskej republiky v transformačnom období," ["Enterprise Conversion in the Slovak Republic in Transition"] *Ekonomický časopis*, 41, 4 (April 1993): 265.

centrally planned economy into a market system was moderated by selective measures designed to restore the economy's industrial base. The transition from the soft budgets of state enterprises to the hard budgets of the market was expected to lead to significant changes in industry. At the same time it was also clear to the government that some industries faced substantial microeconomic problems. In particular, it was evident that heavy industry, and especially arms producers, would have difficulty selling their products.

Production of arms thus had begun to drop under the pre-revolutionary government. But the decline was relatively gentle. According to official statistics, the decrease in arms production "was triggered especially by the over-all military and political situation in the countries of the Warsaw Pact (WTO), including the growing problems of sales of arms production among the member countries and further, by the limitation of exports of this production to developing countries in view of outstanding payments on the government's long-term loans."[7]

In the post-revolutionary period, just after November 1989, the pace of policy change increased dramatically. Because the arms industry was located primarily in central and northwest Slovakia while policy decisions were made in distant Prague, the consequences of policies taken by the center were felt disproportionately by these two regions. As conversion progressed, the federal government passed a set of resolutions concerning a reduction in and an ending of the manufacture of tanks (resolution 84/1989), an effective utilization of industrial capacities in the manufacture of special technology (resolution 159/1989), as well as in the manufacture, export, and conversion of special technologies, including an end to the manufacture of infantry combat vehicles (resolution 42/1990). These resolutions had a longer lasting effect on Slovak policy. For example, an enclosure to federal resolution 326/1991, the "principles of federal bodies' attitudes to a solution of arms production conversion," subsequently guided the Slovak government as it sought to assist enterprises undergoing conversion. Specifically, this legislation was designed by the federal government to ameliorate the negative economic consequences of change.

7. Jozef Belcák, "Problems of the Conversion of Armament Production in Slovakia," in *Conversion of the Military Production: Comparative Approach* (Bratislava: Slovak Academy of Sciences, Institute of Economics, and Friedrich Ebert Foundation, 1993), p. 62.

In addition, institutional measures were developed to protect both enterprises and the labor force. In June 1990, Labor Offices were established in the most affected regions (in Martin, Dubnica, and Detva) to provide statistics on vacant jobs and to create conditions for new jobs. To provide support for enterprises during conversion, the Fund for Special Technology was established at the federal level. In 1991, federal sources for stabilization provided 1.2 billion ČSK for thirty Slovak enterprises (sixty-three projects) compared to 0.79 billion ČSK in 1992 expended on forty-seven projects in twenty-five enterprises. In 1993 direct support from the Slovak state budget dropped to 0.5 billion SK. All policy makers agreed that this was an insufficient sum.

A change in Czechoslovakia's policy on the export of arms had serious consequences for the speed of the conversion process. Most important, the collapse of both the WTO and the CMEA made the decline of the Slovak arms industry inevitable. Exports were dominated by sales to the WTO member states, with the Soviet Union as the leading customer. WTO countries absorbed approximately 80 percent of total arms exports. With the breakup of the WTO, exports declined from 6.1 billionČSK in 1988 to 4.4 billion in 1989 and 0.1 billion in 1992.[8] But Czechoslovak policy was not merely dictated by developments beyond its borders. For the government had compiled a list, kept secret for reasons of security, which listed countries henceforth excluded from arms exports. According to Czechoslovak Television, the list contained two categories of countries. The first group consisted of approximately twenty "prohibited area" countries to which exports were not permitted; the second consisted of twenty-six "risky area" countries where exports would be possible only with special permission. In addition, the federal government also exported arms to some "dangerous areas." For a number of reasons third world states had been the major markets for Czechoslovak weapons. The type, simplicity, and quality of Czechoslovak arms were well suited to the demands of third world countries, many of which had an ideological affinity with socialist Czechoslovakia and were among the largest importers of traditional arms.[9]

Czechoslovakia's new identity as a democratic state and its wish to join Western international institutions such as NATO, the

8. Jaroslav Bartl, "Peripetie zbrojárskej vyroby," ["Peripheral Armaments Production"] *Hospodářské noviny* (26 July 1993): 4.

9. The top arms importers between 1985 and 1989 were, measured in billions of U.S. dollars: India ($17.3), Iraq ($12.0), Saudi Arabia ($8.8), Syria ($5.9), and Libya ($3.2). See *Hospodářské noviny* (6 February 1992): 3.

EU, WEU, and the CSCE were an important reason for a reorientation in the government's domestic and export policy. For example, after 1989 the Czechoslovak government supported a proposal for establishing a conventional weapons sale register under UN auspices and participated in a wide range of activities furthering disarmament. In a new international system, the federal government could no longer afford to neglect the political aspects of Czechoslovak weapons exports. This was particularly true regarding arms shipments to the Middle East to such countries as Iran and Syria. While former federal Vice-Premier Pavel Rychetsky stated in a television debate that Slovakia is an independent state that makes its decisions freely, the spokesman of the Federal Ministry of Foreign Affairs, Egon Lánsky, has pointed out that the pro-Israeli lobby in the United States could easily change its positive attitude towards Slovakia should the Slovak government continue to export arms to countries such as Iran and Syria.

As it happened, the decision of the Czechoslovak federal government to sell arms to Syria generated a note of protest from the U.S. administration to Czechoslovakia's Deputy Minister of Foreign Affairs, Martin Palous. Democratization and pressure from new international allies thus also helped to diminish the market for Czechoslovak weapons exports. During his visit to Hungary, the U.S. Deputy Minister of Defense, Donald Atwood, declared that the U.S. government had no objections to either a strong defense in former Eastern bloc countries or to arms production or exports, provided the latter went exclusively to friendly states.[10] The Deputy Director of the U.S. Agency for Arms Control and Disarmament, Michael Moodie, voiced a similar opinion. And in its 1991 annual report the World Bank stated that it was necessary to cut Czechoslovakia's military expenditures.[11]

The social and economic consequences of these policy changes were nothing short of dramatic. They varied both in the nature of their economic, security, and social impact and in their local, regional, and national effect. There occurred an enormous drop in military production from 19.3 billion ČSK in 1988 to 4.5 billion ČSK in 1991. In 1990 alone the reduction amounted to almost eight billion ČSK.[12] This dramatic decline weakened what remained of

10. *Hospodářské noviny* (22 July 1991): 14.

11. *Hospodářské noviny* (7 July 1991): 14.

12. Karol Droppa, "Conversion of Armaments Production in the Slovak Republic," in *Conversion of Military Production: Comparative Approach* (Bratislava: Institute of Economics, Slovak Academy of Science and Friedrich Ebert Foundation, 1993), p. 7.

Slovakia's defense industry.[13] The breadth and speed of the conversion process, together with the simultaneous decline of important R&D programs, eliminated Czecho-Slovakia's comparative advantage: information, knowledge, and organizational capacity eroded; avenues for export and budget revenues decreased; and the armed forces became increasingly dependent on foreign arms.

Production at the thirty-six Slovak arms producers dropped by 9.5 billion ČSK in 1989; further reductions of eight billion ČSK occurred in 1990 and 6.3 billion ČSK in 1991.[14] All told between 1988 and 1992 production dropped by an astounding 90 percent.[15] In 1988 arms accounted for almost 9 percent of Slovak exports compared to only 2 percent in 1992. WTO members absorbed about 80 percent of Czechoslovak arms exports in the late 1980s. With the breakup of the WTO those exports declined from 6.1 billion ČSK in 1988 to 0.1 billion ČSK in 1992.[16] And the share of arms production in total Slovak industrial production declined from 6.3 percent in 1988 to 0.9 percent in 1992.

The impact at local and regional levels was disastrous. Slovakia's major arms producers laid off thousands of workers.[17] Between 1987 and 1992–93 Slovakia lost between 40,000 and 50,000 jobs in the arms industry, about 70 percent of the total job loss suffered by the Czechoslovak economy.[18] Regionally, the impact was also highly asymmetric inside Slovakia, with the northwest region bearing 70 percent of the total reduction while the south-central region took cuts of "only" 18 percent.[19] These dramatic reductions reinforced the widely shared Slovak sentiment which held that political decisions in Prague had disastrous consequences only in Slovakia. While it is difficult to assess or quantify the effect, conversion undoubtedly contributed to the dissolution of Czecho-Slovakia. But most observers agree that the deterioration in Slovakia's economic situation and the disparate regional

13. Oldřich Čehák, Ladislav Ivánek, Miroslav Krč, and Jan Šelešovský, *Zbrojní výroba, konverze, obranyschopnost* [*Armament Production, Conversion, and Defense Capacity*] (Prague: Magnet-Press, 1993), pp. 88–100.

14. Droppa, "Conversion of Armaments Production," p. 7.

15. Schmögnerová, "Enterprise Conversion in a Slovak Republic in Transition," p. 265.

16. Bartl, "Peripheral Armaments Production," p. 4.

17. Čehák, Ivánek, Krč, and Šelešovský, *Armament Production*, p. 78.

18. Droppa, "Conversion of Armaments Production," p. 7.

19. Ludmila Kormanová, "Conversion of Arms Production at a Regional Level," in *Conversion of Military Production: Comparative Approach* (Bratislava: Institute of Economics, Slovak Academy of Sciences, and Friedrich Ebert Foundation, 1993), p. 185.

effects of the federal government's economic policy influenced Slovak voters. Indeed, some go so far as to argue that the post-November 1989 decision to close down the arms industry was an important factor in the growing conflict between Czech and Slovak representatives, which peaked with the dissolution of Czecho-Slovakia.[20] In 1991, 70 percent of the Slovaks were highly critical of the federal government's policies which were closely associated with the name of President Václav Havel.[21] To be sure, the conversion process led enterprises toward normal competitive environments; it reduced overstaffing; and it created small and medium-sized firms producing goods for civilian markets. But whatever the policy's long-term benefits, its short-term effects on the Slovak economy were enormously harmful.

The Northwest Region

To illustrate some of the specific effects on Slovakia's regional and local political economies, this section offers a case study of the deeply affected northwest region of the Slovak Republic. This region is characterized by a very high share of arms production and includes the biggest weapons plants in Slovakia. It bore 70 percent of the decline in arms production between 1989 and 1991, while the south-central region experienced what amounted to 18 percent of the decline. Conversion has affected these regions more strongly than others in Slovakia.[22] At the local level the impact was also very destructive. For example, more than 90 percent of the 3,100 employees of ZŤS Dubnica's who were laid off between 1988 and 1991 were in the arms sector. During the same period ZŤS Martin laid off 3,900 employees (one thousand from arms production), and PPS Detva let go 2,415 employees.[23] The process of conversion also affected companies tightly linked to the large weapons producers. A strategic decision to reduce, relocate, and re-organize the armed forces also contributed to the decline of many smaller firms.[24]

20. For example, Berthold Kohler of the *Frankfurter Allgemeine Zeitung* held to this view, as reported in *Hospodářské noviny* (26 July 1993), p. 12.

21. Pavol Frič et al., "Aktuálne problémy slovenskej spoločnosti-máj 1991" ["Actual Problems of Slovak Society—May 1991"] (Bratislava: Institute for Social Analysis, Comenius University, 1991), pp. 49–50.

22. Kormanová, "Conversion of Arms Production at a Regional Level," p. 185.

23. Čehák, Ivánek, Krč, and Šelešovský, *Armament Production*, p. 78.

24. It would be a mistake to disregard some positive aspects of the conversion process. Among them, at the enterprise level, were an accelerated transition

We define the northwest region as including the six districts located in the northwestern part of the Slovak Republic.[25] As the site of nearly 60 percent of Slovak military production, it is the area most affected by conversion. In comparison, the second most important region, south-central Slovakia, accounts for only about 25 percent of total military production. The six districts of the northwest region are Martin, Považská Bystrica, Čadca, Žilina, Dolny Kubín, and Liptovsky Mikulás. Of these, the Považská Bystrica district has the highest concentration of military production (36 percent of Slovak arms production), while the Martin district ranks second (21 percent).[26] The region is dominated by three large enterprises: ZŤS Martin in the Martin district, and ZŤS Dubnica nad Váhom and ZVS Dubnica nad Váhom in the Považská Bystrica district. ZŤS Martin was a giant holding company, consisting of twelve plants and several R&D institutes. Sixty-four percent of its output was military equipment. The proportion was even higher for ZŤS Dubnica (70 percent) and ZVS Dubnica (87 percent).[27] In 1988, ZŤS Martin produced tanks valued at 5.5 billion ČSK, and military production made up 47 percent of its total production in 1989. Not only were these shares very high, but these enterprises, taken together, accounted for a very high share of total Slovak military production in 1988 (ZŤS Martin 23 percent, ZŤS Dubnica 22 percent, and ZVS Dubnica 8.5 percent).[28]

The sub-region Dubnica nad Váhom, which is part of the Považská Bystrica district, is heavily industrialized and is the site of two big firms, ZŤS (8,100 employees) and ZVS (1,400 employees), as well as four medium-sized building companies, four medium-sized R&D and electronics companies, and nearly three thousand small businesses, of which only a few have more than five employees. The relatively high population density in this sub-region is a result of a recent wave of industrialization that commenced in the 1960s, when ZŤS and ZVS, as well as the Electronic Research Institute, were established.[29] The sub-region has two

---

towards a normal competitive environment, a reduction of overemployment, and the creation of small and medium businesses producing for civilian markets.

25. Regions are not administrative units. Officially, Slovakia is divided into districts (named after their administrative centers) and counties (Eastern, Central, and Western Slovakia).

26. Kormanová, "Conversion of Arms Production at a Regional Level," p. 184.

27. Čehák, Ivánek, Krč, and Šelešovský, *Armament Production*, p. 51.

28. Schmögnerová, "Enterprise Conversion in a Slovak Republic in Transition," pp. 253–54.

29. ZŤS itself was established in 1937 as a part of the Škoda Plzeň factory.

TABLE 5.1 ECONOMIC IMPACT OF MILITARY CONVERSION
(IN ČSK MILLION)

Enterprise	Unusable Stock	Unusable Fixed Assets	Interest from Invest. and Oper. Credits	Over-heads not Reflected in Output	Unamor-tized Costs of Future Periods	Penalties, Losses and Non-produc-tive Costs
ZŤS Dubnica n/V.	729.5	234.2	56.9	193.8	146.0	56.0–409.7
ZŤS Martin	367.6	227.2	81.3	127.5	28.7	151.4
ZVS Dubnica n/V.	11.5	7.0	6.4	—	8.8	—
ZŤS Nová Dubnica	27.8	1.3	0.8	0.4	0.8	—

Source: Adapted from Jozef Belcák, "Problems of the Conversion of Armament Production in Slovakia," in *Conversion of Military Production: Comparative Approach* (Bratislava: Institute of Economics, Slovak Academy of Science, 1993), p. 66.

major towns, Dubnica nad Váhom (population 7,000 in 1965 and 25,000 in 1985) and Nová Dubnica (13,000 inhabitants). While enterprises in this sub-region employed 21,770 people and produced goods and services worth 9.5 billion ČSK in 1988, in 1991 production shrank to 6 billion ČSK and the number of employees decreased to 15,862.[30] The sharp decline in production also strongly affected the subcontractors of ZŤS and ZVS. This was particularly evident in the case of building companies working primarily for ZŤS and ZVS. Table 5.1 gives some indication of the costs of conversion, while at the same time offering an indication of the difficulty of carrying out a conversion of enterprises organized according to the principles of socialist accounting and management.

Conversion created fundamental problems for the Dubnica region that engaged the representatives of many stakeholders. A May meeting of employers', trade unions' and state administrations' representatives in Dubnica was initiated by the Slovak Ministry of Labor and was supported by the trade union association, KOVO. Many other organizations were also involved in planning: representatives of local administrations, labor, city governments (in the case of Dubnica, representatives of the Dubnica Regional Council), management and employees, ministries, different agencies operating in

30. The data presented here were taken mainly from an application for regional subsidies "Ako úspesne realizovať hospodárske oživenie regiónov na Slovensku" ["How to Successfully Realize Regional Economic Recovery in Slovakia"] by Stefan Kaliar, Head of the Regional Department at the Local Administration Office in Dubnica nad Váhom.

the region (the Dutch agency START, U.S. AID, and the 600 members of the Association of Entrepreneurs in Dubnica. Some of this activity was not fruitless. Dubnica, for example, was successful in its application for a U.S. AID project for regional restructuring and managed to develop supporting programs with foreign firms. But this did not bring back thousands of jobs, and it did little to help the many firms threatened by bankruptcy.

At the local level, several organizations have a stake in arms enterprises. The most important are the Local Administration Office, the Local Labor Office, the Tax Office, the Local Office for the Environment, and the Subsidiary of the District Social Assistance Office. The Regional Council (with twenty-six members and six working groups) was established in 1991 to pursue regional stabilization programs. One of its tasks was to foster an Association of Entrepreneurs. The Council focuses on short- and medium-term goals, especially those dealing with unemployment, structural changes, and retraining. It also cooperates with the National Agency for Small and Medium Enterprises. One of its most important activities is preparing proposals to be included in the Conversion Law and subsequent national legislation.

Local organizations have identified several market barriers that impair economic change and growth in the Dubnica sub-region. Among these are low economic demand, poor financial discipline among the biggest enterprises which limits the development of a secondary sector, poor credit policy in the banking sector, a lack of capital, and serious ecological problems. These problems are aggravated by external factors, which include the termination of arms production, a collapse of traditional export markets and a serious recession in potential export markets, an average or lower than average technical level for most products, poor knowledge of markets, and the dominance of the public over the private sector.

The position of the Martin district is very similar to that of the Považská Bystrica district and the Dubnica sub-region. The Labor Office has had to deal with the layoff of approximately five thousand employees from ZŤS enterprises. In addition, two smaller companies in the area have been liquidated. At the beginning of October 1993, the unemployment rate was 10 percent, with 5,624 people on the Labor Office's roll.

Privatization is the most important issue for the future of Slovakia's arms manufacturers. Seeking to facilitate the possible privatization of ZŤS Dubnica, the Slovak government liquidated the firm's debts of about 950 million SK. Current debt amounts to about 70 percent of the firm's assets; debt liquidation, it is hoped, will cut the debt to 30 percent of the firm's assets. An employee-owned joint-stock company has also been formed, but approval of the ZŤS Dubnica privatization project is complicated by the fact that there is disagreement about the size of the state's stake in the company. The original project assumed that the state would hold one-third of the company's stock. Subsequent proposals have suggested a majority share. An uncertain defense strategy, made more uncertain by questions regarding Slovakia's possible NATO membership, has made it difficult to determine the extent to which production capacities should be preserved, and how the government can control private owners in the future without relinquishing control over its security policy.

A very similar process is under way in Martin, where employees of ZŤS Martin and Trstená are buying shares in Turčianské strojárne, a joint-stock company established by the management of ZŤS and the town of Martin. There are two plans for privatization. In one, Turčianské strojárne j.s.c. is expected to take over all of ZŤS except for the arms production divisions. In the other a private company, Kriváň, will acquire the company's engine and tractor divisions.[31]

Political Actors

The activism of former Czechoslovak President Václav Havel on behalf of quick military conversion is often considered to have played a crucial role. Havel has been very outspoken on this topic. He declared, for example, that "arms production and profit from its products by the state is an amoral act."[32] Indeed, it would be quite easy to compile a long list of quotations from Havel's speeches in which he speaks against arms production and the economic "advantage" of tank sales, both old and new, and advocates the clear moral "advantage" deriving from a refusal to sell. On more pragmatic grounds Havel has also opposed the sale of obsolete military hardware and unrestricted exports to politically sensitive areas around the globe. He supports conversion because it reflects the situation in the world after the Cold War and agrees with the Vienna disarmament talks.

31. Kriváň was established by several private firms in the region, Perex, Seco, and Ping, among others, which themselves had been set up by former ZŤS managers. See *Trend* (11 November 1993): 2.

32. *Pravda* (9 July 1993): 5.

Havel, to be sure, was not alone in his views. Slovakia had already begun to trim military expenditures as a part of budget restructuring before the end of the Cold War—a process that saw military expenditures decline from $1.2 ČSK billion in 1989 to $1.07 billion in 1990, due to underlying economic and technological changes affecting defense industries everywhere.[33] And the Velvet Revolution also affected, if only for a brief moment, popular responses to the problem of conversion. At the end of 1989, for example, employees of one big arms enterprise, ZŤS Martin, organized a meeting to support the cancellation of military production and criticize the former Communist government's export activities. In a moment of revolutionary fervor the federal government was asked to prohibit the export and production of weapons. This event clearly documents the "revolutionary enthusiasm" that was also visible in other areas of Czechoslovak society.

On balance, however, leading individuals in Slovakia as well as public opinion have not shared Havel's views. Slovak President Michal Kováč, for example, has disagreed with Havel in public. He appointed Vítazoslav Móric (SNS), a former employee of ZŤS Martin, as his advisor for arms conversion. In a television debate Móric stated that "opposition to Slovak arms production was mainly Czech propaganda." In a similar vein one of the former directors of ZŤS Dubnica nad Váhom, a major producer of arms, stated on 26 May 1993 that the government acted in an amateurish

33. For example, SIPRI makes it clear that employment cuts in arms industries are a trend in all European countries that results from a general "disarmament of policy." See Petr Valerián, "Křehký led konverze" ["Fragile Conversion"], *Hospodářské noviny* (1 March 1993): 10. A leading British specialist in defense conversion notices, more provocatively, a broader European-wide trend toward conversion: "It is important to note that, although accelerated by the end of the Cold War, the origins of this industrial turbulence predate the revolutions of 1988 and 1989, and the dissolution of the Soviet Union. Even without Mr. Gorbachev, profound changes would have occurred at the defense industrial level. These were arising from a general over-capacity of production, a shifting balance of leadership as between defense and civil technologies, the indirect effects of the Single European Act, and a concern within defense ministries about the competitiveness of western European defense firms vis-à-vis their United States counterparts. The last of these concerns has grown even more acute following the Kuwait war, as U.S. arms exporters have turned their attention more firmly to both Europe and the markets to which European firms themselves have traditionally exported. It deserves emphasis that international restructuring has come to the defense sector later than to the rest of industry." See Philip Gummett,"Restructuring of the Arms Industries in Western Europe: Market Rationalisation rather than Conversion," in *Conversion of Military Production: Comparative Approach* (Bratislava: Institute of Economics, Slovak Academy of Science and Friedrich Ebert Foundation, 1993), pp. 49–50.

way in 1989 when it suddenly stopped arms production rather than allowing producers to draw on credits for materials worth 900 million ČSK. Peter Magvasi, a former financial director of ZŤS Martin, another major arms producer, expressed a similar view: "The decision on termination of arms production made by the Federal Government in January 1990 was a shock for the Slovak engineering industry. This resolute political decision ... has caused a chaotic and unpremeditated start of conversion in comparison with other countries."[34] Public opinion data from 1991 show that Slovaks were also very critical of Havel's policy. Seventy percent of Slovak respondents believed that conversion was the result of an unjust policy developed in Prague.[35]

The dynamics of the conversion are determined by a wide range of actors who have different stakes in the process. For simplicity we can classify these stakeholders into three categories. The first category includes organizations like the government, political parties, trade unions, the Federation of Industry, and other interest groups operating at the national level. Second, there are regional and local groups, with stakeholders such as district Employment Offices and regional and local governments. Finally, there are stakeholders in the individual companies.

The Slovak government is involved in the conversion process in different ways. Institutionally, an office such as the Department of Special Production at the Ministry of Economy oversees conversion, and less formally, the government discusses both local and national problems of conversion with a variety of interest groups representing those affected most directly (trade unions, management, local governments). Regional councils were created to support activities designed to help mitigate the negative consequences

34. Peter Magvasi, "Approach of the Union of Engineering Industry to the Process of Conversion of Armament Production in Slovakia," in *Conversion of the Military Production: Comparative Approach* (Bratislava: Slovak Academy of Sciences, Institute of Economics, and Friedrich Ebert Foundation, 1993), p. 130.

35. Pavol Frič et al., *Aktuálne problémy Slovenskej spoločnosti* (Bratislava, Comelius University, May 1991), pp. 49–50. Two questions were asked about the sources of conversion. The first was: "Is the conversion process the result of bad policy developed in Prague?" The second was: "Is the conversion process the result of bad company leadership?" Supporters of the DS, SDĽ, SNS, and HZDS were inclined to agree with the first statement, while voters for VPN, KDH, Együttelles, and SZ disagreed. Over 60 percent of respondents not oriented to any particular political party agreed with the first statement, and less than 5 percent disagreed. But only a minority of citizens (36 percent) felt optimistic about arms production in the Slovak Republic or felt that economic factors should have priority over political and moral ones (39 percent).

of economic restructuring in particular districts. In their activities they are supported by associations of private employers.

Management views are exemplified by the former financial director of ZŤS Martin and the chairman of the Federation of Industry's Permanent Working Commission For Arms Production Conversion, Peter Magvasi. He has been a vocal critic of the government's failure to provide the industry with any short- or long-term outlook on its procurement. On the enterprise level trade unions have been on both sides of the issue. On the one hand, there is evidence that working conditions at some plants are dangerous and that some conversion is necessary to ensure future economic survival. On the other hand, unions have been reluctant to support rapid change in state-subsidized firms that had developed social infrastructures and provided employees with relatively high salaries. Because it has become evident that the impact of conversion is much stronger than expected, top trade union officials have started to object that Western countries are also exporting arms to inappropriate countries.

The conflict between these various political actors has become endemic. Although disagreements between management and unions are inevitable, it should be noted that at the outset, when the conversion process was broadly expected to be a relatively short-term and easy process, a broad consensus existed on the necessary conversion measures. But as the first negative effects occurred, the situation changed. Now, according to one top trade union member working for an enterprise caught up in conversion, collective agreements are not generally accepted by management, and the trade unions are closed out of discussions with top management.

Management is also locked in conflict with government. Difficult problems arising from the establishment or definition of property rights, management actions linked to pre-privatization strategies, and management problems during the process of conversion have led to government interference in the operations of particular firms, including the firing of top managers. On the other hand, government has also been actively involved in solving specific problems arising from military conversion. The Union of Engineering Industry of the Slovak Republic (UEI SR) also has attempted to address systematically the problems of conversion. Joint pressure from the Union of Engineering and the Confederation of Trade Unions resulted in the passage of a government decree (no. 6/1991) laying out a system of ameliorative measures designed to counter some of the negative economic and social consequences of conversion.[36] Trade union dissatisfaction with government policies, both federal and Slovak, has led to some collective actions. Usually, these have taken the form of "open letters"—such as the one KOVO, the Confederation of Trade Unions, addressed in May 1990 to Federal Minister of Labor and Social Affairs Petr Miller. Representing fifty Slovak and Czech industrial firms, the foreign trade organization Martimex, and one of the biggest commercial banks, Slovakia—Všeobecná úverová banka (VÚB), both shareholders of ZŤS Martin, used the same method when they sent a statement to Slovak Minister of Economy Jozef Kubečka. Conflict, however, was reduced due to economic growth in the private sector, the departure of Vietnamese workers (in the case of Dubnica), foreign assistance, and a tendency to maintain some overemployment by methods such as shortened working hours. Yet now, as economic problems deepen, conflict has been increasing; in Dubnica nad Váhom workers have gone on strike against unpaid wages and the unsolved economic problems of ZŤS.

A number of international actors, many of them from the U.S., were involved in Slovakia's conversion process. They provided assistance, mostly at the national level, to specific enterprises and regions. Members of the International Executive Service Corps (IESC), for example, gave advice to major firms such as ZŤS Martin, ZŤS Dubnica, PS Považská Bystrica, and PPS Detva, as well as to the Slovak Government. U.S. AID offered technical support to two Slovak companies undergoing conversion. KPMG Peat Marwick, a large consulting firm, was selected to organize the restructuring of both PPS Detva and ZŤS Hriňová. Moreover, the Czecho-Slovak-American Enterprise Fund (CSAEF) was engaged in a variety of support activities that focused primarily on small and medium-sized firms. And one Dutch company, START, has worked in the northwest region to improve the human resource management routines of Slovak firms that are going through the conversion process.

The activities of international organizations in which the U.S. plays a leading role has also been important. The North Atlantic Cooperation Council (NACC), for example, devoted three major meetings to the problem.[37] And the OECD, the International

---

36. Magvaši, "Approach of the Union of Engineering," p. 130.

37. On "Defense Conversion" (20–22 May 1992), on "Interaction between Defense Spending and Economic Development with Particular Emphasis on Defense Budget Issues" (30 September-2 October 1992), and on "The Human Dimension of Defense Conversion" (3–4 December 1992). See Daniel George, "NATO's Economic Cooperation with NACC Partners," *NATO Review* 41, 4 (August 1993): 20.

Monetary Fund, the World Bank Group, and the Bank for International Settlement have also offered assistance at the regional and enterprise level.

Several European institutions and organizations not directly concerned with economic matters have also been involved in conversion, as has the European Bank for Reconstruction and Development (EBRD). Furthermore, should Slovakia choose a Western European path in its security policy, it might be able to join the Independent European Program Group dealing with the coordination of procurement and research and development policies in organizations like the European Cooperation for the Long Term in Defense (EUCLID).[38] In sharp contrast to the involvement of U.S. and European actors, Germany has played no more than a marginal role in assisting Slovakia's conversion. Support typically came from Germany's political foundations, which organized some seminars. Direct German aid was discussed by the Slovak-German Roundtable without any concrete results.

Conclusion

The dramatic change in policy stemming from the Velvet Revolution and the end of the Cold War has left a deep imprint on Slovakia. Even so, in the past few years views have moderated and more pragmatic positions are now common. Václav Klaus, for one, has stated that Czechoslovak arms conversion was "too cruel" a form of economic interference in Slovak affairs,[39] and former Federal Minister of the Economy Vladimír Dlouhy stated, during a visit to ZŤS Martin, that "We have to realize that other countries are also doing business with arms, including those who are criticizing us the most for similar activity."[40] Greater pragmatism is on the rise in both the Slovak and the Czech Republics.

The case of the RDP Group illustrates this trend. Established by eighteen Czech arms producers, it is a holding company established with the aim of reviving the Czech arms industry. The leading company in the group is Škoda Plzeň, a famous pre-World War II arms producer. The group takes a pragmatic and business-like view of conversion. Its CEO said in one interview, "let us give up the naïve post-revolutionary ideals and let us give, by the development of special technologies, employment to the people

38. Gummett, "Restructuring of the Arms Industries in Western Europe," pp. 48, 58.
39. *Národná obroda* (19 October 1991): 13.
40. *Express*, 1992 (No. 12), p. 5.

and a chance for Czech industry to reach world standards."[41] Because of suspicions regarding Prague's motives, the RDP Group's decision to modernize the T-72 tank was not well received in Slovakia at first. Subsequently, more pragmatic steps were taken towards cooperation between the two states in arms production and exports. Peter Končier, director of ZŤS Dubnica nad Váhom, confirmed ZŤS's desire to cooperate with the RDP Group, but only in export activities. Later, cooperation in production was also included as a goal.

Slovak arms executives and government officials have made it clear that the arms industry is to be given a second chance. According to Andrej Sobol, deputy defense minister until the beginning of 1995, Slovakia is committed to exporting weapons in competition with other states.[42] The new policy explains why Slovakia launched in 1994 a major advertising campaign and sent delegations of officials, accompanied by the executives of Slovakia's major arms producers, to India, Vietnam, Indonesia, and Iran, all former importers of WTO arms. Foreign officials also have visited Bratislava hoping to forge closer ties with Slovak arms producers. The government's objective is to raise within a few years the production of arms to at least twenty-five per cent of the 1989 capacity.[43] Topping Slovakia's list of military products is a newly designed howitzer code-named "Zuzana" that fires NATO-standard ammunition. Military experts believe this to be the first of its kind intended for Western markets. The arms producer ZŤS Martin has modernized its classic T-72 tank, which is now also available on the world market. According to experts, there are an estimated 8,000 T-72 tanks in use around the world. While it is very difficult to predict future levels of arms production, there is now a visible movement on the part of companies towards activities that could help them survive. In some cases arms production may again become profitable. The future prospects of conversion companies will hinge both on strategies developed by management and on government policies that determine whether the Slovak armed forces will continue to be a customer of Slovak arms

41. Pavol Janík, "Vojenskopriemyselný komplex: Zbohom konverzia," ["Military Industrial Complex: Farewell to Arms Conversion"], *Národná obroda* (21 July 1993): 7.

42. "We do not want to be known as the gun suppliers of Europe, we just want to provide our citizens with jobs.... It is a strategic fight for the arms market out there, and every tactic and means is fair game. We will do what the rest of the world does," in Interview for "Reuter," Bratislava (24 November 1994).

43. Then Defense Minister Pavol Kanis, as quoted in Reuter (Bratislava, 24 November 1994).

producers, whether it will be possible to modernize arms production and to cooperate with foreign partners or export arms, and whether competitive prices will attract foreign customers.[44] However, even under the most advantageous conditions it is certain that Slovakia will not again attain its previous level of arms production.

The modernization of the Slovak arms industry has also contributed to an increasing compatibility with NATO weapons and has been a frequent topic of discussion with Western defense officials during 1995.[45] However, four scandals and allegations of the smuggling of Slovak arms forced the Foreign Ministry in 1995 to speak up in public against the accusation that Slovakia was shipping arms to extremist groups, terrorists and illegal organizations throughout the world. But the scandals and allegations have continued and thus are possibly contributing to further endangerment of Slovakia's hopes of joining NATO.[46]

Military conversion since 1989 shows the primacy of international economic and political developments that have forced domestic actors to deal with massive dislocations in Slovakia's regional economy. Nationalist resentment of the federal policy initially dominated by Czech influence and of the harsh intrusion of international markets and political pressures are one important consequence that is shaping the distinctive political outlook of Slovakia in contemporary central Europe.

Privatization

Privatization in Slovakia, as is true throughout central Europe, is a basic means to establish a market economy, to create new economic incentives, and to establish ownership control over corporate managers. The distinctiveness of Slovak privatization lies in

44. For example, the price of a Slovak T-72 tank is $0.9 million, while the M-1 Abrams costs $4 million and the British "Challenger" £3.8 million.

45. Among others, meetings of Defense Minister Ján Sitek with British Defence Minister Malcolm Rifkind on 15 February 1995, as reported in *Národná obroda* (16 February 1995), and with U.S. Defense Secretary Perry on 18 September 1995, as reported in *Sme* (19 September 1995). "Armáda Slovenskej republiky" ("The Army of the Slovak Republic") (Bratislava, 1995), pp. 96–97.

46. The allegations were, for example, substantiated by a cargo of Slovak arms that was accidentally detected in the Azores even though the shipment had been declared as medical instruments bound for Ecuador. See *Pravda* (24 March 1995). The Slovak Weapons Export Commission insists that this cargo was properly licensed. Because Slovakia's position differs from that of the Czech Republic, such scandals have different political consequences.

the government's attempt to retain some political control over acquisitions by foreign investors and to privatize in such a way that trusted individuals are placed in key economic positions. Voucher privatization, the government argues, does not redistribute property on the basis of economic efficiency. And because the government does not earn money from sales, voucher privatization contributes to budget deficits. Furthermore, it generates inflation and provides opportunities for money laundering. These shortcomings, however, are balanced by the fact that privatization improves the general economic position of the country and enhances the competitiveness of Slovak industry. Voucher privatization is an efficient method of privatization in at least two additional respects: it is quick and, as the first results demonstrate, generates concentrated ownership through investment funds and companies.

Slovakia's privatization is intimately related to that of the Czech Republic. For privatization programs originated in both states before the breakup of Czechoslovakia. Because Czechoslovakia's public sector comprised 98 percent of all firms the reformers were looking for as fast and irrevocable a break with the past as possible. While virtually all reformers agreed on the overall objective, there was considerable disagreement about the means to accomplish this objective. Some favored direct sales and public auctions; others emphasized the advantages of new forms of privatization such as employee or management buyouts; still others argued in favor of a voucher scheme organized by state investment funds. In the end the federal Czechoslovak government settled on a three-step process of privatization. First, within a few years most of the small state-owned firms were to be auctioned off; in the case of the Czech Republic more than 90 percent within three years. Second, large companies were sold directly to the public or joint ventures were formed with foreign companies. Between 1990 and 1995, for example, foreign firms invested $5.8 billion in the Czech Republic.[47] Finally, and most important, Czechoslovakia decided on a process of voucher privatization.

The five rounds of the first wave were implemented in 1992 prior to the country's breakup. This program aimed at the privatization of large firms valued at 166.5 billion ČSK. The program

47. Hana Pišková, "Přímé zahraniční investice vzrostly" ["Direct Foreign Investment Increased"], *Hospodářské noviny* [*Economic News*] (1 March 1996): 7.

relied on both direct (12.3 billion crowns in 1992) and indirect sales (through the issuing of individual vouchers). In addition, a total of 9,667 out of 11,420 economic units were successfully auctioned off as part of the small-scale privatization program. This resulted in total sales of fourteen billion SK, 1.6 billion more than the original offering price. By the end of 1993 Slovakia's small-scale privatization was virtually complete.[48] The doubling of the GDP produced in Slovakia's private sector, from one-fifth to two-fifths between 1992 and 1994, is largely due to the success of the small-scale privatization program. The same factor accounted for the shift from 40 to 65 percent by the end of 1995.

Subsequently, the Czech Republic followed through with a second round of privatization in 1994. In the first round of voucher privatization each adult citizen had received for a $35 fee coupons nominally worth $1,000 which could be used to purchase shares in hundreds of formerly state-owned firms.[49] In the case of the Czech republic state-owned companies valued at $10 billion, or 70 to 80 percent of the public sector, were thus transferred into private hands within a few years. Most Czechs spent their coupons on investment funds, which received 70 percent of the coupons in the first round, 60 percent in the second.

Yet the common origin of voucher privatization has contributed to increasing tensions between Slovakia and the Czech Republic. Because the Czech government was reluctant to confirm and accept the property rights which Slovak holders of investment vouchers received in the first wave of voucher privatization, the political pressure brought to bear by parties and the public led to a change in policy. A similar problem occurred when representatives of both countries were first not able to agree on the division and later on the exchange of shares of the General Credit Bank (Všeobecná úverová banka, VÚB).[50]

Following independence Slovakia's privatization took a quite different course. The legal foundations for privatization were provided

---

48. These are data from Slovakia's Ministry of Privatization.

49. In the second wave, which occurred in the Czech Republic in 1994, citizens received coupons worth nominally $700.

50. Slovak representatives decided to file a charge against the Czech FNP after the top officials of the Czech Fund (in June 1994) decided to transfer shares of both funds (the Slovak Fund of National Property and the Czech FNP) in Komerční banka and VÚB to the division of federal property. The exchange of Slovak's 14.67 percent share of shares in Komerční banka for a 30 percent share of the Czech FNP in VÚB had not been realized because of the differing market value of shares of both banks in the Czech Republic and Slovakia.

by two privatization acts and the law on restitution.[51] In contrast to their counterparts in the Czech Republic, Slovakian politicians have engaged in an acrimonious debate on issues of privatization. Although rooted in domestic politics, the political struggles over Slovakia's privatization have clear consequences for the institutional structure of Slovakia's emerging capitalist economy, specifically the position of the banking sector and investment funds as well as the type of corporate governance system, American or German, that will eventually prevail. After the breakup of Czechoslovakia, 2.6 million citizens were registered for the first round of privatization in the Slovak Republic.[52] In this round 503 Slovak companies, with a book value of ninety billion ČSK, were offered for voucher privatization. Slovak citizens could also invest in 988 companies in the Czech Republic.[53]

As was true of the Czech Republic, voucher privatization created investment funds that became an important new type of economic actor in Slovakia. Rather than investing directly in companies coupon holders relied on these financial intermediaries for approximately 60 percent of their total investment. VÚB Invest is a good example of how these investment funds are related to other financial institutions. It was founded by Všeobecná úverová banka VÚB, one of Slovakia's biggest commercial banks. It owns 88 percent of VÚB Invest's equity capital. With assets of 534 million SK, this investment company had, between 1993 and 1995, obtained net profits of 194 million SK. VÚB Invest is a founder and administrator of the biggest Slovak investment fund, VÚB Kupón, the recipient of 501 million investment points from 551,000 investors in the privatization process. VÚB Kupón received shares of 238 companies nominally valued at 11.98 billion Sk. In sixty-two companies its equity exceeds 10 percent. VÚB Kupón has a subsidiary company in the Czech Republic, VÚB Consult Ltd. A special feature of this fund was that it invested more in Czech than Slovak companies.

51. The wording of the small-scale privatization act (Act 427/1990) regarding the transfer of state-owned property is included in Acts No. 541/1990, No. 429/1991, and No. 561/1991. The wording of the large-scale privatization act (Act 92/1991) is included in Acts No. 92/1992, No. 264/1992, No. 544/1992, No. 17/1993, and No. 172/1993. The restitution process is regulated by Acts Nos. 403/1990 and 87/1991 and regulations Nos. 458/1990 and 137/1991.

52. This number increased to 3.4 million for the second wave but remained stagnant throughout 1995 and 1996.

53. Individual Slovak investors put 90 percent of their coupons in Slovak companies; the proportion for investment funds ran at about only 65 percent. See *Trend* 3, 13, p. 1.

Part of VÚB Kupón was sold to the Japanese investment company, Nomura, which decided subsequently to sell back its shares and exit VÚB Invest. VÚB Invest also administers two share funds (VÚB Invest Finančny Podielový and VÚB Invest Real Podielový). And for the second wave of voucher privatization VÚB Invest has prepared a new investment fund, VÚB Kupón plus.

The second wave has given rise to an extensive discussion among economists and policy makers over the mode and legal framework of privatization. According to Blommestein and Spencer, investment funds can concentrate share ownership, thus enabling these funds to play an important role in corporate control and, possibly, in the search for investment capital. However, these authors also point out that because the funds are a recent innovation it is still not clear how active they will be in the financing and management of companies. Nevertheless, they argue that it is necessary to build a healthy banking sector as soon as possible, because, in their view, banks are the best source of both capital and oversight.[54]

It is still too early to give a comprehensive evaluation of the efficiency of the new investment funds. But a 1993 survey of the managers of thirty-two investment funds showed that these managers affirmed the right of shareholders to participate in the control of individual enterprises. By a ratio of almost two to one, the fund managers saw corporate governance rather than securities trading as their most important task.[55] The interest in control varied with the degree of a fund's ownership of particular firms; when the stake in a firm exceeds the 10 percent mark, more than a quarter of the managers want to exercise control. Fully one-third of the managers indicated that they are aiming at controlling more than ten enterprises.

It is thus hardly surprising that the funds meet with considerable opposition from both individual shareholders and corporate managers. Associations of individual shareholders are often coordinated by corporate managers or trade union leaders and have no regular legal standing in Slovakia. Because they are legally

---

54. J. Blommestein and M. G. Spencer, "The Role of Financial Institutions in the Transition to a Market Economy," IMF Working Paper No.93/75 (Washington D.C., International Monetary Fund, October 1993).

55. Daneš Brzica and Brigitta Schmögnerová, "Podnikový sektor z pohl'adu investičných spoločností a investičnýoh fondov" ["Enterprise Sector from the Point of View of Investment Companies and Investment Funds"], *EÚ SAV* (Bratislava, Slovak Academy of Sciences, Institute of Economics, April 1993).

unregulated, investment funds view them as unfair. Among a list of possible partners for cooperation, the funds put these associations last. Still, these associations are seeking to exercise political influence. For example, under the leadership of former Minister of Privatization Milan Janičina, an association seeking to protect the rights of individual investment voucher owners began to organize a petition drive in June 1995. In attempting to force a referendum on the stalled second wave of voucher privatization, it hopes to increase the 80,000 signatures it has collected to date to an eventual total of 400,000. Corporate managers are also engaged in at least covert conflict with investment funds. They had expected voucher privatization to leave untouched their prerogatives or to enhance their power through management buy-outs or the purchase of shares from individuals. As matters turned out, investment companies soon became serious competitors in the power struggle for control of firms.

Like Hungary, Slovakia has a public Fund for National Property (FNP) which administers state-owned corporations. It is one of the biggest owners of partially privatized Slovak companies. Between 1992 and 1994 the FNP privatized property valued at about ninety billion SKR. The pace of privatization further accelerated in 1995 when the FNP concluded 292 agreements valued at 32.4 billion SKR.[56] The FNP has become a political football in the 1990s. In a changing political climate its rights and responsibilities have been radically restructured. An amendment to legislation originally passed in 1991 expanded its role in the privatization process while at the same time prohibiting any direct links between the FNP and the Slovak government. Until March 1994, for example, Vladimir Mečiar, then prime minister of the Slovak Republic, was also president of the presidium of the FNP. Top administrators of the FNP are now elected by the Slovak National Council (SNC).

Slovakia's stock exchanges have developed not so much as a response to company needs as to the opportunities offered by voucher privatization. This is a source of their institutional weakness, especially as privatization has stalled. At present in Slovakia there are three stock exchanges: Bratislava Stock Exchange,

56. The government receives 10 to 20 percent of the total price at the time the deal is signed; investors pay the balance of the purchase price on an installment basis stretched over a decade. See Danes Brzica, "History and Recent Development of Privatization in the Slovak Republic: Selected Issues" (forthcoming, European Center for Peace and Development, Belgrade, 1996).

Bratislava Option Stock Exchange, and RM-S System Slovakia. The Association for Capital Market Development was established in October 1993. Its aim is to support ethical behavior in the financial sector and to make recommendations on future or pending legislation. The founding meeting of the Association of Securities Traders was held in November 1994.

Problems associated with the trading of derivatives have resulted in the persistent weakness of the Bratislava Option Exchange. Indeed some political parties argue that privatization creates ample opportunities (especially in the case of direct sales) for the corruption of state bureaucrats. Some sources claim that the exchange has suffered a loss of sixty million SK, which explains recurrent proposals to merge the BOE with the Bratislava Stock Exchange. Initially, initiatives for the proposed merger were fostered by BOE itself, but now the Ministry of Finance supports the idea. It feels that the merger would make it easier to maintain control over the trading activity of investment funds. There is also a proposal to introduce so-called "stock exchange totality," under which shares could be traded only on registered stock exchanges. In 1995 approximately 90 percent of the total volume passed through "direct and registered" trades.

Privatization affects the balance between mercantilism and internationalism. Motivated by the expectation of short-term profits, the only substantial inflow of portfolio investment into Slovakia occurred in the first quarter of 1994. But voucher privatization and investment funds have helped create a capital market for foreign investors in Slovakia as well. As in Hungary, foreign investors have created a market for financial services and alternative investment vehicles, such as option agreements. The door is thus open to a variety of forms of foreign participation in Slovakia's privatization program. Among them are investment funds, which will probably have to sell a portion of their portfolio to foreign investors in order to raise the capital necessary for financing individual companies and paying individual coupon holders. Thus the interest of investment funds may be at odds with those of management, which typically has no interest in ceding control over operations to a foreign owner. In these conflicts the government, specifically the Ministries for Privatization and Finance as well as the FNP, tend to line up on the side of management. Deputy Prime Minister and Minister of Finance Sergej Kozlik, for example, has argued that a clearance "sale of shares abroad is a menacing possibility. We do not know yet who stands behind whom. Personally I see risks rather than positives."[57] Fears regarding international investments are one important reason why Slovakia's second wave of privatization remains mired in controversy; why, in 1994–95, the government changed its policy to favor the issuing of government bonds rather than investment vouchers; and why Slovakia is perceived in many European quarters to be sliding back toward a policy that prefers economic nationalism over a liberal internationalism.[58]

The consequence has been a noticeable cooling of relations between Slovakia and foreign firms and experts. Experts from the World Bank and other international financial organizations reportedly have insisted that for the second wave of voucher privatization to succeed, a minimum of seventy to eighty billion SK worth of assets must be privatized, a larger proportion of the total number of state-owned firms than the government may be prepared to sell.[59] Nomura's widely noted decision to sell its stake in one of the largest Slovakian investment funds, VÚB Kupón, is another indication of the declining interest of the international financial community in Slovakia's economy.

Aware of the importance of privatization for the future health of the Slovak political economy, various Slovak political parties have chosen different stances on the issue of privatization. The political parties clarified their positions in the 1994 national elections. A coalition of three Hungarian parties (Maďarská koalícia) has always been fully supportive of both the principle of privatization and the method of voucher privatization. A coalition of four parties called Common Choice (Spoločná voľba, SV), which is led by the left-wing Party of the Democratic Left (Strana demokratickej ľavice, SDL), has gradually moved to support voucher privatization. Although its representatives initially preferred employee buy-outs (EBOs), now, despite the fact that certain currents inside the SDL still harbor some negative feelings about vouchers, the leadership of the party favors voucher privatization, which has become part of a political strategy directed primarily against the HZDS. The difference of opinion between the SDL and other parties currently in opposition is not over whether to privatize by vouchers, but rather over what should be privatized by this method.

Characteristic of the SV is its fondness for public ownership and control. The Democratic Union (Demokratická únia, DU)

---

57. *Národná obroda* (3 January 1995): 13.
58. Brzica, "History and Recent Development," pp. 12–14.
59. *Národná obroda* (8 May 1995): 121.

holds that the voucher method can also be used for privatizing state property. The Democratic Party (Demokratická strana, DS) also supports the voucher method of privatization, generally along the lines of the views of the Czech ODS (Civic Democratic Party) with whom it shares many views. In June 1995 the leader of the DS, Peter Osuský, said that changing the existing plans for voucher privatization would constitute a breach of confidence and respect toward the Slovak population, seeing as 3.5 million Slovak citizens have acquired investment coupons in response to the government's promise to distribute shares of companies worth eighty billion SK. Because the Christian-Democratic Movement (Krestanskodemokratické hnutie, KDH) introduced the first wave of voucher privatization when its own leader, Dr. Čarnogurský, served as prime minister, it is only natural that this party supports continuing this method. Led by Prime Minister Vladimír Mečiar, the Movement for a Democratic Slovakia (Hnutie za demokratické Slovensko, HZDS) presents itself as a party that wants to keep domestic capital in the hands of employees and Slovak managers. Early on it considered voucher privatization to be of limited importance to the process of economic transformation, but over time leading representatives of the party have become more outspoken about their assessment of the role of voucher privatization, especially during the second wave of privatization. Their view tends to be more supportive of standard methods of direct privatization than the voucher method. This view also entails a strong opposition to any further enhancement of the role of investment companies and funds.

These differences in outlook among of Slovakia's major parties explain why Slovak governments have followed quite different policies on privatization. While former prime minister Moravčík's government supported the process of voucher privatization despite considerable opposition from within the coalition, the Mečiar government is a strong opponent of voucher privatization and favors direct sales instead. After announcing a specific date for the beginning of the second on 5 January 1995, State Secretary of the Slovak Ministry of Finance, Jozef Magula, then announced that the rules for the second wave of voucher privatization would have to be changed.[60]

---

60. The professed reason was that the zero-round (in which citizens are permitted to put their investment points into investment funds but cannot use them to purchase company shares) had not yet started.

Since then, Slovakia's privatization has provoked intense debate that has come to be symbolized by the bitter political and personal feud between the prime minister and the president of the Republic. President Michal Kováč has taken a strong position on the issue of voucher privatization, effectively stalling Prime Minister Vladimir Mečiar's planned modifications prior to the second wave. Specifically, the president has refused to sign three amendments to what is commonly referred to as the Large-Scale Privatization Act (Act No. 92/1991). He objects to legal provisions that would limit the power of investment funds by prohibiting them from putting their representatives on management, as opposed to supervisory, boards of those companies of which they hold significant numbers of shares. And he strongly opposes new legislation which would grant the government a veto right over key corporate decisions such as the sale of a company to foreign investors.

As in Hungary, Slovakian privatization is a profoundly political process, shaped by considerations of political power and expediency as much as by arguments for economic rationality. Specifically, the Mečiar government is proposing to sharply reduce, if not eliminate, voucher privatization in the second round. This policy stance reflects the government's express preference for sharply reducing or eliminating altogether the role of investment funds and international investors in Slovakia's economy. But in sharp contrast to Hungary, the evolution of policy does not feature merely a succession of different approaches to a vexing problem within an agreed-upon political framework. Instead, the future of Slovakian privatization is now cast in terms of a deep personal, political and constitutional conflict between prime minister and president.

What looks like a conflict between two powerful politicians also appears at first to be a conflict between competing economic models for organizing Slovakia's political economy. Czech-style voucher privatization was intended to create an Anglo-Saxon capital market and capitalism. Mečiar's mercantilist approach, and the political machine that he is seeking to build to strengthen his political camp, appears to be modeled after the traditional German and central European style of capitalism that leaves a great deal of power over industry in the hands of a small number of banks and institutional investors. However, the unintended consequence of voucher privatization in the Czech Republic was to leave control over the investment funds in the hands of the Czech banks. In the Czech Republic seven out of the ten largest funds were established by banks, while in Slovakia only two of the ten largest funds were established by banks. In any case, it is likely that the same development would have prevailed in Slovakia even had the Mečiar government not forcefully intervened. Thus personal power politics, not competing institutional models, are at the root of the deep conflict over the preferred method of privatization in Slovakia.

The connection between partisan politics and the investment funds is a murky one. A few political parties have apparently informally participated in the building of some investment funds. But it is very difficult either to describe precisely these delicate and controversial connections or to identify the political loyalties of individual investment groups. There is a commonly shared view, however, that some investment funds are more inclined to the HZDS party while others favor more liberal parties. A proper understanding of the power of institutional investors does not, however, depend on knowing precisely whether the existing structure of investors in voucher privatization represents a low or a high level of ownership concentration. Rather, we wish to show only that institutional investors possess sufficient power to impose efficient corporate governance on the newly privatized companies. Although institutional investors do not presently represent political power, they have started to form interest groups that are comparable to those of industrial firms and banks.

Preliminary evidence based on empirical research into the operation of investment funds and a small sample of industrial companies shows that Slovakia's institutional investors do indeed operate like strategic investors, even in the absence of any legal framework designed to facilitate the playing of such a role. Investment funds have a right to own a maximum of 20 percent of a company's shares (a percentage higher than is permitted by German, French, or U.S. regulations) and their representatives can sit on management and supervisory boards. However, models ranging from "strong management boards," with representatives of owners (usually representatives of investment funds), to "weak management boards," with owners limited to seats on a company's supervisory board, exist in practice, as do various admixtures.

Thus two models exist in Slovakia. The first features a strong supervisory board, the second a strong management board. While owners are present on the supervisory board in the former, in the latter they are present on the management board. The Fund of National Property has supported the German bank-centered model of statutory bodies as the preferred one for Slovakia. Investment funds typically have supported strong management boards. In reality, both models coexist and even interchange when investment funds decide to change the operations of a (successful) company from the second model to the first.

The basic features of the U.S. and the German models of corporate governance in the development of the Slovak economy can be delimited in the following terms.[61] As in the United States, Slovakia's evolving political economy features a large number of corporate listings on the stock exchange; corporate ownership in the hands of a relatively large number of individuals and non-bank financial institutions such as investment funds; and active trading of company shares by investment funds outside of regular financial markets, such as the Bratislava stock exchange. But as in Germany, only a few companies are actively traded on the stock market, illustrating the financial market's low level of liquidity; core investors hold up to 20 percent of each privatized corporation; banks own a substantial proportion of equity capital either directly or indirectly; a two-tier board structure is common; and some banks and funds intend to be active investors.

Although it is too early to speak of any clear tendency of Slovakia to follow the German social market model or the German model of corporate governance, a shift towards direct, rather than voucher, methods of privatization reinforces an evolving approach that aims at imitating the German model of corporate governance. For it offers even more "direct power" to banks than does the method of voucher privatization.[62] And because Slovakia has adopted many institutional arrangements, such as the accounting system, from the German model and moreover has gradually adjusted its institutional framework to conform to EU legislation, it seems likely that the Slovak model will follow the German model more closely than the U.S. one. In addition to adjusting to EU law, Slovakia is developing a system of pension insurance more closely modeled after the German than the American model.

61. Daneš Brzica, "American vs. German Models of Corporate Control in the Slovak Republic," in Pavol Marasz, Jana Plichtová, and Vladimír Krivý, eds., *Economics and Politics: Proceedings from the 5th Bratislava Symposium and 2nd East Central Conference* (Bratislava: Slovak Committee of the European Cultural Foundation, 1995), pp. 207–95.

62. We are using the expression "direct power" because of our need to distinguish cases where banks hold directly shares as a consequence of, for example, a debt-equity swap in the case of companies in trouble from cases where a bank has established an investment company and this investment company has created one or more investment funds. In the latter case the bank is a co-owner, or shareholder, of these funds, not a direct owner of the company.

Even if the German model were to prevail, one significant feature of Slovakia's privatization needs to be underlined. Despite sharp ideological differences on "voucher-style" privatization, economic behavior tends to be pragmatic. There are 3.5 million holders of investment coupons in Slovakia and they expect positive results from holding these coupons, a serious constraint on the policy choices of whatever coalition holds power in Bratislava. Voucher privatization and the large number of investment companies and funds will speed up Slovakia's economic transformation both in the institutionalization of property rights and in the movement toward de facto integration into the EU. The balance of power in corporations is slowly shifting, following the German model, from management, which had been hegemonic, to banks and non-banking financial institutions. Germany's central role as the source of the largest amount of direct foreign investment in central Europe is likely to reinforce these institutional effects.

The Hungarian Minority in Slovakia

Compared to the strength of European standards in the treatment of the German minority in Poland, the position of the Hungarian minority in Slovakia reflects both the powerful hold of traditional, central European conceptions of nationality as well as the intense political infighting in Bratislava. About 15 to 20 percent of the current Slovak population of 5.3 million belong to ethnic minorities. The vast majority consists of about 570,000 Hungarians, 250,000 to 500,000 Romas, and 55,000 Czechs. Spurred by the atrocities and occupation of Nazi Germany, Czechoslovakia's policy of forcible resettlement after World War II left in 1950 only 6,000 of the more than 150,000 Germans who had lived in Slovakia in 1930.[63]

Hungarians are compactly settled between the Danube and the southern border of Slovakia.[64] Incorporated for many centuries in the Habsburg Monarchy, and after 1867 in the empire's eastern half, where it was administered by Hungary, Slovakia became part of Czechoslovakia at the end of World War I. A relatively liberal

---

63. Georg Brunner, *Nationalitätenprobleme und Minderheitskonflikte in Osteuropa* (Ebenhausen: Stiftung Wissenshaft und Politik, 1993), p. 117. Dieter W. Bricke, *Minderheiten im östlichen Mitteleuropa: Deutsche und Europäische Optionen* (Baden-Baden: Nomos, 1995), p. 97.

64. In southern Slovakia Hungarians account for more than 90 percent of the population in 194 villages, more than 50 percent in about 400 villages, and slightly above 10 percent in 508 villages.

minority policy is one reason why the Hungarian population in Slovakia has preserved its distinctive identity. Slovakia's nationalist fervor surrounding the 1993 breakup of Czechoslovakia reinforced latent fears on the part of Slovaks living in the southern part of the country that they were a minority in their newly constituted state. Slovaks and Hungarians have engaged in a symbolic politics that may poison political relations for years to come. For example, while the Slovak Ministry of Transport ordered the removal of Hungarian village signs, the Hungarian minority built memorials commemorating Horthy's occupation of southern Slovakia during World War II. Lurking behind symbolic politics is the specter of violence. The Hungarian parties in Slovakia have, to date, succeeded in blocking the government's attempt to reorganize the Slovak armed forces so that one of its parts would become a Border Guard.

Slovak-Hungarian relations have been influenced by domestic constitutional provisions. Slovakia's constitutional provisions are in full agreement with European standards, such as Articles 20–22 of the Council of Europe Framework Convention for the Protection of National Minorities. And the Slovak constitution of September 1992 contains the same Charter for the Protection of Human Rights and Fundamental Freedoms that can be found in the Czech constitution.[65]

But these constitutional protections of minority rights are not free from criticisms. Some Slovaks, for example, are critical of a constitutional provision that, in accordance with European norms, lets individuals freely choose to join a specific national minority, as members of the Roma minority typically do. And the Hungarian minority was often critical of a relatively liberal version of the language law, in force until November 1995, that regulated the use of minority languages. And it has condemned outright the elimination of many of the provisions protecting minority rights in the new law which prohibits, for example, bilingualism and restricts the use of minority languages in relations with public authorities

65. Chapter 4 of the constitution defines the rights of minority and ethnic groups. And Articles 33 and 34 posit that membership in a national minority or ethnic group cannot be used to the detriment of individual rights. Members of such groups are guaranteed the right to develop their own culture, to disseminate information, to organize themselves in nationality associations, to be educated in their own languages, to use their own languages in their dealings with public authorities, to participate in the issues that affect national minorities and ethnic groups, and to establish and maintain their own educational and cultural institutions.

to instances where the minority exceeds a minimum threshold of 20 percent in a village or town. In addition, the Hungarian minority insists on the official recognition of the Hungarian versions of first and family names; the use of Hungarian street and village signs alongside Slovak ones; the revocation of a decree issued after World War II that declares the Hungarian minority in Slovakia to have been collectively guilty in their conduct during World War II; and the redrawing of administrative boundaries. Hungarians point to the silence in the Slovak constitution and relevant legislation about the necessary financial support for the constitutionally mandated educational and cultural affairs of the national minorities in Slovakia. Most important, the Hungarian minority in Slovakia points to the Preamble of the Slovak Constitution which enshrines the central rather than the Western European tradition of ethnic and national identity. It reads: "we the Slovak nation" rather than "we the people of Slovakia."

In Hungary the Slovak minority experiences difficulties which are not altogether dissimilar. Legally, Hungary guarantees full protection to all members of national minorities, both as an individual and group right. But the new Nationality Act of 7 July 1993 embeds the principle of the self-determination of minorities within a more encompassing principle of dual or plural self-determination that makes it possible for a member of one of Hungary's national minorities to define him/herself simultaneously as a member of a minority and a Hungarian. The use of minority languages in public institutions is legally protected. But an assimilation policy that peaked in recent decades, especially in the 1960s, has led to a significant decline in the use of minority languages, including Slovak.[66] The Hungarian Constitution guarantees freedom of religion and the Nationality Act (Article 50) guarantees that church ceremonies will be conducted in minority languages. This condition, however, is rarely met. Only nine of the approximately one hundred villages in which the Slovak minority in Hungary lives have a Slovak-speaking priest. The Hungarian education system is increasingly neglecting to provide education in minority languages. The number of child care centers (sixty) which offer Slovak language instruction (one hour per week) has been cut back. The school reform of 1960 greatly restricted the schools for national minorities. Slovak is taught only as a foreign language (three to four hours per week) in seventy-one elementary schools. In five schools

66. As a major European language, German, but not Slovak, is a partial exception to this generalization.

three subjects are taught in Slovak. Two secondary schools offer three subjects in Slovak.[67]

In the early 1990s Hungary's constitutional provisions and domestic and foreign policies tended to aggravate the situation between the two countries. The Hungarian Constitution (Article 6, paragraph 3) stipulates that Hungary is responsible for the welfare of those ethnic Hungarians who live abroad, and that the government must support the relations between these minorities and Hungary. Thus the Constitution introduces an ethnic, not a civic, notion of nationality into Hungarian foreign policy, and the Hungarian government has consistently intervened on the side of the Hungarian minority in Slovakia. It intervened particularly strongly when the Slovak parliament rejected a constitutional revision put forward by the Hungarian minority aimed at rewording the preamble of the Slovak Constitution. By sending the complaint of four Hungarian parties in Slovakia to the Council of Europe, the Hungarian government aligned itself with the position of radical elements among Slovakia's Hungarian minority. Given this Hungarian policy it is not surprising that since 1990 representatives of the Hungarian minority in Slovakia have engaged the Hungarian MDF (Hungarian Democratic Forum) rather than the Slovak government in a permanent dialogue on the issue of minority rights. A more nationalist successor to the MDF, which split in March 1996, is likely to adopt a vigilant stance in the future.

The liberal and socialist opposition of the Antall government strongly criticized these contacts and insisted that a recognition of the inviolability of borders should be part of any agreement seeking to secure Hungarian minority rights in Slovakia. When a socialist-liberal government was elected in Hungary in 1994 it organized its foreign policy around three major goals: European integration, the stabilization of relations with Hungary's neighbors, and guarantees for Hungarian minorities living in other countries, including Slovakia. In this manner it sought to preempt NATO fears that a problem of Greek-Turkish dimensions would be recreated should Hungary and Slovakia be admitted to join NATO. The fear persists in some Western quarters that a suppression of the Hungarian minority in Slovakia might trigger in central Europe a crisis of Yugoslavian proportions.[68] In an attempt to

67. Ján Hovorka, "Slováci v Maďarsku" (unpublished manuscript, Bratislava, Ministry of Foreign Affairs, 1994), pp. 20–25.

68. Bennett Kovrig, "NATO Council Seeks a Solution of Minority Issue" ["Az Atlanti Tanács Megoldást Keres a Kisebségi Kerdésben"] *Népszabadság* (18 June 1994): 30.

alleviate NATO concerns, both countries signed in October 1993 a five-year bilateral military cooperation agreement.

Slovakia and Hungary also signed on 19 March 1995 the Basic Treaty regulating the status of minorities on both sides of the border. The treaty focuses primarily on two issues: Hungarian guarantees of the inviolability of Slovakian borders on the one hand, and the protection of Hungarian minority rights in Slovakia on the other.[69] The issue of borders has been solved. And because of Hungary's unwavering European commitment, the treaty's ratification met no resistance in the Hungarian parliament. The issue of minority rights, however, remains mired in ambiguity and controversy. Specifically, in contrast to some of the major international documents signed and ratified at the end of World War II, as well as virtually all domestic legislation, Recommendation 1201 of the Council of Europe speaks of collective as well as individual minority rights. The treaty is thus couched in sufficiently ambiguous terms to allow the two governments each to present to their domestic constituencies the treaty's obligations in a favorable light.

In Slovak domestic politics this game has run quickly into real difficulties. The Hungarian minority, for example, refers to 1201 when it defends its claims for greater autonomy. Because they are adamantly opposed to granting the Hungarian minority anything that might resemble collective rights, parties of both the ruling coalition and the opposition in the Slovak parliament are strongly opposed to meeting this demand.[70] Hence the treaty has encountered stiff resistance in the Slovak parliament which, on this issue, handed the Mečiar government its most stinging defeat in December 1995 when it refused ratification. Furthermore, parliament has further complicated relations with the Hungarian minority by passing in November 1995 the controversial State Language Act, which revokes the relatively liberal provisions of the Language Act of 1990. In both instances nationalist forces inside the ruling

69. The treaty confirms not only the inviolability of borders and the territorial integrity of the two states; it also stipulates, in accordance with European norms, that minorities have not only rights but also obligations. Specifically, minorities relinquish the right to engage in any activity that contravenes international law and that undermines in any way the sovereign equality, territorial integrity, and political independence of the state in which they live.

70. The Association of Slovak Workers (ZRS) and the Slovak National Party (SNS) belong to the government; the Slovak Democratic Left (SDL) and the Christian Democratic Movement (KDH) are in the opposition. All four parties have strongly opposed the Basic Treaty between Slovakia and Hungary, signed in March 1995, that, following Recommendation 1201, endorses collective minority rights.

coalition succeeded in shaping government policy. It took Prime Minister Mečiar until March 1996 to get the Slovak parliament to ratify the Basic Treaty. The Slovak National Party (SNS) coupled its support of ratification to the passing of a far-reaching amendment to the Criminal Code that opens the door to administrative abuse and judicial shackling of the political opposition. The amendment was denounced vociferously and in unprecedentedly strong language by both liberal critics of the government and the Catholic Church. In the view of the Conference of Bishops of the Slovak Republic it is comparable to legislation passed by the Communists in 1948 that provided the basis for "the conviction and torture of hundreds of thousands of innocent victims."[71]

But it is easy to paint the situation in darker colors than is warranted by reality. No Hungarian party in Slovakia expresses irredentist demands. Most politicians of the Hungarian minority realize that they would be the first to suffer the serious consequences of any revival of extremist nationalist tendencies in Hungary or among members of their own minority. These leaders continually emphasize that all they demand is more autonomy, a term that they do not define very precisely, along with a greater devolution of responsibilities and power to local levels of government. A much publicized meeting of mayors and other representatives of the Hungarian minority in 1994 succeeded in easing Slovak fears about the threat of Hungarian separatism. And Hungarian-Slovak relations may well improve following the ratification of the Basic Treaty by the Slovak parliament in March 1996.

Although the minority issue was exploited by important political forces in Slovakia for tactical reasons, the Slovak National Party and its ally, the Movement for Democratic Slovakia, lost a vote of confidence in the Slovak parliament with which they had hoped to bring down the government in March 1994. In the September 1994 election the party barely won the 5 percent of the national voted necessary to enter parliament. Even if Prime Minister Mečiar and those parties supporting his coalition were to exploit it for domestic reasons, it is highly unlikely that the issue would trigger armed conflict between Hungary and Slovakia.

Furthermore, the Hungarian minority has a considerable stake in Slovak politics. It is organized in four different parties and has

71. "Strafrecht in der Slowakei Verschärft," *Frankfurter Allgemeine Zeitung* (27 March 1996): 3. Earlier in 1996, in an exchange of letters with the Hungarian Bishops' Conference, the Slovakian bishops expressed their solidarity concerning the rights of the Hungarian minority living in the Slovak Republic.

elected seventeen members to the National Council. Wherever Hungarians are in a majority they control local government. And they are represented in a variety of official bodies at the national level dealing with minority affairs. The Hungarian minority has a variety of cultural institutions and media at its disposal with financial subsidies totaling 63 million SK, as compared to the 25 million Ft which the Hungarian government allocates in support of the cultural affairs of the Slovak minority in Hungary.[72] About 80 percent of the children of the Hungarian minority attend kindergarten, elementary, grammar, and vocational schools in which the Hungarian language is available either as the only or as a second language of instruction.[73] In technical high schools and secondary occupational schools the proportion declines to 40 percent. At the university level, however, there are no specific institutions or tracks for members of the Hungarian minority.[74] It comes as no surprise, therefore, that the educational qualifications of the Hungarian minority lag far behind the levels regulating the Slovak population. Despite this fact the Hungarian minority remains strongly opposed to the introduction of alternative education schools which would offer some subjects in Slovak and some in Hungarian language. From the Hungarian perspective this most probably would lead to a policy of forced assimilation, as happened to a substantial part of the Slovak minority in Hungary in the 1960s, and to a reduction in the number of classes offered strictly in Hungarian. In sum, the intractability of these issues of minority rights illustrate the extent to which traditional central European notions continue to shape the politics of minority rights in Slovakia.

Defense Policy

The Slovak Republic illustrates the continued relevance of traditional conceptions of national security in contemporary Europe. With only 5.3 million inhabitants, Slovakia borders on Ukraine with its 50 million, Poland with its almost 40 million, Hungary

72. Slovak Ministry of Foreign Affairs, *Situation of the Hungarian Minority in the Slovak Republic: With International Comparisons* (Bratislava, March 1996) p. 10. Interview with Tibor Szabo, Director, Slovak Section, Office for Magyars Abroad, Budapest, June 1995.

73. Ministry of Foreign Affairs, *Situation of the Hungarian Minority*, p. 15.

74. Except for the department of Hungarian language and literature at Comenius University and three Hungarian departments at the Pedagogical University in Nitra which trains future teachers.

and the Czech Republic with 10 million each, and Austria with 7.5 million. The breakup of Czechoslovakia and political developments in East and West has prompted domestic debates about the future position of the Slovak Republic between East and West. A state with no past that is confronting bewildering changes both at home and abroad, Slovakia is more open to a nationalist-populist style of politics than are its central European neighbors. Political elites and mass publics remain deeply divided about the international course that the new state should steer. Although Slovak efforts to join NATO, the WEU, and the EU are not at the center of public concern, according to opinion polls taken in the summer of 1995, Slovakia is the only Visegrad country in which a majority of the public is not in favor of entering NATO.[75]

The breakup of Czechoslovakia in 1993 has had significant implications for Slovakia's security policy. A smaller Slovakia suddenly faced an old enemy, Hungary, in what remained a potentially unstable southeastern border region. While Slovakia officially became independent only on 1 January 1993, it proclaimed international sovereignty immediately following the June 1992 elections.[76] Indeed, Slovak foreign policy analysts and decision makers had been thinking about security matters since the appearance in 1991 of the first signs that the country might be headed towards division. The breakup of Czechoslovakia changed the balance of power in central Europe, and it remains to be seen, in the long run, if this will affect the balance of power in a broader European context.

Although Slovakia does not face any direct military threat, it does have to deal with two sets of security concerns. Hungary, Ukraine, and to some extent even Poland could conceivably present historically substantiated claims on several parts of Slovak territory. Although the governments of Hungary and Ukraine have not suggested any territorial changes, both countries have extremist political groups that are urging a revision of the Trianon borders.[77] But because the ethnic Hungarian and Ukrainian

75. This includes undecided respondents. However, a substantial majority favors joining the EU, even though most respondents know precious little about the economic, political, and security dimensions of EU membership.

76. Following the June elections, the Movement for Democratic Slovakia immediately fulfilled its pre-election promise. After the parliamentary majority had proclaimed Slovakia's international sovereignty, Václav Havel abdicated immediately as the president of Czechoslovakia.

77. In Hungary especially the political group led by István Csurka, and in Ukraine the nationalist movement "Ruch."

minorities in Slovakia are concentrated in border areas, political extremism abroad might in times of crisis be reinforced by political extremism at home.

Slovakia is also threatened by potential instabilities in Ukraine and the Russian Federation. Waves of migrants from the east, using Slovakia as a natural transition country, might complicate Slovakia's relations with Austria and the Czech Republic. Furthermore, the war in the former Yugoslavia is a poignant reminder that in possible future crises Slovakia may not be able to count on any effective assistance from the EU. Moreover, whether a revamped NATO will be able to guarantee Slovak security remains, at best, an uncertain prospect. Until the mid-1990s the lapsed security guarantees by the WTO have not been replaced by any new ones. Slovakia's security situation thus differs not only from states that are NATO members but also from neutral states that have their security guaranteed by international treaties.

Slovakia is the only member of the Visegrad Group of central European states to border on all other members of the organization. The Slovak government perceives more acutely than do the other three member states a need for integration into a reliable security arrangement. Unfortunately, the Visegrad Group is of no more than symbolic importance. The oscillations in Slovak foreign policy should be viewed from this vantage point. The division of Czechoslovakia deprived Slovakia of common borders with NATO—that is, with Germany. Austria's entrance into the EU in 1995 compensated only slightly for this loss, as membership in the WEU has been officially declared to be part of Austria's future.[78]

The armed forces of Slovakia are undergoing changes similar to those in other former Communist states. These changes started immediately after the Velvet Revolution, while Czechoslovakia was still one country. After the election of Václav Havel, Communists still controlled the armed forces, and at the beginning of 1990 they still held power in the Ministry of Defense. The government justified this as an inevitable concession to the Soviet Union and the obligations of the WTO. Soon after Havel's election the government launched a campaign to depoliticize the army and initiated a purge of high-ranking members of the general staff. It abolished mandatory "Marxist-Leninist" education courses in the armed forces and appointed several new deputy ministers of defense. Six

---

78. Austria became the only Western neighbor with a frontier of 117 kilometres. Until 1994 this country was Slovakia's most important Western economic partner; it has been replaced by Germany since 1995.

members of the State Defense Council were dismissed and eight new officials named. Among the new members only two, including the minister of defense, were Communists. President Havel became chief of the armed forces. In brief, since 8 February 1990 the Czechoslovak army has been under non-Communist control.

Until the breakup of Czechoslovakia, however, decision making remained completely in the hands of the federal government in Prague. Slovak influence in defense matters remained secondary. After the split, a civilian minister of defense took over in the Czech Republic. In the Slovak Republic civilian control was also established, but the first minister of defense was a professional military man,[79] an exception among the four Visegrad states.

Based on an agreement with the Czech Republic, after the division of Czechoslovakia the Slovak army was allotted one third of most of the military equipment provided for Czechoslovakia under the Vienna Disarmament Agreement of 1990 (CFE) and one-half of the available military aircraft. Because the Czechoslovak armed forces had greatly exceeded the CFE limits, the Slovak army sharply reduced its size between 1993 and 1995. According to the CFE the Slovak army should not number more than 50,000 men.[80] Military service in the Slovak armed forces is compulsory and lasts twelve months.[81] The age for conscription is eighteen; just under 50,000 men annually become eligible for military service. The total pool of men who could be drafted in the event of war exceeded one million in 1994.[82]

The armed forces also sharply cut back on military equipment. At the time of the division of Czechoslovakia, the Czech Republic and Slovakia together had 3,208 tanks (the CFE limit was 1,475) and 3,414 pieces of artillery (the CFE ceiling was 1,150).[83] Thus Slovakia had to dispose of one-half to two-thirds of its major military

79. General Imrich Andrejčák held office until the fall of the Mečiar government in March 1994.

80. As of October 1995 the Slovak armed forces number about 47,000, according to figures given in interviews by Ivo Samson at the Ministry of Defense of the Slovak Republic, 24 October 1995. The armed forces consist of the Army, Air and Air Defense Forces, and Civil Defense and Railroad Units. Since 1995 Slovakia's Hungarian political parties have successfully resisted the creation of a Home Guard envisaged by Prime Minister Mečiar.

81. Alternative service lasts twice as long as regular military service. Compared to Slovakia's twenty-four months, alternative service is shorter, by six months, in Poland, Hungary, and the Czech Republic.

82. Data and figures taken from Martin Votruba in *Slovak News*, 27 February 1995.

83. The number of tanks was reduced to 570 in October 1995. RFE/RL Research Report, 5 March 1993.

equipment. Due to the high costs of disposal, a preliminary completion of the reductions was announced only in October 1995.[84] According to official statistics, the Slovak Republic's armed forces had been reduced by some 46,300 men (divided equally between conscripts and professional service personnel) by the beginning of 1996; tanks were reduced by 478; armored vehicles by 683; a variety of heavy artillery systems by 383; aircraft by 115; and attack helicopters by 25.

The heavy costs incurred in the process of downsizing the armed forces have meant that the Slovak army now lacks the financial resources necessary to invest in the upgrading of its traditionally poor infrastructure. In 1995 total military expenditures amounted to no more than $270 million.[85] Even such vital assets as airfields and ammunition depots are lacking, as are adequate housing for army personnel, including housing for officers and their families. The funds necessary for constructing proper housing will not be available for many years.

Militarily, it is practically impossible to defend Slovakia were it to confront a serious threat from any of its larger neighbors. The country is often described as "two East-West railways and three North-South mountain valleys."[86] The former integration of Slovakia (as a part of Czechoslovakia) into the Warsaw Treaty Organization (WTO) had left the country's national defense intertwined with that of its neighbors. For instance, Czechoslovak pilots who trained in eastern Slovakia had to start descent maneuvers over Hungarian territory. With the breakup of the WTO after 1990, some Slovak politicians called for the creation of new national "forces for mountain terrain" and also for a "homeguard of territorial defence forces."[87]

Central European security arrangements have not provided a satisfactory option for Slovakia. Hungary developed the Central European Initiative (CEI) so as to have more room for maneuver in its foreign policy while the Soviet Union was relinquishing control over the Eastern bloc. Initially this initiative was called the *Quadragonale* and included Hungary, Yugoslavia, Italy, and

---

84. Data provided by the Slovak military cannot be checked against other sources and are presumably subject to considerable change and reinterpretation.

85. Converted at a rate of thirty Slovak "koruna" for one U.S. dollar.

86. Jan Urban, "The ČSFR-Security Consequences of the Break-up of Czechoslovakia," in Regina C. Karp, ed., *Central and Eastern Europe: The Challenge of Transition* (Oxford: Oxford University Press, 1993), p. 106.

87. Minister of Interior Jozef Tuchnya in his speech in Liptovsky Mikuláš as quoted in *Lidové noviny* (2 November 1992).

Austria. When Czechoslovakia (in 1990) and Poland (in 1991) applied for membership, this informal arrangement was expanded into the *Pentagonale* and then the *Hexagonale*. Following the breakup of the Yugoslav federation, Slovenia, Croatia, Macedonia, and Bosnia also became members of the CEI. The Initiative, it was hoped, would become involved in crisis management in southeastern and central Europe. However, from the beginning it has been troubled by the unequal international standing of its various members. Italy and Austria had both been deeply enmeshed in Western political and security arrangements for several decades and thus had interests that differed greatly from those of the former Eastern bloc countries. Hence, with the exception of minority issues, the annual prime ministerial meetings of the CEI have sidestepped central political and security issues confronting the political leaders of the member states and dealt instead with problems of the environment, culture, agriculture, and scientific research.

As Valerie Bunce argues in chapter 6, the *Visegrad Group* has also failed to provide Slovakia with a viable regional security arrangement. The framework of cooperation articulated after the Prague summit of 1992 was ambitiously named the "New Pattern of Central European Relations." By 1995, for all intents and purposes, the group, as originally conceived, was dead. The Czech Republic had ceased to cooperate by 1993, and there is no sign that it is willing to reactivate its participation in this arrangement. In the end, economic issues have been the only area on which all parties could agree. Following the gradual weakening of diplomatic cooperation among the Visegrad member states, the integration of the central European states has shifted toward economic issues, specifically under the auspices of the Central European Free Trade Area (CEFTA).[88] But their common quest for membership in the EU has been frustrating for the Visegrad members. The Association Agreements with the EU have not compensated for the security vacuum in the region.[89] Security is not a topic because all the Visegrad countries are seeking membership in NATO and the WEU and do not want the group to be considered a substitute for membership in Western defense structures.

88. It includes the members of the Visegrad Group and, since January 1996, also Slovenia.

89. This is true in particular because EU Association Agreements have been extended to other post-Communist countries and have lost the significance they enjoyed at the beginning of the 1990s.

The Slovak position in Central Europe has been distinguished by a less than fully transparent relationship with Russia. In August 1993, Russian President Boris Yeltsin visited Bratislava and signed a bilateral Basic Treaty with Slovakia. Following objections from Slovak opposition parties, the government dropped, at the last minute, a controversial paragraph in the draft treaty that stipulated that neither nation would assist an attack on the other by allowing an attacking country's troops on its territory. In effect this would have obligated Slovakia to remain neutral in any conflict in which Russia was involved. After renegotiation, the head of the Slovak government, Vladimír Mečiar, signed the agreement in September 1993 but also reaffirmed the country's desire to join NATO; parliament ratified the treaty in August 1994. Since then Slovakia has signed a number of important agreements with Russia, including a five-year cooperation agreement between the Defense Ministries (1993) calling for closer bilateral defense and security ties and for the delivery of Russian military parts to the Slovak army. In addition, the two governments signed twelve agreements in March 1995 concerning the free movement of people and workers between the two countries. An agreement between the Ministries of the Interior of Slovakia and Russia concerning technical cooperation in the arms industry was signed at the same time. By the end of 1995, the Slovak Republic had signed sixty-eight bilateral treaties with Russia, most of which deal with economic and cultural issues.

During talks with a Russian parliamentary delegation in 1995 the chairman of the Slovak Parliamentary Committee for Foreign Affairs, Ivan Laluha, stated that while Russia might have reservations about Slovak efforts to join NATO, Russia nonetheless recognized that every post-Communist country had the "right to decide freely its priorities in foreign policy."[90] In a similar vein, Prime Minister Mečiar has declared that NATO is "the only effective security structure in Europe."[91] All Slovak governments have reiterated their intention of joining NATO, and, officially, there is no doubt on the issue. Since 1993 statements made by Western officials and articles published in the Western press discussing the possibility of Visegrad countries being admitted to NATO have ceased to mention Slovakia as a possible candidate for early membership because Slovakia appears to lack a demonstrated commitment to

90. *TASR* (18 September 1993).
91. Speech of Slovak Prime Minister Vladimír Mečiar in TASR (Press Agency of the Slovak Republic), 29 August 1993.

institutionalizing quickly the principles of a market economy and political democracy. Slovak leaders are aware that Slovakia is becoming isolated and have publicly expressed their apprehension that Slovakia's admission to NATO is "increasingly in doubt from the standpoint of West European nations."[92] A member of the ruling coalition expressed similarly pessimistic views in 1995.[93]

Slovakia has no tradition of state sovereignty, and its domestic politics and foreign policy each betray a high degree of conflict and indecision. The security implications of these divisions have become increasingly evident since the parliamentary elections of November 1994. Before the elections virtually the entire political elite and all of the political parties in parliament favored a defense policy aimed at integrating Slovakia into Western security institutions. Thus President Kováč visited NATO headquarters in Brussels in late 1993 and applied officially for Slovak membership. Slovakia's membership in NATO depends on meeting five basic criteria: civilian control of the army, compatibility between the equipment of the Slovak army and the weapons of NATO members, completion of the democratic transformation of society, development of a free market economy, and friendly relations with neighbors.[94] According to public remarks by the U.S. secretary of defense in September 1995, Slovakia scores high on the first two points.[95] And because Slovakia traditionally has been an exporter, not an importer, of military equipment, its rapid progress in weapons compatibility is viewed as especially noteworthy.

The bitter conflict between Slovakia's President and prime minister that has increasingly poisoned the political atmosphere since 1995 is one reason why its international position in central Europe has deteriorated sharply. Significantly, Slovakia's defense policy is beginning to show a quiet tilt toward a more neutral stance. For example, Slovakia's contribution to international peacekeeping within the framework of UNPROFOR, though relatively modest in absolute terms, is disproportionately large in comparison to that of the Czech Republic.[96] However, reflecting the

92. Slovak President Michál Kovác, quoted in *TASR*, 18 September 1993.

93. See Deputy Foreign Minister Jozef Šesták, as quoted in "Jozef Šesták about USA and NATO," in *SME* (17 May 1995).

94. This means relations going beyond the basic treaties with both neighboring countries and Russia.

95. William Perry as quoted in *Pravda* (19 September 1995).

96. Interview of Ivo Samson, Martin Kahl and Phillip Borinsky at the Slovak Ministry of Defense, 24 October 1995.

general foreign policy orientation of these two states, Slovakia's contingent of about 600 peacekeepers stationed in Croatia and Slavonia were left under the authority of the United Nations UNPROFOR following the Dayton Agreement. In contrast, the Czech contingent of about one thousand were put under the command of NATO's INFOR. During a visit to Slovakia in September 1995, John Shalikashvili, U.S. chief of staff, indicated that the Czech army is leading Slovakia's in seeking convergence with NATO along different dimensions, but Slovakia's armed forces are by no means passive bystanders in this process.[97] This characterization illustrates a growing differentiation between the positions of the two states that had not been evident in the statements of U.S. or NATO officials only a few years earlier. Despite Slovakia's participation in NATO's Partnership for Peace (PFP) program, there is no longer any guarantee that its defense policy is traveling on a road that will eventually turn westward. On questions of national defense Slovakia appears to be charting a course that differs from that of the other three central European states.

Slovakia's vacillation between West and East is explained by the ambiguities inherent in central Europe's international relations after the Cold War. For example, in an effort to expand Slovakia's bilateral security arrangements and demonstrate to NATO its readiness to establish close military ties with its eastern neighbors and support multilateral arrangements in the region, Slovakia has sought to reach agreements with Ukraine and Romania. NATO has a strong interest in winning Russian acquiescence to an inclusion of the central European states in NATO's possible eastern enlargement. This puts Slovakia and the other central European states in the peculiar situation of seeking good relations with Russia while at the same time striving for NATO membership. But because a Western security guarantee or a national policy of neutrality could probably not provide protection from political instabilities in Russia and Ukraine, these potential developments are deeply troubling for Slovakia. For this and unrelated reasons, there is now a substantial political constituency in Slovak politics that since the 1994 elections prefers a policy of neutrality between East and West to a policy of Western alignment.

Although it has searched for security arrangements in a variety of fora, in the end Slovakia, like the other post-Communist states in central Europe, has had to settle for NATO's Partnership for

---

97. Quoted in *SME* (28 September 1995).

Peace (PFP) program. Like others in the Visegrad Group, Slovakia will receive no special treatment or security guarantees within the PFP.[98] Indeed, Slovakia's security policy has made early admission to NATO less likely than for the other Visegrad states. Since joining the PFP, Slovakia has had to face another round of negotiations with Hungary to persuade the West that relations between these two states will not replicate problems similar to those dividing Greece and Turkey and thus do not constitute an obstacle to membership in NATO or the EU. Slovakia's official position on security matters is that it wants to join Western security arrangements while also seeking close ties with Russia. This dual strategy, in the eyes of Western leaders, could make Slovakia either an asset or a liability for NATO as the alliance searches for a solution to how it can accomplish both its eastern enlargement and closer cooperation with Russia. Slovakia's security policy will greatly depend on which way NATO, in the end, decides this issue.

It should come as no surprise that Slovakia is less preoccupied with others—Europe, Germany, Russia, NATO—than with itself, as the case studies in this chapter illustrate. After having briefly been an ill-fated satellite state of Nazi Germany, for the first time in a thousand years Slovakia has become a sovereign state. But the meaning of sovereign statehood in a Europe that has embarked on a pervasive integration process is far from clear. Integration through the balance of power should give considerable clout to Slovakia, with its geostrategic position in the heart of Europe. This at least is the expectation of many members of Slovakia's political leadership who see NATO's dependence on Slovakia as being at least as large as Slovakia's on NATO. But with the end of the Cold War the European balance of power accounts for less than it did in previous decades. Furthermore, integration through markets is occurring at a pace that the government explicitly hopes to control at least partially. Here lies an important difference between Slovakia and the Czech Republic, which is ideologically more committed to processes of marketization and deregulation. But most importantly, beyond the balance of power and markets,

98. Speech made by the president of the Slovak parliament, Ivan Gasparovic, on Slovak television, 11 January 1994.

European integration represents a set of standards regulating the conduct of politics that Slovakia cannot simply disregard without incurring high political costs. Acting against such standards may in the end divert the country onto a path that may differ considerably from its central European neighbors. This would be a very costly choice and one that would deeply divide the country. How Slovak domestic politics evolves over the coming years and attempts to reconcile its newly found statehood with the reality of European integration will have important consequences for both Slovakia and Europe.

6. THE VISEGRAD GROUP

Regional Cooperation and European Integration in Post-Communist Europe

Valerie Bunce

Was ist Europa?
Europa ist ... nicht Russland.[1]

There is no chance for dialogue because 'Europe One' speaks and 'Europe Two' predominantly listens.[2]

It is important to remember that this region has been defined far less by ties binding these countries than by the comings and goings of the great powers that flanked them.[3]

Since 1989, the post-Communist countries of central Europe[4] have been engaged in two sets of changes. The first is domestic and involves the simultaneous construction of capitalist economies

I would like to thank the American Council of Learned Societies and the German Marshall Fund for support of this project. I would also like to thank Włodek Anioł, Daneš Brzica, Miklos Derer, Péter Gedeon, Bogdan Goralczyk, Hynek Jeřábek, Ron Linden, Ivo Samson, Istvan Szonyi and, especially, Peter Katzenstein for their comments on earlier drafts of this paper; Joe Brada for assistance in locating some needed economic data; Geoffrey Harris for providing helpful materials from the European Union and European Parliament; Christine Ingebritsen for helping me delve through the literature on regional cooperation; and Maria Csanadi for arranging interviews for me in Budapest.

1. Conversation with a Lithuanian member of parliament quoted by Timothy Garton Ash. See "Journey to the Post-Communist East," *The New York Review of Books* (23 June 1994): 18.

2. Jiri Musil, "Europe Between Integration and Disintegration," *Czech Sociological Review* 2 (1/1994), p. 17.

3. Sarah M. Terry, "Intraregional Political and Economic Relations," in John P. Hardt and Richard F. Kaufman, eds., *East-Central European Economies in Transitions* (Joint Economic Committee, U.S. Congress, G.P.O., 1994), p. 368.

4. In order to simplify the presentation, the term "central Europe" will be used in this paper when referring to the post-Communist countries of Poland, Hungary, and

and liberal democratic polities. The second is international and involves the integration of central Europe with Western Europe —through the development of similar domestic economic, political and social structures, through the creation of a common European culture and, finally, through the full and equal participation of the central European countries in such Western multilateral institutions as the European Union (EU—formerly, the European Community), the Council of Europe and NATO.[5]

Both the domestic and the international transformations involve a revolutionary break with the practices and institutions of the previous forty-five years of Eastern, as well as Western European history (if not longer, once we add the much longer-term division of Europe into two halves, if not three parts, since at least the Middle Ages).[6] In particular, the domestic transformation in post-Communist Europe means that these countries are attempting to move from state socialism—with its defining characteristics of authoritarian politics, state ownership of the means of production, and central planning—to capitalist liberal democracy—with its diametrically opposed features of liberal politics, private ownership of the means of production, and market exchange. The sheer distance to be traveled between these two political-economic systems, the rapid pace of change in eastern Europe, and the absence of an historical precedent for simultaneously building capitalism and liberal democracy time point to the radical character of the changes now being implemented throughout the region. Like all revolutionary processes, moreover, these promise to be de-stabilizing, long in the making and without any guarantees.

Czechoslovakia (or the Czech Republic and Slovakia, beginning in 1993). In strictly geographical terms, of course, this list should include also Austria, Greece, and Germany, along with the south-central post-Communist countries of Bulgaria, Romania, Albania, Slovenia, Croatia, Bosnia-Herzegovina, Macedonia, and rump Yugoslavia. The more expansive term "eastern Europe" will be used when referring to Poland, Hungary, the Czech Republic, Slovakia, along with Latvia, Lithuania, Estonia, Belarus, Ukraine, Moldova, and Russia. Again, a strictly geographical perspective would add to this list Austria, Greece, and Germany. Finally, when I use the term "Eastern Europe" I will be referring to the Communist period and, in terms of countries, to Poland, Hungary, Czechoslovakia, Bulgaria, Romania, Yugoslavia, and Albania.

5. For a discussion of the remarkable expansion of multilateral institutions in post-World War II Western Europe, see John Gerard Ruggie, "Multilateralism: The Anatomy of an Institution," in John Gerard Ruggie, ed., *Multilateralism Matters: The Theory and Praxis of a Institutional Form* (Columbia University Press, 1993), pp. 3–47.

6. See, especially, Jeno Szucs, "The Three Historical Regions of Europe," *Acta Historica* 29 (1983), pp. 131–84.

Uncertainty and instability, in short, are likely to characterize post-Communist Europe for many years to come.[7]

The international side of the post-Communist agenda is equally revolutionary—and just as daunting. It involves adjusting to the dramatic changes in the international system as a consequence of the end of bipolarity, the division of Europe and, indeed, the very superpower that helped define the structure of the postwar international order—the Soviet Union. In practice, this means joining the global economy, adjusting to the seemingly sudden development of a stronger and unified Germany and a weaker and dismembered Soviet Union and, finally, moving from membership in the now defunct Warsaw Treaty Organization (WTO) and the Council for Mutual Economic Assistance (CMEA)—two hierarchical regional systems (the first political-military and the second economic) defined by state socialism in the domestic arena and by Soviet dominance and competition with the West in the international arena[8]—to full economic and political-military integration with the West. As with the domestic side of the transition, these revolutionary shifts in the foreign policies of post-Communist Europe will no doubt be destabilizing—for the east and, one can argue, for the West as well.[9] To further echo earlier arguments about the domestic transformation, the international transformation will also take a long time and will proceed without any guarantees—with respect to achieving security, growth, stability, or full integration with the West.

The two revolutions under way in eastern Europe are, not surprisingly, closely entwined with one another. It is not just that they are both based on the notion of "joining Europe"; it is also that progress in the domestic arena is understood by policy-makers in eastern *and* Western Europe alike to determine the future of what happens in the international arena—and vice-versa. Just as the consolidation of the emerging liberal orders in eastern Europe is

7. See, especially, Valerie Bunce, "Democratization, East and South," *Journal of Democracy.*

8. On the development and impact of these two Cold War institutions (including their self-destructive consequences), see Valerie Bunce, "The Empire Strikes Back: The Transformation of the Eastern Bloc from a Soviet Asset to a Soviet Liability," *International Organization* 39 (Winter: 1984/1985), pp. 1–46.

9. See, especially, the comments by Endre Erdos (Ambassador of the Permanent Mission of Hungary to the United Nations) in the "Roundtable on Domestic Challenges," *Harriman Institute Forum* 7, Nos. 3–4 (1994), p. 6; Strobe Talbott, "Why NATO Should Grow," *The New York Review of Books* 42, no. 13, 10 August 1995, pp. 27–30; Przemyslaw Grudzinski and Andrzej Karkoszka, "East Central Europe in an Uncertain World," In Jeffrey Laurenti, ed., *Searching for Moorings: East Central Europe in the International System* (United Nations Association of America, 1994), pp. 9–38.

understood to be a necessary condition for full participation of these countries in Western European institutions, for example, so the construction of liberal orders in the east is understood to depend heavily on the support provided by Western governments and Western international institutions.[10] Their inter-relationships take other forms as well. As Alois Mack, the foreign minister of Austria, succinctly put it: "If we do not succeed in *ex*porting stability to the Eastern half of the continent, we shall soon find ourselves *im*porting instability from there."[11]

Regional Cooperation

Residing at the intersection between the domestic and international transformations has been a series of recent efforts to forge regional linkages among the post-Communist states in eastern Europe. One can point, for example, to a number of new regional organizations that cross the east-west divide. For example, the Central European Initiative (the successor to the Pentagonale that was established in November 1989 and that now includes Italy and Austria, along with Croatia, Slovenia, Bosnia-Herzegovina, the Czech Republic, Slovakia, Poland, and Hungary—with Bulgaria, Romania, Belarus, and Ukraine pressing as well for full participation) and the Black Sea Economic Cooperation (established in June 1992 and composed of

10. The interdependence between domestic economic and political liberalization, on the one hand, and European integration, on the other, is not a new argument. Similar arguments were made when other authoritarian states in post-World War II Europe underwent a transition to democracy. On the German case, see Peter Katzenstein, *Policy and Politics in West Germany: The Growth of a Semisovereign State* (Temple University Press, 1987). On the Greek case, see Susannah Verney, "The European Community as Exporter of Democracy: Lessons From the Greek Case," paper presented at the European Community Studies Association Conference, George Mason University, Fairfax, Va., 22–24 May 1991. On the Spanish case, see Jonathan Story and Benny Pollack, "Spain's Transition: Domestic and External Linkages," in Geoffrey Pridham, ed., *Encouraging Democracy: The International Context of Regime Transition in Southern Europe* (St. Martin's Press, 1991), pp. 125–58; and Michael Marks, "Spain and European Integration in the New Europe," paper presented at the Workshop on Unified Germany in an Integrated Europe, Budapest, 1–3 June 1995. A clear statement of this argument for eastern Europe can be found in Ronald Linden, "The Price of a Bleacher Seat: East Europe's Entry into the World Political Economy," paper presented at the International Political Science Association, Berlin, 21–25 August 1994.

11. As remarked on in "Roundtable on Domestic Challenges," in "Between Russia and Germany: East Central Europe After the Collapse of the USSR," *Harriman Institute Forum* 7, nos. 3–4 (1994), p. 4. Emphases in the original.

nine post-Communist states in addition to Turkey and Greece)—as well as a number of regional formations that are limited to the post-Communist region—for example, the Visegrad Quadrangle (founded in February 1991 and composed of Poland, Hungary, the Czech Republic, and Slovakia) and the Baltic Council of Ministers Commission (founded in 1993 and composed of Latvia, Lithuania, and Estonia).[12] While specific emphases differ, the overriding purpose of *all* of these regional organizations is essentially the same. It is to promote economic growth, the consolidation of capitalism and liberal democracy, the stabilization of the region, and the integration of the eastern half of Europe with its Western half. Of concern, then, is providing a *regional mechanism* for encouraging as well as reconciling the domestic and international transformations now underway throughout eastern Europe.[13]

The purpose of this paper is to examine in detail one such regional group, the Visegrad Quadrangle, composed of Poland, Hungary, the Czech Republic, and Slovakia. This regional grouping was selected for intensive study, because it features a number of distinctive characteristics. It is the oldest cooperative grouping within the post-Communist region, and the one with the most wide-ranging agenda (combining as it does both economic and security issues). In addition, the member states (especially Hungary, the Czech Republic, and Poland) are understood by Western countries and Western multilateral institutions to be the most stable and the furthest along in the transition to capitalist democracy of any of the remaining twenty-four countries that make up the post-Communist region.[14]

12. On these and other cooperative ventures (including developments in the Commonwealth of Independent States), see, for example, Terry, "Intraregional Political ad Economic Relations"; Daniel A. Connelly, "Black Sea Economic Cooperation," *RFE/RL*, vol. 3, no. 26, 1 July 1994: 31–38; Andrejs Plakans, "Historical Considerations of the Prospects for Baltic Regional Unity," Discussion Paper no. 39, Woodrow Wilson Center for International Scholars, no. 39, November 1993: 5–20; Brudzinski and Karkoszka, "East Central Europe"; Jenonne Walker, "European Regional Organizations and Ethnic Conflict," paper presented at the Conference on Regional Stability in Eastern Europe, Krakow, August 1992; Pal Dunay, "Stability and Instability in Europe: The Contribution of Hungary," paper presented at the conference on Regional Stability in Eastern Europe, Krakow, August 1992.

13. See, especially, Alpo Rusi, "Military Threats to Regional Security," paper presented at the Conference on Security in Central Europe, Krakow, Poland, 25–26 August 1992; Joseph Camilleri, "Alliances in the Emerging Post-Cold War System," unpublished manuscript, Cornell University, 30 March 1992; August Pradetto, "Transformation in Eastern Europe, International Cooperation and the German Position," *Studies in Comparative Communism* 25 (March 1992): 23–33.

14. This is a primary reason why the distribution of Western aid to the post-Communist states is skewed in favor of the Visegrad states. Thus, by the end of

Finally, the Visegrad Group has had an unusually eventful history during its five years of existence. It began by registering a number of foreign policy successes and managed to create, within a mere two years of its formation, a regional custom's union. However, since 1993, cooperation among the Visegrad states—aside from the area of trade—has declined. This is despite the strong support for such cooperation expressed repeatedly by the European Union, and despite the overarching rationale for the existence of the Visegrad Group as a vehicle for accelerating the process of the integration of these countries into Western Europe.

All of this would seem to suggest that an analysis of the Visegrad Group will allow us to get at a number of important questions. One set of questions concentrates on the development of cooperation among states[15]—a topic that has received considerable attention in recent years among specialists in international relations.[16] Here, we will concentrate on two key issues. The first key is why and how did the Visegrad Group come into being—and so quickly after the formation of new regimes in the region? This is puzzling because inter-state cooperation is the exception, not the rule, in international politics. States do not tend to form cooperative linkages with each other because there is an appeal and a logic to

1993, for example, in per capita terms, Hungary received $1200, Poland $659, and the Czech Republic and Slovakia $535. By contrast, Bulgaria received $356 and Romania $266. See Linden, "The Price of a Bleacher Seat," Table III. His data come from *The Wall Street Journal* (23 February 1994): A10.

15. Inter-state cooperation will be defined here as the agreement among three or more states to coordinate their policies.

16. See, for example, Ruggie, "Multilateralism;" Joseph Grieco, *Cooperation Among Nations: Europe, America and Non-Tariff Barriers to Trade* (Cornell University Press, 1990); Arthur Stein, *Why Nations Cooperate: Circumstances and Choices in International Relations* (Cornell University Press, 1990); Kenneth Oye, ed., *Cooperation Under Anarchy* (Princeton University Press, 1985); Janice Gross Stein, "Cooperation as Risky Choice: Framing the Problem," paper presented at the Working Group on International Cooperation, Department of Political Science, the University of Toronto, August 1991; Duncan Snidal, "International Cooperation among Relative Gains Maximizers," *International Studies Quarterly* 35 (December 1991), pp. 387–402; Helen Milner, "International Theories of Cooperation among Nations: Strengths and Weaknesses," *World Politics* 44 (April 1992); Neta C. Crawford, "A Security Regime Among Democracies: Cooperation Among the Iroquois Nations," *International Organization* 48 (Summer 1994), pp. 345–86; Bernt Schiller, "At Gun Point: A Critical Perspective on the Attempts of the Nordic Governments to Achieve Unity after the Second World War," *Scandinavian Journal of History* 9 (1984), pp. 221–37; Andrew Moravcsik, "Liberalism and International Relations Theory," paper presented at the Program on International Politics, Economics and Security, the University of Chicago, 1993; Charles Lipson, "International Cooperation in Economic and Security Affairs," *World Politics* 37 (October 1984), pp. 1–23.

"going it alone" as a consequence of such factors as the anarchy of the international system; the considerable variations in the interests and the domestic political economies of states; the commitment of political leaders to maximize their policy flexibility and to guard state sovereignty; the usually asymmetric gains derived from cooperation; and, finally, the constraints on international institutions and major powers to provide the incentives necessary for states to develop a coordination of their policies. The second key issue is what explanation can there be for the cooperation among these states breaking down nearly as rapidly as it had sprung up? What, in short, distinguishes the 1991–92 period from 1993–96?

In the process of answering these questions, we will necessarily address the issues posed at the beginning of this chapter; that is, the relationship between domestic and international politics and policy in a time of considerable flux. Put in more concrete terms, the analysis of the rise and fall of the Visegrad Group allows us to address the following questions. First, how have the domestic transitions under way in post-Communist central Europe shaped the foreign policies of these new regimes—with respect to each other and with respect to their relations with Russia, Germany, the European Union, and NATO? To reverse the causal arrow: how have the actions of Russia, Germany, the European Union, and NATO affected domestic and foreign developments in central Europe?

The analysis that follows is divided into four parts. In the first part, I trace the development of the Visegrad Group from 1989 to 1992, discussing in the process its origins and its accomplishments. In the second part, I present an explanation of why this cooperative grouping came about. As we will discover, the key factors seem to have been leadership commitment to cooperation, international incentives supporting cooperation, and a remarkable, if transitory, convergence among the member states in their domestic and foreign policy agendas. What then follows is a discussion of the decline of cooperation, beginning in 1993 and continuing to the present day. In the final part of the paper, this is explained as a function of shifts in the very same factors—that is, in domestic politics, in international institutions, in the geopolitical location and, thus, in the interests of these states—that had earlier encouraged the development of cooperative relations among Poland, Hungary, the Czech Republic, and Slovakia. In the conclusion, I discuss what all this seems to suggest about the two issues that framed this paper; that is, the determinants of cooperation among states and the relationship between domestic and international change in central Europe.

Inventing the Visegrad Grouping

The origins of the Visegrad Group[17] can be found, first, in the support for such a venture expressed by two new leaders in the region very soon after the end of state socialism. Thus, in the early fall of 1989, the new prime minister of Poland, Tadeusz Mazowiecki, floated the idea of establishing closer regional ties among Poland, Hungary, and Czechoslovakia. His call for cooperation was based in part on arguments made during the 1980s by dissidents in Poland, Hungary, and Czechoslovakia regarding the value and necessity of building regional ties among the central European states. At that time, regional ties were understood to have a number of positive consequences. They would expand linkages among dissidents and thereby create some safety in numbers while laying some of the groundwork for the creation of a liberalized island within Eastern Europe; they would carve out autonomy within the Soviet bloc (in part, by introducing horizontal ties that would undermine its radial structure) and thereby enhance the bargaining power of these states; and they would build bridges to the West. All of these arguments made even more sense, given developments in 1989; that is, the fall of state socialism, the commitment of the new and liberalized regimes in central Europe to building capitalist liberal democracies and integrating with Europe, and, finally, the threats to the achievement of these goals as

17. The summary of the evolution of the Visegrad Quadrangle is based, first, on interviews conducted in January 1995 in Budapest, with Andras Balogh, director of the Institute of Foreign Affairs; Andras Szabo, regional affairs minister, the Ministry of Foreign Affairs; Csaba Tabajdi, assistant to the prime minister; Tamas Kende, professor of law at ELTE and advisor to the Free Democrats in foreign affairs; and Sandor Meizel, specialist in European integration and the European Community, the Institute of the World Economy. It is also based upon the following sources: Dunay, "Stability and Instability"; Jan de Weydenthal, "The Cracow Summit," *Report on East Europe*, no. 43 (25 October 1991), pp. 27–30; Foreign Broadcast Information Service, 8 October 1991 (reports and speeches from the Cracow meeting); Rudolf Tokes, "From Visegrad to Cracow: Security and Cooperation in Central Europe," *Problems of Communism* 40 (November-December, 1991), pp. 3–24; Bogdan Goralczyk, "Visegrad Group: Is Real Cooperation in Central Europe Possible?" commentary presented at the Workshop on Unified Germany in an Integrated Europe, 1–3 June 1995; Miklos Derer, "Visegrad: A Buzzword for the West," commentary at the same workshop.

a consequence of the significant residues left by forty-five years of state socialism—for example, international isolation, economic disarray, weak civil societies, and competition between the rooted institutions of the socialist period versus the embryonic institutions of the emerging liberal order.

In February 1990, Václav Havel, the new president of Czechoslovakia, responded with enthusiastic support for Mazowiecki's idea by arguing that regional cooperation would further four inter-related goals: the construction of capitalist democracy, the building of regional security, the enhancement of regional stability, and the laying down of the groundwork necessary for the full integration of central with Western Europe. Havel, therefore, expanded on Mazowiecki's notion of regional cooperation. In large measure this was because, in comparison with Poland, Czechoslovakia had in effect more room for maneuver, given a more secure geopolitical location and a sharper break in 1989 with the state socialist past. At the same time, these were issues that had long preoccupied Havel. During the course of his dissident activities, he had developed a broad and nuanced understanding of security—something he saw as flowing directly from the creation of stable liberal democracies in central Europe and the economic and cultural, as well as political-military, integration of these countries with Western Europe.[18] That he combined his concerns with security with a call for more Western aid to the Soviet Union (as he outlined in his speech before the U.S. Congress in the fall of 1990) also allowed him to sidestep the uncomfortable question of whether heightened cooperation among the Visegrad states would isolate the Soviet Union—a question that was to come up repeatedly in the future during the continuing debates over collective security arrangements in Europe after the Cold War.

The Visegrad Group also came into being for another reason, aside from the strong interest in such cooperation expressed by the leaders of Poland and Czechoslovakia. This was the highly uncertain position of these new regimes in the emerging post-Cold War European order. This uncertainty can be explained in terms of what could be called the "in-between" problem of the countries of central Europe. It was not just that these countries fell (as they usually had) "in-between" the two Europes at a time when central Europe was "in-between" domestic economic and political systems and when the European international order itself

18. As Havel was to elaborate in his address at the Cracow meeting in October 1991. See FBIS-EEU-91-195, 8 October 1991.

and, thus, the institutions that defined that order, were also "in-between" the postwar era and the "post" postwar era—with the latter yet to be defined. It was also that the central European countries fell "in-between" the multilateral economic and political-military institutions of Western Europe and the now outmoded international institutions, such as the WTO and the CMEA, that had once monopolized international security and international economics in central Europe. In addition, the Visegrad countries also fell "in-between" the two major powers of the new Europe. One was a reunified and increasingly powerful Germany, which had strong historical ties to central Europe and had very quickly become after 1989 the "point guard" for central Europe within Western European multilateral institutions. The other was the Soviet Union, a downwardly mobile power, the regional hegemon for forty-five years and a highly unstable country with an unclear future with respect to both its domestic and foreign policies.

Of the two, moreover, the Soviet Union was by far the more worrisome for post-Communist central Europe. This was because the Visegrad countries were economically dependent on the Soviet Union, given the high percentage of trade between these states and the Soviet Union (ranging from 40 to 60 percent of their trade prior to the collapse of state socialism[19]), the dependence of these states on the Soviets for their primary products, and the collapse, beginning in 1990, of the Soviet market and thus the Soviet means of payment.[20] The Soviet Union, in short, was in a position to deploy considerable economic pressures on central Europe. These pressures were all the more compelling given the continuing presence of Soviet troops on Hungarian, Polish, and Czechoslovak soil and the continued existence of the two major institutions that had defined Soviet control over Eastern Europe—the WTO and the CMEA. Finally, there were growing indications of instability in the Soviet Union and the real possibility of reinvigorated Soviet designs on the region. The first was indicated, for example, by the battles between Gorbachev and Yeltsin over the course of reform, the relationship between Russia and the remaining fourteen Soviet

19. See, for example, the figures presented in Morris Bornstein, "Issues in East-West Economic Relations," in Morris Bornstein, Zvi Gitelman and William Zimmerman, eds., *East-West Relations and the Future of Eastern Europe* (Allen and Unwin, 1981), pp. 105–26.

20. See, for example, Joseph Brada, "Regional Integration in Eastern Europe: Prospects for Integration within the Region and with the European Community," unpublished manuscript, Arizona State University, 1994.

republics, and the very structure of the Soviet state (the new Union Treaty); the continuing conflicts between the Soviet legislature and the executive; and, finally, the growing challenges to the authority, if not the territorial integrity of the Soviet state as a consequence of an increasingly mobilized periphery seeking political and economic autonomy.[21] At the same time, the possibility of Soviet designs on the region was indicated, for instance, by Gorbachev's policy shift to the conservatives beginning in mid-1990; the Soviet military attack on Lithuania in January 1991; and the resolution of the Central Committee of the Communist Party of the Soviet Union, published in January 1991, which stated in strong terms Soviet opposition to membership of any of the Eastern European states in Western European security structures and the compelling logic of extending greater Soviet economic pressure on Eastern Europe as a way of keeping the region within the Soviet zone of influence.[22]

All of this meant that high uncertainty and shared fears—the latter figuring prominently in the beginning of many new cooperative ventures[23]—played a major role in encouraging the Visegrad countries to cooperate with one another. Thus, within days of the crisis in Lithuania, the foreign ministers of the three Visegrad states issued a joint appeal calling for the immediate dismantling of the WTO military structure and a stepped-up timetable for disbanding the CMEA. This was followed up in particular by the Hungarians who, influenced no doubt by the events of 1956, if not 1848, took the lead following the elections of May 1990 on the specific question of ending the Warsaw Pact. Towards that end the new government, led by the Democratic Forum, pressed Poland and Czechoslovakia to join Hungary in a united demand for the immediate disbanding

21. The irredentist tendencies of the Soviet republics also had a clear economic implication. Most of the oil and natural gas to Eastern and central Europe was piped through the Ukraine—a Soviet republic that was showing more and more evidence of joining the movement for independence from the center. On the influence of the Baltic independence movements on developments in the Ukraine at this time, see Nils R. Muiznieks, "The Influence of the Baltic Popular Movements on the Process of Soviet Disintegration," *Europe-Asia Studies* (formerly *Soviet Studies*) 47 (1995), pp. 3–25. Also see Joseph Kun, "In Search of Guarantees: Hungary's Quest for Security," Potomac Foundation monograph, McLean, Va., September 1993.

22. See *Izvestiia* (22 January 1991): 12–17.

23. See, especially, Schiller, "At Gun Point" and Robert Axline, "Regional Cooperation and National Security: External Forces in Caribbean Integration," *Journal of Common Market Studies* 27 (September 1988), pp. 1–25; Kenneth Oye, "Explaining Cooperation under Anarchy: Strategies and Institutions," In Oye, ed., *Cooperation Under Anarchy*, pp. 1–25.

of the WTO and for the commencement of state-by-state negotiations on the question of Soviet troop withdrawal.

The final factor pushing for regional cooperation—which entered the equation *after* these three states had laid the groundwork for such cooperation—was provided by the European Community. By mid-1990, the European Community had made it clear in its communications to the Visegrad states that their future membership in the Community—and the preliminary stage of Associate membership in the Community—rested heavily on their ability, among other things, to demonstrate that they could cooperate with one another.[24] The logic of this position was not just to define regional relations as a litmus test of the capacity of these countries to work within a cooperative framework, to use regional cooperation as a mechanism for "socializing" the elites in these states to embrace the norms of compromise, reciprocity, and the like,[25] or to argue (echoing the postwar experience of Western Europe in general and the German Federal Republic in particular) that regional cooperation was essential for political stability and the consolidation of capitalist liberal democracy in new and uncertain democracies. It was also to render more manageable the demands made by the central European countries on the European Community. It would be far easier, for example, for the European Community to deal with the Visegrad grouping as a whole than to bargain, separately, with each of the member states.[26]

The end result of these factors—that is, strong interest in regional cooperation expressed by the new leaders in the region, high uncertainty and shared fears, a clear agenda for regional action and strong support for such regional initiatives expressed by the European Community—was a meeting held among the leaders of these three countries in February 1991 in Visegrad,

24. This position was stated most clearly in the Randzio-Plath Report of April 1991. See Geoffrey Harris, "The European Parliament in a Wider Europe," unpublished manuscript, September 1995.

25. See, especially, the arguments by Steven Burg, *War or Peace? Nationalism, Democracy and American Foreign Policy in Eastern Europe*, unpublished manuscript prepared for the Twentieth Century Fund, Brandeis University, February 1995; and Patrick Morgan article in John Gerard Ruggie, ed., *Multilateralism Matters: The Theory and Praxis of an Institutional Form* (Columbia University Press, 1993).

26. See, for instance, Craig Whitney, "West Europeans Cast a Cautious Line Eastward," *New York Times* (1 December 1994): A14; Joseph Kun, "In Search of Guarantees: The Case of Poland," Potomac Foundation, McLean, Va., December 1993; Kun, "In Search of Guarantees: Hungary's Quest"; Heinz Kramer, "The European Community's Response to the 'New Eastern Europe'," *Journal of Common Market Studies* 31 (June 1993): 213–44.

Hungary.[27] It was at this meeting that the formal agreement to cooperate resulted in the Visegrad Declaration.[28] This said simply that these three countries agreed to work together to maximize their shared goals of building independent, democratic, and capitalist states; expanding and guaranteeing freedom and human rights; dismantling the totalitarian order; and proceeding rapidly with the process of full integration with Europe.[29]

At the two regional summits that followed—that is, near Krakow in October, 1991 and in Prague in May 1992—these goals took on more concrete form. In particular, the Visegrad Group agreed, first, to establish a regularized exchange of information through the establishment of cross-regional working groups and direct intergovernmental exchanges. The primary emphasis here was on policies dealing with the environment and human rights, as well as with domestic approaches to reform of the security police, the military, the legal system, the educational system, and the economy.

Second, beginning in 1991–92 the Visegrad states established regularized consultation in response to major international developments. For example, the Visegrad foreign ministers met within hours of the attempted coup d'état in the Soviet Union in August 1991. This was a key precedent that led very soon thereafter to their joint appeal in October 1991 to be included in some way in the activities of NATO. It also laid the groundwork for regularized meetings among their foreign ministers.

Third, the Visegrad Group very quickly identified areas where they could coordinate their policies—specifically, migration,

27. There was an earlier meeting held in April 1990 in Bratislava, then Czechoslovakia. However, this meeting proved to be relatively contentious because the leaders representing the central European states were primarily holdovers from the Communist era. However, there were still some complications at the meeting in Visegrad. In the Hungarian case, for example, there were disagreements between President Arpad Goncz and Prime Minister Jozsef Antall, over who had the constitutional authority to represent Hungary in Visegrad. The solution was that both attended. The disagreement was a function of two factors: the absence of constitutional clarity with respect to the role and powers of the president (who had been elected by the Hungarian parliament) and the considerable ideological differences between Goncz—a candidate of the Free Democrats—and Antall—the leader of the Democratic Forum.

28. For a full text, see "Text of the Visegrad Summit," *Report on East Europe* 2, 1 March 1991, pp. 31–33. Also see Jan deWeydenthal, "The Visegrad Summit," *Report on East Europe* (2 March 1991), pp. 28–31.

29. See, for example, Zoltan Barany, "Visegrad Four Contemplate Separate Paths," *Transition* 1, no. 14, 11 August 1995, pp. 56–59; Goralczyk, "Visegrad Group"; Terry, "Intraregional Political and Economic Relations."

refugees,[30] and trade. At the Prague summit, for example, a decision was made to establish a regional custom's union—the Central European Free Trade Area, or CEFTA. This was implemented in March 1993, with commitment to establishing full liberalization of regional trade by the year 2001.

Finally, members of the group agreed to work together in preparation for admission to the European Community (which, along with the establishment of CEFTA, became the major focus of the Visegrad Group). In practice, this meant two kinds of activities. One was technical and involved sharing information on and approaches to designing and implementing the new banking, communication, legal, trade institutions and like which were necessary for eventual full membership in the European Community. Later, this was expanded to include coordination of military reforms necessary for full membership in NATO. The other was political; that is, to work together to form a regional interest group capable of exerting strong influence on decision making in European multilateral institutions—most notably, the European Community.[31] The assumption at the time was that the whole—that is, the region—would be a more effective lobby in support of European integration than would be the case if the three member states were to "go it alone."[32]

There are two conclusions that can be drawn from this discussion of the development of the Visegrad Group from 1989 to 1992. First, the decision to establish cooperative relations by Poland, Hungary and Czechoslovakia proceeded very quickly. The Visegrad Declaration was issued a mere two years after the conclusion of the roundtable between Solidarity and the Polish United Workers Party—the event that set off a chain reaction that led within a year to the end of Communist Party rule in all of Eastern Europe

30. In September 1991, for example, the Hungarian, Czechoslovak, and Polish offices on refugee affairs agreed to cooperate and are now using uniform legal criteria. See FBIS-EEU-91-195, 8 October 1991, p. 1. On the concerns with respect to these issues, especially given instability in the Soviet Union, see Vladimir Kusin, "Refugees in Central and Eastern Europe: Problem or Threat?" *Report on East Europe* (2 January 1991): 33–43.

31. See, especially, Havel's statement at the May 1992 summit in Prague.

32. See, especially, the comment by Jiri Dienstbier, the former foreign minister of Czechoslovakia, quoted in *Prague Radiozurnal*, 10 January 1994, translated in FBIS-EEU-007. This is an argument made explicitly by the EU as well. See "Toward a Closer Association with the Countries of Central and Eastern Europe," communication by the Commission to the Council, in view of the meeting of the European Council in Copenhagen, 21–22 June 1993.

and the establishment of new regimes throughout the region.[33] This is in direct contrast to the slow pace of development of other regional groupings in the international system—for example, the evolution of the European Community, beginning with the founding of the European Coal and Steel Community in 1951 to the Treaties of Rome in 1957 and to the establishment of an embryonic economic community the following year.

At the same time, speed in this case did not mean symbolic achievements. Instead, a great deal was in fact accomplished in a short period of time. In particular, just two years after the Visegrad Declaration, Poland, Hungary, the Czech Republic, and Slovakia could boast of two important regional initiatives: the coordination of their military policies (with their defense ministers meeting twice a year) and the creation of a regional custom's union—a single market now comprising (with the addition of Slovenia in January 1996) sixty-seven million people.[34]

To these accomplishments, we can add a more subtle, but nonetheless important achievement. In its early years, the Visegrad Group seemed to have contributed to stability in eastern Europe in a time of enormous, destabilizing changes. It did so, for example, by creating full military transparency; by drawing the Visegrad states closer to European multilateral institutions; by functioning

33. This is not to argue, of course, that a single event can explain the collapse of Communist Party hegemony in Eastern Europe. The reasons why this happened are complex and are best understood by analyzing the structure of the Soviet bloc as a domestic and as a regional system and its impact over time on the economics and politics of the member states and on the development of the Gorbachev reforms. See Valerie Bunce, "Two-Tiered Stalinism: A Self-Destructive Order," in Kazimierz Poznanski, ed., *Decline of Communism, Rise of Capitalism* (Westview Press, 1992) and the earlier article that predicted much of what happened in the Soviet Union and Eastern Europe, beginning with Gorbachev's rise to power in 1985, "The Empire Strikes Back." However, it is nonetheless the case that Poland—that is, the events of 1980–81 and the later developments in the fall of 1988 through the spring of 1989— functioned as a catalyst for what followed in the rest of the region.

34. See, for example, Miroslaw Glogowski, "Not Quite the EC, But," *Warsaw Voice* (10 January 1993): B1, B3; Karoly Okolicsanyi, "The Visegrad Triangle's Free-Trade Zone," *RFE/RL Research Report* 2, 15 January 1993, pp. 19–22; Brada, "Regional Integration"; Andras Inotai and Magdolna Sass, "Economic Integration of the Visegrad Countries: Facts and Scenarios," Working Papers of the Institute for the World Economy, Hungarian Academy of Sciences, no. 33, Budapest, May 1994; Barbara Durka, "Problem Areas in the Development of Economic Cooperation with Poland and the other CEFTA Countries," and Danes Brzica and Richard Outrata, "The Development of Foreign Trade in the Slovak Republic," both in *Proceedings of the First Roundtable Conference*, Budapest, 2–3 March 1994 (Budapest Institute for the World Economy, 1994), pp. 230–44 and 194–201, respectively.

as a regional lobby to press these multilateral institutions to move more quickly in integrating eastern Europe into a European-wide economic and security structure (for instance, their role in the establishment of the North Atlantic Cooperation Council in 1991 and the ratification of Associate Member Agreements by all the member states by 1993); and by embracing the norm of multilateral cooperation. The final point is crucial—as John Ruggie, among others, has argued.[35] By legitimating multilateralism, the Visegrad Group functioned to help re-socialize decision makers in central Europe *and*, by virtue of its precedent and its successes, to encourage other states in the region to embrace multilateralism and establish their own cooperative ventures with their neighbors.

Why Cooperate?

We can now step back for a moment from these details and address the larger question of why this cooperative grouping formed. The rapid creation of the Visegrad Group, along with its considerable accomplishments in a mere two years, is quite surprising, not just because of the considerable obstacles to building multilateral cooperative relations among states, but also because of the constraints on doing so in eastern Europe in particular. Having just won in effect their independence from the Soviet empire, the central European states would seem to have been understandably wary of doing what regional cooperation requires; that is, compromising their hard-won state sovereignty[36] and their increased flexibility in foreign policy. Moreover, one can point at the same time to the existence of a number of factors that should have at least slowed the development of a cooperative agreement. For example, tensions which were in place even before the end of Communist Party rule between Hungary and Czechoslovakia with respect to the Hungarian minority in Slovakia and the Gabcikovo-Nagymaros dam project (which the Hungarian media referred to as "Dunasaurus")[37]; there was also competition among these states in the immediate post-Communist period to attract

35. "Multilateralism."
36. On the question of sovereignty, see Wlodzimierz Aniol, "Miedzy odzyskana suverennoscia a oczekiwana integracja," in Janusz Stefanowicz, ed., *Bariery na dradze Polski do EWG* (Polish Academy of Sciences, 1992), pp. 15–27.
37. On the dam project, see, for instance, Andrzej Jonas, "Hungary: Picture of Progress," *Warsaw Voice* 24 May 1992, p. 5; Juliusz Urbanowicz, "Together to the

foreign capital, expand trade with the West, and join Western multilateral institutions; finally, there was the absence of an historical
precedent for cooperating with one another.[38]

The final point requires elaboration.[39] The last time leaders of
these three states had pledged themselves to a coordination of their
policies was in 1335 when Kings Casimir, John, and Robert Charles
met.[40] The six hundred and fifty-five years separating these two
"rounds" of regional cooperation in central Europe, moreover, had
produced one of two models of inter-state relations in the region,
neither of which was conducive to cooperation among these states.
The first was isolation from one another (as when they were encased in different empires prior to World War I or when they were
encased in the Soviet bloc and separated from one another as a
consequence of the radial structure of the Soviet bloc[41]) or conflict
with one another (for example, the establishment of the Little
Entente during the interwar period, when Czechoslovakia, Romania, and Yugoslavia were allied against Hungary).

What factors, then, seemed to have produced the "deviation" of
1990–92? The discussion above leads to a rather straightforward
list of factors. Cooperation in this case seems to have arisen in
response to: 1) strong leadership commitment to cooperation; 2)
the uncertainties and the considerable threats facing these states
as a consequence of their geopolitical location, and; 3) the incentives for cooperation offered by the European Community. However, embedded in this discussion is a fourth and very important
factor: the presence of what could be termed remarkable similarities from 1990–92 among the three central European states. These
similarities ran the full gamut—from similar domestic political
and economic profiles and similar ideological commitments of
their leaders to similarities in the definition of their foreign policy
interests and in the policies their leaders considered best suited to
maximize these interests and these values.

EC," *Warsaw Voice* (17 May 1992): 4; Judith Ingram, "Slovaks Pushing Danube Project," *The New York Times* (25 October 1992); and Tadeusz Olszanski, "Accord in
Deep Water," *Warsaw Voice* (24 May 1992): 4.

38. See, especially, Ronald H. Linden, "The New Security Environment in East
Europe," unpublished manuscript, the United States Institute of Peace and the
University of Pittsburgh, April 1996.

39. See, for example, the arguments by Plakans, "Historical Considerations."

40. Tokes, "From Visegrad."

41. See Bunce, "The Empire." Also see Andras Koves and Gabor Oblath, "The
Regional Role of the Former Soviet Union and the CMEA: A New Assessment," in
Hardt and Kaufman, eds., *East-Central European Economies in Transition*, pp. 355–66.

Let me now elaborate on this observation. The collapse of communism in Eastern Europe in 1989 had one common consequence: the subjection of Communist parties to political competition. However, within that commonality was considerable variance. In some cases, this merely meant the victory by 1990 of the Communists—in various renamed parties—in the first competitive elections held after the end of Communist Party hegemony (as in Romania, Bulgaria, Serbia, Macedonia, and Albania). In other cases, this led to the victory of the opposition (as in Poland, Hungary, Czechoslovakia, and, along with these states, the newly formed states of Slovenia, Croatia, Bosnia, Latvia, Lithuania, and Estonia). This is important because this divide structured not just the composition and ideology of the new governments in the region, but also subsequent developmental trajectories—succinctly put, the commitment to and the speed of the transition to capitalism and democracy.[42] By 1990, then, the Polish, Hungarian and Czechoslovak regimes featured an unusually similar domestic and foreign policy agenda—similarities that were only deepened by their shared geopolitical location and the absence of all those complications introduced by having to construct new states and new national economies (in direct contrast, for example, to Lithuania, Slovenia, and the like, which had likewise featured a clear break with the Communist past).

What also contributed to their similarities was the fact that these countries shared a protest tradition during the Communist period (for instance, Hungary in 1954–56, Czechoslovakia in 1953 and 1967–68 and Poland in 1956, 1970–71, 1976, and 1980–81). This tradition, which distinguished them from their neighbors, pointed to the existence of comparatively developed civil societies, and which had obvious relevance as a consequence of the events of 1989, meant that there were established linkages among the dissidents-now-rulers in Poland, Hungary, and Czechoslovakia[43]—linkages that had been forged in particular through the Helsinki process[44] and through increased interactions among these

42. See, especially, Valerie Bunce, "The Return of the Left and the Future of Democracy in Central and Eastern Europe," paper presented at the Annual Conference of the Council for European Studies, Chicago, 15–17 March 1996.

43. While dissidents long known to each other came to power in Poland and Czechoslovakia, this was not the case in Hungary following the May 1990 elections. However, the party representing the dissident intelligentsia—the Free Democrats—had reasonable representation in the Hungarian parliament.

44. See Daniel Thomas, "International Norms and Political Change: The Helsinki Accords and the Decline of Communism in Eastern Europe and the Soviet Union, 1972–1990," Ph.D. dissertation, Cornell University, 1996.

dissident communities from the mid-1980s onward as a consequence, among other things, of a loosening of the Soviet bloc.

Thus the history of these three countries under state socialism,
the victory of the opposition in the first competitive elections
after socialism, and the similarities of their geopolitical location,
as well as their agendas for transformation, all worked to ho-
mogenize in effect the structure, the experiences, the interests,
and the goals of the new regimes in Poland, Hungary, and Czechoslovakia. In this way, an unusually supportive environment for
regional cooperation developed over the course of 1990–92.
However, what was also at work was what could be termed the
"abnormal politics" of the early transition period. What is striking about the policy agenda of Poland, Hungary, and Czechoslovakia immediately following the collapse of state socialism was
its *generality* and its *optimism*. In particular, in the heady days of
1990–91 the leaders of these three countries found it easy to identify and to agree upon what they didn't want—that is, state socialism, the WTO, and the CMEA—and what they did want—
that is, capitalism, democracy, stability, security, and membership
in the European Community. They were also very confident that
they could dispense quickly and easily with the former, while
achieving the latter—without delays or trade-offs. At the same
time, similar platitudes with similar levels of optimism came out
of the mouths of Western leaders. This is reminiscent of an old
joke often heard during the Communist period: "We know what
the future will bring and that it will be wonderful. We also know
exactly what happened in the past, and that it was terrible. But
the present is a complete mystery."

What all this meant with respect to the issue of inter-state
cooperation was that the similarities among the three Visegrad
states in their domestic structures and in their domestic and foreign policies were a function of both real and false similarities.
By the latter, I refer to the absence of what usually divides even
like-minded and like-situated states; that is, the details of the present, the uncertainty surrounding the future, and the diverse
range of possible strategies and painful trade-offs that necessarily accompany the movement from the present to the future.
Cooperation among Poland, Hungary, and Czechoslovakia from
1990–92, then, was easy, in part because politics during this period was shorn of its complications and its uncertainties. As we
will see below, once politics had again normalized—that is, when
the transitions "settled" at both the domestic and international

levels—similarities evolved into differences and the case for co-operation weakened considerably.

Decline of Visegrad Cooperation, 1993–96

The year 1993 marked a turning point in the development of coop-erative relations among Poland, Hungary, the Czech Republic, and Slovakia. This is evident, first, when we construct a "time-line" of initiatives and accomplishments. Beginning in 1991–92, we see the establishment of inter-state working groups and regular consulta-tion among defense ministers; the formation of a regional interest group pressing the European Community and NATO for member-ship; and the construction of a consensus around the development and the design of CEFTA. It was also during this period that the Visegrad Group succeeded in carrying out the withdrawal of Soviet troops from the region (with Soviet troops leaving Hungary and Czechoslovakia in June 1991, but due to elongated negotia-tions, in October 1993 in Poland); the termination of the WTO and CMEA (which took place, respectively, in June and September of 1991); the creation of the North Atlantic Cooperation Council (1991), which laid the groundwork for the participation of these countries in NATO; the negotiation of Associate Member Agree-ments with the European Union; and membership in the Council of Europe. By contrast, after 1992 there are no new initiatives and few collective accomplishments to which one can point.

Indeed, by 1993 one can see the beginning of what was to be-come a relatively linear decline in cooperation among the Viseg-rad countries. This is indicated, first, by the fact that *no* summits have been held among these states since the Prague meeting in May 1992. Moreover, as we will see below, there are good reasons to assume that this will continue to be the case in the near future.

Moreover, the various intra-regional working groups that formed in 1991–92 around such issues as migration, legal reform, and selected aspects of the economic transition have in fact rarely met and have virtually no policy impact in their respective coun-tries, let alone at the regional level.[45] Of more impact, it should be added, have been the working groups organized through the

---

45. As observed by Andras Szabo, minister charged with responsibility for regional affairs, Ministry of Foreign Affairs, Budapest, in an interview taking place in Budapest on 17 January 1995.

Central European Initiative and through the European Union and European Parliament.

At the same time, the *only* regional institution that the Visegrad Group has in fact constructed is CEFTA. While one might argue that this is an impressive achievement,[46] there are in fact reasons to be skeptical given the expansion of member states and given the adherence of the member states to the original timetable of trade liberalization. One reason is that the institutional development of CEFTA has been minimal. Thus while the EU has its Commission and the European Free Trade Area its Secretariat, CEFTA has *no* permanent bodies. At the same time, trade among the central European states amounts to only 4 to 8 percent of their total trade. This reflects the redundancy of the central European economies as a consequence of the Soviet bloc structure; the inescapable economic logic of expanding trade with the West, not the east; and the understandable fear that increased trade within central Europe would only increase the output of uneconomic sectors.[47] Regional trade liberalization in this case, then, has not had—and will not have in the future—the desirable consequences it has had elsewhere; that is, the creation of regional institutions, expansion of trade, and growing economic efficiency.

There are good reasons, moreover, to suspect that CEFTA will be the last, as well as the first, institution established by the Visegrad process. Policy makers and influential policy analysts in central Europe seem to be reaching a consensus that: 1) their states do not need to add any new bureaucratic structures and, instead, need to reduce their institutional density; 2) the creation of new regional institutions would merely duplicate what already exists in the EU and NATO, but without the same level of effectiveness; and 3) the construction of regional institutions would merely give members of NATO and the EU an excuse to put off the question of full membership of the central European countries in these international institutions.[48] Empirical support for the final argument, moreover, has been readily available. The European Union does in

46. See, for example, Open Media Research Institute Report on Eastern and Central Europe, 1 December 1995 and 7–8 December 1995, along with Lida Rakuszahova, "Raczej CEFTA," *Gazeta Wyborcza* (15 April 1994): 12–13.

47. On the limits and costs of CEFTA trade, see, for example, Brada, "Regional Integration"; Malkiewicz, "CEFTA, Past and Future."

48. See Kun, "In Search of Guarantees: Hungary's Quest"; Malkiewicz, "CEFTA, Past and Future"; Václav Havel, "A Call for Sacrifice," *Foreign Affairs* 73, no. 2 (March–April 1994); Inotai and Sass, "Economic Integration." This was also a dominant theme in the interviews I conducted in Budapest in January 1995.

fact seem to be moving rather slowly on the admission of these states—at least in the perception of decision makers in central Europe.[49] This interpretation was all the easier to draw, moreover, given disturbing comments by Western European political leaders—especially those who were less supportive of the rapid inclusion of these states in the European Union. For example, in 1993 President Mitterrand of France commented that these countries should focus on cooperating with one another rather than trying to get into the European Union so quickly.[50]

Tensions among the Visegrad countries have also grown since 1993. Hungarian-Slovak relations have continued to be testy, given Slovak commitment to the Gabcikovo-Nagymaros dam (which they see as economically necessary and as a symbol of their political, as well as economic, independence) and continued Hungarian objections (on ecological and economic grounds) to this project and its diversion of the Danube. However, beginning in 1993 three additional factors have further strained relations between these two states: the breakup of Czechoslovakia on 1 January 1993, the assumption several months later of full Slovak ownership of the dam and the loss as a result of the Czech role of mediator; the Hungarian threat to vote against Slovak admission to the Council of Europe (which created strains between the Hungarians and the Czechs as well); and the passage of a new language law in Slovakia in 1995 as well as the consideration of a new treaty between Slovakia and Hungary in the same year,[51] both of which have focused—and are continuing to focus—attention on the combustible issue of the position of the Hungarian minority in Slovakia (which comprises 10 percent of the Slovak population).[52]

49. Their model, of course, was Greece—which had been admitted quickly, once the colonels were out of power. However, this was because Greek membership had been put on temporary hold, and the European Community had promised that the end of the military dictatorship would win quick admission to the European Union. The Greek case, however, is exceptional. More typical is the Spanish case, where eight years lapsed between Spain's formal application to join the European Community (two years after the death of Franco) and the decision to admit Spain.

50. As noted in Terry, "Intraregional Political and Economic Relations," p. 374.

51. It is telling, for example, that when the Hungarian-Slovak Friendship Treaty was submitted to parliament for ratification in Hungary, *all* the opposition party members, Left and Right, either abstained or voted against it. See Linden, "The New Security Environment," p. 20.

52. This was a central theme in the interview I conducted in Budapest on 18 January 1995 with Csaba Tabajdi, assistant to the prime minister with particular responsibility for ethnic relations.

Tensions have also arisen because of the growing sense among leaders of these states that their continued cooperation with one another will not contribute very much to their goal of becoming full members of the European Union and NATO. On the one hand, the Visegrad Group is no longer distinctive or privileged. Like Bulgaria and Romania, for example, these states are Associate Members of the European Union, members of the Council of Europe, members of the North Atlantic Cooperation Council, and members of the Partnership for Peace Program (a combination of institutional affiliations that will also cover, very soon, the Baltic states and Slovenia as well). This not only means that they have been reduced to "one of many" and, thus, derive no special benefit from their regional connections to one another. It also means that distinctions among the post-Communist countries are blurred, which, in the view of many central European policy makers "... brings a danger of the politically and economically least developed countries setting the criteria and date for membership in the primary institutions (the EU and NATO)."[53] The Visegrad states, in short, seemed to have lost their regional "edge" by being "lumped" with Bulgaria and Romania—not to mention the Baltic states and Slovenia.

All of this means that, since 1993, these states have had increasingly strong incentives to play up their distinctive assets, to reject any "partners" (such as Slovakia) that would undermine the strength of their claims to joining Europe quickly, and to view one another as competitors, rather than collaborators. This is why, for example, over the past few years the Hungarians have played up the historical roots of their economic reforms, the stability of their governments, and their long parliamentary tradition; why Vaclav Klaus has emphasized the economic and political stability of the Czech Republic and, following the Polish parliamentary elections in the fall 1993 and the May 1994 parliamentary elections in Hungary (not to mention the Polish presidential election of December 1995), the fact that the Czech Republic now exists as a "liberal island" in a regional Communist sea[54] (though the Social Democrats, it must be noted, are doing very well in the polls these days[55]

53. Andras Inotai and Miklos Derer, "The World in 1993: A Hungarian View," Center for Security Policy and Defense Studies, Budapest, 1993, p. 16.

54. Points emphasized as well by other representatives of the Czech government—see, for example, the commentary by Karel Kovanda, ambassador of the Czech Republic to the United Nations, in "Between Russia and Germany," p. 6.

55. See *SME* (8 March 1996): 5.

and are the second largest party in the Czech parliament); and why the Poles have emphasized their role in 1989, their shock therapy, their democratic traditions in pre-partition Poland, and their important geopolitical location.[56]

Actions by Western governments and international institutions, as well as statements by Western leaders, have only encouraged such individualistic rather than collective claims, of course. For every statement that the European Union makes supporting regional cooperation in central and eastern Europe, there are a variety of statements and actions that encourage competition and division among these states—for example, the bilateral negotiations to join the Partnership for Peace Program, the recent decision by the OECD to admit the Czech Republic as its first post-Communist member (though Hungary has now also recently been admitted), the comment by Helmut Kohl in a December 1995 speech that the enlargement of the EU should focus on the Visegrad countries, but minus Slovakia,[57] and the recent comment (in August 1995) by U.S. Defense Secretary William Perry that the Czech Republic would seem to have the strongest case for joining NATO.[58]

All of this has had predictable consequences. There has been a growing tendency since 1992 for these states to defect from the regional grouping and to prefer unilateral and bilateral actions over multilateralism. One can point, for example, to the individualistic approach each of these states has taken since 1993 regarding the question of joining NATO and the EU; the recent agreement between Poland and Hungary to coordinate their activities on both fronts (thereby substituting bilateralism for multilateralism and excluding the Czech Republic and Slovakia); and the intense negotiations between Hungary and Slovakia over their bilateral treaty and the Slovak language law.

What this also suggests is that the commitment to regional cooperation among the Visegrad states has declined. This is most evident in the speeches and actions of the Czech leadership.[59] For example, just five days after the birth of the Czech Republic, the

56. Missing from this list, of course, is Slovakia. Of the four Visegrad states, this state is least able to make arguments about the strength of its case for joining Europe quickly. Thus, not surprisingly, Slovakia has been far more of a team player than its neighbors—though the Poles have also been relatively supportive of the Visegrad grouping.

57. As reported in Kinzer, "West Says Slovakia."

58. As noted by Whitney, "Despite Russian Objections."

59. See, for example, Edward Krzemien, "Razem-nie osobno," *Gazeta wyborcza* (15 April 1994): 12–13.

prime minister of the Czech Republic, Vaclav Klaus, said in an interview in *Le Figaro* that he was not very interested in the Visegrad process, that the Visegrad Group was "artificial," and that the end of Czechoslovakia provided a useful pretext for rethinking the value of regional cooperation.[60] Klaus then followed up these comments in 1994 by arguing that the Visegrad Group should rename itself CEFTA and cease all those activities that fell outside the province of intra-regional trade liberalization.[61] Klaus, however, was not alone in his thinking. When asked about the future of Visegrad military cooperation (the only area, aside from economics, where significant progress had been made), Antonin Baudys, the Czech defense minister, said that: "The Visegrad grouping is—from our point of view—obsolete." He then went on to argue that the bilateralism of the Partnership for Peace Program and the high probability of eventual membership in NATO were in effect all the security activities the Czech Republic needed—while nonetheless recognizing that Poland and Hungary, with their more vulnerable geopolitical locations, were entitled to a different position.[62]

By the beginning of 1994, then, the future of the Visegrad Group was in serious question. Events in January of that year did a great deal to cement these developments. In anticipation of President Clinton's visit to Prague, President Lech Walesa of Poland called for a consultation in Warsaw among the Visegrad foreign ministers. But Klaus refused to send his minister. He then demanded a major change in the structure of the discussions to take place with Clinton. The original plan—supported by Poland, Hungary, and Slovakia—was to hold a joint meeting of the Visegrad countries with the American president. Klaus proposed, instead, bilateral meetings—and this is what in fact took place.[63] All this led the leaders of the Visegrad countries to agree on two points. One was

60. As reported in *RFE/RL New Briefs* (11 January 1993): 12. See also Endre Aczel, "The Czech's Separate Way," *Nepszabadsag* (6 June 1994): 3, translated in FBIS-EEU-007, p. 11.

61. See, especially, Jiri Pehe, "The Choice Between Europe and Provincialism," *Transition* 1, no. 12, 14 July 1995, pp. 14–19.

62. See "Perhaps We Will Welcome NATO Troops in the Czech Republic: Interview with Defense Minister Antonin Baudys by Jan Stetka," *Lidove noviny* (14 January 1994), in FBIS-EEU-94-012 (19 January 1994): 14.

63. However, when pushed on the question of regional relations, Klaus did say the following on 10 January 1994: "… if we protest sometimes, it is rather a protest against a certain empty regionalism, against artificial concepts, that lead nowhere. As for real and good regional relations, we, I believe, say clearly yes," quoted from "Prague CT Television," 10 January 1994, translated in FBIS-EEU-007, 11 January

that the Czechs "are eager to be released from any obligations in order to run a lonely race toward the West" (as the Slovak ambassador to the United Nations put it subsequently[64]), and the other was that the group would disband, unless a major effort were made to revive it.[65] Thus far, little has been done to resuscitate the group—though Poland, Slovakia, and Hungary have at least maintained their verbal support of regional cooperation.

This leads us to the final question that will be addressed here. Why, especially after such a promising beginning, did regional cooperation decline in central Europe? Putting the question another way: what changed in 1993–96 and what does that say, more generally, about why states do and do not cooperate with one another?

The Decline of Cooperation: Changes in the International System

The decline of cooperation among the Visegrad states can be explained by tracing changes, beginning in 1993, in the international system, international institutions, and domestic politics and economics.[66] Let us turn, first, to changes at the international level; that is, shifts in the structure of power in the international system, the interests and capabilities of states, and the payoffs attached to pursuing multilateral versus unilateral and bilateral actions in the international system. What is striking is that all three of these factors changed, beginning roughly in 1992. First, three states in the region disintegrated beginning in 1991–92; that is, the Soviet Union, Yugoslavia, and Czechoslovakia.[67] This had a number of important consequences. One was to draw much sharper distinctions among the geopolitical locations of the Visegrad states. Poland, never

---

1994. See also the interview of Klaus by Roman Krasnicky, "The Free Trade Zone is a Test of Cooperation," *Lidove noviny* (8 January 1994): 1, 3 in FBIS-EEU-007, p. 3.

64. See the comments by Eduard Kukan in "Between Russia and Germany," p. 23.

65. As reported by Barany, "Visegrad Four." See also Pehe, "The Choice."

66. See also the insightful analyses by Gorzlczyk, "Visegrad Group," and the commentary by Kovanda, "Between Russia and Germany," pp. 21–22.

67. Arguments about why these states disintegrated—and, just as important, did so at different times, in different ways, and with different levels of violence—can be found in Valerie Bunce, "From State Socialism to State Disintegration: A Comparison of the Soviet Union, Yugoslavia and Czechoslovakia," paper presented at the conference on Post-Communism and Ethnic Mobilization, Cornell University, 15–17 April 1995.

lucky in its geopolitical location (to put it mildly), became even more unlucky by now having seven, rather than three, states on its borders; that is, not just Germany, but also Lithuania, the Czech Republic, Slovakia, Belarus, Ukraine, and Russia (because of the presence of the heavily militarized Kaliningrad oblast).[68] None of these newly formed states (with the exception of the Czech Republic), moreover, could be considered very stable. For example, Belarus has an increasingly doubtful status as a state, given its domestic turmoil and its increasingly close economic, as well as political, ties with Russia; Ukraine has serious strains between its eastern and western halves, a very large Russian minority (which constitutes nearly half of the twenty-five million Russian diaspora living in the "near abroad"), and a Polish minority as well; it also has continuing problems associated with economic reform, the construction of durable and democratic political institutions, and in its relations with Russia (now eased a bit as a result of the victory of the pro-Russian Kuchma in the recent presidential elections). For its part, Slovakia seems quite divided and potentially quite unstable, given the recent return to power of Vladimir Mečiar and his Movement for a Democratic Slovakia. The most threatening neighbor, however, is Russia, because of its domestic instability, its sheer size, its military capacities, and its imperial nostalgia, especially evident during electoral periods (which, unfortunately, has meant much of the time, from 1993 onward).

Two other states within the Visegrad Group were also rendered more vulnerable as a consequence of state breakup—Slovakia, because it shared a border with Ukraine (a potentially powerful country, given its size and military capacity), and Hungary, because it shared a border not just with Slovakia but also with the former Yugoslavia. The one state that could be said to have improved its geopolitical location by virtue of state disintegration was the Czech Republic—which experienced some complications due to its former integration with Slovakia, but which is now physically separated from the former Soviet Union and thus outside the Russian sphere of influence.[69]

68. The proclamation of a treaty between Russia and Belarus in mid-March 1996, moreover, has generated further geopolitical problems for Poland. This treaty calls for considerable cooperation, if not integration, between Belarus and Russia. While there are protests within Belarus over the question of lost sovereignty, the end result is that the Russian border with Poland may very well be in the process of expanding.

69. The division of Czechoslovakia was also quite beneficial for the Czech economy, given the substantial political and economic obstacles to a rapid transition to capitalism in Slovakia.

What all of this meant was that the interests of the Visegrad states, so similar in 1990–91, began to differentiate. For example, Poland, the Czech Republic, and Slovakia were less concerned about the war in Yugoslavia than was Hungary, and carried fewer costs from that war. There are 500,000 Hungarians in the former Yugoslavia (primarily in Vojvodina); it was Hungarian air space that was violated by the Yugoslav National Army in the brief Slovenian war of secession in the summer of 1991; and it was Hungary that has had to absorb the largest number of refugees from that war—about 100,000. It is also Hungary that serves to-day, of course, as the staging area for the implementation of the Peace Accords. At the same time, Slovakia and Poland are much more threatened by developments in Russia and the Western successor states of the former Soviet Union than are the Czech Republic and Hungary. What all this meant was that Polish foreign policy had a much more complex set of tasks before it than the foreign policies of the other Visegrad states; that Russia functioned as a major factor in the shaping of Polish and Slovak foreign policy, but not in the determination of Czech or Hungarian foreign policy; that Poland, Hungary, and Slovakia became much more concerned about security issues by the beginning of 1992; and, finally, that the Czechs were relatively free to build their foreign policy around one key issue—integration with the West.

The breakup of the three federalized Communist states in the region also affected the balance of power within the Visegrad constellation. On the one hand, the Czech Republic (for domestic, as well as international, reasons—more on that below) was empowered because of its reduced geographical vulnerability. This meant that the development of regional security structures were less important to the Czechs than to their neighbors, and this resulted an additional reason for the Czechs to defect.[70] NATO, very divided over the question of expansion, found the Czech Republic an ideal place to start—or at least to experiment with— an expansion of NATO to the east (with the Czechs arguing all the while that Prague sits to the west of Vienna). This is because the Czech Republic would be the easiest state in the region to defend; it seemed to best meet the preconditions for membership in NATO as laid out in the 1995 blueprint; and its membership in

70. However, it is interesting to note that in a *New York Times* poll taken in mid-1994 in the Czech Republic, Hungary, and Poland, the percentage of those viewing the Russian threat as "big" was as follows: 34 percent in the Czech Republic, 5 percent in Hungary, and 24 percent in Poland.

NATO would cause far fewer problems with Russia than the membership of, say, Poland.

Here, it is important to insert the Russian position on NATO enlargement.[71] A recent paper on this question, co-authored by a cross-section of academic specialists in Russia (including a large number of liberals) and appearing in full in a liberal Russian newspaper, makes the Russian perspective quite clear via the following arguments. First, this paper warned of expanding German power in Europe—which was expressed, among other things, in German support for extending NATO eastward and isolating Russia in the process. Second, it asserted that NATO membership for the former members of the Soviet bloc was in effect a consolation prize being offered to these countries for negligible progress in their full incorporation into the European Union (with a hint that the European Union was just playing games with central Europe). Finally, while noting that the central and eastern European countries have legitimate security concerns, the authors also noted that "... Russia does not consider membership of these countries in NATO to be an optimal or a balanced answer to their security, since in this case the security of the CEE countries would threaten the interests of Russia."[72]

If the Czech Republic was to some degree empowered by boundary changes, so was Poland, albeit in another way. Poland became by far the largest country in eastern and central Europe (with a population more than 50 percent larger than its three Visegrad neighbors combined); the country with the most important geopolitical location (there are advantages to be had from bad geography); and an emerging counterweight to Ukraine. This meant that Poland was strongly committed to building security structures wherever it could—through Visegrad, through bilateral treaties, and through NATO. This also made the other Visegrad states less willing to cooperate with Poland—for fear of getting dragged into Polish conflicts with their many neighbors and for fear of being dominated by Poland. The end result, of course, is that regional cooperation was undermined.

71. There are also considerable differences of opinion at the mass level on this question. For example, in a recent survey in Russia and Poland, 70 percent of the Poles and only 18 percent of the Russians denied that Polish entry into NATO would threaten Russian security. See the report by CBOS (the Polish Public Opinion Research Center), February 1996.

72. "Rossiia i NATO: Tezisy soveta po vneshnei i oboronnoi politike," *Nezavisimaya gazeta* (21 June 1995): 2. See especially sections 1.1.1; 1.2.2 and 1.2.3.

There were three other changes in the international system that affected the interests and thus the behavior of the Visegrad countries. One was the war in Yugoslavia—which, in addition to the effects already noted, had, along with the rise, beginning in 1994, of at least aggressive talk in Russia, the effect of sensitizing all of these countries to their continuing isolation from European collective security structures. Here one can point to growing awareness among these states that: 1) NATO had a great deal of trouble responding to crises in Europe that straddled the domestic/international divide and that fell "out of area" (both of which resonated all-too-well with the present and future situation of central Europe); 2) the Western European states were in fact very divided in their foreign policies; 3) the Russians were a "wild card" and had increasingly returned to their historic role of demonstrating their power in the international system through disruption rather than a show of force; and 4) multilateral institutions, such as the OSCE (which had been the focus of the eastern and central European regimes from 1991–92), were even less capable of guaranteeing regional security than was NATO.[73] This led all of these states to be more concerned about the security vacuum in the region and to step up pressures on NATO to admit them as members. NATO's reticence to do so, the increasingly varied profile of these countries with respect to their geopolitical location, their interests, and their capabilities, along with the growing sense among the central European states by 1993 that NATO, like the EU, was a theater with a limited number of seats, all led, quite predictably, to growing incentives for these states to deal with security by acting unilaterally rather than multilaterally. Thus, by 1994—reinforced by the bilateral basis for negotiations to join the Partnership for Peace—the Visegrad states increasingly defined their security needs in individualized terms.

This leads us to a final change in the international system, beginning at the start of 1992: the increasing importance of Germany.[74] As the largest, most stable, and most economically robust country

73. On the security deficits of OSCE, see, especially, Istvan Szonyi, "The False Promise of an Institution: Can Cooperation Between the OSCE and NATO be a Cure?" unpublished manuscript, the University of Rochester, 1996; and Szonyi, "Caught between Wealth and Security: Alternative Futures for the OSCE," unpublished manuscript, the University of Rochester, 1996.

74. See, for instance, August Pradetto, "Transformation in Eastern Europe, International Cooperation, and the German Position," *Studies in Comparative Communism* 25, no. 1 (March 1992), pp. 23–30.

in what is in precise geographical terms central Europe (the German GNP, for example, is ten times the GNP of Poland, Hungary, the Czech Republic, and Slovakia combined), Germany quickly emerged as *the* key Western European player in eastern Europe as a whole.[75] To understand the German role, we must begin with the principles underlying German foreign policy since the collapse of state socialism: that the greatest threat to German security comes from the east; that Germany has a responsibility, because of its location and its history (given its historical influence in the region, the burden of its Nazi past, and the Europeanization of Germany in the post-World War II period), to play a central role in stabilizing and integrating the new capitalist democracies in eastern Europe; and that the German economy is in an ideal location to derive considerable benefits from expanding its markets to the east. While these principles do not always combine in felicitous ways (as witnessed by, for example, German pressure for rapid recognition of the secessionist Yugoslav republics of Croatia and Slovenia—which contributed in certain ways to the wars that followed in Croatia and Bosnia),[76] they were so with respect to central Europe. They transformed Germany into the Visegrad states' strongest advocate in Western Europe for trade, aid, and membership in European multilateral institutions.[77] At the same time, they rendered Germany

75. Moreover, the importance of Germany is widely recognized in public opinion polls in the Visegrad states. For example, in a recent poll in Poland, Germany and the United States (in that order) emerged as the two countries considered most important for the establishment of cooperative relations. See CBOS (Newsletter of the Institute for Public Opinion Polling, Warsaw), October 1995.

76. See, especially, Susan Woodward, *Balkan Tragedy: Chaos and Dissolution After the Cold War* (Brookings Institution, 1995). This is not to argue, though, that the cause of the wars of secession and Serbian expansion in the former Yugoslavia can be reduced, by any means, to the German decision to recognize Croatia and Slovenia (and, belatedly, Bosnia-Herzegovina). A careful construction of the sequencing of events would suggest that many of the factors that led to the wars in Slovenia, Croatia, and Bosnia—for instance, the rise of nationalist parties in Serbia, Croatia, and Slovenia, Serbian commitment to the end of Yugoslavia and to a "Greater Serbia," and the deal struck between Presidents Tudjman and Milosevic to divide Bosnia between them, were in place prior to the German decision. Moreover, the German decision had two positive consequences: it forced the West to reconsider its policy of holding Yugoslavia together, and it contributed to the recognition by the West and eventually by Western multilateral institutions that this was a war among states, not a civil war.

77. See, especially, Angela Stent, ""Between Moscow and Bonn: East Central Europe in Transition," in Hardt and Kaufman, eds., *East-Central European Economies*, pp. 441–56. Germany is the largest aid donor and the largest trade partner of the Visegrad states. However, in 1993 the United States surpassed Germany in one

the single most important trade partner of the Visegrad states. Thus, while these states comprise about four per cent of German exports and about 3.8 percent of German imports (1993 data), the reverse figures are as follows: 25 percent of Czech imports and 26.9 percent of Czech exports; 11.7 percent of Slovak imports and 15.3 percent of Slovak exports; 21.6 percent of Hungarian imports and 26.6 percent of Hungarian exports; 28 percent of Polish imports and 36 percent of Polish exports.[78]

The question then becomes: how does this affect regional cooperation? The long answer is that: 1) the central European economies have become quite dependent on Germany and are likely to become even more so in the future (thereby repeating the interwar experience); 2) European integration has increasingly translated in practice into German integration; 3) the central and eastern European states are more and more in the position of competing with one another for German aid, trade, and investment (especially seeing as the costs of German unification, much higher than Helmut Kohl originally envisioned, have, along with a recession in global trade by 1992, rendered German domestic demand much more limited than the eastern and central European states originally had hoped); and 4) the road to Europe and, thus, the road to economic growth and political stability, seems to run through Germany—because of the factors already mentioned, and because of the growing realization among central Europeans, most evident by 1993, that full membership in the European Union is not "around the corner."

This leads us to a much simpler answer to the question. German dominance in central Europe has worked, along with the actions of NATO and the EU, to encourage competition and conflict rather than cooperation among the Visegrad states. This in turn means that the international incentives to defect from regional cooperation grew, beginning in 1993, with the predictable consequence that cooperation among these states declined.

It could be argued, then, that the major reason why regional cooperation among Poland, Hungary, the Czech Republic, and

---

important economic statistic for the region: foreign direct investment. Germany comes in a very close second. Moreover, German investment in the Czech Republic in particular is quite high—36.4 percent of all foreign direct investment from 1989 to March 1995. See Zschiedrich, "Die Freihandelszone" and Steve Kettle, "Foreign Investment and the SPT Telecomm Deal," *Transition* 1, no. 17, 22 September 1995, p. 53.

78. See Harald Zschiedrich, "Die Freihandelszone der 'Visegrad-Staaten'" Neubeginn einer Intraregionalen Koooperation?" *Sudosteuropa* 42, no. 9 (1993), pp. 491–511.

Slovakia declined after 1992 was that the structure of power in the international system changed and, with that, the interests of the Visegrad states and the incentives they had to cooperate with one another. What could be termed a realist understanding of the causes of and constraints on inter-state cooperation, then, would seem to be well-supported by the ups and downs of the Visegrad experience from 1991 to 1995. Thus the factors noted in the analysis of the rise of regional cooperation would seem to be relevant as well to the question of the decline in regional cooperation. Changes in the international system meant that fears were no longer the same nor shared; international incentives for cooperation declined; and absolute gains from cooperation also declined, while relative gains—more as perceived by the Visegrad states—were highly unequal. We can even apply the "shadow of the future" to this case. With CEFTA trade limited, with rapidly expanding trade with Germany, with the growth of bilateral negotiations through the Partnership for Peace Program, and with the growing likelihood that these states would eventually join the EU and NATO (and not necessarily as a group), the future appeared to be one in which these states would interact more and more with Western European states on a bilateral basis or within multilateral institutions dominated by Western Europe. Thus the notion of repeated interactions in the future was increasingly revised after 1992 by the reality of "semi-joining" Europe. While this did not mean that the absence of cooperation led to more conflict, it did mean that competition among these states was heightened and the willingness and capacity to coordinate their policies reduced.

International Institutions

The explanation for declining cooperation among Hungary, Poland, the Czech Republic, and Slovakia, however, is incomplete without reference to a second set of factors; that is, the role of international institutions. What is crucial to understand here is that multilateral institutions, embracing the norm of cooperation, can under certain circumstances encourage quite different behavior, especially by states that are "out" and want "in." With this in mind, let us look more closely at the behavior of two such institutions; that is, NATO and the EU.

From 1991–92, the leaders of the central European states, while calling for their admission to NATO, seemed to agree that their security needs could be met, at least minimally, by regional military cooperation and by their participation in OSCE. By late 1992, however, they had come to realize that there were limits to what they could do at the regional level—because of their military weakness and the strength of their neighbors (including not just Russia and Germany, but also Ukraine), and because the creation of a regional military alliance would necessarily threaten their neighbors and thereby reduce, rather than enhance, security. At the same time, it became clear that OSCE was too unwieldy (having moved from thirty-five to fifty-two active members), lacked military muscle, and was best equipped to work with conflicting parties prior to the outbreak of actual conflict (a role that it played with some limited success in the Estonian citizenship controversy).[79]

All this, plus the security concerns already noted, led the central European leadership to two conclusions. They could expect little from regional security cooperation, and they had to join NATO as soon as possible.[80] NATO, however, was—and still is—quite divided on the question of expansion, given the monumental changes in its mission with the end of the Soviet threat and the unification of Germany,[81] the increasingly blurred boundaries between international and domestic conflict in contemporary Europe, Russian hostility to NATO expansion (which had been placated for awhile by the Partnership for Peace Program—though the Russians complained about this as well, until they finally joined), the varying interests of its members with respect to eastern Europe, and finally, the many costs—economic and political—of expanding to the east.[82] In the interface between NATO's

79. Paul Gallis, Julie Kim, and Francis Miko, "Regional Security Relations and NATO," in Hardt and Kaufman, eds., *East-Central European Economies*, pp. 393–411.

80. While leaders throughout the region of central Europe seem to support NATO membership, there is some division on the ground on this question. For example, Romania Mare, a nationalist party, published a memorandum in 1995 signed by 300 members of the military accusing the Romanian government of "high treason" for cooperating with NATO. See Linden, "The New Security Environment," pp. 17–18.

81. A succinct summary of the NATO mission was offered by a British diplomat, Lord Ismay, who argued that the function of NATO is " to keep the Russians out … the Americans in and the Germans down," quoted in Michael Mihalka, "Creeping Toward the East," *Transition: Year in Review, 1994*, part I, vol. 1, no. 1, 30 January 1995, p. 80.

82. See, for example, Douglas Clarke, "Uncomfortable Partners," in *Transition: The Year in Review, 1994* (15 February 1995): 27–31; Michael Mihalka, "Creeping Toward the East," *Transition: Year in Review, 1994*, part I, vol. 1, no. 1, 30 January 1995, pp. 73–78; Laszlo Tolnay, "Hungarian Quest for Security and the West European Union,"

ambivalence on this question and growing concerns among the central European countries about their security, then, lies the growth of incentives, beginning in 1993, for the Visegrad states to deal with their security concerns by slowing down the process of regional military integration and by making their cases individually for NATO membership.

Similar dynamics have taken place with respect to the EU. Like NATO, the EU has faced identity problems as a consequence of the collapse of state socialism. As Michael Shackleton puts it:

> ... the democratic legitimacy of the Community had at least in part been assured by the contrast in political forms between the two parts of Europe. Once that contrast disappeared, there was much room for questioning the democratic credentials of the Community. This was particularly so in view of ... the declining confidence among publics as to the democratic character of their own national societies.[83]

Moreover, the EU, like NATO, is quite divided.[84] For example, it has its own "north-south" problems and its own economic problems, and these two difficulties together have caused quite differing levels of support for admission of the central European states. For example, ratification of the Associate Membership agreements for the three Visegrad states was put off from September to December 1991 because of French threats to veto these agreements (with the French concerned, among other things, about the influx of agricultural products from central Europe). The European Union is also constrained by a backed up agenda for admitting

Policy paper 1, Center for Security and Defense Studies, Budapest, 1994; Stanley Kobar, "The U.S. and the Enlargement Debate," *Transition* 1, no. 23, 15 December 1995, pp. 6–10; Stephen Connors and David Gibson, "Caution and Ambivalence over Joining NATO," *Transition* 1, no. 14, 11 August 1995, pp. 42–46. For a succinct statement on why NATO should not expand, see Trevor Taylor, "NATO and Central Europe," *NATO Review* 5 (October 1991), pp. 17–22. As Secretary of State Warren Christopher put it in 1994: "Swift expansion of NATO eastward would make a neo-imperialist Russia a self-fulfilling prophecy," quoted in "NATO Plus," *Washington Post* (9 January 1994). For a succinct statement on why NATO should expand, see Strobe Talbott, "Why NATO Should Grow," *New York Review of Books* 42 (10 August 1995): 27–30.

83. "The Internal Legitimacy Crises of the European Union," Europa Institute, Edinburgh Occasional Paper, no. 1, 1994, p. 7, quoted in Harris, "The European Parliament."

84. This is not aided, moreover, by the sharp decline in public support for their democratic governments in western Europe. In 1993, the Eurobarometer registered for the first time since it began in 1973 a higher proportion of citizens dissatisfied with the operation of their national democracies than satisfied. See Shackleton, "The Internal Legitimacy Crisis."

Switzerland, Malta, Cyprus, and Turkey (and, perhaps, Norway as well, if its mind were to change); by the fact that the size of the Union could go up to twenty-five (standing at fifteen now), if all the Associate Members were to join; by the economic and bureaucratic costs still being worked out as a consequence of the recent admission of Finland, Sweden, and Austria; and by growing pressures, especially in light of the failure to ratify the Maastricht Treaty, to reconsider the relationship between "deepening" and "widening" and the current institutional format of the EU. While the EU evidenced more support of eventual membership of the central European states at both the Copenhagen and Cannes meetings in June 1993 and October 1995, respectively,[85] the EU's response to central Europe has nonetheless been quite cautious—whether the issue is full membership or the willingness of the EU to open up its markets.[86]

As with NATO, these delays and these difficulties have had important consequences for regional integration in central Europe. The major incentive for regional cooperation—that is, European integration—is less powerful than it once was because of the declining certainty that: 1) this benefit will be delivered in the near future; and 2) the Visegrad countries will be admitted to the EU more quickly if they come as a unit than if they come as individual states (which they would necessarily do anyway, seeing as applications are state-by-state, as are negotiations).[87] At the same time, the promise made in 1995 to move more quickly after 1996 has not contributed to regional integration. If membership is guaranteed, then regional cooperation is necessarily devalued. More-

85. See, in particular, "Conclusions of the Presidency," European Council of Copenhagen," Europe Documents, no. 1844/45, 24 June 1993; and "White Paper: Preparation of the Associated Countries of Central and Eastern Europe for Integration into the Internal Market of the Union," (Brussels: European Commission, 1995).

86. It is unfortunate that the three economic strong suits of the central and eastern European countries—steel, textiles, and agricultural products—are precisely those areas where the European Union is most protectionist. Thus it is unclear whether the EU can be considered unfair to central and eastern Europe. Compare, for example, the following two arguments. Brada, "The European Community," versus Bartlomiej Kaminski, "Central European Access to EC Markets: Hard or Easy?" *Transition: The Newsletter about Reforming Economies* (The World Bank), vol. 4, no. 7, September 1993, pp. 6–8.

87. Another factor that seems to have been crucial, but which has received little attention from theorists, is the importance of having a concrete set of objectives which can be realized in a short period of time. While integration with Europe does not fit this stipulation, negotiations over Soviet troop withdrawals from eastern Europe and the dismantling of WTO and CMEA do.

over, if this theater, like the other multilateral institutions in Western Europe, has limited seats (which the divisions within the EU would certainly support, as would the history of how other states have become full members), then why take the chance of bargaining as a unit, especially when that unit contains one country—Slovakia—that has a substantially weaker case? Thus, while the uncertainty of EU membership from 1992 through mid-1993 worked against regional cooperation by encouraging competition, the greater certainty of membership subsequently has had a similar effect.

The role of international institutions in the Visegrad case, then, underwent some important changes from 1991 to 1995. While functioning initially as a powerful international incentive for the central European countries to establish cooperative linkages, the EU and NATO functioned after 1992 as a *disincentive* for the continuation, let alone the expansion, of regional policy coordination among Poland, Hungary, the Czech Republic, and Slovakia. Competition among multilateral economic and security institutions, therefore, led to competition within each of these regional constellations and to what might be termed the "bankruptcy" of the weaker regional competitors. This process was further hastened along, moreover, by defection to those regional institutions that represented a true "halfway house" between multilateral eastern and Western institutions; that is, the Central European Initiative.[88]

This leads us to the final factor influencing the downturn of cooperation among the Visegrad states—domestic politics.

Domestic Setting

The story of the decline of regional cooperation in central Europe is dominated, as is the story of its rise, by the actions of specific political leaders and their ideological perspectives. As noted above, Vaclav Klaus, the prime minister of the Czech Republic, contributed a great deal to the decline of cooperation among the Visegrad states—by downgrading it, by repeatedly preferring unilateral and bilateral actions to multilateral ones, and by attempting to reduce the Visegrad initiative to a matter of trade

88. See, especially, Terry, "Intraregional Economic and Political Relations." This was also an argument made by Andras Szabo, the Minister of Regional Affairs, the Hungarian Foreign Ministry, in an interview I conducted with him on 18 January 1995.

liberalization in a handful of economic sectors. But as with any discussion of the role of political leadership, this leaves us with problems of interpretation. Are we to assume that the issue is Klaus as an individual, Klaus as a "transmission belt" for the interests of the Czech Republic, or Klaus as an ideologue? While all three interpretations have merit, it is the third that seems to be the most important. In particular, one needs to understand Klaus' ideology as an economic liberal. This has led him in the area of regional cooperation, as in other areas that fall within his decisional purview, to be opposed to bureaucratization; to favor individualism, whether expressed by human beings or states; to see security issues through economic lenses and, thus, to assume that economic growth and economic integration are processes that necessarily further security; to view politics, like economics, as a competitive, rather than a cooperative, game; and to assume that the benefits go not to those who stand on the sidelines and watch history happen, but rather to those (one is tempted to say "Leninists") who make history and engage in aggressive entrepreneurial behavior (which is one reason why he, alone among the "finance tsars" of eastern and central Europe, jumped into politics and formed his own political party).[89]

Domestic political coalitions are also important players in this story. Here the case of Hungary is instructive. From 1990 to 1994, Hungary was governed by a coalition dominated by the Democratic Forum. The ideology of this party was nationalist and Europeanist. This combined in ways that led the Hungarian government at this time to pursue policies that supported regional integration when it came to dealing with the Soviet threat, but that undermined regional integration, once the issue shifted to security, European integration, and the treatment of Hungarian minority populations outside of Hungary. Thus the Antall government had quite testy relations with Romania and Slovakia. In May 1994, the Democratic Forum was thrown out of power in a decisive manner and was replaced by the Hungarian Socialist Party (the former Hungarian Communist Party)—a party that had done very badly in the first competitive elections but now returned to power with a

---

89. This perspective on Klaus is drawn from sources already listed, along with an extended interview with Klaus (and with Leszek Balcerowicz and Peter Bod). See Mario I. Blejer and Fabrizio Coricell, *A Dialogue with the Reformers in Eastern Europe: Conversations with Leszek Balcerowicz, Peter Bod and Vaclav Klaus*, unpublished manuscript, the World Bank, 1993. My thanks to Leszek Balcerowicz for sharing this manuscript with me.

majority of the seats in the Hungarian parliament (54.1 percent). Hungarian public opinion strongly supported the creation of a coalition government with the second most popular party—the Free Democrats—which had won 18 percent of the seats. Because of this and the desire of the Socialists to reach out to the Communist-era opposition and to expand their legitimate claims to power in a democratic order, the coalition was formed, with the result that the coalition enjoys more than a two-thirds parliamentary majority.

This government has a complicated set of ideological commitments. It has a strong commitment to rapid economic reform and finally bit the bullet in 1995 by introducing austerity measures; it has embraced regional cooperation and the improvement of relations with Hungary's neighbors; and it has campaigned strongly for the admission of Hungary to NATO and the EU.[90] We can understand these actions not by simple reference to Hungary's geopolitical location, military capacity, state interests and the like, but by understanding that this government has combined some leftist principles—in particular, anti-nationalism and pro-internationalism—with a strong concern, on the part of the Socialists in particular, to reach out to their most skeptical constituencies—those who doubt their commitment to the transition to capitalism and those who doubt their commitment to European integration. The end result is that the domestic politics and economics of Hungary since 1994 help us to understand the two tracks of Hungarian foreign policy since 1994: the commitment to European integration and the commitment to improved regional relations. Both have meant an expansion of Hungarian bilateral relations with neighbors and with European international institutions, but without the "Klausian" antagonism to regional cooperation.[91]

All of this points to a final domestic factor—and one which resonates with our earlier discussion of why these states decided to establish cooperative relations. Václav Havel provides a clue:

90. This is my interpretation. Others perceive more lukewarm support for joining NATO in particular (as argued to me in January 1995, for example, by Tamas Kende, a member of the ELTE law faculty and an advisor in foreign affairs to the Free Democrats).

91. See, especially, Ivan Scipiades, "Wegry: Wyszehrad jest gdzie indziej," *Gazeta Wyborcza* (15 September 1994): 13. See also the Government Program of the Hungarian Socialist Party, October 1994, part 13. One could make, I would argue, a similar argument about the Polish and Lithuanian leftist governments. On Polish support for regional cooperation, see Jozef Wiejacz, "Urgopowania regionalne w nowej Europie," *Polska w Europie*, no. 11 (April 1993).

What is at issue now is finding a new identity and a new form of regional cooperation that will be in keeping with the present time. The fact is that at the present time, when the interests of individual countries are beginning to differentiate, when differences in the historical identity of these countries are coming to the surface, it is becoming clear that things are slightly different in this period than they were in the initial phase. Thus, cooperation will have a different form.[92]

A very important reason why regional cooperation among the Visegrad states declined, then, was what could be called the *differentiation* of these states, beginning in 1992. As already noted, what was striking about the period of 1991–92 was that these states shared a large, clear, but very vague agenda; that is, building capitalism and democracy and integrating with Europe. What was also striking was that these states were sure that they could achieve these goals quickly. Finally, they were similar—or at least more similar than their neighbors—in their governing coalitions. To put it succinctly: non-Communists were in power. However, these coalitions were in all three cases broad anti-Communist fronts (though the Hungarian Democratic Forum fell far closer to the notion of a party, and anti-Communists in Hungary were divided between several parties). Their agenda and their constituencies, in short, were poorly defined. As these broad fronts splintered, as the population began to diverge in terms of the costs it paid for the economic transformation, and as the complexities—political, economic, and social—of the transformation began to make their presence felt, political parties began to take the place of these broad fronts, agendas and constituencies became more refined, politics became more ideological and more competitive, and the directions these countries took began to diverge. This process, of course, was not purely domestic; it was influenced as well by all the changes that were taking place in the international system.

The result was that these regimes began to move in different directions. They began to develop their own identities, and, with that, their own specific constellation of preferences. We can support this observation with two examples. One is the political support enjoyed by the ex-Communists. As already noted, in Hungary the ex-Communists won a majority of the seats in parliament in the last election; in Poland the ex-Communists now hold the office

---

92. Translated from Prague Radiozurnal Radio Network, 16 January 1994 by FBIS-EEU-94-012, p. 12.

of the Presidency and are the senior member of the governing coalition, *but* their dominance is far less than it might seem, given that they won only 20 percent of the vote in the last parliamentary election and less than 2 percent of the vote separated the victor, Aleksander Kwasniewski, from the loser, Lech Walesa, in the November 1995 presidential election. In the Czech Republic the ruling party is liberal, the next most popular party is social democratic (from the interwar period), and the ex-Communists (who keep splintering) have minimal support. In Slovakia the ex-Communists are divided among several parties, including the now dominant party of Vladimir Mečiar, Movement for a Democratic Slovakia. The other example comes from public opinion. In a mid-1994 poll conducted by the *New York Times* in the Czech Republic, Hungary, and Poland, for example, we find the following average scores on a one to ten scale, with one being the position that incomes should be more equal and ten being the position that there should be incentives for individual effort. In the Czech Republic, the average score was 7.02; in Hungary, 3.96; and in Poland, 6.75. To cite another result from the same poll, 32 percent of the Czechs surveyed said they were better off now than in the past, as compared to 12 percent of the Hungarians and 18 percent of the Poles. Substantial differences were also registered with respect to the international questions posed in this survey. For example, in response to the question—"We can only solve our problems by joining the European Union"—25 percent of the Czechs agreed, as opposed to 48 percent of the Hungarians and 33 percent of the Poles.[93]

Thus what differentiated 1991–92 from 1993–96 was that the blanks, the grandiose goals, and the heady optimism created by the collapse of state socialism—all of which facilitated the development of regional cooperation—were replaced by political and economic details, middle-range goals, and quite varying degrees cross-nationally in optimism and pessimism. The end result was that these states had developed varying domestic politics and economics, varying governing coalitions and varying ideologies, varying kinds of leaders, and varying understandings of where they fit in the European scheme. Their identities, in short, were taking shape. Thus, with greater certainty about who they were but great uncertainty about where they were going and when and

93. As reported in a summary mailing by the *New York Times*, with the polls taken on 7–14 July in the Czech Republic; 8–12 July in Hungary; and 28 June–3 July in Poland.

if they would achieve "their radiant future," came greater differentiation. And with greater differentiation came expanding opportunities and incentives to move individually in international politics, rather than collectively. Knowledge, experience, political and economic "settling," and a strong dose of realism worked against collective action, just as ignorance, inexperience, flux, and naivete had once worked in support of collective action.

Conclusions

In a recent paper on international monetary cooperation, Jonathan Kirshner argues that a robust explanation of cooperation among states must begin not with the question of why such cooperation is unusual, but rather with why it ever occurs. What he is suggesting, then, is that there are considerable obstacles to inter-state cooperation, and that these obstacles are surmounted only under exceptional circumstances.[94]

This analysis of the rise and fall of the Visegrad Group provides considerable support for Kirshner's observation. What we see in 1990–92 is in fact the appearance of some quite unusual circumstances that paved the way for the establishment of cooperative relations among Poland, Hungary, and Czechoslovakia. In particular, the following factors presented themselves: 1) strong leadership support for cooperation; 2) similarities in the geopolitical location and the interests of the Visegrad states; 3) powerful international incentives for cooperation; and 4) striking and to some degree artificial similarities in the domestic politics and economics of the central European post-Communist states. However, when all is said and done, these factors can be boiled down to a relatively simple point. With an international system and domestic systems in transformation, there came a convergence between the desire and the capacity of the central European states to establish a cooperative relationship with one another. In this way, ironically, the instability of the post-Communist order generated an important element of stability—at least in the case of the central European states and their foreign policies from 1990 to 1992.

This was, however, a fleeting moment. By 1993, normal politics had begun to return to the European stage. The similarities among

94. "The Puzzle of International Monetary Cooperation," unpublished manuscript, Cornell University, April 1996.

the Visegrad countries began to evaporate as each of these states took on separate economic and political, domestic and international identities. At the same time, the international system began to take on more structure and thereby functioned to define differences in the geopolitical location and the interests of these states. Finally, international institutions also settled, and began to communicate a more complex array of incentives and disincentives for cooperative activity. Competition and not cooperation, details and not generalities, realism and not idealism, strategies and not goals, and, finally, differences and not similarities—that is, the usual stuff of the day-to-day politics and economics of regimes and states—became the order of the day. The result was that there was a decline in regional cooperation in central Europe. The Visegrad Group dispersed, almost as quickly as it had come together.

We can now return to the two issues that framed this paper: what the Visegrad experience suggests about the evolution of cooperation among states and about the relationship between domestic and international politics in a time of considerable flux. Here we can highlight several conclusions—aside from the difficulties inherent in the project of inter-state cooperation. First, the story of the rise and fall of the Visegrad Group would seem to suggest that it makes little sense to choose among the factors now highlighted by different theories of international politics and their competing perspectives on cooperation among states. In particular, what seems to be important is the structure of power in the international system and its impact on the interests and capabilities of states (the concerns of neo-realists); the role of international institutions and international norms in shaping the behavior of states (liberal institutionalists); the domestic structure, governing coalitions, and leadership of states and their consequences for foreign policy (the "domesticists"); and the culture and identity of states and, thus, state definitions of what it is, what it opposes, and what it wants (the "culturalists"). Put another way: if every school seems to have a point, every school at the same time seems to be deficient. For example, we could hardly understand the key factor shaping the fate of cooperation among the central European regimes—that is, the similarities of these states from 1990 to 1992 or their growing differences from 1993 to the present—without reference to changes over the course of this period (which began to make themselves felt in 1993) in the position of these states in the international system and their definition of state interests; in the messages put forward by international institutions and state responses to these messages; in the political leadership, governing coalitions, and ideological profile of these states; and in the state's definition of itself, its place in the region, and its place in Europe.

Second, it is in the details of these factors, in how these details relate to one another and how this interaction changes over time, that we can understand the evolution of cooperation among the Visegrad states. This point is at variance with the usual approach to analyzing cooperation among states. Here the common concern has been to focus less on details and more on the presence or absence of certain facilitating factors—to take some examples from the literature on cooperation, whether there is a shared security threat; whether there is a hegemon supporting multilateralism and willing to carry the costs of regional cooperation; whether international institutions embodying the norm of cooperation are in a position to provide incentives for inter-state cooperation; whether states are similar and are "stuck with one another" and thus have incentives to regularize their relationship (the "shadow of the future"); and whether states evidence similarities in their domestic political and economic structures and, thus, in their international preferences. What the Visegrad case seems to suggest is that these "empty vessels" must be filled and then combined before they can tell us much about patterns over time in inter-state cooperation.

Finally, it appears that the question of cooperation in this case cannot be separated from the question of the relationship between domestic and international change. To put the issue succinctly: it seems that the latter can be used to explain the former. The movement from flux to settling—at the levels of domestic regimes, international institutions, and the international system—seems to explain the movement as well from multilateralism to unilateralism in the foreign policies of Poland, Hungary, the Czech Republic, and Slovakia from 1990 to 1996. The abnormal politics of the transformation, in short, laid the groundwork for cooperation, just as the return to normal politics led to its decline.

Looking beyond matters of interpretation, the future international relations of central Europe are indelibly linked to developments in both West and East. Central Europe will be affected deeply by the balance between a broadening (in terms of the number of policy sectors and member states) and a deepening (in terms of the pooling of national sovereignties) of the European integration process. With the possible exception of Slovakia, relations among the central European states are likely to accommodate to the specific mixture of broadening and deepening that will shape the pace and quality of the European integration process in the coming years. Hence, as I have argued in this chapter, the special type of cooperative international relations that the Visegrad Group experienced between 1990 and 1992 is likely to remain an exception as central European international relations become increasingly linked to the European integration process.

Developments in the East are likely to reinforce the Europeanization of central Europe's international relations. Increasing political stability and growing economic prosperity in Russia, Ukraine and the other successor states of the former Soviet Union would strengthen further the relaxation of international tensions after the end of the Yugoslav war. And they would facilitate NATO's Eastern enlargement and the building of special political relations between NATO, Russia, and Ukraine. Instability and crisis in the East, on the other hand, which I judge to be the less likely scenario, would accelerate both the rush of the central European states to join NATO and the EU and Western receptivity to accommodating central Europe.

With the spreading of the process of European integration during the last two decades the international relations of Europe's northern and southern subregions have lost most of their specific content. The international relations of central Europe in the 1990s and beyond are confirming this broader political development. Central Europe had a come-back after 1989. But the available evidence suggests that it was only a short-term engagement.

Contributors

Włodek Anioł is Associate Professor, Warsaw University.

Daneš Brzica is Research Associate, Institute of Economics, Slovak Academy of Sciences.

Valerie Bunce is Professor of Government, Cornell University.

Timothy A. Byrnes is Associate Professor, Colgate University.

Péter Gedeon is Associate Professor, Budapest University of Economics.

Elena A. Iankova is Instructor, School of Industrial and Labor Relations, Cornell University.

Hynek Jeřábek is Associate Professor, Charles University, Prague.

Peter J. Katzenstein is Walter S. Carpenter, Jr. Professor of International Studies, Cornell University.

Zuzana Poláčková is Research Associate, Institute of Political Science, Slovak Academy of Sciences.

Ivo Samson is Research Associate, Slovak Institute of International Studies and University of Giessen.

František Zich is Research Associate, Institute of Sociology, Czech Academy of Sciences.

INDEX

New in Paperback

TOWARD A GLOBAL CIVIL SOCIETY

Edited by Michael Walzer

The demise of communism has not only affected Eastern Europe, but also the countries of the West where the far-reaching examination of political and economic systems has begun. This collection of essays by internationally renowned scholars of political theory from Europe and the United States explores both the concept and the reality of civil society and its institutions.

Michael Walzer is a permanent faculty member of the School of Social Science, Institute for Advanced Study, Princeton.

ISBN 1-57181-054-4 hardback
ISBN 1-57181-138-9 paperback

New

THE POLITICAL ECONOMY OF GERMAN UNIFICATION

Edited by Thomas Lange and J. R. Shackleton

Although German unification has had a profound impact on European integration and economic development, very few studies of the East German economy exist. The editors of this volume have therefore brought together specialists in economics and politics who analyse such important issues as privatisation, monetary reform and unemployment. The aim is to provide scholars and generally interested readers with a critical understanding of the complex processes of German unification, and to identify the general lessons that can be learnt from their analysis for economies and societies that undergo such profound transformations as has been the case in East Germany since the early 1990s.

Thomas Lange is Quintin Hogg Research Scholar in Labour Economics and Member of the Research Group 'Education, Training and the Labour Market' at the University of Westminster, Adviser for the Deutsche Gesellschaft für Technische Zusammenarbeit, and also teaches at the School of Public Administration and Law at Aberdeen University.

J. R. Shackleton was Economic Adviser in the Department of Social Security and now teaches as Principal Lecturer in Economics and Associate Head in Economic and Business Studies at the University of Westminster.

ISBN 1-57181-880-4 hardback

DATE DUE

GAYLORD			PRINTED IN U.S.A.